MW01069388

Those for Whom the Lamp Shines

Those for Whom the Lamp Shines

THE MAKING OF EGYPTIAN ETHNIC IDENTITY IN LATE ANTIQUITY

Vince L. Bantu

UNIVERSITY OF CALIFORNIA PRESS

University of California Press
Oakland, California

© 2023 by Vince L. Bantu

Library of Congress Cataloging-in-Publication Data

Names: Bantu, Vince L., author.
Title: Those for whom the lamp shines : the making of Egyptian ethnic
    identity in late antiquity / Vince L. Bantu.
Description: [Oakland, California] : University of California Press, [2023] |
    Includes bibliographical references and index.
Identifiers: LCCN 2023008844 (print) | LCCN 2023008845 (ebook) |
    ISBN 9780520388802 (hardcover) | ISBN 9780520388826 (ebook)
Subjects: LCSH: Coptic Church—Egypt—History. | Egyptians—Ethnic
    identity. | Ethnicity—Religious aspects—Christianity. | Egypt—
    Religion—332 B.C.–640 A.D.
Classification: LCC DT61 .B3225 2023 (print) | LCC DT61 (ebook) |
    DDC 932/.02—dc23/eng/20230315
LC record available at https://lccn.loc.gov/2023008844
LC ebook record available at https://lccn.loc.gov/2023008845

Manufactured in the United States of America

32 31 30 29 28 27 26 25 24 23
10 9 8 7 6 5 4 3 2 1

For Naniki, my spirited one

CONTENTS

CONTENTS

ACKNOWLEDGMENTS

My doctoral dissertation formed the foundation of this book, which has now undergone significant revision and expansion with the help of many. Several faculty members of the Department of Semitic and Egyptian Languages and Literatures at the Catholic University of America provided valuable guidance in the preparation and defense of my dissertation, most notably my Coptic advisor, Janet Timbie, as well as Sidney Griffith and Monica Blanchard. Scott F. Johnson also provided helpful support as part of my dissertation committee. I am grateful for the support and advocacy of Eric Schmidt and the University of California Press. Several friends provided helpful feedback on this project, most especially Mary Farag, Gregory Lee, and Brian Howell. The community of Fuller Theological Seminary supported this project tremendously. I would like to especially thank my Fuller community for the Johnson-Barsotti Emerging Scholar Grant and my dean Amos Yong for his support. The research assistant for this project—Deirdre McClain—aided in this project immensely. I am grateful to the Meachum School of Haymanot and Beloved Community Church for the space and support they provided for me in developing this project. I also thank my family—Diana, Taína, and Naniki—for their grace with me during this process. Most of all, I would like to thank Tilli, to whom all thanks are due.

ONE

Egyptian Ethnicity in Late Antiquity

JAMES BALDWIN ONCE WROTE that "any real change implies the breakup of the world as one has always known it, the loss of all that gave one an identity, the end of safety."[1] It is the purpose of this book to understand the ways that late antique Egyptians formulated and asserted their social identity. In light of Baldwin's comments, it is not surprising that the clearest articulation of an emergent Egyptian identity occurred on the heels of significant political, ecumenical, and cultural change. At the dawn of the Christological controversies of the fifth century, a particularized Egyptian identity came to the fore in an unprecedented manner.

In late antiquity, Roman imperial culture co-opted the universalizing element of the Christian tradition.[2] The present study focuses on Egypt as a means of investigating one side of the double-edged sword carving out ethnic identity. Egyptian Christian identity in late antiquity promulgated a Christian universalism that placed Christianity as the primary locus of identity—a global identity that placed all Christians in union across lines of ethnicity, language, empire or social class. At the same time, the "Egyptian" element in the Egyptian church was emphasized in distinction and sometimes, in conflict, with other Christian communities beginning in the fifth century. The double-edged sword of Egyptian Christian identity framed itself with religious universalism on one side and social particularity on the other. While Roman imperial Christianity promoted universality, Christians leveraged social factors such as ethnicity to frame theological divisions. In the case of Egypt, the role of ethnic difference as a means of framing theological discourse became increasingly evident after Chalcedon. Egyptian identity formation had already taken an ethnic turn well before the Arab Muslim conquest of Egypt. Scholarship on late antique Egyptian Christianity tends to point to this as the decisive event that instigated a pronounced ethnic consciousness in the Egyptian church.[3] The following study will demonstrate how this awakening of ethnic consciousness actually happened two centuries earlier.

The Council of Chalcedon convened under the authority of Emperor Marcian in 451 CE to respond to growing differences in Christology between Egypt and the bishops of Constantinople and Rome. During the decades leading up to this council, theologians across the Roman Empire diverged in their attempts tó explain how Jesus could be fully God, as established at the Council of Nicaea (325 CE) and fully human. A monk named Eutyches taught that Jesus's humanity and divinity persist in one nature (*physis*). Eutyches was supported by the Patriarch of Alexandria, Dioscorus, at the Second Council of Ephesus (449 CE). The decisions of this council and the person of Eutyches were both disagreeable to the bishops of Constantinople and Rome; this led to the Council of Chalcedon's acceptance of the Roman Bishop Leo's *Tome*, which defined Jesus as one person (*hypostasis*) with two natures (*physis*).

But the Council and Leo's *Tome* were disagreeable to the Patriarch of Alexandria and the majority of the Egyptian population. Patriarch Dioscorus was sent into exile for his rejection of the Council and replaced with a Chalcedonian ("two-nature") bishop who was killed by an Egyptian mob. Roman and Constantinopolitan bishops came to Egypt with Roman soldiers and attempted to force Egyptian bishops and monastic communities to accept the *Tome* of Leo and the Council of Chalcedon. Emperor Zeno's subsequent compromise proposal did not work. During the sixth century, Emperor Justinian attempted to force the Egyptians into Chalcedonianism, which only pushed them further away from Roman imperial authorities and church officials. During the early seventh century, Emperor Heraclius enacted similar policies in Egypt, exiling the Egyptian Patriarch Benjamin and replacing him with a bishop named Cyrus from the Caucasus region. Egypt came under Persian control for a decade and briefly returned to Roman dominance before the Arab Muslim conquest. When the forces of 'Amr ibn-al-As conquered Egypt, Christians had mixed reactions. Some lamented the new rule of "heathens," but others rejoiced at freedom from the Roman Chalcedonian "heretics." Even in the earliest years of Islamic dominance in Egypt, Christians displayed greater anger towards Roman Chalcedonians than their Muslim rulers. This demonstrates the importance of the anti-Chalcedonian movement for Egyptian identity.

The defining characteristic of Egyptian Christianity after Chalcedon was Miaphysite doctrine. The term "Miaphysite" ("one nature"), originally used by Cyril of Alexandria, refers to the central claim of this group: that Christ exists in one united nature, both human and divine.[4] The majority of recent scholarship has avoided the term "Monophysite," a polemical term originating outside the communities that it labels.[5] While "anti-Chalcedonian" or "non-Chalcedonian" are certainly more appropriate, they are also not optimal as the communities that did not accept Chalcedon include other groups inside and outside of Egypt, such as Eutychians and the Church of the East.[6] I will employ the terms "anti-Chalcedonian" as well as "Miaphysite," while avoiding use of "Monophysite."

The Chalcedonian schism motivated the Egyptian church to mark its indigenous origin.[7] The framing of Egyptian identity by means of boundaries defined by Miaphysite doctrine is not a process that began with the Arab Muslim conquest but two centuries earlier, with the Chalcedonian schism.[8] The later conquest reinforced a process already well underway. While the Copts' *dhimmi*—or religious minority—status under Islam generated an even more pressing need to define a distinct identity, Egypt's Christians had already experienced minority status as a "heretical" faction within the Byzantine Empire. The elements that defined Egyptian identity—martyrdom and resistance to governmental oppression—were therefore strengthened, not created, at the time of the Arab Muslim conquest. Since Ptolemaic times, indeed, Greeks had represented Egyptians as oppressed martyrs. The adoption of martyrdom as a central theme in the life of the Coptic church came about during the period of the Great Persecution at the beginning of the fourth century CE.[9]

After the Chalcedonian schism, the Roman Emperor Justinian persecuted the Egyptian church, prompting Coptic leaders to resist through martyrological rhetoric. The hagiographical sources of the fifth and sixth centuries surveyed in the following chapters demonstrate that Egyptian preoccupation with forming ethnic identity along Miaphysite lines resulted from a new need to differentiate from the imperial church of Constantinople.[10] Anti-Chalcedonians wanted to demonstrate that their position was in agreement with the Christian voices of the past. This was not, therefore, a new position taken at the time of the Arab Muslim conquest. An earlier example of this strategy is found in the *Life of Longinus* when the Lycian monk summoned the voices of his deceased predecessors at the Enaton monastery who unanimously condemned the *Tome* of Leo.[11] Likewise, Romans were not "gradually" depicted as hegemonic, foreign oppressors; indeed, there was a swift development of anti-Byzantine rhetoric in the writings of mid-fifth-century figures like Timothy Aelurus and Dioscorus of Alexandria.[12] The works of Timothy mark the beginning of theological resistance framed in ethnic terms.[13] Texts such as these were some of the most powerful instruments of identity formation in late antique Christianity.[14] From the perspective of Egyptians, Chalcedonianism was rapidly associated with the Roman Empire. However, awareness of the new perspective developed only gradually and authorities in Constantinople did not fully understand what had happened for another century.[15]

Ethnic identity development in late antique Egypt is evident primarily in hagiographic, homiletic and historical works. It has become common in studies of late antiquity to prioritize documentary sources that are legal, administrative, and/or economic in nature.[16] While documentary papyri may be the most useful source in attempting to reconstruct the social and economic context of late antique Egypt, readers can gain understanding of religious and ethnic identity through hagiographic, homiletical, and historical material in which the attitudes of Egyptian Christians are most clearly presented.[17] Indeed, documentary papyri often leave one in the dark regarding the social and religious convictions of a particular community.[18] Primary attention here will be given to the anti-Chalcedonian/Miaphysite texts of Egypt written after the Council of Chalcedon (451 CE) into the period immediately following the Arab conquest (642 CE).

This book presents events and figures of the Egyptian church in the chronological order in which they have been traditionally commemorated during the late antique, medieval, and modern periods, both within the Coptic church and in other religious communities around the world. Furthermore, texts that likely were written in very different time periods yet focus on similar events and people will be considered alongside one another. The book is organized first by time period, covering the pre-Chalcedonian period, the late fifth century, the sixth century, and the seventh century. Within these periodizations, the chapters are organized primarily by leading figures who are thought to have lived and operated in Egypt during these periods. However, several of the texts I treat were written much later than the date they claim. All the same, texts regarding certain individuals emerging from different periods are considered together. The danger in such an approach, of course, is that texts often reveal more about the period in which they were written than in which they are set. I have endeavored to signal such instances throughout the book. The benefits of my approach, however, are twofold. One, many of these texts have a long, complicated redaction history, and their origins are often uncertain. This leaves open the possibility that many of them may have an oral or written origin during the time period in which they are set. Two, authors often labored to keep the details of a text set to its appropriate time. For example, texts written after Chalcedon that are set before Chalcedon leave the schism out of their contents and present Roman authorities in a vastly different manner than their contemporaries. Such examples demonstrate the continuity in which communal memory was fashioned, built upon, and maintained in the making of Egyptian identity.

While the following study will include an assessment of Egyptian identity from various religious communities, anti-Chalcedonian literature will be especially highlighted as the Miaphysites produced the majority of Coptic literature during this period and, as it will be argued, the dominant articulation of Egyptian identity. Events such as the reign of Justinian and the Islamic conquest continued to shape the Egyptian identity that took form in the aftermath of Chalcedon. The ethnic rhetoric present in Egyptian texts will be analyzed through the lens of contemporary anthropological methodology. However, I should first establish the utility of "ethnicity" as a useful interpretive category for late antique Egyptian Christianity, as opposed to alternative categories such as "race" or "nationality."

THE FALSE THESIS OF LATE ANTIQUE
EGYPTIAN NATIONALISM

The topic of Egyptian ethnic identity development has not been addressed in scholarship directly, but instead enters in the form of a debate regarding the existence of nationalism in Coptic literature. Scholars working in the late nineteenth and early twentieth centuries alleged that an anti-Hellenistic sentiment motivated early Coptic writers in Upper Egypt to formulate a religious movement interested not in profound theological engagement but in Egyptian nationalistic propaganda that was both anti-Byzantine and anti-Alexandrine. This argument focused heavily on the writings of the fifth-century monastic leader and Coptic author *par excellence,* Shenoute of Atripe. Scholarship in the later twentieth and early twenty-first centuries has seen a complete rejection of this analysis. While the modern rejection of an anachronistic nationalist lens is accurate, scholars have not offered a helpful alternative for how to interpret Egyptian-centered rhetoric in late antique texts.

The nationalism thesis originated in the work of Émile Amélineau. Amélineau claimed that Christianity was adapted and fused with various elements of pre-Christian Egyptian religion and culture, while Islam entered Egypt as an opposing force demanding the rejection of indigenous religious practice.[19] Johannes Leipoldt went further and posited a sharp distinction between Greek-speaking, wealthy landowners and Coptic-speaking peasants. He operated under the assumption that the Greek language remained largely unspoken in Upper Egypt due to hostilities between "Greeks" and "Copts."[20] E. L. Woodward suggested that theological controversies of late antiquity were, in fact, political power struggles between the various regions of the Roman Empire.[21] Jean Maspero claimed that Egyptian nationalism manifested in pagan religious practice[22] and even referred to Egyptians as a "vain people."[23] Maspero's analysis is laden with bias as he characterizes Miaphysite doctrine as "an assembly of disconnected assertions, contrary to orthodox theories."[24]

Harold Idris Bell advanced a blunter version of the nationalism thesis, asserting an alleged racial purity of Egyptian Christians. Bell claimed that the Egyptian church was of "a strongly nationalist character," bolstered by his belief that Egyptians were "without an admixture of Greek blood" and that they demonstrated "no capacity for abstract philosophical thought."[25] Indeed, he even described Greek-speaking Egyptian leaders like Cyril as "ardent nationalists."[26]

A. H. M. Jones was one of the first scholars to challenge the nationalism thesis. For Jones, Egyptian solidarity was motivated not by national sentiment but ecclesiastical unity.[27] While later-twentieth-century analysis was characterized by conflicting responses to the nationalist thesis and the challenge raised by Jones,[28] Ewa Wipszycka's 1996 refutation of the nationalist thesis put a complete end to any nationalist analysis of late antique Egypt. Focusing solely on Egypt, Wipszycka argued that the exaltation of Greek speakers from other parts of the empire discredits any kind of Coptic anti-Greek sentiment.[29] Wipszycka's study has influenced recent studies of late antique Egypt to the extent that there has been no support for the nationalist thesis in the last three decades of scholarship.[30]

Wipszycka's claim is congruent with leading studies on nationality and nationalism finding that national identity is inherently political and that ethnic boundaries must exist within the political interests of the state.[31]

Nationalist movements seek political legitimacy. Following the schism between the Egyptian church and the dominant Roman church centered in Constantinople, the theological resistance movement was characterized by an increase in rhetoric centering the people of Egypt. However, this rhetoric was not political. There was no military resistance or move for political separation from the Roman Empire. Egypt was not a nation but a province of the Roman Empire; and the Miaphysites who resisted Chalcedon displayed no interest in changing that reality. Since Egypt was not a nation in the modern sense nor even in a manner equivalent to the modern concept of nationality, nationalism is not helpful in understanding the anti-Chalcedonian movement in Egypt.

However, there is a reason that scholars of the late nineteenth and early twentieth centuries were drawn to the question of social identity in anti-Chalcedonian texts. And that is because the land and people of Egypt are centered in unprecedented ways during this period. Prior to Chalcedon, Egyptian Christian texts did not mention being Egyptian very much; after Chalcedon, Egypt and Egyptians appear much more frequently. Contemporary scholarship on Egyptian Christianity has rejected the nationalist thesis, but has not yet provided an adequate framework to understand the role social factors *did* play in Christological controversies.[32] Jason Zaborowski argues that ethnic rhetoric in medieval Coptic texts are not assertions of Coptic pride, although he asks "when or how did Copts come to see themselves as an 'ethnochurch'?"[33] Bagnall accurately summarizes the state of the current discussion of Egyptian ethnic identity development: "Nationalism is a doubtful interpretive concept for this emerging world, but was there an Egyptian consciousness detaching itself and reconstructing its past to justify such a detachment? If so, when did this come about? This is still a frontier for study."[34] There is still a need for a better framework for the analysis of the "égyptocentrisme" present in Coptic texts.

PARADIGMS OF ETHNICITY

Studies have yielded a multiplicity of definitions and manners of conceiving of ethnicity. My working definition of ethnicity is: a form of social organization where the group continually fashions its membership along changing cultural, linguistic, or religious characteristics in order to distinguish itself from neighbors.[35] Leading anthropologists guide my definition as it builds upon extant descriptions of ethnicity in applying this concept to the category of "Egyptian" in late antique Egyptian Christian literature.

Nationalism has failed as an analytical tool in assessing anti-Chalcedonian Egypt. The phenomenon of nationalism refers to a transition from agrarian to industrial forms of political economy. Furthermore, a desire for political autonomy undergirds any nationalist movement.[36] None of these defining characteristics of modern nationalism best characterize the ways in which late antique Egyptian identity was framed. If a spirit of nationalism fueled anti-Chalcedonian polemic, then solidarity with Egypt's past would be a defining characteristic of this nationalism.[37] However, late antique Egyptian Christians often distanced themselves from their own pre-Christian, Egyptian past. Nationalism maintains the nation to be the primary and highest locus of identity.[38] Late antique Egyptian Christians were not nationalists because their highest loyalty was neither to Egypt nor to the Roman Empire; it was to the global Christian church.[39] Furthermore, modern sociologists recognize that contemporary instances of Coptic nationalism have their roots in the nineteenth century.[40] Modern Coptic nationalism may indeed have roots in the anti-Chalcedonian resistance movement.

Religion is another modern concept that in large part correlates to the designation "Christian" that appears in late antique Egyptian texts. It is true that "Christian" was the community's highest sense of identity. However, this study explores the language of "Egypt" and "Egyptian"—modifiers that correlate to the modern concept of ethnicity—and how this layer of identity intersected with religious identity. Late antique Egyptian Christians understood themselves as Christians first; but as they split from the dominant expression of Christianity, the Egyptian part of their identity rose to the surface of their collective consciousness as a means of distinguishing themselves from other Christians. This ethnic segment of the Christian religion even differentiated itself from other communities that Egyptians would have considered orthodox, Miaphysites in places like Syria or Palestine. For this reason, ethnicity is the most useful category to understand "Egyptian" in anti-Chalcedonian literature. It is also important to keep in mind that ethnicity is understood in this context as a marker of social identity that overlaps and incorporates other categories such as religion, language, culture, race, and political boundaries.

This book will interpret Egyptian-centered rhetoric not from the perspective of nationalism but of ethnicity. Max Weber defines ethnicity primarily along the lines of common descent and shared customs.[41] Contemporary anthropological and sociological studies of ethnicity, however, have largely moved away from the primordialist, Weberian understanding of ethnicity as common descent.[42] In the mid-twentieth century, Fredrik Barth proposed a method of understanding ethnicity that has continued to be influential in the discipline of anthropology. A useful concept in analyzing Egyptian-centered rhetoric is Barth's "ethnic boundary maintenance."

> First, it is clear that boundaries persist despite a flow of personnel across them. In other words, categorical ethnic distinctions do not depend on an absence of mobility, contact and information, but do entail social processes of exclusion and incorporation whereby discrete categories are maintained *despite* changing participation and membership in the course of individual life histories. Secondly, one finds that stable, persisting, and often vitally important social relations are maintained across such boundaries, and are frequently based precisely on the dichotomized ethnic statuses. In other words, ethnic distinctions do not depend on an absence of social interaction and acceptance, but are quite to the contrary often the very foundations on which embracing social systems are built.[43]

Barth introduced a radical shift in the way ethnicity was previously undestood. Ethnic studies needed to shift from investigating internal constitution to the maintenance of ethnic boundaries: "The critical investigation from this point of view becomes the ethnic *boundary* that defines the group, not the cultural stuff that it encloses."[44] While cultural content will always change, the boundaries maintained by ethnic groups signal the (often shifting) limits of exclusion and acceptance. Furthermore, ethnicity is a form of peoplehood that is broader than a tribe and may transcend or exist within larger categories of nationality or race. "Egyptian" is a bounded category in anti-Chalcedonian literature that is not coterminous with linguistic, religious, or political boundaries. "Egyptian" refers to a highly codified sense of peoplehood that is best defined as an ethnic group. Yet, "Egyptian" emerged in ways that factored in categories of language, race, empire, and religion. For example, Macarius of Tkôw and Dioscorus of Alexandria were both Egyptian, but they spoke different languages (Coptic and Greek). Conversely, Egyptians embraced Severus of Antioch for his shared theology, but he was not Egyptian. Ethnicity is the most helpful category to describe such an interconnected, non-political layer of identity.

Barth's methodology has been very influential in studies of ethnicity.[45] Scholars such George De Vos and Richard Jenkins have grounded much of their ethnicity research in Barth's concept of boundary maintenance.[46]

While the field of anthropology continues to develop Barth's theories, *Ethnic Groups* achieved its goal of providing a new theoretical framework within which to understand ethnicity. Various disciplines now have an accessible concept of ethnicity to apply to new areas of research. The goal of the present study is to demonstrate the way in which Egyptian-centered rhetoric functions as ethnic boundary maintenance. However, studies in late antiquity utilizing modern methods of social science often encounter accusations of anachronism.[47]

An increasing number of scholars working in antiquity have interpreted ancient categories of identity through modern anthropological terms.[48] While it is crucial to avoid anachronistic attempts to equate ancient social phenomena with those of the present day, there is an equally dangerous tendency to neglect the socio-cultural dynamics of religious discourse in antiquity. Recent studies on late antique ethnic identity have demonstrated the utility of modern conceptions of ethnicity as a dynamic, fluid process of identity negotiation. A primordialist approach that frames ethnicity as a static, fixed entity is unhelpful when analyzing late antique Egyptianness. The boundaries of "Egyptian" shifted dramatically following the Chalcedonian schism, and the reframing of Egyptian identity is evident in the frequent juxtaposition of Egyptian Miaphysites and Roman Chalcedonians. By extension, the post-Chalcedonian Egyptian majority rejected the idea of an Egyptian Chalcedonian. Furthermore, while the earliest opponents of Chalcedon desired a return to orthodoxy (that is, Miaphysitism), the idea of a Roman Miaphysite quickly became seen as an impossibility. Ethnicity is a useful tool in identity politics as it can fashion and refashion group identity around a particular cause. However, before considering the ethnic rhetoric emerging from Egypt during late antiquity, it is necessary to clarify the distinctions between ethnicity and race. What do "race" and "ethnicity" mean in both modern and ancient contexts? Why is ethnicity the most appropriate category for understanding references to Egyptian identity in late antique Christian literature?

THE QUESTION OF RACE

Like nationality and language, ethnicity is formed in overlapping intersections with race. The claim of the existence of something approximating the modern concept of race in antiquity has engendered even harsher backlash than ethnicity.[49] This forms no small part of the reason as to why ethnicity is seen as a "safer" category than race.[50] It has been amply demonstrated that a social category equivalent to the modern concept of "race" was indeed operative in the ancient world.[51] However, this present study claims that it is ethnicity, not race, that is the most accurate way for modern scholars to speak of Egyptian identity in late antique Christian literature. This claim is not an attempt to avoid race nor to posit that race and ethnicity are wholly distinct. The degree to which these two categories are distinct is the area where ethnicity emerges as a more accurate interpretive category for the Egyptian-centered rhetoric in anti-Chalcedonian texts.

Without specifying the differences, Buell claims that "'race' and 'ethnicity' can function in particular socio-historical moments to signify different things."[52] It is difficult to specifically parse the distinctions between the ways that *ethnos* and *genos* were used in late antiquity—especially by Christians. This difficulty is largely rooted in the reality that these terms are often used in intersecting and interchangeable ways. However, as Byron pointed out, race often evokes "external factors," such as genotype and phenotype. All forms of social identity are meant to distinguish one group from another. "Race" is the category that differentiates a larger collection of various people groups from another assortment of groups based on perceived physical commonalities.[53] Perhaps the best examples in both the ancient and modern world are the invented categories "Black" and "white," two overarching categories that encompass a wide variety of ethnicities while transcending boundaries of nationality, language, and religion and which are based on physical characteristics and beliefs about biological commonalities.[54] For example, the Scetan ascetic hero Moses was named for his skin color—Moses the Black. He contrasted his Blackness with being "white," which was associated with purity.[55] Such instances of racial imagination in Christian literature followed broad Roman constructions of race. The Roman poet Ausonius associated Blackness with depravity and whiteness with purity, a practice common to the Greco-Roman world.[56] The work of Erich Gruen affirms the association of "race" with physical characteristics, especially skin color. Interestingly, Gruen questions the accuracy of the term "race" in analyzing ancient texts, and yet proceeds to use the term to refer to ancient descriptions of Blackness/Aithiopianness. This is because of Gruen's conflation of "race" with "racism" or "colorism." He is actually questioning the validity of the term "racism" as applied to antiquity; "race," however, he continues to acknowledge.[57]

Avoiding anachronism is of utmost importance; and so is acknowledging the social realities that shaped ancient texts. It is as dangerous a mistake to impose modern definitions of ethnicity or race into the ancient world as it is to deny the existence of ethnicity and race in the ancient world. As Erich Gruen puts it: "The ancients were not color-blind."[58] Despite his claim that the ancient world did not harbor the kind of anti-Black sentiment that has characterized the modern Western world, Frank Snowden still acknowledges that classical writers certainly noticed differences in skin color, especially when it came to Black people. More importantly, Snowden's assessment of the term "Black" (*aithiopos*) demonstrates that this term referred to a multitude of ethnic groups across the African and Asian continents that exhibited dark skin.[59] This further demonstrates the distinction between race and ethnicity in ancient contexts. The definition of race in the work of Benjamin Isaac also posits a social category that highlights common color and a common physique, which derive from a common ancestry. Isaac distinguishes race from ethnicity, as he also distinguishes racism from ethnic prejudice—again, with physicality at the center of the distinction.[60] What the two have in common is the belief that the inhabitants of a specific region share commonalities. The distinction, however, between racism and ethnic prejudice is that the former holds behavior to be stable and unalterable while the latter allows for the possibility of change at the individual or collective level.[61]

While these concepts may conflate, doing so will actually make it more difficult to identify race and racism in ancient texts. Race most often refers to a collection of ethnic groups that are assumed to share certain physical traits.[62] But as I will show, late antique Egyptian Christian sources do not deploy the category "Egyptian" in contexts that situate this modifier in terms of physicality. Like nationality, race is not a helpful social category with which to interpret Egyptian-centered rhetoric in late antique Christian literature. It must be stated that modern definitions of race, ethnicity and nationality do not correlate to those of the ancient world. Indeed, the Greek-speaking world used a variety of words such as *genos, ethnos*, and *phulos* to describe human social difference. These words were often used interchangeably, with different nuances than the modern nuance between race and ethnicity. However, the ancients certainly did notice human difference and use distinct categories to talk about it. Indeed, the modern world interchangeably uses categories of social difference with equally puzzling inconsistency.

Therefore, this study will proceed with the modern distinctions between race, ethnicity and nationality and will demonstrate that ethnicity is the most apt modern category with which to interpret Egyptian-talk in late antique Coptic literature. The reason for this is simple: ancient Egyptian Christians did not write out a clear definition of exactly what they meant by *ethnos, genos,* or *rōme.* This approach is therefore not anachronistic, but a bridge to aid modern readers in correlating ancient Egyptian expressions of identity using the definition established above. An analogy would be using terms like "Byzantine" or "Near Eastern," which aid modern readers but were irrelevant in the ancient context to which they refer. Throughout this study, I will most often translate the various terms used in the languages surveyed as "ethnicity" while placing the original word in parenthesis. In some rare cases, I will use the word "race" when the definition outlined here is evident in the text.

Chapter 2 will examine the construction of Egyptian identity during the fourth and early fifth centuries, prior to Chalcedon. To understand the significance of Chalcedon for Egyptian identity, it is important to survey how Egyptian identity persisted prior to this event. The core of the book begins with chapter 3, which analyzes the beginning of Egyptian ethnic rhetoric in the aftermath of the Council of Chalcedon. Chapter 4 continues this survey by analyzing the anti-Chalcedonian literature of sixth-century Egypt. The majority of texts from this period focus their attention on the imperial policies of Emperor Justinian. Chapter 5 examines texts from the period immediately following the Arab Muslim conquest. This chapter also considers medieval texts that discuss the seventh-century figures in order to demonstrate the normative ethnic imagination that emerged during late antiquity and continued in the succeeding periods. The anti-Chalcedonian movement was a global faith that was not exclusive to Egypt. Therefore, it is necessary to consider this book's claim that anti-Chalcedonianism was a central marker for Egyptian identity, given that not all anti-Chalcedonians were Egyptian. This final chapter will analyze the degree to which Egyptians distinguished themselves among other Miaphysites.

The overwhelming majority of studies on ethnicity and other forms of social identity in the ancient world have focused on the Greek and Latin literature of the Roman world. However, scholarship has paid little attention to ethnicity in the literature of other language groups from the Eastern Roman, Persian, and Caucasian Empires. How were the Greek concepts such as *genos* and *ethnos* appropriated, for example, in the Coptic or Syriac-speaking world? And how did these compare to Syriac or Coptic categories we translate "people"?[63] While a comprehensive study of Near Eastern Christian models of ethnicity is still needed, this book contributes to a broader understanding of social identity in the ancient world by shifting focus to a body of understudied literature produced or transmitted in Egypt during the late antique and early medieval periods.

TWO

Egyptian Christians and Ethnicity
Prior to Chalcedon

EGYPTIAN ETHNIC IDENTITY BECAME INCREASINGLY framed by Christian—specifically Miaphysite—identity during the late antique and early medieval periods. This process was bolstered by the Egyptian church's newfound place of opposition to the Roman Empire and its dominant church. The majority of this study will focus on the Christian literature from Egypt's leading figures following Chalcedon. However, before consideration of post-Chalcedonian texts, this chapter will focus on how Egyptian Christians framed ethnic identity prior to Chalcedon. Several texts in this chapter have a redaction history that lies primarily after Chalcedon—notably, the *Apophthegmata Patrum* ("Sayings of Our Fathers") and the *Life of Pachomius*. While it is possible that the various translations and recensions of these texts emerged from fourth- or early-fifth-century material, most recensions come from the late fifth century or later.

However, the central figures of these texts lived before Chalcedon and as such, the texts endeavor to represent a worldview prior to the christological schism. These texts are considered alongside material more confidently dated to the fourth and early fifth centuries in order to demonstrate the commonalities of ethnic rhetoric in texts prior to and assumed to be prior to Chalcedon. I will demonstrate that before Chalcedon, Egyptian Christians placed very little emphasis on their unique ethnic identity. Rather, the Egyptian church identified principally as a part of the Roman imperial church due to the relative theological harmony between these communities. At the same time, aspects of Egyptian ethnic boundary maintenance that would come to the fore following Chalcedon are discernable in the period preceding the christological schism. While theological schism did not take on ethnic framing in the fourth century, the model of Egyptian ascetic resistance to imperial oppression was already present and would become an archetype for Egyptian ascetic identity following Chalcedon. However, ethnic rhetoric was largely absent from Egyptian Christian literature before Chalcedon while articulations of Christian universalism were much more frequent. Such universalism continued after Chalcedon, but was diminished due to Egypt finding itself surrounded by a predominately "heretical" empire.

CHRISTIAN UNIVERSALISM

Like many Christian communities during late antiquity, the Egyptian church primarily framed its identity as part of a larger Christian "people."[1] Perhaps the most influential Egyptian Christian prior to Chalcedon was Athanasius, archbishop of Alexandria. In his famous biography on the monastic hero Antony, the rhetoric deployed by Athanasius highlights Christian identity more than Egyptianness: "We Christians, however, do not have the mysteries by means of the wisdom of Greek rhetoric."[2] The foil for Christian is "pagan." In the anti-Chalcedonian period, both sides of the conflict were Christians. "Christian" was suddenly not enough to distinguish the Egyptian Church; "Egyptian" then becomes the marker of difference that significantly increases. The *Life* again uses the language "we Christians," further demonstrating the Christian universalistic rhetoric common to this time period.[3]

The *Life* draws universalizing language from the Apostle Paul. Many of the converts that Antony taught about the ascetic life were said to have "registered themselves for citizenship in heaven."[4] Language highlighting universal Christian identity with a lack of emphasis on particular ethnic categories was more common for Egyptian Christians prior to Chalcedon. Athanasius deploys the term *genos* with regard to all of humanity throughout his writings, seldom with reference to Egyptians or any particular ethnic group.[5] The beginning of the *Life of Antony* represents the end of the earliest stage of Egyptian Christianity—the period of the Egyptian church enduring persecution under Roman religion. The first three centuries of Christianity in Egypt were characterized by intermittent persecution, and Antony lived before and after the early-fourth-century transition to Christian legitimacy in the empire. The persecution of Christians generated a sense of unity of identity across various regional and ethnic affiliations throughout the Roman Empire. For this reason, the term "Christians" appears in the *Life* as a primary locus of identity, especially in contrast to the "Greeks." Antony went to

Alexandria out of a desire to be martyred and he stood boldly before a pagan magistrate, thus "representing the determination of the Christians."[6] The genesis of Egyptian pride was already present in pre-Chalcedonian literature such as the *Life of Antony*, which highlights Antony's Egyptian ethnicity and language. More will be said about this at the end of this chapter.

Christian identity was also contrasted with heretical groups. The *Life of Antony* uses universal Christian language and contrasts Christian identity with the Arians: "Therefore, you better not have any kind of fellowship with the wicked Arians, for 'light has no fellowship with darkness.' You are devout Christians; but those people, saying that the Son—the Word of God—is a creation of the Father, are no different from the ethnic groups[7] 'worshipping the creature rather than God, the Creator.'"[8] Note that the juxtaposed categories are religious and do not pinpoint specific ethnic groups. This occurred again when an Egyptian prefect and imperial military commander began to impose Arianism in Egypt. Antony prophesied divine judgment of these two leaders, which duly occurred when they were attacked and killed by their own horses.[9] Imperially-sponsored impositions of Arianism during the fourth century were intermittent, unlike the sustained schism that resulted after Chalcedon. Furthermore, Arianism was not associated with any particular ethnic or political entity. This dynamic would change following Chalcedon, when Chalcedonianism became associated with Roman identity and many, if not most, Miaphysites with Egyptian identity.

The universalism and ethnic inclusivity in pre-Chalcedonian Egypt is most visible in the *Life of Pachomius*. Egyptian saints such as Pachomius are still highlighted and presented as exemplars of the faith. Pachomius is often reported as one whose reputation spread all over Egypt and beyond.[10] The Bohairic *Life* tells readers that "in fact, the fame of our father Pachomius and of his charity reached everyone. His name was heard even abroad and among the Romans, and they came to become monks with him. And the man of God Pachomius treated them well with every word and with every doctrine, 'like a nurse comforting her children.'"[11] The *Life of Antony* gives a similar impression of Egyptian ascetic heroes being models for the global church: "And people came from foreign lands to see him. And those people, like all others, gained profit and returned as though escorted by a father."[12] While "Romans" and imperial authorities were, for the most part, depicted as allies of the Egyptians, there was yet a tendency among pre-Chalcedonian Egyptian Christians to highlight the influence and leadership of Egyptian saints in the global church. Pachomius and the Coptic-speaking monks of Pbow were even elevated over the Greek-speaking Christians of Alexandria and Lower Egypt. At times, philosophers from "the city" came to test the wisdom of the Pachomian monks, which resulted in the intellectual victory of the humble Upper Egyptian monks over the Alexandrian philosophers.[13]

While Egypt was certainly a multilingual and multicultural society, there were still degrees of distinction and stratification between Greek- and Coptic-speakers, Alexandrians and Upper Egyptians. An Alexandrian monk named Theodore who lived under the tutelage of Athanasius for twelve years found some of the Pachomian monks on a trip in Alexandria one day and asked them, through an interpreter, if he might come to Pbow and live as an ascetic there. In the text, Pachomius embraces Theodore and "assigned him to a house in which an ancient old man lived who, as he understood the Greek language, could converse with him and comfort him." After Theodore's embrace at the monastic community of Pbow, a dialogue ensues that entails a sharp critique of the Alexandrian Christian community: "Our father Pachomius asked him (Theodore) through an interpreter about the faith of those who lived as anchorites in Alexandria, and about their spiritual practices."[14] Theodore replies that the Alexandrian monks have an unshakable faith. However, Pachomius declares that their purity had been compromised due to their excessive reliance on food and drink.[15] While Theodore is initially confused, later some Pachomian monks visit Alexandria and indeed discover that the monks there had fallen into impure lifestyles brought on by excessive reliance on food and drink. Theodore was amazed at Pachomius's knowledge and was embraced in Pbow as the ambassador for ethnic outsiders: "When our father Pachomius saw that Theodore had advanced in the knowledge of God, he appointed him Man of the House for the foreigners[16] who were coming to become monks under him. And our father Pachomius earnestly tried to learn Greek, so that he could strengthen them regularly by the Scriptures and to show Theodore the way to guide the brothers that were under him."[17]

Not only did Pachomius begin to learn Greek to accommodate the "foreign" monks at Pbow, but Theodore begins to learn "the Egyptian language"[18] so that, after hearing the teaching of Pachomius, he "would say it in Greek to those for whom he was Man of the House over them."[19] The supplemental material to the *Life,* or the *Paralipomena,* claims that Pachomius received the ability to speak "all the languages" instantly after praying. This was in response to the arrival of "a Roman" who desired to confess his sins to Pachomius, but did not want to use an interpreter. Pachomius then prayed: "Give me, O Master, the knowledge of their discourse I may for the restoration of their souls."[20] While the *Life* at times displays a spiritually-superior position of the community of Pbow vis a vis Alexandria, there is still an attitude of solidarity, especially with episcopal figures such as Athanasius. Theodore eventually becomes fully bilingual, enabling him to solidify the unity between Greek-speaking Alexandria and the Coptic-speaking monks of Upper Egypt:

> For that which our father Theodore explained to them was a help to them. He ordered them to translate the letter of the Archbishop, Apa Athanasius, and they wrote it in Egyptian.[21] He placed it in the monastery, as it remained a law for them. After he rose, he prayed for the brothers. Each one of them went to their monastic cell marveling at what they had heard from our father Theodore from the holy Scriptures of God.[22]

The unity displayed in the *Life* between Greek- and Coptic-speaking Egyptians cautions against overemphasizing the distinctions between these language communities in late antique Egyptian Christianity. It is important to avoid the other extreme of ignoring the clear cultural distinctions within Egyptian identity, especially those evoked by linguistic and cultural differences. Theodore is called "the city-man, the Man of the House of the Greeks."[23] Titles such as these set Theodore up as a cultural "Other" among the predominately Egyptian-speaking community of Pbow.

The pre-Chalcedonian period lacked the anti-Roman rhetoric that became common following the council. However, there was a higher frequency of socially-disparaging rhetoric common to the broader Roman Empire in Egyptian Christian texts written in Greek.[24] Such varieties in the social formation of identity across languages and cultures in Egypt no doubt exacerbated the Greek/Coptic distinctions present in Egyptian Christian literature. In late antique Egypt, there was no sense that "Greek" and "Coptic" signaled opposing cultural communities.[25] However, the presence of patronizing language towards Egyptian identity and language in Greek texts complicates the cultural dynamic in late antique Egypt. The multilingual nature of this area was complex and it is equally insufficient to posit an ethnic division between Greek and Coptic speakers as it is to state that there was no division at all between these communities.

Another example of the cultural distinctiveness of Alexandria from Upper Egypt is a letter from Emperor Constantius preserved in Athanasius's *Apology* to the emperor. In this letter, the emperor addresses the people of Alexandria as bearers of Hellenistic civilization:

Your city, maintaining its patriotic nature[26] and remembering the virtue of its forefathers, has consistently been obedient, and has continued to do so . . . you, who were established as the first teachers of wisdom and who were the first to recognize God.[27]

Constantius emphasizes the Alexandrian allegiance to Roman imperial identity and yet acknowledges its unique cultural heritage. Yet, for Constantius, this heritage is not traditional Egyptian culture, but that of the imposed Greek civilization. Attitudes of Hellenistic superiority appear more vividly in late antique Christian literature in Greek than in Coptic. The Greek version of the *Life of Pachomius*, for example, comments on the Egyptian land and people in more disparaging ways than the Bohairic. The Greek *Life* refers to the site of Pachomius's first monastic community, Tabennesi, as a "desolate village" and the residents as "commoners."[28] Such condescending language referring to the land and people of Tabennesi is absent from the Bohairic *Life*, which instead calls the land Pachomius chose for his monastery a "large acacia forest" and says that "there were a lot of people all around that place."[29] Similarly, the Bohairic *Life* takes greater care to name several of the original Tabennesiotes who helped build the monastery. The Greek *Life*, at one point, names several of the leaders at Pbow and then states that it is "excessive to name each of these who were all strong in spirit and true athletes of Christ."[30] "Excessive," applied to this situation, is a descriptor that is uncommon to Coptic-language monastic literature. Rather than referring to the inhabitants as "commoners," the Bohairic *Life* speaks to the social conditions of the community: "He was very attentive in providing for them, since they were in great poverty."[31] In his preface to his translation of the Pachomian *Rules*, Jerome calls the Egyptian language "simplistic" in comparison to his own native Latin.[32]

The multilingual interchange and diverse ethnic makeup of Pbow demonstrates the inclusivity and universality of Egyptian Christianity. This was also true following the Chalcedonian schism. However, there was already a tendency in the pre-Chalcedonian period to elevate Egyptian saints as teachers to the global Church—a rhetorical strategy that would be intensified following Chalcedon. This is evident in the Greek *Life* where the Pachomian monks refer to Apa Anthony as the "light of this entire world," whose "fame has reached the Emperors, and they glorify God because of you."[33] After Chalcedon, Egyptians would often be presented in contrast to "Romans," a dynamic that is absent from pre-Chalcedonian texts. In Pbow, a unity of faith and identity included an increasing number of foreigners. Among

Theodore's disciples was a multiethnic group of monastics including "Alexandrians, Romans Armenians" and other individuals who were not ethnically identified (perhaps Egyptian?): "Theodore, the City Man[34] ... translated every word of teaching he heard from his (Pachomius's) mouth."[35] Eventually, Theodore was able to recruit more translators who aided him in making the teachings of Pachomius available to the growing Greek-speaking community at Pbow: "The brothers who were his interpreters for the remaining words into Greek for those who did not understand Egyptian[36]—because they were foreigners or Alexandrians—these people heard him speak many times about the way of life of our father Pachomius. They paid complete and passionate attention to what he said to them (the brothers) concerning him (Pachomius), they wrote these things down for them (the brothers)."[37]

The renowned Coptic author Shenoute of Atripe also betrayed a social worldview of Christian universalism that was devoid of any special emphasis on the Egyptian people. Shenoute gives thanks to God for the victory at Ephesus using universalizing ethnic rhetoric: "Blessed are You, who summons every race of humanity[38] to get away from the deception and all the traps of the devil, and to know You."[39] Shenoute frames orthodoxy and heresy using extant categories of human social organization: "Blessed are You, who poured Your blessings of every kind upon Your people[40] and not on any godless nation."[41] However, for Shenoute, the Roman Empire fit the category of a "godly" empire. This would drastically change for his immediate Egyptian successors.

The distinctions between "Greeks," "Romans" and "Egyptians" were already extant in pre-Chalcedonian literature, as was the tendency to elevate the spiritual status of Egyptians. This occurred in the context of claims of Christian universalism. In the *Apophthegmata Patrum,* Christian universalism is vividly expressed in ethnic terms: "One of our Fathers said, 'There is no ethnicity under heaven like that of the Christians.'"[42] This statement is repeated later in the *Apophthegmata Patrum* when one of the "Egyptian fathers"[43] travelling to Athens is told that he was "greater than all the philosophers of the Greeks."[44] This Father reiterates the teaching that "there is no ethnicity[45] under heaven like that of the Christians." While post-Chalcedonian Egypt still maintained a universal scope of the universal Church, the texts surveyed below demonstrate that such strong language (Christians as a universal *ethnos*) is absent from literature following Chalcedon. Furthermore, Egyptian Christian universalism held a nuanced view of ethnicity and religion—Christians were both a distinct race/ethnicity as well as a religious community made up of all ethnic groups. Athanasius expresses this in his *Orations against the Arians:* "Not only Israel, but all the ethnic groups[46] from this point forward, as the Prophet has already said, have left their idols and discover the true God, the Father of the Christ."[47] Similarly, Theophilus of Alexandria said that non-Jewish Christians "belong to the ethnic groups,"[48] that is, Christians continue to identify with their "Gentile" ethnic background even after becoming Christians.[49]

The *Life of Pachomius* represents a similar Christian universalistic worldview, yet a distinct appropriation of Jewish identity. The concept of "race/ ethnicity" (*genos*) only appears in universalizing instances: "The Lord's will is to minister to the race of humanity[50] and to unite them to himself."[51] The Sahidic version of the *Life* records a lengthy prayer from Pachomius that includes a similar statement: "The Lord God is blessed, the One who created all the races of humanity from one,[52] so that they cover the face of the earth."[53] Christians are present among every ethnicity and their persecution only strengthens their resolve as it gives rise to asceticism. Because the Roman Empire, along with all other empires, is the enemy of Christianity, Egyptian Christians are not especially singled out. Not only is there a lack of emphasis on the category "Egyptian," but ethnicity is deployed in more expansive ways. Pachomian leaders, such as the successor Apa Horsiesios, is described multiple times as "the true Israelite," a reference to Jesus.[54] Rather than emphasizing Egyptian identity, the category of "Israelite" is appropriated to emphasize ascetic piety.

Cyril also betrays a vision of race/ethnicity (*genos*) in universalizing Christian terms. In his *Commentary on John,* Cyril distinguishes between corporeal *genos* and spiritual *genos:* "For the way of the Gospel is exceedingly more ancient than that of the Law. That is to say, that which is by faith and friendship of God, then shaped first in Abraham, as in the beginning of his ethnicity of the flesh,[55] that is of Israel, but now coming as from a symbol to truth, beautifully fulfilled in the holy disciples themselves, as in the beginning of a spiritual ethnicity,[56] safeguarded as a people[57] for God's own keeping, which also is known as a holy ethnicity[58] and a royal priesthood."[59] The *Commentary on Luke* has a similar universalizing concept of a Christian *genos:* "And the Spirit also again came down as if it were a second beginning of our race:[60] and upon the Messiah first."[61] In fact, Egyptian visions of Christian universalism were tied to the political and theological status of the Roman Empire.

Prior to the Council of Chalcedon, the Egyptian church often found itself on the side of the leading theological voices and political authorities across the Roman Empire. Because of this, Egyptian Christians before Chalcedon placed very little emphasis on their unique Egyptian identity.[62] Since pre-Chalcedonian Egyptians espoused a Christian universalism that centered on the Roman Empire, this period was characterized by expressions of political and theological solidarity with Rome.

The *Life of Pachomius* provides an Egyptian Christian view of the Roman Empire before and after the reforms of Constantine. The biography of the fourth-century Egyptian ascetic begins with reflection on God's universal plan of salvation through the call of Abraham: "The word of God, who made all things, came to our father Abraham and ordered him to sacrifice his only son. He said to him, 'I will shower blessings on you. I will make your descendants as many as the stars of heaven; all the nations of the earth shall be blessed in your seed.'"[63] God continued to speak through the various prophets and figures in the Hebrew Bible, culminating in the appearance of Jesus: "For he had promised to him a blessing for the nations, and he commanded his disciples, 'Go and teach all the nations, baptizing them in the name of the Father and of the Son and of the Holy Spirit.'"[64] The *Life* then recounts how Christianity spread "in every land"[65] following the time of the Apostles, with special emphasis on the persecution of Christians in the Roman Empire.[66] The *Life* also emphasizes Peter of Alexandria as chief among all the early Christian martyrs in the Roman Empire, highlighting Egyptian Christian leaders. The *Life* frames the genesis of Christian asceticism as a result of continuing the rigorous spiritual lifestyle of the Old Testament prophets, especially those that challenged political authorities. It is curious that the *Life* sees the first three centuries of Christian history as characterized by persecution "in every land and island,"[67] especially as there is no evidence for wide-scale Roman-style persecution of Christians in the kingdoms of Osrhoene, Persia, or India. This further attests to the tendency of Christians in the Roman Empire to interpret world events through a Roman-centric perspective.

As in the anti-Chalcedonian period, Egypt is presented as the faithful opponent of Roman imperial authorities: "In Egypt and the Thebaid there had not been many of them. It was only after the persecution under Diocletian and Maximian that the conversion of the pagans increased in the Church." However, the pagan leadership of the Roman Empire would change during

Pachomius's lifetime, and this would be celebrated by his ascetic community: "After a little time, when the persecution ceased, the great Constantine became emperor; he was the first Christian emperor from the Roman emperors.[68] And it wasn't long that he was king when a tyrant of the Persians attacked him, desiring to take the kingdom away from him. Then he summoned from the entirety of his empire[69] so that he could establish big and strong recruits to go to war against the enemy of God."[70]

Now, not only were Roman emperors of the late fourth century the allies of the Egyptian church due to their shared Christian faith, but the military actions of the Roman Empire were seen as an extension of God's will, as Constantine's enemies are also called "the enemies of God." Pachomius himself joins Constantine's army and serves faithfully before returning to Egypt to begin his monastic community. Pachomius obtains permission to return home after "the godloving emperor Constantine,[71] with God's help, was victorious over those who waged war against him."[72] Whereas once, the Roman emperors were enemies of Christianity, now they were among its strongest patrons. This shift in tone represents a sense of solidarity among Egyptian Christians with Roman imperial authority during the mid-fourth to mid-fifth centuries. This comes forth strongly in Athanasius's *Apologia ad Constantinum*, where the patriarch defends himself against accusations of conspiracy to aid the usurper Magnentius. Athanasius responds by declaring his loyalty to Constantius and his prayers for Magnentius's defeat: "I never would have slandered you before him (Constans); and since I see him (Constans) in you, I would never have written to him (Magnentius), instead of praying for your deliverance."[73] Athanasius views Constantius's reign as the will of God, "who has given this Kingdom to your servant Constantius."[74] Furthermore, the *Apology* represents the Roman Empire as the bearer of the Christian tradition to surrounding kingdoms. While Athanasius was in exile, Constantius wrote a letter to Ezana, king of Axum, issuing paternalistic commands for the newly-ordained bishop Frumentius to be brought under Roman imperial authority:

The knowledge of the Almighty is altogether of the greatest concern and zeal. For indeed, I think that the community of the human species[75] is worthy of the same rights in this area, so that they might live out their life in hope, knowing such things about God, and having no discrepancies concerning the inquiries into justice and truth. Accordingly, since you are worthy of divine providence and an equal share as the Romans, we command that the same doctrine reign in the churches.[76]

The *Life of Antony* supports the idea of a Christian empire but cautions excessive attention paid to Christian kings. The fame of the desert hermit gains the attention of Emperor Constantine and his son Constans, who write Antony a letter in support of his ascetic ministry. Antony has no desire to read the letter among the monks, telling them that such attention from worldly authorities pales in comparison to the written Word of God. However, the monks encourage Antony not to offend the emperors, stating "They are Christians!"[77] Antony begrudgingly reads the letter but then reminds the monks to focus on Jesus, who is "the only true, and eternal Emperor." The only reason Antony allowed the reading of the letter was "because they worshipped Christ." Egyptian Christians expressed support of Christian governmental officials; and when the Egyptian church saw the imperial government as orthodox, Egyptian identity was not notably emphasized.

The solidarity on the part of the Egyptian church with the broader Roman Empire/church was due to a shared faith. It makes sense then that when the dominant church of the Roman Empire went the "wrong" way following Chalcedon, countless Egyptian Christians saw this as a loss for world Christianity. On an occasion where a disciple of Pachomius travelled to Alexandria and reported regarding the rise in Arianism across the Empire, Pachomius asks: "How is the Church? For he was grieved for Her then, for the blasphemous Arians with a certain Gregory had risen up like bandits against Her. He prayed to God about this, pained in his heart because of this injustice against the people of God[78] who were now without the archbishop Athanasius, the Christbearer."[79] It is curious that the *Life of Pachomius* here acknowledges the exile of Athanasius but does not implicate the Roman emperor in this act. Despite support for Arians by Constantine and his son Constantius, this community was rejected by the dominant Roman church by the late fourth century and following. Therefore, Egyptian Christians such as the Pachomian communities could look upon the Roman Empire with favor prior to Chalcedon.

Moreover, the Egyptian church was part of the universal (catholic) church that was supported by the Roman government. In his *De Decretis,* Athanasius defends the anti-Arian theology that was affirmed at Nicaea by the "holy catholic church."[80] Prior to Chalcedon, the catholic or universal church was envisioned by Egyptian Christians as globally-dispersed and patroned by the Roman Empire. Athanasius claims that the catholic church was the only hope for refuting the false teachings of the "Greeks."[81] Shenoute of Atripe interpreted the decision at the Council of Ephesus—the imperially-sanctioned condemnation of Nestorius—as tantamount to God's victory:

> I understood it now during this year after we came from Ephesus; that is to say, 'When the Son of Man comes'—the Son of Man according to the distribution (of the Trinity), God and the Son of God according to divinity—'then He will sit on the throne of His glory, and every ethnicity of humanity[82] will be gathered together through His angels. They will stand in His presence, and He will divide them one from another, like a shepherd divides the sheep from the goats.'[83]

In other words, a win for the dominant church of the Roman Empire is a win for God. What is important here is the degree to which Egyptian Christians tied their optimism or despair regarding Christian orthodoxy to the decisions of imperially-sanctioned councils in the Roman Empire.

After Chalcedon, the language of catholicity referred specifically to Alexandria/Egypt and the Roman government is often depicted as the enemy of the catholic church. In the case of Theophilus of Alexandria and his polemic against the Origenists, the archbishop claims that the churches of Rome and Alexandria were united in their rejection of this movement: "Therefore anathematize Origen and the other heretic, just like us, and also Anastasius, the bishop of the holy church of the Romans, who was appointed revered governor of a renowned people."[84] The theological unity between Rome and Egypt led to flattering language toward the Roman pontiff, a situation that shifted for the successors of Theophilus a few decades later. Theophilus claimed that the "Western" bishops rejected Origenism due to the "decree of the Church of the Alexandrians," thus emphasizing the role of the Egyptian church in promoting orthodoxy.[85]

However, the *Life* does recall the persecution of Athanasius at the hands of the Roman Empire. A Roman imperial official named Artemios, in collaboration with the governor of the Thebaid, comes to Pbow to search for Athanasius during one of his exiles.[86] Artemios brings a garrison of soldiers to surround and detain the monks at Pbow, initially declaring that they are searching for a "Persian" enemy of the Roman Empire. Speaking through translation to the Egyptian monks, Artemios searches the entire *koinonia*. An Armenian monk speaks in Greek to the duke, declaring the community's innocence. After hearing from this "foreigner,"[87] the duke reveals their true intention to the monastic superior: "'Athanasius, the archbishop, is the enemy of the emperor. He is the one we are searching for because the emperor has sent for him and we have not found him. But we have heard that he is hiding among you.' The elder (Domnius) answers the duke, 'Archbishop Athanasius is our father through God; but we testify to you before God that not only is he not hiding among us, but I have never seen his face.'"[88]

The monks of Pbow even refuse the duke's subsequent request for prayer due to obedience to an episcopal decree not to pray with potential Arians.[89] This ban on praying with any outsiders was to stand "until the Church is set right again." Such a statement indicates that this manuscript of the *Life* emerged at a time when the Church had been "set right"; that is, Nicene orthodoxy was the position of the Empire again. This is evident in that the soldiers and officials leave the monks unharmed, despite their loyalty to Athanasius and refusal to pray. The monks celebrate their safety and that God protected them from harm from the Roman imperial officials. This is in stark contrast to post-Chalcedonian interactions between Egyptian ascetics and Roman officials, which often ended in the latter persecuting the former. The short-lived oppression of the Egyptian Church at the hands of the Roman Empire was decried; however, the Empire was still embraced overall due to its ultimate allegiance to orthodoxy in the late fourth century. In Athanasius's *Letter to Serapion,* the patriarch acquits Emperor Constantine of any culpability in supporting the Arian heresy and implicates Eusebius of Nicomedia. According to Athanasius, Constantine summoned Arius at the behest of Eusebius. Arius gave an incomplete report of his doctrine and left out the points for which Alexander of Alexandria excommunicated him; therefore, Constantine dismissed Arius in peace.[90]

Athanasius did not exonerate Constantine's son Constantius, who "oppressed the bishops for the sake of (Arianism)."[91] However, Athanasius's treatise addressed to Constantius was written with a respectful, conciliatory tone: "We know that you have been a Christian for many years and that you are of God-loving descent.[92] Now I, for my part, gladly present a defense . . . Your piety, as a lover of the truth and a lover of God, will observe that we are free from all suspicion, and will declare concerning our opponents that they are false accusers."[93] The *Apology* takes the position that Constantius's concern about Athanasius was merely the result of misunderstanding and slander against the patriarch. Athanasius claims that his opponents slandered him by alleging the patriarch's support of Constantius's enemy Magnentius as well as attempting to create enmity between the emperor and his brother Constans. However, Athanasius claims throughout the *Apology* that there is no truth in these claims and he even reports leading the Egyptian people in prayer on behalf of the emperor: "I only said, 'Let us pray for the well-being of the pious Constantius Augustus,' and all the people immediately shouted with one voice, 'Christ help Constantius!' and they remained praying in this way."[94] Athanasius claims that his lack of compliance with Constantius's order to appear before the emperor was concern that this verbal order may have been an inauthentic ploy of the Arians to replace the patriarch in his absence. Further, the letter appeals to his father Constantine: "Your pious father Constantine Augustus, of blessed memory, honored them (the virgins) above all the rest. And your piety in many writings has given them honorable and holy names. But now these wonderful Arians . . . have slandered me."[95] Prior to Chalcedon, Egyptian patriarchs and monastic leaders engaged in theological debate under the assumption that they were on the same side as the "Christian emperors" of the Roman Empire.

When Cyril of Alexandria came into conflict with Nestorius of Constantinople, he did so with a sense of support of Roman imperial and ecclesiastical authority, casting Nestorius as the rebel: "It follows that . . . you understand and teach the things which we all do, the bishops and teachers and leaders of the people[96] throughout the West and East."[97] Unlike the rhetoric of Egyptian patriarchs following Chalcedon, Cyril did not see the theological disagreement as coinciding with geographical or cultural lines. Cyril's successor Timothy Aelurus used the same language of "East and West." In the case of Timothy, however, East and West were divided. For Cyril, East and West were united in their doctrine while Nestorius was the outlier. Cyril expresses similar statements of ecclesial unity across geography in his response to the Formula of Reunion with John of Antioch: "It behooves us to form an alliance for the peace of the church, and to silence the mockery of the heterodox, and for this (purpose) to blunt the blade tips of the hostility of the devil."[98] Even in times of theological dissent with Roman authorities, the pre-Chalcedonian Egyptian church engaged in polemic with an underlying sense of imperial unity.

This Egyptian strategy of interpreting Roman imperial success and failure through the lens of theological orthodoxy continued to be vital in the anti-Chalcedonian resistance. One of the most notable opponents of the church of the Roman Empire during the fourth century was Julian the Apostate.[99] When Julian is mentioned in the *Apophthegmata Patrum,* he is contrasted with a monk whose prayers actually aid in the Persian overthrow of the Roman emperor. However, this monk is not Egyptian. In this passage, then, Egyptian Christians are not reported as having enmity against the empire.

Furthermore, the religious reforms of Julian were a relatively short-lived period in an otherwise Christianized fourth century. Christian dominance in the Roman Empire created an atmosphere where it was not necessary for Egyptian Christians to strongly assert their identity, a situation that drastically changed after Chalcedon. The stories of the sixth-century Abba Daniel of Scetis were written during the anti-Chalcedonian period and therefore, display a more antagonistic portrayal of Emperor Justinian. Daniel, along with a disciple of his, care for a Scetan ascetic who, upon her death, is found out to not only be a woman in disguise but a member of Justinian's palatine order.[100] In this later addition to the *Apophthegmata Patrum*, the Alexandrian patriarch, Abba Daniel, and select Scetan monks conspire against the Roman emperor by aiding a Roman imperial refugee who was on the run from the emperor. This contrasting story demonstrates the shift in tone on the part of the Egyptian church towards imperial authority. Egyptian Christians displayed loyalty to political leaders who adhere to Christian standards. When this failed to be the case, both Roman and Egyptian governmental leaders fell under sharp critique on the part of Egyptian Christians. Critique of Egyptian "pagan" leaders appears in late antique sources in the form of rejection of pharaonic leadership during Old Testament times.[101] Critique of the Egyptians of the Hebrew Scriptures is evident in an apothegm which defends the murder of the Egyptian at the hands of Moses: "When he killed the Egyptian, he looked this here and there and did not see anyone; that is to say, he looked into his thoughts and saw that he was doing nothing bad, but what he was doing was by means of God. And so, 'he killed the Egyptian.'"[102]

Late antique Egyptian Christians did not blindly embrace all things Egyptian; they rejected much of the indigenous religious practices of Egypt.[103] The *Life of Antony* included Egyptian religion in Antony's invective against Greek philosophy: "Tell us now, where is your magic? Where are the spells of the Egyptians? Where are the illusions of the magicians? When did all these things become weak and cease come except at the time when the cross of Christ appeared?"[104] This rejection is significant for matters of ethnic identity as well as religious polemic. While early Christian rejection of traditional religious practices were commonplace, the Egyptian religion was a core part of Egyptian ethnic identity prior to Christianization. Indeed, the Egyptian gods, temples, and rites were a significant factor in how Egyptians were "Otherized" by the broader Roman Empire.[105] Therefore, a rejection of this previous religious and ethnic identity would necessitate framing a new sense of being Egyptian.

Any tensions between the categories "Christian" and "Egyptian" that were present prior to Chalcedon dissolved afterwards. Athanasius articulates similar critiques of Egyptian traditional religion in his other writings, and situates Christianity as the corrective to such religious practices.[106] Any government or ethnic group that stands against the Christian gospel loses the loyalty of the Egyptian ascetic community. The *Life of Antony* critiques traditional Egyptian culture that is incongruent with Christianity. After predicting his death, Antony expressed his desire not to be mummified and rebuked this traditional practice outright: "Egyptians love to prepare for burial the bodies of prominent people, especially those of the holy martyrs. They wrap them in linens but they do not cover them under the ground; but they place them on small couches and watch over them all night long in their homes. They reckon that by doing this they honor the departed."[107] The *Life* argues that this practice is problematic because the patriarchs and Jesus were buried in tombs, and claims that the practice of mummification among Egyptian Christians ended from this time on. What is of note for us is the way the *Life* here speaks of Egyptians as a cultural group distinct from Antony and the monks. The *Life* highlights and celebrates Antony's Egyptian ethnicity in some areas, but distances him from it when it perceives Egyptian culture as antithetical to Christian practice. Similarly, in *On the Incarnation,* Athanasius critiques the Egyptian practice of venerating water and calls non-Christians to worship God, the creator of the water.[108]

Unlike traditional Egyptian religion, the Egyptian church embraced the Roman Empire and its church prior to Chalcedon. Archbishop Theophilus participated in a controversy regarding the celebration of the Pascha. However, in a letter to Emperor Theodosius, Theophilus expresses solidarity with the emperor on behalf of the Egyptian church:

> Certainly, your piety's love for God has been celebrated throughout all the churches. But surpassing all things like the splendor of the sun, you establish blessed and salutary laws that you may secure the souls of the lost. Because of this, the glory of your name will endure for many ages because of your imitation of God and your orthodox faith (*recta fide*). Indeed, glory and virtue are for the emperor who, being drawn closer to God, also has an impregnable piety which is firm and persevering. But I, Christ-loving emperor (*amice Christi imperator*), having reflected on the firm contributions of the Church of Alexandria, in no aspect of human life can I imagine being able to offer sufficient thanks to your goodness, seeing that of all the things here come from God, we enjoy a proper joy and favor through you.[109]

While Theophilus offers a correction on the date of the Pascha to the emperor, he expresses strong sentiments of unity with the Roman government and the belief that the Roman emperor is the representative of God on earth. Theophilus's successor, Cyril of Alexandria, demonstrates a similar attitude towards Theodosius in his polemic against Emperor Julian:

> And give me your indulgence that I have resolved not only to speak against a king, but also for the glory of Christ, the Great King, who rules together along with His Father over everything. For it is only through Him that it is appropriate to say: 'Through me kings reign,' for He is the Lord of Glory in heaven and upon the earth. The consequent result is that the enforcers of the divine doctrine—which is obviously us, ordained into this by Him—oppose those who desire to harm His glory.[110]

Cyril praises Emperor Theodosius, to whom the work is dedicated. The patriarch also outlines the Egyptian Christian response to imperial authority: Christians are to support imperial "godly" governments and oppose those that are "heretical."[111] The Egyptian Christian community's participation in Christian dominance in the Roman Empire engendered acts of religious violence against practitioners of Greco-Egyptian religion: "Some fathers once went into Alexandria, having been summoned by the blessed Theophilus the Archbishop, in order to offer prayer and tear down the temples."[112] Shenoute of Atripe defends his actions of breaking and entering the home of a local wealthy citizen of nearby Panopolis named Gesios, and destroying Gesios's religious idols. Shenoute incurred the criticism of the populace of Panopolis—likely including many Christians—to whom he defended his actions as congruous with the Christian emperors of the Roman Empire:

> But now someone has made for himself an icon of Kronos and icons of other demons, while not being satisfied with icons of effeminate men and licentious and promiscuous women, whose deeds are shameful to talk about, just as you saw them all, each according to its kind, even icons of priests with their heads shaved and altars in their hands, everything that was in the temples at the appointed time when the one whose memory is of good repute, Theodosius the righteous emperor, had not yet commanded that they be destroyed, just as his honored progeny, the present righteous emperors who rule the entire earth,[113] have commanded in their letters to destroy and dig up the foundations of the other remains until there is no stone among them that is left on top of another.[114]

Shenoute likely delivered this sermon at the White Monastery complex during the early fourth century, when Emperor Theodosius's grandson was continuing much of the pro-Christian reform across the Roman Empire. While practitioners of traditional Greco-Egyptian religion were still numerous throughout the Nile Valley during the fifth century, Christian leaders such as Shenoute felt emboldened by the Christian emperors and their public support of the church. Indeed, Shenoute felt that his actions were a logical extension of the policies of Christian emperors:

> If it is illegal to take icons of demons from that one's (Gesios's) house, is it also illegal to take them from their temples? Because the things on account of which the righteous emperors commanded destroy the temples and to raze them down to their foundations and to smash their idols that are placed inside them, these are the things that we took from that place.[115]

Shenoute expresses no remorse to his critics in Panopolis and even criticizes them as faltering in their Christian resolve for not being supportive of destroying relics of Greco-Egyptian religion. In another discourse defending his actions against Gesios, Shenoute claims:

> For just as there is no thievery for those who have Jesus in truth—regarding what you have said to me because I took your gods secretly and that I caused your condemnation and shame to be tied to the doorposts of your house, written on papyrus, as your urine vessels, which were in bottles like wine, were broken upon the steps of your house and into your doorway and the door of those who resemble you—there is freedom for those who put their trust in Kronos, that is, you and those who are like you in unbelief and every uncleanness.[116]

Shenoute wrote these justifications during the late-fourth/early-fifth century when the two most infamous instances of Christian violence upon practitioners of Greco-Egyptian religion occurred: the destruction of the Serapeum in 391 CE and the murder of the Neoplatonist philosopher Hypatia in 415 CE. Indeed, these decades may have been the most significant window of time where the Egyptian church found itself most in line with the religious worldview of the dominant Roman Empire.[117] In the first three centuries of Christianity, Egyptian Christians were persecuted by patrons of traditional Roman religion; during the fourth century, Athanasius and the Egyptian church were persecuted for their defense of Nicene Christology; and following Chalcedon, the Egyptian church was persecuted for its rejection of two-nature Christology. However, the half-century between the Theodosian reforms and the Council of Chalcedon witnessed theological agreement between Alexandria, Constantinople, and Rome the likes of which had not existed before and would never exist again.[118] It is not surprising then, that some of the most extreme acts of Christian violence in Egypt occurred during this time period. Prior to Chalcedon, Egyptian Christians strongly identified with their "Christian emperors."

FOUNDATIONS FOR EGYPTIAN ETHNICITY AND RESISTANCE

The Egyptian church before the Chalcedonian period primarily identified with the universal church, placing little emphasis on its unique ethnic identity due to its alliance with the Roman imperial church. However, the heightened emphasis on Egyptian identity following the Council of Chalcedon did not emerge from nothing. Indeed, there were foundations of Egyptian-centered rhetoric and imperial resistance before the Council of Chalcedon.[119] The following analysis simply demonstrates that the category of "Egyptian" existed prior to Chalcedon and that Egyptians had a collective consciousness as a people. The difference, however, is that this identity was not pronounced nor in opposition to competing Christian identities that were framed ethnically.

People in the ancient world organized humanity into various levels of social identity; they noticed physical, linguistic and cultural differences. In the fourth- and fifth-century collection of monastic sayings the *Apophthegmata Patrum*, some monks were identified as "Egyptian" and non-Egyptians were labelled as "foreigners."[120] The *Life of Antony* opens by highlighting Egypt as the context where Anthony entered the noble contest of asceticism. After the preface to the *Life*, the first thing that Athanasius asserts about Antony is that Antony was an Egyptian, or his "ethnicity was Egyptian."[121] The *Life* contains both ethnic and racial language.[122] One of Athanasius's first stories of Antony's spiritual engagement in the desert deploys racial rhetoric. When the devil is unable to draw Antony into sinful behavior, "he appeared to him in the image of a Black boy."[123] When Antony resists and causes the devil to flee, he is simply called "the Black One,"[124] rather than one who had dark skin. Athanasius's successor Theophilus of Alexandria makes a similar statement disparaging Blackness when he argues against the anthropomorphite Aphou: "How can you say that a Cushite[125] is in the image of God? Or a leper, or a cripple, or a blind person?"[126]

The Greek term *melas* used for Antony's devil is a racial term, rather than referring to ethnicity, for the word means "burned-faced one." Similarly, the Coptic word may derive from the Cushite people, but it is used to refer to Africans who reside south of the First Cataract of the Nile. This word applies alternatingly to Blemmyes, Nubians, or Axumites and, therefore, is a racial category akin to "*Aithiopian*," rather than a specific ethnic category. These words referred to people with dark skin across various kingdoms and ethnic groups such as Nubia, Axum, Southern Arabia, and the Indian subcontinent. Athanasius's use of concepts referring to skin color help to illustrate the physical dimensions of race, in contrast to ethnic categories such as "Egyptian." Ultimately, the significance of highlighting Antony's Egyptianness at the beginning of his *Life* is that Egyptian Christians expressed pride in their ethnicity from the earliest periods of Christianity.

The *Life* calls Antony "a physician given by God to Egypt."[127] When Antony taught his ascetic disciples, the *Life* highlights the fact that he did so in the "Egyptian language."[128] It is of note that the *Life* elevates an ascetic hero who speaks the Egyptian language, which the broader Roman world commonly disparaged.[129] In fact, Athanasius claims that Greeks looked down upon Egyptians because the Egyptian gods are the victims of Greek gods.[130] By contrast, the "Greeks" appear in the text in a manner common to early Christianity in the Roman Empire: "The Greeks leave home and cross the sea in order to become learned in letters, but we have no need to leave home for the Kingdom of Heaven nor to cross the sea for virtue."[131] Athanasius's use of the term "Greeks" may have a more religious sense. In other writings, Athanasius seems to understand "Christian" and "Greek" as opposing identities: "Those from among the Greeks who now come into the church, having abandoned their superstitious idolatry, take the name, not of their catechists, but of the Savior, and begin to be called Christians instead of Greeks."[132] However, the ethnic dimension is also important.[133] At various points in his writings, Athanasius distinguishes between the pagan practices of the Greeks and other ethnicities such as Egyptians, Assyrians, Persians and many more.[134] He consistently juxtaposes all of these "pagans" with Christians. Similarly, Cyril of Alexandria speaks against "Greek religion."[135] The specificity of "religion" that is "Greek" illustrates the inseparability of the religious and ethnic dimensions of identity in antiquity. Therefore, while "Christian" is a religious concept that emerges through ethnic rhetoric, writers such as Athanasius did not see all "pagans" as one united entity. "Greeks" should not be understood to represent all "pagans"; Christian writers knew how to distinguish pagans of various ethnicities.

Later in the *Life of Antony*, "Greeks" and "Christians" are contrasted: "The Greeks they deceived through illusions, while envying us Christians, disrupting everything, desiring to prevent us on our way up to heaven so that we will not enter that which they left behind."[136] The distinction between Christian and pagan identities in the *Life* comes to the fore most poignantly in the clashes between Antony and Greek philosophers. It is here that the *Life* highlights Antony's illiteracy: "It was amazing that although he was not learned in letters, he was a smart and discerning person. And then two philosophers—Greeks—came to him under the belief that they could put Antony to the test." Antony replies to the Greek philosophers by inverting the Greco-Roman social stratification that elevated those educated in imperial culture: "Why did you so greatly inconvenience yourselves, O philosophers, for such a foolish person?' When they said that he was not a fool but that he was very wise, he said to them . . . 'Since you came to me, be like me, for I am a Christian.'"[137] Other philosophers come to test Antony and go home defeated and impressed with the wisdom of such "a simpleton. For even though he was raised on the mountain and grew old there, his lifestyle was not uncivilized but it was graceful like an urbanite."[138] The text inverts conventional Roman social stratification, presenting the illiterate Egyptian as the philosophical superior to the Greeks. Antony needs an interpreter to debate the philosophers further about the veracity of the Christian faith, indicating that he would have been speaking in Coptic.[139] Yet, the philosophers are convinced of the veracity of Antony's argument. The construction of Egyptian identity is absent here, but the strategy of elevating Egyptian Christians of a lower socioeconomic status over the cultural-capital-bearing "Greeks" is important. This strategy of identity maintenance—that is, setting Egyptian/Christian identity against a powerful yet theologically aberrant "Greek/Roman" Other—would be crucial for the post-Chalcedonian period.

Sayings in the *Apophthegmata Patrum* also express preference for Egyptian culture and language rather than the cultural capital of knowledge of Greek:

> When Abba Arsenios was asking an Egyptian elder about his own worldview, another person, when he saw him, said, 'Abba Arsenios, how is that you, who have such an education in Roman and Greek knowledge, are asking this peasant about your worldview?' But he said to him, 'I am educated in Roman and Greek knowledge, but I have not yet learned the alphabet of this peasant.'[140]

Statements of Romano-centrism that disparaged non-Roman "barbarians" and even peripheral ethnic groups within the Roman Empire were common in Late Antiquity.[141] The most common theological motif of the *Apophthegmata Patrum* is the cultivation of ascetic humility. In this example, the text inverts the common ethnocentrism of the Greco-Roman world: the text presents Abba Arsenios as a humble ascetic leader who does not glory in his knowledge of the more prized cultural systems of knowledge. Rather, he desires to learn the alphabet of the "peasant." The *Greek Life of Pachomius* also deploys the Roman social category of "barbarian" in contrast to ascetic humility. Some "barbarians" raid the *koinonia* of Pbow and threaten a monk to pour libations for traditional liturgy, which he did. This disappoints Pachomius. who admonishes that the monk should have died for the Gospel.[142] The category of "barbarian" in the rhetoric of late antique Roman Christians appropriated this term for ethnic outsiders with respect to Roman borders and imbued it with spiritual significance. For Roman Christians, "barbarians" required the saving faith of Roman Christianity just as the "barbarians" of old required the civilizing presence of Roman civilization.

Infusing social stratification with spiritual, moral and theological value also appeared within Egypt's various regional identities. The *Apophthegmata Patrum,* at times, draws distinctions between the Scetan residents of Lower Upper—the text's central characters—and "Egyptians" as a distinct people and "Egypt" as a region separate from Scetis. In one episode, some "monks came into Scete from Egypt" and received food as they were extremely hungry. However, the text depicts the "Egyptians" as impulsively eating, offending the Scetan monks who rebuke the "Egyptians."[143] In this example, "Egyptians" are ethnically distinct from the ascetic community at Scetis, with the former being morally critiqued by the latter. The ethnic distinction is curious, given that sometimes "Egypt" is exchanged for the "Thebaid" which is also used in contrast to Scetis.[144] Indeed, the geographical purview of the term "Egypt" displayed variety in ancient parlance. Another example of this is an apophthegm regarding Abba Longinus who encounters "an Egyptian" on the shore. This man comes on a boat "from Egypt" and dies shortly after meeting Longinus.[145] The text portrays this "Egyptian" in a positive manner, unlike the hungry "Egyptians" in the above excerpt. Indeed, the "Egyptians" are depicted as spiritually inferior and in need of reproval.[146] In another example, the Alexandrian bishop Ammon refers to himself and other Alexandrians as "Greeks," in contrast to residents of Pbow, who he calls "Thebans."[147]

However, such negative depictions of Egyptians were absent during the anti-Chalcedonian period, as is demonstrated below. This negative vision of Egyptians was also rare in the *Apophthegmata Patrum*. The text even contains sixth-century stories that illustrate the continuance of linguistic diversity across the regions of Egypt. One story involving the anti-Chalcedonian hero Daniel of Scetis relates that he travelled with other Scetan monks to the Thebaid and spoke to a community of monks there, where his words had to be translated into "Egyptian."[148] While Greek is often associated with Lower Egypt and Coptic with Upper Egypt, the post-Chalcedonian period exhibits a diminished presence of any preference between the two languages. However, in the pre-Chalcedonian period, the *Apophthegmata Patrum* praises the piety of monks by referring to their Scetan rather than Egyptian identity.[149] The pre-Chalcedonian period was characterized by more specific social descriptors than "Egyptian," referring to one's town or region. Similarly, in the *Life of Pachomius,* ascetics from the Pachomian *koinonia* were often called "Tabennesiotes."[150] In the anti-Chalcedonian period, regional identity shifted to emphasize a more overarching Egyptian identity.

Likewise, celebration of Egyptian ascetics does not refer to a specific town or region, but to Egypt as a whole. The *Apophthegmata Patrum* celebrated Egyptian ascetics and their humility in rhetorical contrast against the Roman Empire:

> An Egyptian monk lived in a suburb of Constantinople during the reign of the emperor Theodosius the Younger. Passing along the road, the emperor abandoned everything and came alone knocking (at the door) of the monk. He opened (the door) and recognized who it was, but received him as though he were an official. When he came in they prayed and sat down. And the emperor began probing him about the fathers of Egypt. He said: 'They are all praying for your well-being.' And he said to him: 'Eat a little.' He moistened some bread and added a little oil and salt, and he ate. And he gave him water and he drank. The emperor said to him: 'Do you know who I am?' But he said: 'God knows you.' Then he said to him: 'I am the Emperor Theodosius.' And the elder immediately prostrated himself before him. The emperor said to him: 'Blessed are you who has no preoccupation for your life. Truly, even though I was born in the palace, I have not enjoyed bread and water like today; I have eaten with great delight.' From then on, the emperor began to honor him. However, the elder got up and fled again and went to Egypt.[151]

Egyptian Christians expressed pride in the faith and people of Egypt, despite common disparaging attitudes in the classical world towards

Egyptians. Another example of this is an apophthegm regarding a Palestinian ascetic named Seridos who meets a "beloved Egyptian" who brings him a letter from Egypt. After delivering the letter, the "beloved Egyptian" returns to Egypt to fulfill further obligations, but dies due to heavy storms on the river.[152] The text celebrates this Egyptian as the model of humility and obedience. It is important to note that this Egyptian pride was not set against the dominant Roman Empire.[153]

Egyptian-centric rhetoric in fourth-century literature presented the Egyptian church as the theological compass of the Roman Empire. The monk Paphnutius "won over" the bishops of Nicaea over the issue of marriage and conjugation for lay ministers. Emperor Constantine paid great honor to Paphnutius.[154] Again, the Egyptian Christian leader advised broader Roman ecclesial and political entities who, in turn, follow the advice given. For this reason, the Empire is not the villain and Egyptian identity is not significant. A similar sentiment appears in the letter of Theophilus of Alexandria to Emperor Theodosius concerning the proper date of the Pascha. While the patriarch embraces an imperial Roman Christian identity, he highlights the unique contributions of the Egyptian church on "correcting" the imperial Paschal traditions: "But it was important during your blessed times to verify the correct date of the divine Pascha through diligent examination in the Alexandrian church, which, by praying for you always, desires your name to remain among all people (*omnes homines*) forever."[155]

Some outside of Egypt also bolstered the perception of the Egyptian church as a guide to the broader Christian world. In his preface to the Pachomian monastic *Rules,* Jerome expresses his desire to translate the *Rules* from Greek (via Coptic) into Latin so that "our brothers would follow the example of the Egyptian—or, Tabennesiote—monks (*Ægyptiorum, hoc est, Tabennensium monachorum*)."[156] Likewise, the anonymous author of the *History of the Monks of Egypt* expresses profound admiration for Egyptian ascetics and reports that there was a high demand throughout the Christian world to have a detailed report of the *ascesis* of Egyptian monks: "The brothers of the holy Mount of Olives have continuously asked us, out of their piety, to write about the way of life of the monks of Egypt and what we saw of their great love and their great spiritual discipline."[157]

Critical statements towards Alexandria, meanwhile, are wholly absent during the anti-Chalcedonian period, when Alexandria was Egypt's bold leader in the fight against Constantinople and the Chalcedonian faith of the empire. Prior to the Chalcedonian schism, ascetics in the Egyptian wilderness considered themselves the moral and theological compass of the ecclesiastical center of Alexandria. An apothegm regarding Abba Pambo relates an instance when he sent his disciple to Alexandria for commerce. The disciple spends a great deal of time at the Church of Saint Mark and laments that the desert monks do not have beautiful singing like the churches of Alexandria. Abba Pambo rebukes this, stating that the humility and *ascesis* of the desert monks far surpassed the glorious singing of the Alexandrine churches.[158] Egyptian asceticism retained a spiritual vigor that was intentionally distinct from the mainstream Christianity in major metropolitan areas. This was in large part because monks considered major cities to be spiritually dangerous places that are full of temptations to sin.[159] This is also apparent in the *Life of Antony* when the desert hermit comes "down from the mountain and went to Alexandria and denounced the Arians."[160] A Scetan critique of Alexandrian Christians—lay and ascetic alike—was writ large in the teachings of Abba Isaiah in the *Apophthegmata Patrum*. Abba Isaiah is met by "brothers from Alexandria" who come to "put him to the test." After asking how they could be saved, Abba Isaiah proceeds to offer a blistering critique of urban ascetics who attempted to live the monastic life and yet were still surrounded by worldly temptations.[161]

Perhaps the most famous example of tension between Alexandria and Upper Egypt is the anthropomorphite controversy at the turn of the fifth century during the tenure of Theophilus of Alexandria. The patriarch taught that humans could not be created in the literal image of God, which incurred the rebellion of many ascetics across Egypt. According to the *Life of Apa Aphou,* the bishop from Pemje came to Alexandria and convinced Theophilus to change his mind on this point. Theophilus then praised the wisdom of the monk: "Tell me, what is your life story? Where are the members of your people from?[162] For I see that your appearance is like that of a simpleton, but I hear that your words are exalted above that of wise people."[163] Again, the humble Upper Egyptian ascetic surpassed the Alexandrian elite—this time, the patriarch himself. Significantly, then, these pre-Chalcedonian Egyptian examples provide a hint of spiritual superiority on the part of the desert monks with regard to Alexandrian Christians.

Egypt was on the side of the Roman Empire and its dominant church for the majority of the pre-Chalcedonian period. However, in one of the rare instances of an Egyptian Christian vehemently denouncing a Roman emperor, the foundations of Egyptian Christian resistance that would later become commonplace are clearly seen in the pre-Chalcedonian period. In his

History of the Arians, Athanasius vehemently condemns the pro-Arian tactics of Constantius in a manner similar to post-Chalcedonian Egyptians. Athanasius decries the imposition of a Cappadocian bishop named George in Egypt who Constantius had sent due to his Arian allegiance. Athanasius presents this George as a financially corrupt businessman from Constantinople who was "an invader" in Egypt accompanied by a military cadre.[164] Athanasius also critiques the Meletians, seeing them as collaborators with the Arians. He contrasts these heretical groups with "us Christians," a global view of Christian identity. However, Athanasius does emphasize Egypt as a particular bastion of Christian orthodoxy in a statement rare to the pre-Chalcedonian period: "For only in Egypt has orthodoxy been completely and boldly professed."[165] Athanasius's conflict with Constantius represents fundamental components of what would become foundational Egyptian Christian visions of ethnic identity. These components include representing Egypt as theologically homogenous in contrast with heretical imperial forces. However, Athanasius's identity language is primarily universalistic. Furthermore, Egyptian ethnic rhetoric such as this was rare in the pre-Chalcedonian period because the Arian schism was relatively temporary. However, in the post-Chalcedonian schism—which persists to the present day—this type of rhetoric became commonplace.

Totalizing discourse on Egyptian Christian identity set against the Roman Empire and its patron church would become archetypal of anti-Chalcedonian Egyptian resistance.[166] Such language was infrequent prior to the Chalcedonian schism and was never contrasted against the Roman Empire. The Greek *Life of Pachomius* provides one of the only examples of an over-arching "Egyptian" expression of ecclesial and ethnic solidarity. After the death of Pachomius, Theodore reports one of his statements providing an assessment of the three greatest theological resources of Egypt during the fourth century:

> I heard, and you elders were present, as our father said, 'In our generation in Egypt I see three ascendant leaders increasing up by God for the aid of all those who understand: the bishop Athanasius, the athlete of Christ for the faith unto death; the holy Abba Anthony, the perfect example of the anchoritic life; and this *koinonia,* which is an example to all those who want to gather souls into God's presence, to guiding them until they become perfect.'[167]

This statement precedes the confrontation of Governor Artemios and the Pachomian monks. This is one of the rare examples in the pre-Chalcedonian period where the Egyptian church stood against imperial authorities that temporarily imposed heretical doctrine. Since the Egyptian church was in agreement with the imperial church, ethnic distinctions that stratified Egyptians, such as "Alexandrian," "Scetan," or "Theban," were more common than the broader "Egyptian" category that would be elevated after Chalcedon. For the Pachomian monastic of Pbow, Alexandria was culturally "Other" and was the connecting point to the rest of the "universal Church."[168] Following Chalcedon, Alexandria was the center of the catholic church while the empire beyond it was largely ruled by heresy. Pre-Chalcedonian Egyptians placed their confidence in the Roman Empire, which was seen as God's representative on earth. When this empire became "heretical," confidence shifted to Egypt, the center of global orthodoxy. The double-edged sword of identity formation shifted from universalism to ethnic particularity. To be sure, Egyptian Christians continued to frame their universal Christian identity with other orthodox of various ethnicities, both inside and outside of Egypt. However, Christian universalism diminished and was no longer centered in the Roman Empire, but in opposition to it.

During the mid-fifth century, the rhetoric of Cyril of Alexandria began to speak of Alexandria and Egypt as a unified whole in ways uncommon to his predecessors: "To the devout and God-loving minister Nestorius, Cyril and the assembled synod in Alexandria of the province of Egypt,[169] greeting in the Lord."[170] The Egyptian church was unique in the late antique Roman Empire in the relatively absolute and consolidated authority of the Alexandrian patriarch. The "Pope of Egypt" did not appoint metropolitan bishops, as was practiced in other regions of the Roman Christian world. Especially after the rise of communal asceticism in Egypt during the fourth century, Egyptian Christianity was further marked by a close affiliation between the Alexandrian patriarch and monastic communities throughout the region. The Egyptian church submitted to a highly-venerated Apa located in Alexandria whom the monastic communities supported. The unique combination of these factors within Egyptian Christianity—the importance of the patriarch and his extensive support across the community—likely contributed to the comprehensive and swift resistance to the Roman imperial church following Chalcedon.

In sum, Egyptian strategies of ethnic boundary maintenance were distinct from those following the Christological schism of the mid-fifth century, while the foundations of post-Chalcedonian identity were extant. Pre-Chalcedonian Egyptian Christians placed little to no emphasis on their

Egyptian identity; rather, they focused on their universal Christian identity. This was the result of the theological unity that existed between the patriarchate of Alexandria and the dominant church of the Roman Empire centered in Constantinople and Rome. Even texts composed after the Chalcedonian schism and set prior to Chalcedon displayed such unity with the pre-Chalcedonian Roman government. However, awareness of and pride in Egyptian identity were present prior to Chalcedon, though minimal. Furthermore, pre-Chalcedonian Egyptian Christians displayed vigor in combating heresy and a sense of theological unity across the land of Egypt, led by the Alexandrian patriarch. When the "Roman church"—the center of Egypt's universal Christian identity—became the enemy, a new sense of ethnoreligious identity rose to prominence that jointly centered Miaphysite orthodoxy and Egypt.

THREE

Aftermath of Chalcedon

THE FOLLOWING THREE CHAPTERS will investigate ethnic boundary maintenance in anti-Chalcedonian literature during the fifth, sixth and seventh centuries. The structure of this analysis is based largely on the three periods of anti-Chalcedonian literature outlined by David Johnson: 1) texts focusing on the immediate aftermath of Chalcedon composed in the early sixth century, 2) texts focusing on the religious policies of Justinian composed in the mid- to late sixth century, and 3) texts focusing on Cyrus the Caucasian composed during the aftermath of the Islamic conquest.[1]

This chapter will explore the anti-Chalcedonian texts relating the events immediately following Chalcedon in the late fifth century. Some of the most significant figures in this period are Timothy Aelurus, Longinus, and Macarius of Tkôw. While many scholars affirm that anti-Chalcedonian doctrine emerged as the rubric for Egyptian identity, this chapter will demonstrate that this process of identity politics did not begin with the Arab Muslim conquest.[2] Ethnic identity formation was already evident in fifth-century sources. The ethnic rhetoric of seventh-century Coptic texts is certainly more overt than those of the fifth century. However, the earlier sources reveal that Egyptians began a process of equating Miaphysite doctrine with Egyptian identity immediately following Chalcedon.[3] In light of this, Chalcedon is the event that sparked a perceived need among Egyptian Miaphysites to distinguish themselves from their newfound Byzantine Chalcedonian adversaries, a need that did not exist before the Byzantines became "heretics."[4]

The ethnic element of these early-fifth-century texts is not blatant. The development of Egyptian Christianity as an ethnic-specific church began at Chalcedon and takes full shape after the Islamic conquest. I will proceed chronologically (as opposed to thematically) in order to demonstrate that ethnic rhetoric in anti-Chalcedonian Egyptian texts became more intensified and obvious in response to historical events in the history of Christian Egypt. Therefore, the three periods of texts surveyed in the following chapters represent a gradual progression of increasingly ethnicized religious polemic.

TIMOTHY AELURUS

Timothy was archbishop of Alexandria in the decades following the Council of Chalcedon and mounted the first sustained resistance to the Christology promoted at the council. Timothy equated Egyptian ecclesiastical authority with universal Christian orthodoxy. Egyptian Christianity, as epitomized in the Alexandrian patriarch, became the normative measure of Christian orthodoxy from his perspective. Timothy Aelurus was a controversial figure in late antiquity, and historical sources present him with varying degrees of partiality in ancient and modern sources. Relying heavily on the epistles of Leo and the *Collectio* of Giovanni Mansi, a nineteenth-century biography entry presents Timothy as an "intruder" who gathered a "motley band of ignorant and turbulent men" to stage a coup on the episcopal see of Alexandria after being consecrated "without the countenance of a single legitimate prelate."[5] It is indeed very common to find ancient sources depicting Timothy as a murderer, thief, and even sorcerer, as in this passage from his enemy Theodore Anagnostes:

> Timothy the Cat [Weasel], having had recourse in magic, went round at night to the cells of the monks, calling them each by name, and when there was a reply, he would say, 'I am an angel and I have been sent to tell everyone to refrain from communication with Proterios and the party of Chalcedon, and to appoint Timothy the Cat [Weasel] bishop of Alexandria.'[6]

Even the origin of Timothy's epithet ("Aelurus") depends upon one's attitude toward the fifth-century patriarch; Timothy's opponents understood the Greek word *aílouros* as "cat," alluding to Timothy's alleged stealthy activities at night. Timothy's supporters, meanwhile, claimed that the name refers to his extremely thin frame, due to his monastic lifestyle, and *aílouros* is often translated as "weasel" by the latter group.[7]

Writing with a positive take, John Rufus, also known as John of Maiuma, records Timothy as accurately predicting the fall of the Western Roman

Empire and labelling it as God's judgment for the acceptance of Leo's *Tome*.[8] The use of eschatological motifs in his attack on the Chalcedonian position was a tactic Timothy shared with Peter the Iberian.[9] The anti-Chalcedonian historian Zacharias of Mytilene gives this explanation of Timothy's name at the time of his forced ordination:

> And the faithful people of the city [said], 'Ordain him [even] by force and unwillingly and seat him on the chair of Mark!' He was weak in body from much [self-]mortification, and on account of his emaciation the members of the party of Proterius used to mockingly call him 'The Weasel.'[10]

The fragments of the *Life of Timothy Aelurus* also reports that Timothy's ordination came at the behest of the people of Alexandria.[11] According to Zachariah, the Roman general Dionysius deposed the anti-Chalcedonian patriarch Timothy and supported the Chalcedonian Proterius, which resulted in massive rioting and death in Alexandria. Dionysius is forced to bring in the monastic leader Longinus to restore Timothy to the patriarchate and stop the violence. Longinus, a foreign monk from Lycia, leads the monks of Enaton in a revolt against the imposition of the *Tome* of Leo by the Byzantine prefect Acacius:

> When Saint Apa Longinus received the letter, he gathered together all the brothers and read the copy to them. When they heard it, they cried out as one, 'Anathematize that abominable ordinance and everything in it, ungodly Leo too, and everyone in communion with him!'[12]

This hagiographical account goes on to describe the miraculous triumph of the monks of Enaton over the Byzantine army without bloodshed, which leads to the establishment of anti-Chalcedonianism as the Egyptian faith. Although the sixth-century *Life of Longinus* does not mention Timothy,[13] monastic communities such as the Enaton supported his doctrinal position.

Timothy's popularity is evident again in the *Chronicle*, which mentions "countless numbers of children" who came to him for baptism during Holy Week, while only six children came to Proterius.[14] Proterius is murdered shortly thereafter by an angry mob and Timothy reinstated as undisputed patriarch. However, by command of Emperor Leo I, Timothy goes into exile at Gangra in Asia Minor in 460 CE.[15] Timothy then goes to a more distant location, Chersonesus, due to further pressure from his Chalcedonian opponents in Constantinople.[16] The *Life of Timothy Aelurus* identifies the bishops of Constantinople and Rome as the primary enemies who caused Timothy's exile.[17] Their success, per the *Life*, was the result of bribes and the actions of lawless men, characterizing Byzantine (and Roman) Chalcedonians as both heretical and corrupt.[18] Timothy remained in exile for nearly twenty years, though he briefly returned to Alexandria when Basiliscus succeeded Zeno as emperor.[19] Timothy died in 477 CE, only a few years after his return to Alexandria.[20] Upon his return, Timothy's position as leader of the people of Egypt was unchanged as he was welcomed with crowds chanting "Blessed is he that comes in the name of the Lord" (Matt. 21:9).[21] Timothy's exile may have deprived him of direct ecclesiastical authority in Alexandria, but the trials of exile may have earned him greater respect from the Egyptian population.[22]

It is during this time of exile that Timothy composed several letters, almost entirely preserved in Syriac,[23] from which we gain insight into his life in his own words. Perhaps the best-known work written during Timothy's exile is his treatise *Against the Definition of the Council of Chalcedon* (*Against Chalcedon*), a work that became important in the florilegia of Christian theology formed in late antiquity.[24] This text and the other large-scale treatise composed by Timothy, *On the Unity of Christ,* surviving completely only in Armenian, are likely epi*tome*s, that is, later summaries written by a different author.[25] Timothy also wrote a church history in an attempt to establish patriarchal authority derived from his place in the line of succession from his Alexandrian predecessors, and at the same time present Miaphysite doctrine as the faith of Egypt.[26]

It is especially through a collection of Timothy's letters—preserved primarily in Syriac and in Ethiopic translation[27]—that we learn most about his unique style of pastoral leadership and doctrine.[28] In these letters, Timothy wages war both on Chalcedonianism and Eutychianism, a strategy that would be followed by Severus and other Miaphysites.[29] Although both Timothy and Eutyches denounced the Council of Chalcedon, their concepts of the hypostatic union were not the same.[30] Timothy was a theologian, church leader and polemicist who used his monastic background to gain the support of ascetic communities in establishing anti-Chalcedonianism as the faith of the Egyptian people. The anti-Chalcedonianizing of Egypt is a process that began with the episcopal career of Timothy Aelurus. This attests to the importance of the fifth-century patriarch for world history.[31] Even from the perspective of his opponents, Timothy's tenure as patriarch represented a turning point in Egyptian religious identity.[32]

The developing ethnic dimension of anti-Chalcedonianism is present in the opening of his letter: "Again while writing to all of Egypt, the Thebaid, and Pentapolis, and instructing them concerning those who are called Diphysites he writes thusly."[33] Timothy writes to "all Egypt," presenting the Egyptian people as completely Miaphysite. Such language describes not so much the reality of fifth-century Egypt but the identity Timothy is prescribing for Egyptians. Timothy believes that it is his duty to instruct the Egyptian Church on matters of the orthodox (that is, anti-Chalcedonian) faith as they endure Chalcedonian hegemony as part of the Byzantine Empire.

Egypt and Byzantine imperial authority were juxtaposed in the period following Chalcedon. The biographical *History of Dioscorus* represents this ethnicized polemic in its depiction of Pulcheria: "Satan, the cursed serpent, continued his previous battle with the woman. He whispered to the impure heart of Pulcheria thusly, 'You are turning and remaining silent; the empire of your fathers will belong to another ethnicity,[34] and you who are a daughter of the Romans[35] are despised.'"[36] Egyptians are orthodox for Timothy while the Romans are heretics, deserving of conquest by another "ethnicity" (*gensā*). Timothy here is using a Greek loan word, which, as argued above, is used interchangeably with *ethnos* in late antique Christian literature. As was also stated above, it is difficult to understand the distinctions between these two signifiers of peoplehood. However, this study has demonstrated that the modern distinction of race come to the fore in rhetoric framing larger collections of humans organized by physical difference, especially skin color. This is not what is happening here in the *History of Dioscorus;* therefore, the mention of Romans and Egyptians and the allusion to the Goths as a "race" correlates to the modern concept of ethnicity. Timothy's labelling Romans as being under the influence of Satan illustrates the beginning of a new phase in which Egyptian Christians depicted Constantinople in increasingly polarized terminology.

Even in the Syriac-speaking world, in a work from John of Maiuma, Timothy, along with "Alexandria and all Egypt," is associated with the anti-Chalcedonian movement: "My Lord, Father, will that orthodox bishop (Timothy) remain in exile and the city (Alexandria) and all of Egypt perish and be captured by impiety?"[37] The specific subject taken up in this letter is how Egyptian Christians are to treat repentant Chalcedonians:

> In accordance with what I have said before, anyone who has received ordination (bishop, priest, or deacon by our holy and orthodox fathers and bishops) who has partaken of the impiety of the Diphysites (people who are murderers of their brothers) and who now desires to repent and acknowledge God with tears—let them return our clergy or orthodox monks of their region to the bishops, so that they may be witnesses of his repentance.[38]

The term Diphysites (or Dyophysites) is constantly employed by Timothy as reverse polemic against his opponents who pejoratively label the anti-Chalcedonians "monophysite." This term remains unsatisfactory to Egyptian Christians who understand the hypostatic union as consisting of two *united* natures (that is, "miaphysite"). Indeed, scholars have described the writings of Timothy as "the origin of the monophysite sect."[39] It remains clear that Timothy "emerges as the first of the major figures of the movement opposed to Chalcedon."[40] Timothy labels the "Diphysites" as "murderers of their brethren," a curious accusation given the involvement of the anti-Chalcedonian party in the murder of Proterius.[41] Although Timothy's concern in this letter is primarily with priestly converts from Chalcedonianism, he opens with some brief instructions concerning "foreigners":

> Of the foreign monks[42] who come to you that you don't know, first acquaint them with the harm of the heresy of those who are called Diphysites, even if it has escaped their notice. If they agree and will be with us, let them anathematize those who are like they were, namely the Council of Chalcedon and the *Tome* of Leo.... Let them be received into communion.... But if they take upon themselves communion with the heretics as well ... then neither pray nor eat with them.[43]

Timothy goes on to exhort the Egyptians to allow Chalcedonian monks safe passage home while demonstrating charity and hospitality, perhaps in hopes of gaining them for the anti-Chalcedonian side. Such hospitality is required, especially for foreigners.[44] Likewise, Timothy instructs the Egyptians to receive laymen[45] into communion after rejecting the Chalcedonian faith. In addition to discussing foreign monks, Timothy provides instructions regarding previously ordained officials and laymen.[46] Interestingly, Timothy provides more detailed information as he moves up the ranks of church hierarchy: the attention given to laymen accounts for one sentence, there is one paragraph for monks, and the majority of the letter focuses on priests.

Employing the imagery of the prodigal son, Timothy instructs the church of Egypt to require a one-year penance from clergy who convert to anti-Chalcedonianism. After this, converted clergy may resume their ecclesiastical office. Severus of Antioch, the most prominent anti-Chalcedonian leader and theologian, also adopted this policy.[47] Timothy expected his rule for converting priests to anger Egyptian Christians who disagreed with the Patriarch's leniency.[48] This is clear when Timothy exhorts his followers in terms that imply the presence of anti-Chalcedonians who had no desire to receive Chalcedonian converts: "Let Christian love return to him from those who live in Alexandria, pious and orthodox clergy of mine, you who are worthy of the rank of priesthood, as you lift up to us the perfection of sincere canonicity and the unity which we pray may exist among all the orthodox."[49] If Timothy calls for loving acceptance of recent converts from the Chalcedonian faith, he then demands strict anathematization of the Chalcedonian formula on the part of recent converts: "Let the penitent's anathematization be in writing with his own hand. . . . For good works occur not only before the Lord but also before people."[50] Timothy wants the Christians of Egypt to embrace former Chalcedonians, just as the father embraced the prodigal son, but he also wants the Chalcedonian converts to demonstrate their allegiance to the anti-Chalcedonian faith.

That Timothy sees Egypt as the guardian of Christian orthodoxy is evident in his writings on church history. Timothy refers to Dioscorus as both "patriarch of the church of Alexandria" and as the "guardian of the faith,"[51] thus combining Alexandrian patriarchal authority with universal Christian authority. Such a rhetorical strategy further represents Timothy's early attempts at identifying the Miaphysite movement with Egyptian ethnic identity. Timothy depicts the Alexandrian patriarch as the sole champion of orthodoxy, rescuing the universal Church from heresy.

Timothy ends his short letter to Egypt with a string of biblical quotations in order to encourage the people of Egypt to endure their present difficulties by maintaining unity: "Those who desire to live in fear of God in Christ will be persecuted . . . A great storm has come upon the Church of God dear brothers, and it is required of us that we suffer together."[52] Timothy also states his ultimate goal of "attaining unity of the Spirit among ourselves" in order to "do battle with our Lord Jesus Christ's enemies" who cause "division."[53] Timothy's short letter to the faithful of Egypt is ultimately concerned with the promotion of the orthodox faith (anti-Chalcedonian) through outreach to foreigners, inclusion of clerical, monastic and lay converts, and the unification of the entire Egyptian church under the banner of anti-Chalcedonianism as a witness to all the enemies of Christ. While there were many non-Miaphysites in the geographic region under the jurisdiction of Alexandria, Timothy prescribes a totalizing, anti-Chalcedonian position for "all Egypt."

Timothy's letter to his homeland deploys resistance rhetoric that lays the foundation for anti-Chalcedonian, Egyptian ethnic identity development. In this way, the dynamic between Byzantine Chalcedonian forces and Egyptian

Miaphysites in the period following Chalcedon was akin to a colonial dynamic.[54] Anti-colonial rhetoric such as that of Timothy increased in the following centuries in the literature of this area, especially in monastic circles.[55] The rich Egyptian history that Timothy and his contemporaries inherited played a role in the ethnic boundary maintenance present in the anti-Chalcedonian movement.

Timothy's letter assumes that the anti-Chalcedonian doctrine is the truest expression of Christian faith and is the faith of the Egyptian people. Language in his letter that has direct communal address ("you," "us," or "our") can be understood as speaking to the entire Egyptian people who are assumed to be anti-Chalcedonian (for example, "let such a one repair to the bishops, the *clergy of ours* in his vicinity").[56] This collectivist tone underlines an appeal for the unity of the Egyptian people in a single cause based on the common struggle of oppression: "A great storm has come upon the church of God, *dear brothers;*"[57] "So let us be diligent, *beloved*."[58] While the ethnic rhetoric present in anti-Chalcedonian texts becomes more obvious in the sixth and especially the seventh centuries, Timothy lays the foundation here for Egyptian Miaphysite strategies of identity formation.

A similar "us"/ "them" dialectic is present in *Against Chalcedon* as Timothy champions the archbishop of the Egyptian people ("our") against an elusive "them" associated with the majority party of Chalcedon: "And yet, they endeavored to enact the deposition of the blessed and holy one, our father and archbishop Dioscorus, who was an utter praise and wonder to them at the synod in Ephesus only a little while ago."[59] However, Timothy includes many non-Egyptians whom he understands to be orthodox in the list of the faithful. In *Against Chalcedon,* this is done primarily through appeal to previous church fathers. This demonstrates that, while Egyptian-centric rhetoric increasingly characterizes this period, there was an important relationship between ethnic boundary maintenance and religious identity.

While Cyril is his main authority, Timothy also quotes several non-Egyptian figures such as Julius of Rome and Theodotus of Ancyra.[60] While Egypt and her inhabitants are most highlighted, Egyptian Christian writers at all times understand their Christian identity to unite them with many outside the boundaries of Egypt. This theme emerges in Timothy's letter to Claudianus in which he quotes 1 Peter 2:9, referring to the orthodox faithful suffering at the hands of "heretics" as "an elect generation, a royal priesthood, a holy nation,[61] an alien people,[62] with a zeal for good works."[63] In this context, the "people" to whom Timothy and his audience ultimately belong is the universal church.

In fact, Timothy offers a direct rebuttal of the nationalism thesis when he accuses the supporters of Chalcedon of being motivated by political rather than by theological concerns, a criticism often levied against anti-Chalcedonians by nationalist scholars: "And it was not in zealous fear of God but in obsequiousness of the ruler at that time that they affirmed this impiety."[64] Timothy's accusation of political sycophancy towards his opponents renders untenable the prior assessment of the anti-Chalcedonian movement as a nationalist movement. However, Timothy's words here also further demonstrate the lack of political motivations behind his populist rhetoric. There is no aspiration for political gain; in fact, the Egyptian Miaphysites rejected such aspirations. This is also the perspective of the CCH, which depicts Marcian offering the patriarchal throne as a bribe: "And the emperor sent the Tome to Alexandria saying, 'The one who will subscribe first, he is the one who shall sit upon the throne and be archbishop.'"[65] The Egyptian-centered rhetoric was a strategy of mobilizing the Egyptian ethnicity around a specific theological cause, not a political or national movement.

Egyptians did not desire to secede from Byzantium but to define the area as the theological and moral center of the empire. The History of Dioscorus presents a similar picture when the empress Pulcheria attempts to trick the patriarch Dioscorus through flattery: "Then she went to the saint where he was. She fell at his feet weeping and begging him saying, 'I am your servant and your daughter; you are the father and the head of the entire kingdom of the Romans.'"[66] Pulcheria's plea to Dioscorus did not work; the patriarch spurned the empress, declaring her a heretic.

As argued above, a desire for a political revolution against the Byzantine state was not a motivating factor in Egyptian anti-Chalcedonian polemic. In fact, the tone of Timothy's writing often exhibits a desire for cooperation with Constantinople.[67] Timothy's letter to the abbot Claudianus ends with an expression of hope for an imperial return to orthodoxy:

> And I sent you a pamphlet so that I might encourage the fear of God which is in you. It was composed by us a year ago when the Emperor summoned us from exile that I might examine the increase in the seditions of the Church, the solution of the heresies mentioned above and help on orthodox decrees. Although the Emperor who summoned us regretted it, we pray that our Lord's will be done, rejoicing in our Lord.[68]

However, there is a steady pro-Egyptian tone in the works of Timothy, which is often critical of imperial Chalcedonianism. An interesting detail is the way he addresses fellow Miaphysites outside of Egypt as "dear friends,"[69] often drawing the wording directly from the Apostle Paul. However, it is only when writing to his fellow Egyptians in Alexandria that he opens and closes the letter by addressing them as "my brothers."[70] The early reaction to Chalcedonian hegemony in the writings of Timothy represents resistance rhetoric in the form of statements of collective consciousness framed in ethnic terms. That Timothy addresses the people of Egypt and begins his letter with attention to "foreign monks" reveals Timothy's assumption that outsiders visiting churches in Egypt require instruction in the faith of its people (that is, anti-Chalcedonianism).

That there were many Chalcedonian Egyptians is evident in the massive conflicts that took place during this period. The Egyptian people were not a monolithic, anti-Chalcedonian group. Furthermore, the fact that the anti-Chalcedonianism became the dominant, popular position in Egypt does not preclude a translocal element in anti-Chalcedonianism. For example, many Armenian Christians accepted the writings of Timothy Aelurus as orthodox during the sixth century.[71] However, Timothy's letter—and the majority of Coptic literature immediately following this period—testify to an anti-Chalcedonian majority in Egypt. More importantly, from the perspective of Egyptian writers, anti-Chalcedonianism was the faith of their people.[72]

To underscore the social, ethnic, and political realities surrounding the Christological controversies and their effects in Egypt is not to ignore the warning of Ebied and Wickham:

> What matters for Timothy and his followers is the simple assertion of a real and true incarnation by the truly divine Word of God. When such emotions are misunderstood or insensitively passed over, the controversy inevitably becomes patient only of interpretation as a logomachy masking political and economic conflicts. Such an interpretation, though superficially appealing, and having perhaps also a measure of truth . . . is, none the less, as this brief extract poignantly reveals, quite unfaithful to the way Timothy, and men like him, understood and experienced the conflicts in which they were involved.[73]

The anti-Chalcedonian movement ignited a process whereby Egyptian ethnicity aligned closely with religious identity. This is in agreement with conceptions of ethnicity in anthropological circles as a category distinct from but shaped by race, language, politics, and religion.[74] It is significant that Timothy and his followers truly believed their faith to be the revelation of God and consistent with the teachings of the apostles and church fathers. Any attempt to dismiss religious rhetoric, such as the letters of Timothy, as political maneuvering in theological dress would be an inaccurate analysis. Timothy's theological conviction was "that Christ was really buried as a dead man, lying in the ground."[75] To point out the role of social and ethnic realities surrounding these theological issues is congruous with the reality that these controversies are fundamentally theological. As the ancient world did not embrace the modern concept of the separation between church and state, theological layers of identity were not thought of as separated from ethnicity.[76] In the case of post-Chalcedonian Egypt, ethnicity became inextricably bound with religious affiliation.

By understanding social conditions, readers of these texts gain more clarity on their meaning and intention. As stated above, attempts to understand the religious life of fifth-century Egypt without bringing in anachronistic factors should not lead to denying the effect of political, social and economic systems on the religious landscape of late antiquity. In conclusion, what we see in Timothy's letter addressed to the people of his patriarchate, comprised of Egypt, the Thebaid, and Pentapolis, is an early move on the part of the exiled patriarch to unite his people under an anti-Chalcedonian statement of faith by rhetorically structuring it as the faith of the Egyptian people. Indeed, the *Plerophoria* credits Timothy with "bringing together the people."[77]

Perhaps the most vivid example of ethnic boundary maintenance present in the theological work of Timothy Aelurus is in his summary of church history. Timothy attributes the fall of Rome to the Chalcedonian schism: "And they were the cause of the schisms and divisions of kings for it was not long after the council of the oppressors[78] that the destruction of Rome occurred. Up until those days there was strife, division, and schisms in the ecclesiastical ranks who were among the kings. Because of this, the Westerners have not reconciled with the Easterners to this day."[79] Here Timothy uses geographical terminology to distinguish the "Westerners" (Rome and Constantinople) with the "Easterners" (Alexandria and Jerusalem). While Timothy's words here in and of themselves do not deploy ethnic categories, they reveal how this theological controversy was largely perceived to divide along geographical lines. Taken together with other statements surveyed above, it is clear that Timothy framed the anti-Chalcedonian resistance through ethnic identifiers ("Egyptian"/"Roman"), communities ("Alexandria"/"Constantinople") and geography ("Westerners"/"Easterners").

As the first prolific anti-Chalcedonian author from Egypt, Timothy laid the foundation for a strategy of Egyptian self-definition that would take further shape in late antiquity.

Timothy links Chalcedonian doctrine with imperial authority and claims that it is "a lie and not faith which prevailed throughout the land (*ar'ā*)."[80] Timothy contrasts imperial Chalcedonian doctrine with the anti-Chalcedonian faith of the East: "Indeed what church in Egypt, Libya, or the East has not mourned over the exploits of their persecution and their impiety? What region or city has forgotten the murders against the sheep of Christ from that time until today as well as the exiles and assaults?"[81] Timothy laid the foundation for a trend in Egyptian anti-Chalcedonian literature of contrasting imperial Chalcedonianism with Miaphysite doctrine. And that Miaphysite doctrine is coterminous with Egyptian identity, even though it is also a translocal movement.

The praise for Timothy and his achievements on behalf of his people found in the *CCH* attest to the function of this patriarch in subsequent Egyptian Christian memory:

> And Pshoi[82] died upon the throne, because he himself was an orthodox. When he died, all the clergy and the archimandrites and the entire country[83] set Timothy on the throne. Then all schisms in the church were brought to nothing [. . .] was in it again,[84] without any offense on any side. But there was peace for all the peoples[85] who hated the *Tome* of Chalcedon.[86]

The totalizing discourse in the CCH presents Miaphysitism as the faith of the "entire country" of Egypt and a light for "all other peoples." Motivated by a commitment to theological orthodoxy, Timothy labored to promote anti-Chalcedonianism as the faith of Egypt, a mantle that he passed on to his successors.[87] The contextualization of anti-Chalcedonianism in the Egyptian ethos, making one-nature Christology a feature of Coptic identity, simultaneously connected Egyptian-ness to the international Miaphysite movement.

LONGINUS

Longinus was a non-Egyptian monastic figure who resisted Chalcedon and therefore is a central figure in Egyptian Christian history. In the introductory material of the *Life of Longinus*, both the universality of Egyptian

Christianity's understanding of belonging to a larger orthodox church and the particularity of elevating the land and people of Egypt are evident. Longinus's foreign ethnicity is made clear, yet, as an orthodox monk, the Egyptian people embraced him. The text folds a universal incorporation of Christians of various ethnicities into the centralized elevation of Egypt. Subordinating the Byzantine political and military forces to the spiritual authority of the Egyptian saints of Enaton makes evident the theological and ascetic superiority of Egypt over against Byzantium. This rhetorical strategy simultaneously sets Egypt up as the orthodox light to the nations and portrays it as welcoming outsiders who ascribe to the orthodox (anti-Chalcedonian) faith.

The *Life* is a compilation based on several texts including homiletic and biographical material with a prologue and title added later.[88] The text demonstrates parallels and potential instances of borrowing from other sources such as the *Apophthegmata Patrum,* the *Life of Peter the Iberian,* the Copto-Arabic *Synaxarium,* and the *Panegyric on Macarius of Tkow.*[89] The primary function of the material that appears in the *Life* serves as spiritual direction for the monastic community.[90] Like much of ascetic hagiography in Egypt and otherwise, promoting the monastic value of humility is of utmost importance.[91] While hagiographical works such as the *Life* provide invaluable insight into the mindset of late antique Egyptian Christians, the historical information needs to be taken with a grain of salt.

For example, while the *Life* claims that Longinus spent significant time as *hegoumenos* (superior) of the Enaton monastery, the silence on this matter in the *Apophthegmata Patrum* casts doubt on this detail.[92] Equally questionable is the identity of the victim of mob violence by the Alexandrian Miaphysites. While the *Life* reports that the prefect of Egypt (Acacius) was burned in the Hippodrome, the Chalcedonian Evagrius claims that Proterius was murdered at the order of Timothy Aelurus.[93] What is clear is that the violence in Alexandria resulted in the exile of Timothy Aelurus and his replacement by the Chalcedonian Timothy Salofaciolus at the order of Emperor Leo I.[94] This Chalcedonian presence in Alexandria during the tenure of Longinus at the Enaton calls into question the depiction of Egypt as completely anti-Chalcedonian in the *Life.*[95] In the *Life of Peter the Iberian,* John of Maiuma presents Longinus as having a central role in the installation of Timothy Aelurus as patriarch:

They had as their head and chief the blessed ascetic and great prophet Longinus, the father of the monks, who was inspired and provided for them according to the will of God for this (purpose). They all reached an agreement to send men who were suited for the task. By force (and) without his foreknowledge nor his being at all aware (of it) beforehand, they took from the desert the holy Timothy, that famous confessor and true martyr, who already had been honored with the dignity of the priesthood by the great Archbishop Cyril. . . . They brought him to the city, to the church called *Kaisarion*, where the whole city was assembled as one, so to say, together with the women and the children. Together with the holy monks they made haste to perform his ordination and to raise him up as high priest, preacher, and fighter for the fear of God.[96]

The *Life*, however, is the primary source of information concerning Longinus. The *Life* contrasts the oppressive tactics of the Chalcedonian Roman forces with the humble, orthodox monks of Egypt. This rhetorical and literary contrast further shapes Egyptian ethnic identity in the immediate aftermath of Chalcedon. The panegyrist began with the customary self-abasement common to Coptic hagiographic material: "Like someone standing under an extremely high rock attempting to lift the rock or climb it, I am at an utter loss for how will I be able to climb it?"[97] Such examples of exaggerated humility usually precede an expression of resolve motivated by awareness of spiritual duty to "write the history of the saints and to further our remembrance of their way of life."[98]

Longinus is said to be from a city in Lycia, a mountainous country in southwest Asia Minor, which attests to the reality that anti-Chalcedonians in Egypt were a cosmopolitan group with many non-Egyptian leaders. The ethnic diversity that characterizes the Egyptian people—in antiquity as well as today—is an example of the manner in which ethnic boundary maintenance develops through contact and incorporation with outside groups.[99] A more inclusive vision of the orthodox community coexists with pro-Egyptian rhetoric. It is interesting that while the panegyrist introduces Longinus and identifies his foreign race,[100] the writer also provides something of a disclaimer: "He was from a city of Lycia according to his race[101] as it is reckoned on earth, but he was a citizen of heavenly Jerusalem for his citizenship was in heaven,[102] according to the teaching of the wise Paul."[103]

This leaves the impression that the panegyrist feels a slight pressure to legitimize a non-Egyptian's place on the roster of proud Egyptian anti-Chalcedonians. By appealing to Longinus's place in the heavenly (orthodox) community, the panegyrist immediately rebuts any ethnically based criticism of Longinus's contribution to the Miaphysite cause. However, as will be shown in the discussion of other texts, such explanations are not necessary when the saint has an Egyptian background. The disclaimer in the *Life of Longinus*, coming at an early stage of the anti-Chalcedonian movement, attests to the significance of ethnic identity and the author's awareness of the Egyptian people's need for Egyptian heroes. Finally, note again the use of a Greco-Coptic word meaning "race" when, indeed, this correlates to the modern concept of ethnicity. "Race" here refers to Longinus's ethnicity, his origin in the Lycian people, and does not refer to a broader racial category. This also further demonstrates how "race" and "ethnicity" appear interchangeably not only in Greek and Latin sources, but in Coptic literature as well.[104]

Longinus is said to have begun monastic life in Lycia at the monastery of Apa Hieronikos under the guidance of Lucius. Lucius and Longinus left the monastery due to a conflict that arose over Lucius's leadership and the two began healing many people in Lycia. Their immense fame caused them to flee in order to cultivate humility. Lucius tells Longinus to go to the Enaton monastery west of Alexandria. Upon reaching the Enaton, Longinus chooses not to identify himself as a monk out of humility. The text then reports that he was not wearing the "foreign" monastic habit that would have identified him as foreign and as a monk: "There was no cowl upon him nor scapular nor habit which the foreign monks[105] wear."[106] The gatekeeper nonetheless correctly identified Longinus as "a young foreign monk"[107] who stood at the door for days because he wanted to enter the monastery.

Impressed by Longinus's patience, the *hegoumenos* allowed Longinus to enter and serve in the monastery. After two years of menial labor, Longinus emerged as a monastic figure by "a Lycian merchant, (from) Apa Longinus's land."[108] After hearing of all the miraculous deeds done by Longinus and Lucius in their "land,"[109] the *hegoumenos* ordered them to shave Longinus's head and clothe him "according to the monastic habit of Alexandria."[110] However, after becoming famous, Longinus left his monastic community again and settled near the sea as a rope maker.

Lucius came to Longinus by divine guidance and the two of them performed miracles, the news of which "filled the great city of Alexandria and all of Egypt."[111] Once again, Alexandria and Egypt are referred to as distinct geographic and cultural units. Byzantine Egypt contained many administrative units, not merely Alexandria and Egypt. Therefore, "Egypt" in Egyptian texts is itself comprised of multiple administrative *nomes*.[112] However, the frequent reference to "Alexandria and Egypt" refers to linguistic and cultural differences as opposed to governmental ones.

The final section of the *Life* discusses Longinus's place in the anti-Chalcedonian movement and scholars take this as the only section of the *Life* with historical value.[113] At the outset of introducing the Christological controversy, the encomiast depicts Chalcedonian doctrine as an imposed force that is synonymous with Byzantine hegemony: "And it happened at that time when the emperor Marcian desired to send a magistrate to Alexandria with the *Tome* of the impious Leo, he commanded that the city of Alexandria, and especially the monks of Enaton, subscribe to it."[114] It is Longinus's mobilization of the monks of the Enaton in opposition to this "polluted doctrine"[115] that launches him into the position of *hegoumenos* of the monastery. Following the rejection of the *Tome* at the Enaton, the text associates Chalcedonian hegemony with the local Byzantine authorities in Egypt: "The emperor instructed Acacius, the prefect ruling at that time, to force the monks at the laura to subscribe to the defiled *Tome* of Leo."[116]

The ecclesiastical and political tension grew because of the response from the Enaton as the monks refused acceptance of the *Tome*, while setting the emperor (*autokratōr*) and God (*pantōkratōr*) in opposition,[117] expressing rejection of the former out of obedience to the latter. It is interesting that in the midst of such rebellion, Leo is the one Longinus labelled "lawless."[118] The depiction of both imperial and local Byzantine authority as wicked continues in the text, as the magistrate and prefect dispatch a group of soldiers to murder the monks at the Enaton.

Byzantine authority is again contrasted with that of God as Longinus becomes aware of the threat by the Lord, who "sets aside the designs of rulers."[119] When the soldiers attacked the monks, who were bearing palm branches, their arrows miraculously missed them. The text contrasts the power and wealth of the Byzantine forces with the humble monks of Egypt: "The wicked have drawn their swords, they have stretched their bows to cast down a poor and wretched one, to slay the upright of heart."[120]

After seeing the miraculous survival of the monks, the imperial troops prostrated themselves before Longinus and came to the Enaton monastery. After the monks reached the monastery and besought the deceased fathers through prayer, the fathers called out from their tombs for the monks to renounce the *Tome* of Leo, as it divides Christ into two natures. Upon hearing the voice of the deceased saints, the court official and the whole army were astonished and prostrated themselves before Longinus.[121] Many soldiers decided to renounce[122] their "military status and the vain deeds of this life."[123]

In this narration, we see again several strands of Egyptian ethnic boundary maintenance present in anti-Chalcedonian literature. The entry devoted to Longinus in the *Synaxarium* highlights this event only in its brief recollection of his life.[124] However, the mention of converts to the orthodox faith—in this case the Byzantine soldiers—attests to the transregional, multiethnic nature of the anti-Chalcedonian movement. Furthermore, the depiction of political and military figures (soldiers, emperors) as representatives of the Roman Empire and as a contrast to the Egyptian faithful do not represent nationalistic aspirations of political autonomy. There was no movement for separation from the Roman Empire or any unique form of political legitimacy. Casting the emperor and his solders as the villains merely highlights the faithfulness of the Egyptian people. Egypt would still be part of the Roman Empire and the writer of the *Life* did not express any desire to change that.

In the text, the court official and other soldiers return to Alexandria proclaiming the deeds of Longinus in the manner of those who have an encounter with Jesus in the Gospels. The citizens of Alexandria then storm the praetorium, seize the prefect Acacius, and burn him in the middle of the city. The panegyrist offers this explanation of the violence of the mob: "I say this, they did not condemn him to death only because of this, but it was a judgment of the justice of God by the mouth of the great Apa Longinus and the brothers who were with him as a prophecy that our father David spoke in the tenth psalm, which he sang in this way, 'Fire and sulfur are the portion of their cup.'"[125] Following the assassination of Acacius, the "bishop of that heresy" fled the city after taking off his ecclesiastical garments and putting on layman's clothing.

The author then reports that "the Church openly proclaimed the teaching of the faithful orthodox."[126] It is interesting that, despite the minority status of Miaphysitism in the Byzantine Empire during the fifth century, the *Life* attributes an anti-Chalcedonian confession of faith to "the Church." Such a universalizing statement, which stands in contrast to Byzantine religious dynamics of the fifth century, further attests to the early attempt at framing Egyptian orthodoxy as an ecclesiastical standard. This Egyptian-centric language supports the ethnic boundary maintenance that permeates texts such as the *Life*. Following the conflict with the Chalcedonians, Longinus spent his last twenty years as leader of the monastery, during which time his mentor Lucius died.

That the text reports Longinus as having ruled "in their midst as a bishop"[127] attests to the dominant role played by ascetic *hegoumenoi* in late antiquity. Longinus's humility is the attribute most accentuated in the *Life* as he "commanded them to flee from vainglory"[128] and "he was humble in every way; his face was cast down as he walked, a walk of wisdom."[129] The *Life* concludes with a short passage about Longinus's death that again casts Alexandria and Egypt as anti-Chalcedonian bulwarks: "Oh how great was the mourning that occurred the day in which he went to rest. Not only the monastic brethren but even the city of Alexandria and its environs, especially those in the surrounding countryside."[130]

This comment indicates that the interior of Alexandria may have been Chalcedonian while the surrounding countryside may have been anti-Chalcedonian.[131] While there were other theological concerns on the part of the Miaphysites,[132] the Chalcedonian dogma that was often associated with Lower Egypt was of primary concern. The distinction between Alexandria and Egypt appears often in the anti-Chalcedonian literature of this period[133] and also appears in the *Life of Longinus*. In sum, the *Life* presents a picture of Longinus as a champion of orthodoxy who established anti-Chalcedonian doctrine as the faith of the Egyptian people despite Byzantine interference.[134]

MACARIUS OF TKÔW

"One is the God of this Egyptian elder[135] who is on board with us!"[136] The Egyptian monk Macarius, bishop of Tkôw, had performed miracles of healing. The biography of Macarius contains ethnic rhetoric that highlights the Egyptian ethnicity of its hero at a level higher than contemporary literature. Drawing on similar themes of ascetic humility and Roman imperial resistance, the story of Macarius adds to the strategies of Egyptian ethnic identity development by frequently referencing Egyptian ethnicity and refuting dominant Roman stereotypes of Egyptians.

The *Panegyric on Macarius of Tkôw* was likely first composed in Greek and is attributed to Dioscorus of Alexandria.[137] As one reads the *Panegyric*, it becomes evident that the story does not unfold in chronological order.[138] The patchwork of unrelated stories contained in the *Panegyric* has led scholars to doubt that the work was written by a single person and, instead, see it as a compilation of separate accounts.[139] Since the historical figure Dioscorus is likely not the author of the *Panegyric*, its date of composition cannot be in the mid-fifth century. The erroneous version of the death of Timothy Salofaciolus in the *Panegyric* is evidence of a *terminus a quo* no earlier than the early sixth century; it is not likely that an author who lived during the mid-fifth century would have made such a significant omission.[140]

The *Panegyric* opens with the identification of the scribes Peter and Theopistus as the authors of the work, who are recording the life of Macarius as reported to them by the patriarch Dioscorus when they visit him in exile at Gangra.[141] As soon as he enters the narrative, the text describes Macarius with a characteristic that is central to understanding the ethnic boundary maintenance in the *Panegyric:* he did not "know how to speak Greek."[142] The text likens Macarius to a soldier who, despite his unfitness for battle (that is, his linguistic handicap), "nevertheless ... did not stop wanting to come with us to the war of Chalcedon."[143] After Dioscorus summoned the Egyptian bishops to accompany him to Constantinople, Macarius was one of the few bishops who did not desire to "remain on their throne."[144] Though he lacked money, Macarius initially turned down the offer to travel with the bishops in the ship and expressed a desire to travel by foot.

Describing Macarius as poor and spurning physical comfort enhances his monastic credentials. Macarius traveled instead with the archbishop, whereupon his linguistic handicap immediately became clear:

> I said to him (Macarius): 'Come, father, and sit next to us.' But he did not understand my speech. However, he walked toward me when I motioned with my hand. He said to me: 'Behold, I have come because you called me.' And I too would not have understood his speech if Peter, the deacon, had not interpreted his speech for me, for he knew the Egyptian language.[145] And Theopistus, the deacon, said to me: 'My father, what are you doing with this mouthless one who is on board with us? ... But I said to him: 'No, my son, do not utter words of this sort against God's just one. ... Theopistus fell to his feet, weeping and saying: 'Forgive me, my father. I have sinned against your holiness.' When Peter had interpreted these words for him, the holy man in his exceedingly great humility said: 'I have sinned, my son.' I said to him: 'Believe me, my father, if you do not absolve him, I will excommunicate him.' And this holy man said to him: 'God forgive you your sins, my son.'[146]

The meekness displayed by Macarius in the face of mockery served as an example of ascetic humility, and providing such examples is a major aim of hagiographical compositions such as this. The text presents Macarius's humility throughout. Like other texts from this period, the *Panegyric* contrasts the humility of the Egyptian monks with oppressive imperial Chalcedonians. This juxtaposition further frames Egyptian ethnicity as the humble guardian of orthodoxy against the imperial heretics. Upon arriving at Constantinople, Macarius is dressed in "dirty garments,"[147] which he feels appropriately express his attitude toward the emperor.

The aspect most relevant to the present study is the role played by ethnicity/language in the case of Macarius. Macarius, as a Coptic-speaker without knowledge of Greek, has a certain kind of marginalized status. However, the laudable humility he displays in the face of prejudiced behavior depicts Macarius and the Coptic-speaking Egyptian people—often called "barbarians"—as spiritually advanced. The multilingual environment of fifth-century Egypt, in which some are monolingual in Coptic, others monolingual in Greek, and others bilingual, contradicts the common assumption of Egypt's cultural homogeneity.[148] However, the marginalization of Coptic-speakers as less prestigious than those who spoke Greek was common in the ancient Mediterranean.[149]

The *Panegyric* highlights the Coptic-speaking Macarius as a pillar of Egyptian ethnicity. Ethnicity, again, is a form of social identity that cannot take form without interaction with other layers of identity, including nationality, race, and religion. Language is another core marker of ethnic identity. The boundaries of Egyptian ethnicity were not coterminous with the Coptic language, for many Egyptians spoke and wrote in Greek and were not considered less Egyptian. However, following the Council of Chalcedon, the Coptic language became increasingly elevated above Greek as an "act of identity." Indeed, ethnic identities are often reified through a variety of oral tools that a "speech community" may deploy.[150] In the case of late antique Christian Egypt, language—especially the Coptic language—became a core marker of Egyptian identity. This will become even more evident in some of the early-medieval texts surveyed below.

As the Egyptian delegation prepared to set sail from Alexandria, Macarius had a midnight vision in which the emperor Marcian and empress Pulcheria appear in the likeness of the dragon and harlot of Rev 12 and 17, respectively. These villainous characters implore the bishops from "every land"[151] to cast down their crowns (Rev 4) and to assemble. However, the voices of Athanasius and Psote implore the bishops not to throw away their crowns (that is, subscribe to the Council of Chalcedon). After the bishops ignore the exhortation of Athanasius and Psote, their crowns pass to Macarius and Dioscorus.

Macarius often appears in the text as the only bishop who stayed the course of orthodoxy: "Apa Macarius did not desire to remain upon his throne corruptly like the rest of the bishops who desired to remain on their thrones. They subscribed to the impious *Tome*. Macarius did not desire to remain upon his throne. Rather, he desired the One who seated him upon the throne of Tkôw, the humble city."[152] In Macarius's vision, Byzantine imperial figures appear as oppressive, demonic forces while anti-Chalcedonian Egyptians are steadfast orthodox martyrs. The text rhetorically contrasts the hegemonic imperial capital against the "humble" Egyptian city of Tkôw. These rhetorical strategies of ethnic boundary maintenance are common to Coptic literature of this period. Dioscorus and Macarius are the sole champions of orthodoxy, while the bishops from "many lands" are apostates. This strategy casts Egypt as the source of orthodox belief for all of the Byzantine Empire. However, the text does not contrast Egyptian ethnicity with an opposing ethnic group, but with imperial officials. This should not lead to the conclusion that the concern here is political or nationalistic. It is a function of ethnicity in a culturally-plural state—such as the Byzantine Empire—for ethnic groups to assert their identity through forms of resistance against state leaders when a sense of injustice is felt.[153]

While aboard the ship heading for Constantinople, Macarius heals a sailor with an inflamed eye. The text places attention on ethnicity and language: "And when the holy man, Apa Macarius, saw him with the pain that was upon him, he had compassion on him and said to him: 'Come, my son, behold the path.' He drew him to himself. And the sailor spoke to him in Egyptian,[154] for he was an Egyptian himself."[155] After the healing took place, the sailor exclaimed: "One is the God of this Egyptian elder[156] who is on board with us!"[157] This is one of the clearest expressions in the late-fifth-century Miaphysite literature of how "Egyptian" functions as a late-antique social category equivalent to the modern concept of ethnicity. In a more pointed manner than that which appears in the literature surrounding Timothy Aelurus or Longinus, Macarius and the unnamed sailor are both called Egyptians and speakers of the Egyptian language.[158] Again, language emerges as a marker of Egyptian ethnicity.

As demonstrated above, language is one of the various intersectional layers of ethnic identity.[159] However, ethnic and linguistic boundaries are not coterminous; and this is visible in the *Panegyric*. Macarius is not necessarily more Egyptian than Peter and Theopistus, who do not understand the Egyptian language, or Apa Dioscorus, who likely communicated primarily in Greek. All of these figures belong to the Egyptian ethnicity and the text contrasts them as the faithful orthodox against the imperial heretics in Constantinople. "Egyptian," therefore, is primarily an ethnic category here and not a primarily political or linguistic one (although these categories influence Egyptian ethnicity). Macarius's inability to speak the dominant language of Byzantium and his monofluency in Coptic highlights the Egyptian ethnicity through the elevation of its unique language.

Immediately after these events, another miraculous event is recorded, again highlighting Egyptian ethnicity. A businessman on board the ship stole the tunic of one of Macarius' monastic brothers. Upon hearing Macarius reassure the brother that the tunic would return to him, the servant threw it in the sea out of fear of Macarius' prophetic abilities.[160] When the tunic miraculously appeared to the brother of Macarius, the servant persuaded the sailors to beat the brother. While beating and spitting on the brother, the only recorded words on the part of the assailants were: "All Egyptians are liars and perjurers."[161] When Macarius intervened and implored the servant to tell the truth, the servant confessed, to the amazement of the rest of the ship as they exclaimed, "Truly this man is a saint."[162]

The text inverts typical Roman prejudiced attitudes towards Egyptians as Macarius again emerges as the archetype of humility. However, the fact that the encomiast desires to depict Egyptians as victims of prejudiced ideology attests to the minority discourse at play in Egyptian anti-Chalcedonian literature.[163] These remarks express prejudiced attitudes towards Coptic-speaking Egyptians.[164] Ascetic humility emerged by means of well-established racist attitudes, as in the case of stories about Moses the Black in the *Apophthegmata Patrum*.[165] While the discrimination that Egyptians are facing in the *Panegyric* do not appear to be based on skin color, as in the case of Apa Moses, there is a similar dynamic wherein various levels of social discrimination (in this case, ethnocentrism) are accepted by Christian ascetics with the expectation that the perpetrators will face divine retribution. However, the fact that the author of the *Panegyric* includes the ethnocentric perspective toward Coptic-speaking Egyptians only enhances the laudable humility displayed by Macarius and further commends the piety of the Egyptian people.

En route to Constantinople, Pinution told Dioscorus about various miracles that Macarius performed, including combating paganism alongside Besa, the successor of Shenoute at the White Monastery. Upon arriving at Constantinople, the text emphasizes Macarius's meekness as he is only allowed to enter the proceedings as a servant to Dioscorus. Following the dismissal of the adherents to the *Tome*, fellow Palestinians accused Juvenal of adhering to the "foreign faith"[166] of the "Diphysites."[167] The use of the word "foreign" emphasizes the cultural layer of the Chalcedonian faith from the perspective of Egyptians, Palestinians, and other Near Eastern cultures that would continue to embrace Miaphysitism for centuries to come. While Miaphysites often refer to the *Tome* and Chalcedon as "defiled," "wicked," "impious" and "heretical," the use of "foreign" demonstrates the degree to which this theological controversy also retained layers of social identity.

Again, the text contrasts the imperial forces of the Byzantine Empire with the meek, faithful orthodox, this time in Palestine. Indeed, Palestine and Egypt often appear as strongholds of Miaphysite resistance in the late fifth and early sixth centuries.[168] The text presents Juvenal and the emperor Marcian as heretical oppressors who work together, as Juvenal is then said to return to Jerusalem with four hundred imperial troops.[169] The *Panegyric* reports that "all the people"[170] were reciting the Miaphysite Trisagion at the shrine of Holy Mary while surrounded by soldiers:

> For they were proclaiming the Trisagion at that time: 'Holy is God,' that is to say, 'Holy are you, God.' 'Holy is the Strong One,' that is to say, 'You are holy, Strong One.' 'Holy is the Immortal One,' that is to say, 'You are holy, Immortal One.' 'Who was crucified for us, have mercy on us,' that is to say, 'Who was crucified for us, have mercy on us.'"[171]

As the crowd not only cursed Juvenal, but "even the lawless emperor,"[172] the *Panegyric* states that Juvenal gave the order to murder everyone in the church. In a confrontation between Juvenal and the priest Silas, Juvenal appeals to Scripture to persuade Silas to "not speak evil against the ruler of your people."[173] Silas's response to this request to first "honor God and the king" further clarifies the parameters of ethnic boundary maintenance present in anti-Chalcedonian texts: any allegiance expressed towards one's *laos* is subordinated to adherence to orthodox belief.

In his argument with Juvenal, Silas alleges that Shenoute intended to have Juvenal excommunicated, but Cyril did not support this. Shenoute is introduced as "Apa Shenoute, the Egyptian, the citizen of the barbaric region of Egypt."[174] The social designation "barbarian" was common to Roman constructions of the ethno-political Other, especially in times of social antagonism.[175] Egyptians were full Roman citizens during the fifth century; therefore, the Egyptian panegyrist highlighting how dominant Roman civilization viewed the Egyptian people further demonstrates the ethnic aspect of theological resistance.

After Silas's lengthy statement, Silas and the entire congregation were murdered, and their "blood reached the ankles of the soldiers."[176] Due to these violent events in the narrative, the text depicts Juvenal as the one whose "impiety and madness was more evil and accursed than anyone."[177] Juvenal then takes his troops to the monastery of Longinus in order to enforce their acceptance of the faith of Chalcedon.[178] Longinus's response to the decurion illustrates the close relationship between monastic communities throughout Egypt and the Alexandrian patriarchate: "Has the throne of Alexandria also subscribed? If so, bring it and I too will subscribe."[179] The *Panegyric* then describes the event, which also appears in the *Life of Longinus,* where the soldiers enter the tomb of the deceased fathers of the Enaton, who order Longinus to renounce the *Tome* and the Council of Chalcedon. Like the *Life,* the *Panegyric* also reports the immediate conversion of the soldiers while adding the detail of their becoming monks. The *Panegyric* explains the background of the decurion convert, Nestorius Andragathes, who was victorious in battle against the "barbarians who are called Arabs,"[180] and whose name was outlawed due to the association with the Nestorius who was condemned at Ephesus I. The *Panegyric* uses Roman social categories of Otherizing ("barbarian") both with reference to distant groups and themselves (Egyptians).

The story then shifts back to the events surrounding the meeting between the emperor Marcian, Macarius, and Dioscorus at Constantinople. Dioscorus opposes the Chalcedonian definition because it unnecessarily adds to that which the orthodox fathers established, a position often taken by anti-Chalcedonians. Protesting against Chalcedon, Dioscorus exclaims: "I am orthodox, the descendant of orthodox people."[181] The frequent contrast between Egyptian Miaphysites and Byzantine/Constantinopolitan Chalcedonians during the fifth and sixth centuries contradicts the idea that this ethnicized religious polemic was an innovation of Egyptians under Islamic rule.[182] As stated above, the domineering Byzantine Other as the foil for Egyptian-ness is not an expression of political or national identity, for there was no attempt on the part of the Egyptian church to secede from Rome. Rather, Byzantine authority serves as a contrast to the category of "Egyptian" which, if it is not being used in a political sense, can only refer to what we today call an ethnic group.

The archbishop and others in attendance express agreement with Dioscorus and beseech the emperor to accept the doctrine laid out by the Alexandrian patriarch: "Cast away these Manichaean deceivers from you, do not allow them to deceive you, O emperor."[183] The fact that, from the beginning, anti-Chalcedonians appealed to imperial authorities to accept the orthodox (Miaphysite) faith attests to their strong desire for theological unity throughout the empire and further disproves any hint of nationalist separatism.[184] The goal was not to separate from the Roman Empire but to bring it back into what the Egyptians viewed as orthodox theology. As the empire continued to reject Egypt's vision of orthodoxy, the Egyptian church continued to emphasize its ethnic identity as an orthodox people amidst a heretical empire.[185]

Religious literature of this period asked governmental leaders to align themselves with theological orthodoxy for the good of the empire or a particular region. Such admonition would not come from Egyptian Miaphysites if their ultimate desire were to become politically independent from the Byzantine Empire. Rather, the Egyptian church saw itself as the moral center of the empire, called to return its leadership to theological orthodoxy.

Egyptian leaders also took to task the leaders of the foreign lands in which they were in exile. Dioscorus accused Sabinus, the bishop of Gangra where Dioscorus was in exile, of leading his city astray through "innocent" heresy: "He (Sabinus) said what Abimelek, the king of Geras said, 'Lord, do not destroy an ignorant ethnic group.'"[186] After Dioscorus's successful protest, Marcian dismissed the bishops at the behest of Nestorius Andragathes who was, at that time, a heretic (that is, a Chalcedonian). Marcian then met with his advisors and devised a plan to murder Macarius. However, a child named Misael came to warn Dioscorus, telling him to allow "this Egyptian elder"[187] to flee lest the Chalcedonians kill him. The text refers to Macarius twice more as "this Egyptian elder"[188] in the story of his healing a woman who had leprosy. When the woman and her husband praise Macarius for his miraculous deed, Macarius angrily implores them to honor only God, again emphasizing his great humility. References to his ethnic identity again associate Egyptian ethnic boundaries with those of the orthodox, monastic *politea*.

A synod occurred in Alexandria in which an imperial courier[189] named Sergius and the future Chalcedonian patriarch of Alexandria, Timothy Salofaciolus,[190] commanded the bishops of Egypt to subscribe to the *Tome*. In order to emphasize the corruption of the Byzantine Chalcedonian movement, the courier offered the throne of the archbishop to the first bishop willing to subscribe to the *Tome*. This is another example of Egyptian Miaphsyites portraying Chalcedonianism as appealing merely for political bribery. Proterius signs the document, thus beginning his rule as patriarch through imperial corruption. Macarius rebukes Proterius, declaring that "all Alexandria is a witness against you."[191] The *Acts of the Council of Chalcedon* indicate that Dioscorus's anti-Chalcedonian teaching had more influence among the people of Egypt than any imperial policy.[192] In the same way, the *Panegyric* depicts the powerful influence of Dioscorus and by association, Macarius.

However, the *Panegyric* reports that all the bishops subscribed to the *Tome* "through fear,"[193] leaving Macarius as the lone pillar of orthodoxy in the manner of Elijah against the priests of Ba'al (1 Ki. 18). John of Maiuma (John Rufus) also identifies Dioscorus as the only bishop to oppose the Chalcedonian definition.[194] The Alexandrian *Synaxarium* speaks of Dioscorus similarly: "But Marcian was made emperor and Pulcheria empress, and no one resisted their profession of faith except Dioscorus, Patriarch of Alexandria."[195] The *Panegyric* uses Dioscorus's international reputation as the chief opponent of Chalcedon to raise the standing of Macarius.

There was also an underlying criticism of the Egyptian bishops who accepted the *Tome* when coerced. The text implies such criticism through the counter-example of Dioscorus and Macarius, who stood as champions of Egyptian orthodoxy. In doing so, the boundaries of Egyptian ethnicity aligned with Miaphysite resistance. The panegyrist holds the Egyptian bishops accountable to a group-specific standard that supports ethnic boundary maintenance. Ethnic boundaries involve judging and being judged by a common set of standards relevant to that identity.[196]

After Macarius's continued refusal to subscribe, the enraged Sergius grabs him and "gave him a kick under the genitals, and he fell and died immediately."[197] Although the text states that the majority of Egyptian bishops subscribed to the *Tome*, it claims that "Alexandrian citizens"[198] wrapped Macarius's body and placed him in the *martyrion* of John the Baptist and Elisha the prophet. This greatly angered Timothy Salofaciolus who asked: "People, what are you doing with this unclean Egyptian,[199] burying him in the sanctuary of the saints?"[200] Timothy was immediately struck by lightning and died.[201]

The constant labelling of Macarius by his ethnic identity enhances the role played by ethnicity in this polemical text.[202] After Timothy's reported death, a young mute child was cured at the sight of Macarius with John the Baptist and Elisha the prophet embracing one another. At the sight of his child's miraculous healing, the father exclaimed: "One is the God of this Egyptian elder!"[203] Immediately following this event, the same exclamation occurred when a hunchback was healed by the corpse of Macarius.[204] The text creates the boundary of Egyptian ethnicity as coterminous with adherence to anti-Chalcedonian doctrine.

After the narrator described these events, Pinution exclaimed: "All Egyptians[205] have died a single time. But you have died many times, O my father."[206] Such a statement could have easily been addressed to "all people" as opposed to "all Egyptians." Again, the ethnic label rallies the Egyptian people by means of the anti-Chalcedonian teaching. This text models the construction of boundaries for Egyptian ethnicity around the Miaphysite confession of faith. The *Panegyric* ends with an exhortation to follow the orthodox example of Dioscorus, just as Macarius did. Such an exhortation reveals the purpose of the *Panegyric:* to serve as a model for Egyptian Christians to follow the example of Macarius who suffered as a martyr for the cause of orthodoxy. There is a similarity here with how the *Life of Anthony* was written by the Alexandrian patriarch to show how a renowned ascetic lived obediently to the theology of the patriarch. However, the difference in the mid-to-late-fifth century is that now Egypt found itself marginalized by a lasting theological schism with the dominant Roman Empire. It is for this reason that this period began a process of ethnic boundary maintenance that expanded during the sixth century.

The imperial policies of Justin and his nephew Justinian during the better part of the sixth century engendered new resistance movements against Chalcedon. However, the resistance against Chalcedon was already well underway in the fifth century. Egyptian bishops and monastic leaders used Egyptian ethnic identity to juxtapose the faithful of Egypt against an oppressive Roman Chalcedonian administration. While the late fifth century witnessed variation from imperial authorities in Constantinople with regard to Chalcedon and the *Tome*, the sixth century was marked by a decidedly heavy-handed approach that exacerbated the emergence of ethnic rhetoric in Egyptian Miaphysite literature.

FOUR

Response to Justinian

THE SURVEY OF EARLY-SIXTH-CENTURY sources describing mid-fifth-century figures has demonstrated the degree to which Egyptian Miaphysite leaders immediately responded to Chalcedon by rallying their congregants around the anti-Chalcedonian banner. The mid to late sixth century brought further changes for Egyptian Christians, most notably during the reign of Justinian I. The imperial policies of Emperor Justin I, his nephew Justinian I and the Second Council of Constantinople (553 CE) played a larger role than Chalcedon in the schism between Antioch and Constantinople. Syriac-speaking leaders of the sixth century played an integral role in forming a Syrian Christian identity coterminous with Miaphysite doctrine because of the imperial policies of the mid-sixth century.[1] The reign of Justinian provided an impetus for the Syrian church to construct a new identity in opposition to Byzantine Chalcedonians in a manner similar to Egyptian Miaphysites. By contrast, Egypt's resistance to Justinian was not the beginning of a new identity but the continuation of one that began after Chalcedon in the fifth century. The Egyptian response against Chalcedon was immediate and unified across every level of ecclesiastical authority.

A contributing factor to Egypt's swift reaction was its uniquely unified ecclesiastical structure under the Alexandrian patriarch.[2] The exile of the Egyptian patriarch Dioscorus at the time of Chalcedon resulted in a swiftly negative reaction on the part of the Egyptian church. The reign of Justinian is the central event that intensified anti-Byzantine and pro-Egyptian rhetoric. The Egyptian church's perception of itself as persecuted by the Byzantine Empire is present in sixth-century sources and is not a later "recasting of Byzantine rule."[3]

The main figures of sixth-century anti-Chalcedonian Egypt who feature in the following chapter are Apollo of Hnēs, Daniel of Scetis and Abraham of

Farshut. The hagiographical texts relating the lives of these Egyptian ascetics include significant evidence of anti-Chalcedonian polemic framed in ethnic terminology. Indeed, the role played by these monastic figures in the fight against Chalcedon emerges as their greatest achievement, solidifying anti-Chalcedonianism as the most important feature of Egyptian Christianity.

While Chalcedon and the *Tome* of Leo are important targets for the Miaphysite invective present in these texts, the person and administration of Justinian receive greater attention. A unique feature of these texts, as opposed to those dealing with fifth-century figures, is the inclusion of other theological concerns apart from Chalcedonianism, such as Meletianism. Yet, as will become evident, Chalcedonianism is the primary concern for Egyptian Christians continuing into the sixth century. The following texts will illustrate how these dogmatic concerns continue to shape the boundaries of Egyptian ethnic identity.

THE *PANEGYRIC ON APOLLO*

The biography of Apollo appears in the *Panegyric on Apollo*, which develops Egyptian ethnic identity around Miaphysite doctrine and rejects Egyptians who do not embrace this view. The author of the *Panegyric* expresses sorrow at the presence of heretics (that is, Chalcedonians) among his people (that is, Egyptians), which is another attempt on the part of the Egyptian anti-Chalcedonian party to make the Miaphysite position coterminous with Egyptian identity. Ethnic boundaries must eventually re-classify or exclude group members who violate the "assumption of shared homogeneity" that defines the ethnic group.[4] According to dominant views of ethnic boundary maintenance, the process by which late antique Egyptian ethnicity was asserted in the context of Miaphysite resistance was perhaps most acute when this community rejects Egyptian Chalcedonians. Egyptian Miaphysites excluded Egyptian Chalcedonians as traitors not only to orthodoxy, but to the Egyptian people. Ethnic boundaries are indeed perceptible in these variegated strategies of inclusion and exclusion.

The author of the *Panegyric* identifies himself as Apa Stephen, bishop of Hnēs[5] who was a monk in the Monastery of Isaac during Apollo's tenure as archimandrite. While neither the *Panegyric* nor the *Panegyric on Elijah* provides any further information on Stephen, the similarity in style of both works removes any significant cause for doubting his authorship.[6] The question of the original language of the work, whether Greek or Coptic, remains open in the case of the *Panegyric* as well for most Egyptian literature of this period. It is common to assume that if a text has an intended audience outside of Egypt that the original language was Greek, while if the intended audience was Egyptian, the text was written in Coptic.[7] Apollo's central role in the *Panegyric* would indicate its composition in Coptic. The extremely high and wide-ranging amount of Greek loan words (a pattern that becomes evident even in the excerpts below) might indicate a Greek composition if the provenance assumption holds water.[8] However, a third option is that a bilingual author who wrote primarily in Coptic wrote the text but was deeply infused with Greek thought.[9] The multiethnic and multilingual nature of Byzantine Egypt lends weight to this possibility.[10]

This further attests to the utility of highlighting ethnicity as the category with which to interpret rhetoric centering "Egypt" and "Egyptians" in anti-Chalcedonian texts as opposed to, for example, language. The deeply infused relationship between Greek and Coptic in late antique Egypt, evidenced strongly by the writing style of Stephen of Hnēs, illustrates how language was not the primary boundary for inclusion in Egyptian identity. Indeed, ethnic identity often takes shape by including multiple language communities.[11] Egyptians asserted belonging primarily through acceptance of the Miaphysite faith for both Greek and Coptic speakers alike. The grammar of the *Panegyric* itself, a Coptic text with copious Greek vocabulary and hybrid grammatical constructions, is an apt symbol of Egyptian ethnicity. That is, like all ethnicities, "Egyptian" is a bounded concept that is constantly renegotiated through contact with neighboring groups across various layers of social organization.

Stephen claims to describe events that took place during the reign of Justinian (527–65 CE) and states that Apollo met Severus shortly before the latter's death (538 CE).[12] Given the knowledge of sixth-century events present in the *Panegyric,* a sixth-century composition is possible. The *Panegyric* describes the monastery of Isaac as existing in two locations: one for men and a convent to the north for "virgins who struggle to acquire the contentment of the incorporeal ones."[13] After formulaic introductory remarks, Stephen expresses the universal appeal of Apollo's *politeia,* which has "spread abroad" for the benefit of the "communities" (*nepoikion*) and the "lands" (*nxōra*).[14]

That Stephen addresses his audience as the "Christ-loving people"[15] indicates his understanding of the faithful orthodox as being a *laos* comprised of all *epoikion* and *xōra*. Such comments demonstrate Egyptian ethnic boundary maintenance in the sixth century. The *Panegyric* highlights the role of the Egyptian faithful, bolstering the spirit of Egyptian anti-Chalcedonians while also encouraging the faithful orthodox outside of Egypt. The use of terms denoting social forms of organization (*laos, genos*) in the context of religious polemic is characteristic of early Christian literature.[16] In this context, as in the *Panegyric,* the audience for these texts is a people that is both Christian and Egyptian.

At the same time, Egyptian Miaphysites do not hesitate to distance themselves from the negative depictions of Egypt as presented in the Old Testament,[17] testifying further to the dominant importance of the Christian faith for the land and people of Egypt. Stephen clearly presents the vision of unity in diversity so prevalent in late antique Egyptian thought: "Even if those that come forth from it (the monastic community) are many, there still exists to all the holy brethren of the community one single focus, that is the holy way of life, even if the good conduct for which each one strives is different."[18]

The *Panegyric* begins by praising one of Egypt's most treasured sons, Apa Pachomius. Pachomius is compared to Abraham for both were called to leave their "country, people and father's household"[19] and come into the "land flowing with milk and honey."[20] Pachomius is actually given greater credit than Abraham who "went on the road up to the mountain of his sacrifice for three days,"[21] while Pachomius "endured to such an extent from this district[22] until he went up to the monastery established on the mountain."[23] And, while Abraham maintained all his possessions after he "left his country behind,"[24] Pachomius's only possession was his virtue.[25]

The comparison between the two figures, which highlights the strengths of the *politeia* of Pachomius, is predictable as the Egyptian abbot is compared to the biblical figures of Moses, Joshua, David, and Elijah in a manner consistent with late antique hagiographical literature.[26] However, comparing Pachomius with Abraham in light of their respective sojourns is more interesting. Pachomius's journey to Pbow is comparable to Abraham's climbing the mountain of Moriah as both figures left their "country" (*kah*).[27]

While Pachomius left his hometown in the diocese of Latopolis in the Thebaid,[28] Abraham left his home in Ur on a journey of far greater geographic and cultural distance. Latopolis in the Thebaid is a different *kah* than Pbow, and it is in a symbolic sense as he leaves "the world" for ascetic life. The comparison with Abraham demonstrates the broad usage of *kah*.[29] The Thebaid and Pbow are distinct *kah,* a word most often referring to a distinct country, but here having symbolic meaning. The primary function of the comparison in the narrative is to highlight Pachomius's sacrifice to take up the ascetic life. However, the use of a social designation of identity that refers to land illustrates yet another layer of Egyptian ethnic identity—geography.

The diverse layers of social identity that constituted Egyptian-ness during this period are significant when encountering the pro-Egyptian ethnic rhetoric in anti-Chalcedonian texts. The *Panegyric* provides evidence of diversity in Byzantine Egypt with regard to theological affiliation. While late antique Egypt is commonly thought of as entirely anti-Chalcedonian, the *Panegyric* indicates that the Pachomian monastic community of Pbow had become Chalcedonian. After comparing Pachomius's arrival at Pbow to Abraham's coming into the "land flowing with milk and honey," Pbow is "the holy community . . . even if that true grapevine which was beloved at first has now turned to bitterness."[30]

Stephen quotes from Jeremiah 2:21 as he derides the monastery of Pbow in an intentional effort to cast himself in the role of an Old Testament prophet who vehemently appeals to his people to turn away from their sinful ways (that is, adherence to Chalcedon). The depiction of a homogenously anti-Chalcedonian Egypt is inaccurate, but it is also significant that Egyptian Chalcedonians are members of the same ethnicity who have fallen from grace and are also vastly outnumbered.

Background information on the Pachomian monastery provides context for Apollo's story. The Pachomian monastic *koinonia* thrived in Egypt and was renowned throughout the late antique Christian world. However, this community eventually experienced a decline in influence in Egypt primarily due to its leadership ascribing to Chalcedonian doctrine, causing much of the community to depart. The Pachomian community's decline in the sixth century is a major dynamic with significant repercussions on the subject of this present study. The details of this controversy are below. However, for now it is important to note the way that the *Panegyric on Apollo* briefly laments the Pachomian *koinonia* and its "apostasy" of accepting Chalcedonian doctrine. The crown jewel of Egyptian Christianity is "polluted" by the Chalcedonian theology of the dominant Roman Empire. While Chalcedonianism in any place is a concern for Egyptian Miaphysites, it is especially tragic on Egyptian soil and in sacred Egyptian institutions. This strategy of ethno-theological exclusion on the part of Egyptian Miaphysites—wherein Egyptian Chalcedonians are traitors to the Egyptian people—is the other side of the double-edged sword that demonstrates late antique Egyptian ethnic boundary maintenance. On the one hand, Chalcedonianism is associated with the "Romans" and Miaphysitism with Egyptians; therefore, the other side of the sword is that Egyptians who embrace Chalcedonianism are no longer Egyptians, but followers of the Roman king ("Melkites").

Despite lengthy praise of his ascetic virtue that is packed with biblical references, the text does not provide much specific information about Apollo's life before entering the monastery at Pbow. The *Panegyric* reports only that Apollo "chose for himself wisdom since his youth" and that he "became holy in his hands but pure in his heart."[31] Stephen then describes Apollo's practice of keeping many vigils and barely sleeping for three years. Apollo received spiritual support as an angelic host regularly transported him into their presence, "making him all the more eager for virtue."[32] Apollo's capacity for suffering was one of the defining characteristics of his *politeia* and his experience of divine encounters evidently raised suspicion: "Why do you doubt concerning the meeting with him of the species of incorporeal ones?"[33] In an effort to verify Apollo's heavenly interactions, Stephen tells a story about how Apollo encountered the crucified Christ after falling ill of exhaustion from labor. Stephen also describes some of Apollo's self-inflicted suffering, such as praying through the night on top of a heated oven or while wrapped in a wet garment in the freezing cold.[34]

Stephen uses these examples as instruction for his audience about the proper monastic attitude toward suffering: "For those who submit to God shall be transformed in their strength."[35] Ascetic suffering fits with the high emphasis placed on martyrdom throughout the Coptic tradition.[36] This also reinforces the anti-Chalcedonian position of the *Panegyric*. Indeed, immediately following the commendation of Apollo's ascetic suffering, the text compares the adherents of Chalcedon to the smoke rising from the pit in Revelation 9:

> This very pit of the abyss was opened again in the days of the Emperor Justinian. Again that soul-destroying madness, again the torrents of lawlessness flowed in their ravines to shake[37] the house of the faithful. For after Marcian, the culprit of the peril of the faith, perished, and after Basiliscus and Zeno and still others after these, the bad weed sprouted again in the kingdom of Justinian like a hidden fire in chaff which continues to produce smoke. Now the wretched bishops who had gathered together at Chalcedon became fodder for destruction and death and heresy, but their sins continue to be active. And their wickedness was unending and even their retribution was unceasing. For the fire of apostasy which those wretched bishops kindled everywhere drew to itself the laments and tears of the holy prophets until the end.[38]

That the *Panegyric* numbers Basiliscus with the pro-Chalcedonian figures, such as Marcian and Justinian, whom the Egyptian Miaphysite community despised, is curious given the more positive image of Basiliscus found in other anti-Chalcedonian texts. The *Chronicle* of Zacharias of Mytilene indicates that Basiliscus demonstrated a more relaxed attitude toward anti-Chalcedonians than his rival Zeno.[39] Indeed, the text even presents Zeno in a positive light, for his *Henoticon* is "aimed at the annulling of the Synod of Chalcedon and of the *Tome* of Leo."[40] It is possible that the different perspective of the *Panegyric* indicates a more strictly anti-Chalcedonian stance taken by Egyptian Miaphysites than that of other communities throughout the empire. It is important that the association of Chalcedonianism with Roman imperial authority is a continuing trend into the sixth century. This strategy of ethnic boundary inclusion and exclusion will expand below as Egyptian Miaphysites begin to frame "Roman" identity—and not just individual leaders—using Chalcedon.[41]

The Egyptian faithful (Miaphysites) are the central focus here, with Byzantine hegemony as the Chalcedonian foil. Stephen speaks as an Old Testament prophet as he cries "woe to the peoples,"[42] referring to Byzantine imperial authorities loyal to Chalcedon. Stephen supplies the usual objection to Chalcedon with regard to Christ's nature: "Indeed he is not divided into two natures (*phusis*), may it not be so, or two persons (*prosopōn*) as it seemed to the corrupt council, but he is one Lord, one Christ, one and the same without change and division."[43] Stephen uses similar wording to that found in the *Tome* in a rhetorical maneuver aimed at discrediting his opponents.

Polemical rhetoric expressing anti-Jewish sentiment was commonplace in early Christian literature and appears in the *Panegyric*: "By means of Jewish thinking, they divided this unified one, our Lord Jesus Christ, into two natures and two persons, and instead of the holy Trinity they brought forth an unlawful quaternity."[44] The Miaphysites' practice of labeling the Chalcedonian position as "Jewish" relies on the view that the Chalcedonians did not uphold the divinity of Christ. This is rooted in the common Christian assumption that the Jews disrespected Christ in the gospel accounts.

Despite the caricature of Chalcedonian doctrine, Miaphysite communities such as the Monastery of Isaac used it to portray themselves as the faithful remnant in an apostatized empire. Miaphysites frequently labelled imperial authorities "lawless." However, the Egyptian Miaphysites engaged in expressions of violent rebellion. The *Panegyric* vividly depicts the Chalcedonian Byzantine administration, with a special focus on the emperor

Justinian, as an evil oppressive force under which the Egyptian church must suffer and endure:

> For truly it was not only the apostolic throne of Alexandria which manifested its light, the holy Dioscorus, which Christ set upon the lamp stand of the high priest at that time, but almost the whole land of Egypt[45] and also the holy community of Pbow. The aforesaid calamity reached it not only in previous times but also in the days of the Emperor Justinian. And who will be able to see, or who will be able to hear the suffering of the orthodox at that time? For the pillar of orthodoxy and the true athlete of election, the holy Severus, the holy patriarch of Antioch, committed to many sojourns while being watched over, especially by God, as herald of orthodoxy. The emperor even called the patriarch of Alexandria, our father Theodosius, to him to Constantinople, openly as if honoring his holiness, but truly he wanted to seize him in order to annul ordination. 'I will stop up,' said that emperor, 'these great rivers, so that their canals and their backwaters will dry up. I will hide,' he said, 'the light under the bushel, so that the feet of those who run to it will be impeded.' What lament does not occur for the orthodox at that time? The churches were abandoned, your[46] clerics were few. The majority of the orthodox bishops[47] had fallen asleep in the faith, having been perfected by the teaching of their father. Thus then when the darkness of the error had spread abroad, the wild beasts boldly proclaimed, wolf after wolf, to hunt the sheep of the Lord. They who came together at Chalcedon mixed the cup of Judaism,[48] and the one who will drink it, his reward is the office of archimandrite of Pbow. O wicked demand, O bitter conflict! The command occurred, the wolf set out, the order of the emperor proceeded. And as it is written, that emperor sent out his arrows. He disturbed the brethren of the holy community. He increased his intimidations to disperse the sheep of the Lord, for[49] they did not want to transgress the faith of the Lord.[50]

Stephen makes extended use of Jesus's analogy of the light of believers which must not be hidden.[51] For Stephen, it is not only Apa Dioscorus, but the "entire land of Egypt" which stands as the lamp of Christ to illumine the darkened empire of Justinian.[52] Despite the fact that Justinian attempted to "hide the light under the bushel" by bribing the Pachomian monastic leadership into Chalcedonianism, Stephen yet describes the community of Pbow as being predominately "orthodox" (Miaphysite). Again, Chalcedonian theology appears through anti-Semitic language. The references to Judaism serve to enhance Egyptian ethnic rhetoric in ways distinct from the association of Chalcedonianism with *romanitas*. The political foil that was the Roman Empire served to contrast the Egyptian ethnos or *rōme* ("people"). In the same way, Egyptian ethnicity contrasts with the Jewish religion through anti-Semitic polemic.[53] Ancient authors shaped ethnic identity through a complex intersection of various levels of social identity.

Stephen paints the picture that it was not only a top-down embrace of one-nature Christology, but that the Egyptian community wholly embraced this doctrine. Indeed, notice the interchangeable ways that Stephen here uses "the whole land of Egypt" and "orthodox." Again, there was no move for political separation; rather, Stephen is portraying Egypt as the moral "light" to bring the empire back into orthodoxy. Likewise, "Egypt" here does not refer to a racial/phenotypical or linguistic category. Religious identity also supersedes "Egyptian" here as Severius of Antioch is among the faithful.[54] If "Egypt" does not refer to a political, racial, linguistic, or religious layer of identity, ethnicity emerges as the best category with which to interpret what it means to be Egyptian in late antique Miaphysite literature.[55] Orthodoxy (Miaphysitism) is not exclusively Egyptian, but "Egyptian" is exclusively orthodox.

Egyptian Miaphysite texts refer to theological apostacy in ethnicized terms ("becoming foreign"). Justinian's efforts at Pbow resulted in the archimandrite Abraham of Farshut being "taken away from them" and a "transgressor"[56] appointed in his place by Justinian.[57] Those loyal to the Miaphysite position, including Apollo, left Pbow with Abraham and came "to this very mountain" (the Monastery of Isaac)[58] in order not to "make themselves foreigners[59] to the God of their fathers."[60] After leaving Pbow, Apollo wandered as "a sojourner in an alien region,"[61] with no specific details on where exactly he went. Perhaps this "alien region" was again simply a neighboring district to that of Pbow and it was "alien" because it was not his monastic home. Given that Apollo's entrance to the monastery of Isaac is likened to the journey of the patriarch Jacob, who was instructed to "return to the land (*pkah*) in which you were born,"[62] this seems unlikely. Unless Apollo was born in the environs of Hnēs, the reference to his returning to the land in which he was born must refer generally to Upper Egypt. This might indicate that Apollo spent some time outside of Egypt. Despite these uncertainties, what remains clear is the manner in which the *Panegyric* again depicts Apollo as a prophet called to lead his people, indicating the theological diversity that was present in late antique Egypt.

Not only did Apollo's monastic career involve extensive disputations with Chalcedonians, but his arrival at the monastery of Isaac led to his confrontation with the Meletian community in the area: "I am referring to the Meletians who were active in this mountain at that time and were acting as a stumbling block in every way to this saint's way of life."[63] Unfortunately, the *Panegyric* does not provide any more information about the Meletian community of Hnēs or Apollo's dealings with them.[64] While one would hope for more information regarding this aspect of religious life in the area of Hnēs, the relative lack of information provided about Meletians in comparison to that for Apollo's conflict with Chalcedonians demonstrates that the latter was much more important for the monastery of Isaac.

The *Panegyric* shifts abruptly from the Meletians to more stories about the miraculous deeds of Apollo and his work overseeing the construction of a church at the monastery of Isaac. The text highlights Apollo's ability to discern hidden realities as he identified those who were worthy and unworthy of receiving communion.[65] In another story, Apollo discerned the thoughts of two young men, one desiring to leave the monastery and another desiring to enter.[66] One of the many visions Apollo receives includes news of a visit from the patriarch, Severus of Antioch. The patriarch came in "the habit of a foreign monk,"[67] and reported that Apollo's "prayers and way of life" reached "high heaven." Apollo bowed before Severus, and then departed joyfully for having seen the countenance (*prosopōn*) of Christ, the holy Severus."[68]

Because of his connection with Severus, the global Miaphysite community hailed Apollo as a champion of anti-Chalcedonian orthodoxy. The panegyrist Stephen praises Severus as the *prosopon* of Christ while also identifying his ascetic practices as foreign (*šmmo*). While *šmmo* can often refer to a practice being "strange" or "erroneous," in this case, *šmmo* must have an ethnic meaning, since it refers to the revered Severus.[69] Severus is highly venerated in the Coptic community, which attests to the existence of a Miaphysite movement that crosses ethnic boundaries. Yet the labelling of his ascetic practices as *šmmo* also indicates that there is a sense of shared identity among Egyptian anti-Chalcedonians, and awareness of difference from non-Egyptian anti-Chalcedonians. As will become evident in chapter 6 on non-Egyptian Miaphysites, there were ethnic differences that distinguished and even divided Mesopotamian transplants in Egypt and the local Egyptian Christians. The distinctions and divisions between Egyptian Christians, on the one hand, and exiles from Syria and Asia Minor, on the other, persisted despite the fact that most of these were Miaphysite and considered one another orthodox. It is for this reason that Egyptian ethnic identity—not simply religion—is a significant marker of identity in anti-Chalcedonian resistance.

Stephen then describes the last days of Apollo: "He fell into a great sickness as his intestines were plagued. Therefore, he continued to vomit blood and phlegm for the rest of his days."[70] However, this "holy spit"[71] served as a healing agent for many people in the community. Likewise, Apollo bathes in water that then becomes a source of healing for various infirmities. Apollo dies on the 20th of Paōne and Stephen entreats Apollo to "remember your community[72] which you have begotten from the start, this mountain in which you dwelt."[73] In the same vein, Stephen makes his final appeal to "this people, orthodox and of the same belief,"[74] so that they also beseech the Lord for protection and provision. The *laos* that Stephen addresses includes the community of Hnēs and the orthodox, anti-Chalcedonian Egyptian people as a whole.

ABRAHAM OF FARSHUT

One of the most prominent Egyptian Miaphysites from the sixth century was Abraham of Farshut. The longest text providing information about Abraham of Farshut is the *Panegyric on Abraham of Farshut* contained in White Monastery Codex GC. The *Panegyric* adds to sixth-century Egyptian ethnic identity development in framing Egyptian collective memory against the Roman Empire and Chalcedonian doctrine.[75] The "totalizing" discourse present in the *Panegyric* and related literature is ethnic boundary maintenance in full form; it is of note that Egypt is the only province singled out as the object of the Empire's attention despite the widespread presence of Miaphysitism throughout the Eastern Empire.

Although the beginning of the *Panegyric of Abraham* remains missing, internal evidence indicates that the text was most likely delivered on the saint's feast day: "... the great deeds of this saint who we celebrate today, our holy father Apa Abraham."[76] Although the first two leaves from Codex GC are missing, the text that is still available in the codex begins at the end of the customary introductory remarks found in hagiographical material and immediately before the narration of Abraham's childhood: "But in order that we not make the story any longer, let us turn to the matter that lies before us and begin his life from his youth."[77] The text identifies Abraham's birthplace as the "village called Tberčot" in the "district of Diospolis,"[78] which is the modern city of Farshut.[79]

Abraham is the son of "great people"[80] in the village of Farshut and the panegyrist identifies himself as a *suggenia* of Abraham.[81] The lexical range of *suggenia* allows for the possibility of an ethnic sense in this context as opposed to merely expressing a familial bond.[82] Such emphasis on familial and ethnic kinship at the beginning of the *Panegyric* immediately evokes feelings of ethnic solidarity common in anti-Chalcedonian Egyptian texts. Upon reaching the age of twelve, his parents enrolled Abraham (along with his relative, the panegyrist) in a school with devout teachers, in the manner of Moses, who "was instructed in all the wisdom of Egypt."[83]

After successfully completing this education, God called Abraham to the "spiritual land (*pkah*) that is fertile, which the Lord visits every time, I mean the life of philosophy, monasticism."[84] Before entering the ascetic community, Abraham spent a year in mourning over the death of his parents: "He completed the year for his parents according to the custom of the world."[85] This provides an interesting example of the way in which Egyptian Christian texts mark distance between their heroes and cultural practices common in their social milieu.

Such distancing is illustrated by referring to specific mourning practices as being "of the world," as opposed to being derived from the Christian faith. This further demonstrates the manner in which the Christian faith acts as a standard by which Egyptian Miaphysites choose which elements of their ethnic identity they will emphasize and which they will ignore. After mourning his parents, Abraham unsuccessfully attempted to persuade his sister to join him in the ascetic lifestyle. Abraham then entered the Pachomian community and studied the *politeia*[86] of Pachomius, Horsiesius, and Theodore while the monastery was under the leadership of Pshintbahse. Upon the latter's death, Abraham became leader of Pbow and immediately clashed with the Chalcedonian policies of Justinian:

> And at that time, the devil set the storm in motion and raised up a disturbance against the church of the Lord, while an emperor named Justinian was rising up. And his heart was corrupt and his mind went astray, raving in the madness[87] of the heretics. And when he sat on the throne, he dedicated himself to the blasphemies of Arius and Nestorius and the *Tome* of the impious Leo. Then he wrote a letter to the whole land of Egypt,[88] to the bishops in each diocese and the superiors of the monasteries so that they might come to him in the imperial city.[89] He wrote to the saint, Apa Abraham, who was superior of Pbow at that time, so that he might come to the court and appear before him.[90]

The opposition between Byzantine Chalcedonian authority and Egyptian Miaphysite monasticism appears in late antique Coptic hagiography through what Goehring calls "totalizing non-Chalcedonian discourse."[91] The text depicts Chalcedonian figures such as Justinian and Leo as pawns of the devil who persecute "*the* church of the Lord." The panegyrist here casts the anti-Chalcedonian community as the true *ecclesia*. The "whole land of Egypt" and all its bishops oppose the diabolic Justinian, which establishes the Egyptian church as the primary opponent (in the minds of Egyptian Miaphysites) of Chalcedonian oppression. The text contrasts the faithful Egyptian bishops of each region with the daunting "imperial city" in a rhetorical attempt to present the anti-Chalcedonian Egyptians as David going up against Goliath.

Abraham goes to Constantinople with four of his monastic colleagues.[92] Justinian explains the intention behind his invitation in a manner intended to distance the Byzantine emperor, and the doctrinal position he represents, from Egyptian Miaphysites. He does it "so that you might join *our* faith and celebrate the Eucharist with *us,* and I will give you glory and great honor in *my* empire"[93] (emphases mine). The "us/you" language reinforces the Byzantine/Egyptian polarization prominent in the *Panegyric of Abraham*. Just before a significant break in the manuscript, the text reports Abraham's refusal to accept Chalcedonian doctrine because of his desire for eternal glory rather than earthly honor.

Abraham's position indicates that the population around Pbow in the sixth-century was predominately anti-Chalcedonian. The panegyric of a certain Martyrios indicates the construction of a basilica at Pbow during the reign of Timothy Aelurus. Given Timothy's staunch anti-Chalcedonian perspective, it is likely that such a prominent project would have occurred with the blessing of the patriarch.[94]

After Abraham's refusal to accept Chalcedon, the text breaks off and the rest of the confrontation with Justinian appears in the *Panegyric on Abraham*. The *Panegyric* picks up again with Abraham establishing a monastic dwelling at "the mountain of his village."[95] However, due to the limited space in this initial settlement, Abraham constructs a larger dwelling place on the same spot. After another four-page break in the text, some brief miracle stories involving Abraham are included, followed by a gap of twenty pages. The text picks up again when Pachomius, Petronius, and Shenoute visit Abraham, and his monastic predecessors announce the date of his death. The *Panegyric* lauds these iconic figures are lauded as spiritual authorities over both Egypt and the rest of the world:

> You know, oh my beloved, that this righteous one is a great one[96] among the saints and a perfect elect among the monks, like our ancient fathers and forefathers,[97] that is, Apa Pachomius and Apa Shenoute and Apa Petronius and Apa Horsiesius, the fathers of the world.[98]

These Egyptian monastic leaders are introduced as "our fathers" (*nneneiote*), indicating a sense of ownership of their memory on the part of the anti-Chalcedonian community of the White Monastery, where the text was preserved. Yet the authority of these Egyptian ascetics extends beyond the Nile Valley to the *kosmos*. In this rhetorical strategy, the Egyptian Christian tradition is supreme among all Christian communities yet open to receiving anyone sharing its faith. Egyptian Christian identity, therefore, is defined less by notions of common descent than loyalty to a specific set of ideas and to particular historical figures. The *Panegyric* declares that Abraham's "citizenship is in the heavens with his fathers," indicating the priority of his eschatological community over an earthly social identity. Egyptian Christian texts constantly make the claim that universal Christian identity is more important than one's ethnic identity. At the same time, Egyptian identity and figures dominate these texts. Egyptian Christian literature has a complex dynamic, holding in tension Christian universalism and ethnic pride.

These Egyptian fathers, the text claims, are the foundation of the anti-Chalcedonian movement of Abraham, with the implication that, had these fathers been alive in the sixth century, they certainly would have agreed with the Miaphysite position. Such examples of the construction of ethnic identity through building a common memory on past heroes is a common feature in the maintenance of ethnicity in modern and ancient times.[99] Here in the *Panegyric of Abraham,* a distinctly-Egyptian Christian manner of asserting ethnic identity through solidarity with past heroes is deployed; the Egyptian Church continually asserts its identity and communal memory through the lens of its patriarchs and theological heroes, even before Chalcedon. By positioning the Miaphysite community as the true successors of the Egyptian patriarchs, the *Panegyric* draws the boundaries of Egyptian identity in the strongest manner possible.

After his disciples lament the news of his imminent death, Abraham "did not cease from his ascetic practices."[100] Abraham exhorts his disciples at length and then dies, just before a break in the text of six pages. The text picks up again, eulogizing Abraham and telling a story about his healing the affliction of "a man named Elias of Djouboure from the district of Antinoë, a protector of the very rich."[101] More miracle stories follow, including one about how he provided food during a famine and another in which he expelled demons. After a ten-page break in the text, the conclusion describes another exorcism and a miracle that occurred on the day of his commemoration. Tears dripped from the altar as a sign of imminent destruction that would occur "in the whole land of Egypt and Ethiopia."[102] The sign may have indicated the imperial policies of Justinian, which were in force throughout Egypt and Ethiopia, given the strongly anti-Byzantine tone of the text. During this period, Egypt's increased resistance to Byzantine Chalcedonianism was strengthened by its connections to Miaphysite communities outside of Byzantine authority, namely Nubia and Axum (Ethiopia).

The same codex contains another fragmentary text, *On Abraham of Farshut*, which relates the events surrounding Abraham's time in Constantinople in more detail. The text begins (after eight missing pages) with Peter, an imperial secretary, imploring Abraham and his companions to endorse Constantinopolitan doctrine: "My lord, the emperor says, 'Let your fatherhood go to the archbishop and hold fast to him according to the custom of your fathers.'"[103] Peter appeals to the value of staying within the tradition of the ancestors and theological predecessors—a value common both to global Christianity and Egyptian culture.

The author, who is certainly an Egyptian, depicts Byzantine Chalcedonians employing "us/you" language that further emphasizes the Egyptian/Byzantine opposition. Whether or not members of the imperial court actually conceived of Egyptian Christians as having a distinct theological lineage (vis-à-vis *nneneiote*), the division between the two groups is clear. Although Theodosius the archbishop appealed to Theodora on behalf of Abraham, Justinian still demanded Abraham's submission to the Constantinopolitan bishop:

> He (Justinian) said to him (Abraham), 'Why did you not go according to the custom of your fathers?'[104] The elder said to him, 'You ask about the custom of our fathers. We have not heard that faith has changed from the time of our fathers.' The emperor said to him, 'Is your faith that of all?' The elder said to him, 'If you ask the orthodox bishop, the shepherd of the people (*laos*) you will be told. But I am a layman, a peasant in doctrine. And just as Apa Athanasius gave it to our father Apa Pachomius when they were both together in the body, when he gave us the means to do it, we did not avoid the canons that Apa Athanasius had given.'[105]

Two subsequent pages are missing. However, in the extant text the panegyrist communicates the idea that while Chalcedonian doctrine is a change to the Christian faith, the Egyptian Miaphysites are faithful to a line of orthodox teaching that reaches back to Athanasius. The orthodox archbishop Theodosius is the "shepherd of the people." Egyptian anti-Chalcedonians ascribe ultimate authority to the Alexandrian patriarch, the last line of defense for the orthodox. While the Byzantine emperor misunderstood the "custom" (*pethos*) of Egyptian Christians, the true custom[106] of Egypt is an anti-Chalcedonian reading of the teaching of forefathers such as Athanasius. As Goehring points out, Justinian assumes that authoritative teaching belongs to Constantinople, while Abraham asserts Alexandrian authority.[107] Abraham appeals to Egyptian ecclesiastical authority and further enhances the ethnic boundary aspect of his refutation of Chalcedonianism. The significance of this resistance cannot be overstated. During the sixth century, Justinian embarked on extensive campaigns to restore and expand the Roman Empire.[108] A significant component to the emperor's leadership was religious and theological unity; indeed, Justinian took on the role of a bishop-king. This is evident in Justinian's query: "Is your faith that of all?" In the midst of an Egyptian Miaphysite corpus of literature, that constantly emphasizes the faith of Egypt and the corruption of Byzantium, Abraham rejects the faith of Justinian and declares allegiance to the Alexandrian Patriarch. Such statements of allegiance exacerbate Egyptian ethnic boundary maintenance by promoting Egyptian leaders and rejecting Roman imperial authority.

In this text, it is the Byzantine Chalcedonians, and not the Egyptian Miaphysites, who are making a radical break from orthodox Christian faith and thus leaving Egypt to play the role of the lone anti-Chalcedonian hero. After the two-page break, *On Abraham of Farshut* refers to those who have subscribed to Chalcedon as those who have "agreed to a foreign faith."[109] The Constantinopolitan bishop, Theodore, expressed frustration at an Egyptian monk's refusal to persuade Abraham to subscribe to Chalcedon. The monk declared to Theodore that anyone who persuades someone to agree to Chalcedon is "subject to fiery hell and he is outside the catholic church."[110]

By using Egyptian ancestors as their metric of orthodoxy, *On Abraham* emphasizes the people of Egypt as the arbiters of truth. The text presents Egypt as the "catholic church" and the bearer of universal authority. Egyptian Miaphysites such as Abraham engage in the fight for the "right faith."[111] Another passage aligns universal church and Egyptian church: "Even though the throne of the catholic church is disturbed, no servant is greater than his master, nor is a son greater than his parents. And our father Pachomius is the son of the catholic church."[112] While the imperial forces accused Egypt of violating the catholic authority of the ecclesiastical and political authorities in Constantinople, the response was that the imperial church itself diverged from fathers such as Pachomius. As mentioned above, the Pachomian community was a hot topic with regard to Christology in the sixth century. In vivid imagery, the panegyrist compares the Pachomian community and its struggle against Chalcedonianism to a sailing ship:

> The ship is the federation, the rudder is the spirit of our father Apa Pachomius. And the twenty-four ropes tied to it are the twenty-four communities bound to him. The mast is Apa Abraham and all the leaders who were orthodox. The sail is the shadow of the federation. The water it sails through is the population (*plaos*) of monks. The rudder is the image of the cross on which Christ was crucified.[113]

Ethnic boundary maintenance includes a collective memory that is congruous with new ways the boundary changes. Whereas the Pachomian community became divided in the sixth century due to Christological controversies, Pachomius himself is described as the "rudder" which guides the monastic "ship," with the implication that Pachomius would be supportive of Miaphysitism were he alive in Abraham's day. For this reason, the analogy ends with a warning to "not leave" the Pachomian tradition "to destruction." Egypt and its leaders are at the center, but allies from the outside are also celebrated. While the text describes Justinian as a threat[114], it presents Theodora as a supporter of the Miaphysite cause:

> Behold, I have spoken with the emperor about you so that he might release you. But the emperor gave in to his madness[115] saying, "If you are not in communion with me, I will not allow you to be archimandrite." So I sent to you through my secretary saying, "Do not leave the side of the archbishop, because the emperor gave word to me that he would release him, and he would go to Egypt (*ekēme*); and you too will go with him. Now behold [3.5 lines damaged or missing] here I will watch over you and attend to you."[116]

Abraham sent back word to Theodora through her assistant, a monk of the Syrian people[117] named Presbeutes; his ethnic identity comes to the fore and the text claims that "he was orthodox."[118] After requesting permission to return "to Egypt (*ekēme*)," the author reports that Abraham had "renounced"[119] the leadership of the Pachomians, causing discord among the Pachomian monks captive in Constantinople. Abraham's loss of leadership caused great celebration among the "accusers" in Constantinople who "rejoiced greatly like the devil, roaring like lions and wolves of Arabia."[120] The manuscript containing the text of *On Abraham of Farshut* ends in the middle of a discussion between a certain John, from the Pachomian community, and Justinian about the future leadership of the federation.

Further information about Abraham emerges in the *Panegyric on Manasseh* in a lengthy excerpt published by Goehring along with the Abraham texts. The excerpt begins with Abraham succeeding the archimandrite Sebastian as head of the Pachomian monasteries. After briefly introducing Abraham and describing his godly attributes, the *Panegyric* shifts to the encounter with Justinian, giving the impression that it is Abraham's involvement in Christological controversies that is his primary point of interest for sixth-century Egyptians: "Christ spoke through his (Abraham's) mouth, until the time when the profane emperor Justinian ruled the empire."[121]

Unlike the account found in the *Panegyric on Abraham* in which Abraham visits the emperor at Constantinople in response to an invitation, the *Panegyric on Manasseh* claims that Abraham was abducted by individuals whose names were Peter of Nemhaate, Patelphe of Šmin, Pešour of Ermont, and Pancharis.[122] A significant gap in the manuscript follows the introduction of these individuals, leaving details about their role in Abraham's abduction unclear. When the text begins again, an unidentified individual is deriding Abraham to Justinian while vying for the position of archimandrite of Pbow:

> He (Abraham) went into the gathering place, every place where your men stood and where they sat, he had all the brothers draw water and wash the entire assembly hall since he loathed you our lord emperor, and all who are under the authority of the Roman Empire.[123] So now send for him, bring him here and punish him as a criminal until everyone knows what it means to oppose the emperor. Since we will celebrate the Eucharist with our lord the emperor you will give us command[124] of Pbow, and we will carry out every order of our lord the emperor through a command of imperial authority.[125]

The cleansing episode continues a theme that appears in Shenoute.[126] In the same way that Shenoute labored to emphasize moral purity in the monastic *synagoge,* the writer of the *Panegyric on Manasseh* utilizes the imagery of purity and impurity to define orthodoxy and heterodoxy for a new generation. While Shenoute uses the rhetoric of purity and impurity to define proper monastic conduct, the panegyrist here employs the same imagery to shape the boundaries of Coptic orthodoxy.[127] The polarization of Byzantine and Egyptian identity, which is also at work in the discourse, indicates that ethnic boundaries, as well as religious, appear in texts such as these

By subscribing to heretical doctrine, Chalcedonians have both renounced their Egyptian identity and taken on Byzantine identity. Justinian is called "our lord the emperor" by the unnamed Chalcedonian Egyptian, whereas the rebellion of Abraham is likened to criminality. Both sides in the conflict over Chalcedonian dogma represent either allegiance to or rebellion against Byzantium. Egyptian Miaphysites clearly wanted to depict their Chalcedonian opponents as pawns of a devious emperor, "motivated by Satan."[128]

Perhaps the most striking example of ethnic boundary maintenance in literature relating to Abraham is the claim that Abraham loathed both the emperor and "all who are under the authority of the Roman Empire."[129] This statement stands out as it expresses disdain not for heretics, but for Romans. While Abraham and the Egyptian people also were Roman citizens, the context of this statement clearly refers to Roman (Byzantine) *authority,* which, as has been demonstrated, was associated with Chalcedonianism.

The *Panegyric on Manasseh,* composed by an Egyptian anti-Chalcedonian, expresses the views of some segment of the Miaphysite community in sixth-century Egypt. The fact that Egypt was "under the authority of the Roman empire" in the sixth century does not change that its Miaphysite citizens felt a growing distance from the Byzantine Empire. While a literal, political separation was not in the purview of the author, the doctrinal differences necessitated distinguishing the Egyptian Miaphysites through a process of re-drawing ethnic boundaries. This language is "ethnic" precisely because of the absence of any accompanying political movements of separation from the Roman Empire on the part of the Egyptian Miaphysites. While texts such as this must be analyzed cautiously with regard to their historicity, they nonetheless provide invaluable insight into the attitude of their authors, an insight that gains value in a relatively poorly-documented period of Egypt's history.[130] It is also important that the rhetoric of ethnic boundary maintenance intensified as time went on.

What precisely was meant by "Roman" in antiquity is also worthy of consideration here. From the beginning of the Roman Empire in the first century BCE into the late antique period, writers referred to Rome as a "Greek city" that, along with the Greek homeland, was a civilizing presence in the world in which "barbarians," such as Egyptians, could take refuge.[131] Therefore, while Egyptians were Roman citizens, there was a persistent "second-class" dynamic for ethnic groups such as Egyptians who were incorporated into Roman imperial identity. This dynamic increased the plausibility of re-negotiating identity with respect to the empire in times of tension.

Part of asserting ethnic boundaries is contrasting one's ethnic group against the Other (Romans) and excluding group members that violate the ethnic boundary (Chalcedonian Pachomians).[132] From the beginning and throughout Egyptian Miaphysite resistance, individuals such as Roman emperors and patriarchs were used as the foil against Egyptian orthodox. However, in the *Panegyric on Manasseh,* it is the Roman Empire that is being contrasted with the Egyptian church. As stated above, the goal here is not political autonomy but theological orthodoxy. The panegyrist frames theological orthodoxy by highlighting the Egyptian faithful and contrasting this with the Roman Empire. This demonstrates the role of Egyptian identity as an inextricable component to orthodoxy in the author's mind. This is also evident in his need to distance the orthodox Egyptians from the Pachomian leadership that had gained command through imperial bribery.

Enraged by Abraham's refusal to subscribe to Chalcedonian doctrine, Justinian sends a letter to the "duke of Antinoë" demanding that Abraham go to him and that the duke inform him of "the condition of all of Egypt."[133] The oppressive paternalism attributed to Justinian and the Byzantine forces continues as the duke receives Justinian's letter: "Then he (the duke) immediately sent some soldiers to quickly arrest him, because the word of the emperor prevails. When the soldiers entered the monastery, they searched deviously,[134] arrested the holy elder Apa Abraham, and brought him to the duke in Antinoë."[135] Abraham goes to Constantinople "by animals"[136] on a difficult journey of almost three months and is under the control of "savage soldiers."[137] After a break in the manuscript, the texts resumes with Justinian reassigning leadership at the Pachomian federation to its Chalcedonian constituency: "Moreover some people here who belong to the federation of Apa Pachomius are faithful, truthful people who love the emperors. I will give them the office of archimandrite of Apa Pachomius and allow no one to oppose them."[138]

The author again equates Christological doctrine with one's allegiance to the Byzantine emperor. The fact that the *Panegyric on Manasseh* labels Chalcedonian Egyptians as "lovers of the emperors" provides invaluable insight into the perspective of anti-Chalcedonian Egypt toward Byzantine hegemony. Indeed, the implication here is that it is a desire to obtain imperial favor and not theological conviction that motivates the Chalcedonians in the Pachomian community. Abraham, however, desires to avoid the punishment that awaits Nestorius, Arius, Juvenal, and Marcion, so the emperor exiles him.

Theodora attempts, unsuccessfully, to persuade Justinian, who declares: "If he will not celebrate the Eucharist with me, he will never dwell in the federation of Apa Pachomius."[139] Before another significant break in the manuscript, Theodora summons Abraham: "Are you my holy father Apa Abraham, the archimandrite of Pbow?"[140] The text represents Theodora as a faithful Miaphysite as she not only recognizes Abraham's position as archimandrite but also addresses him as "my holy father." After a significant lacuna, the portion of this panegyric dealing with Abraham concludes as Abraham narrates the events surrounding his banishment to the Pachomian monastery and (following ten missing lines) expresses sorrow over being replaced by the Chalcedonian archimandrite Pancharis: ". . . those who were present at the time Pancharis entered the monastery. Grief is listening to them."[141]

Later in the medieval period, the Copto-Arabic *Synaxarium* included some further information about Abraham than that which developed in these late antique hagiographies. The *Synaxarium* briefly relates the confrontation with Justinian but provides more information about the later part of Abraham's life. The *Synaxarium* claims that after his banishment from Pbow, Abraham went to the White Monastery where he copied the rules of Shenoute and sent them to the monastery of Apa Moses.[142] Abraham received a revelation from God to found a monastic community at Farshut where he also became an ordained priest and provided much aid to citizens suffering famine.[143] However, the most significant factor in the literature related to Abraham with regard to the question of Egyptian ethnic boundary maintenance is the role he played in the Miaphysite struggle. The fact that the sixth-century material emphatically presents ethnic rhetoric more than the medieval *Synaxarium* demonstrates the degree to which the sixth century was a period of intense identity formation for Egyptian Miaphysites. This distinction in emphasis across different periods also demonstrates that the process by which the Coptic Church became an "ethnochurch" was well underway before the Arab Muslim conquest of Egypt.

Abraham's banishment along with the other Miaphysites of the Pachomian *koinonia* caused the federation to become primarily Chalcedonian. The "Chalcedonization" of the Pachomian community was the primary cause of the decline in Pachomian monasticism after the sixth century. Subsequently, Pachomius was eclipsed in prominence by Shenoute in Egyptian Christian memory due to the latter's monastery being a stronghold of anti-Chalcedonianism. This is interesting considering Pachomius's greater renown in the Christian world outside of Egypt.[144]

There was a Chalcedonian community in Egypt at the Tabennesiote monastery at Canopus. However, despite the presence of Chalcedonians in Egypt, the decidedly anti-Chalcedonian leanings of Egypt are demonstrated by the dissolution of the Pachomian community precisely because it became Chalcedonian after Abraham's banishment.[145] Indeed, the memory of Pachomian monasticism diminished due to the anti-Chalcedonian White Monastery.[146] Perhaps the most significant factor in the literature relating to Abraham is the way in which Miaphysite doctrine became so strongly associated with Egyptian identity that failure to adhere to this doctrinal position resulted in the demise of one of Egypt's greatest religio-cultural institutions.

DANIEL OF SCETIS

"This is Egypt, and not Constantinople."[147] These were the words of an Egyptian stone-cutter who had fallen from a previous position of wealth and influence and returned to his homeland. In the following section I will explore the distinct ethnic and linguistic dynamics that led to this disparaging remark being present in the Armenian and Latin versions of the *Life of Daniel of Scetis*, while the Geʿez and Coptic versions record the statement very differently. The *Life* continued to frame Egyptian ethnic identity along Miaphysite lines in contradistinction to the Roman Chalcedonian policies of Justinian. Given the wide circulation of the *Life*, Egyptian ethnic framing is highlighted in new ways as we are able to compare Egyptian translations with other language groups and their corresponding visions of Egyptian identity.

Daniel of Scetis is one of the most important figures in the renowned monastic region of Scetis during the Byzantine period.[148] Although Daniel of Scetis is not the Daniel found in the *Apopthegmata Patrum*, it is unclear if he is the same Daniel that Egyptian and Ethiopic tradition identify as the *hegoumenos* of the Monastery of Saint Macarius.[149] The various texts about Daniel of Scetis likely come from Greek sources composed no earlier than the seventh century.[150] While the Daniel stories appeared in various languages over the centuries, the following two strands of transmission are most likely: Greek-Syriac-Arabic and Coptic-Ethiopic.[151]

The Coptic (and later, Ethiopic) strand is unique in that the hagiographer assembled the various stories of Daniel and composed a *Life*. The Coptic is also unique in that it contains material about conflict with Justinian and Chalcedonian doctrine that is not present in the Greek texts. The inclusion of such material highlights the importance of the Miaphysite position for the Egyptian Christians who wrote and read this text. While the story of Anastasia is not included in the Coptic *Life*, a Coptic panegyric relates the story of Anastasia and emphasizes her flight from Justinian into Egypt, which is a symbol of a flight from Chalcedonians.[152]

This section will include an investigation only of the Coptic *Life*, while including other translations at relevant points. The present study does not seek to provide a detailed analysis of the entire dossier related to Daniel, but to understand how stories about Daniel that are preserved in Coptic illustrate the role of ethnicity in the anti-Chalcedonian movement in Egypt.

The historicity of the anti-Chalcedonian material in the *Life* has been called into question.[153] However, the addition of the conflict with Justinian contains similarities with the *Life of Samuel of Kalamun*.[154] Considering the great attention given to Justinian in accounts of sixth-century events, as in the material relating to Abraham of Farshut and Apollo, it is not unlikely that the monastic community at Scetis also came into confrontation with Justinian.[155] In any case, the presence of this material in the Coptic *Life* is significant in that it demonstrates the immense importance of resisting Justinian for late antique Egyptian Christians. The fact that this material appears in the Coptic and Ge'ez versions and not in the Greek is also important.

Just as Justinian tried to force Chalcedonian doctrine on Abraham of Farshut in order to use the monastic community at Pbow to influence the rest of Upper Egypt, he also tried to control Lower Egypt through the monastic community of Scetis.[156] It is possible that the anti-Chalcedonian episodes of the *Life* were originally written in Greek, which would indicate a significant Greek-speaking community with anti-Chalcedonian leanings.[157] However, the fact that the episodes only survive in Coptic and Ethiopic further demonstrates the degree to which Miaphysite doctrine shaped and was shaped by Coptic identity.

The proemium identifies Daniel as the *hegoumenos* of Scetis and emphasizes the virtue and "way of life" of Daniel in keeping with the style of Egyptian hagiography.[158] The *Life* opens with two stories, which the Greek manuscripts share, about Mark and Eulogius. The first story narrates Daniel's encounter with an "idiot" named Mark who had a reputation in Alexandria as a madman.

It was the "custom of the great father of Scetis to go to Alexandria at the Great Festival [Easter] to meet with the archbishop."[159] When Daniel encountered Mark, Daniel, the archbishop, and the people of Alexandria became aware that this imbecile was in fact a monk who was faking insanity as a penance for previous sexual sin. Mark died shortly thereafter and Daniel ordered the monks of the Enaton to come and bury Mark with great honor.[160]

The longest single anecdote in the Coptic *Life* deals with Eulogius, who was a stonecutter in an unidentified village in Upper Egypt.[161] Daniel was traveling with a disciple who complained excessively about stopping at this village on their way back to Scetis, unaware of Daniel's prior acquaintance with Eulogius. As they sat in the village square "like foreigners,"[162] Eulogius saw them and invited them to come to his home.

Eulogius made a habit of "searching in the streets for foreigners" and bringing them to his home for a meal.[163] Daniel and his disciple are Egyptians, but they are called "foreigners," because they are not local residents. The distinction could also derive from regional differences in speech or appearance between different districts of Egypt or between Egyptians of the Upper and Lower regions of the Nile.

On their way back to Scetis the next day, the disciple urged Daniel to tell him about Eulogius. Daniel initially refused, due to the disciple's prior grumbling, but agreed to tell him when the disciple continued to insist. Daniel describes events that brought him to Eulogius forty years earlier, when he visited the same village on business and Eulogius welcomed him to his home. Daniel, impressed by Eulogius, prayed for the success of Eulogius's ministry of hospitality and promised to work for the salvation of his soul. Eulogius then found a cave filled with money belonging to the Ishmaelites.[164]

In order to avoid an attempt by the local landlord to seize his newfound wealth, Eulogius went to Constantinople, where he was made a procurator by Justinian, in the Coptic version. The Greek text identifies the emperor as Justin I[165] while the Ethiopic states that Anastasius was the emperor when Eulogius arrived in Constantinople and that Justinian was emperor when he left.[166] While this difference in the various versions could be the result of translation errors, it is more likely that Justinian plays an important role in the Coptic *Life* due to a more negative attitude toward him in the Coptic-speaking community. It is important to remember that many Greek-speaking and bilingual people were also considered Egyptian, such as Dioscorus or Timothy Aelurus. Furthermore, the *Apophthegmata Patrum* includes stories about Daniel written in Greek that include antagonistic rhetoric towards Emperor Justinian. Daniel aided an escaped Roman elite who was hiding among the ascetics of Scetis disguised as a man. Upon her death, Daniel recounted her life to one of his disciples. This imperial official fled Justinian with the aid of Theodora and took shelter in the Scetan desert with the help of Daniel. The emperor and the "pope of Alexandria and the entire city" were not able to find this woman.[167]

The circulation of this apophthegm in post-Chalcedonian Egypt demonstrates that there were Greek stories regarding Daniel that advanced the agenda of anti-Chalcedonianism (and anti-imperial authorities). The *Panegyric on Macarius of Tkôw* demonstrates that Coptic-speaking Egyptians appeared as a poignant example of Egyptian pride. Yet the fact that language alone does not encapsulate the boundaries of "Egyptianness" is a further indication that ethnicity, rather than language, is the social category with which to interpret the significance of the heightened anti-Chalcedonianism of the Coptic *Life*.

Eulogius's new position as procurator led to a change in behavior and he became "arrogant and merciless."[168] In the Coptic *Life*, Justinian is the source of Eulogius's spiritual downfall since he is the one who showers Eulogius with possessions that compromise his piety. The Greek text reports that Eulogius was given a large estate that was "known as 'The Egyptian's' to this day."[169] Eulogius's ethnic identity comes to the fore in the Greek text in a manner that separates him from his Constantinopolitan neighbors. This example of outside ascription of ethnic identity was not included in the Coptic or Ethiopic manuscripts, suggesting that Greek texts emerging from Egypt maintained a rhetoric of difference between "Greeks" and "Egyptians" in some cases. This example also further illustrates how the late antique concept of "Egyptian" encompassed various languages.

Daniel, alerted to Eulogius's fall from virtue, returns to the village and is dismayed to learn that Eulogius had been appointed procurator. Daniel receives a vision of Eulogius being dragged to court by a man who is identified in the Greek as "an Ethiopian."[170] The Coptic *Life*, however, does not label the race of Eulogius's captor, perhaps indicating the absence of the anti-black/Ethiopian racism prevalent in Greek literature.[171]

However, the Ge'ez text retains the racial dimension of the narrative as Eulogius is dragged away by "black men."[172] It is possible that the Ge'ez story of Eulogius did not use the Coptic text. But the Ge'ez text also identifies the court official as "black" instead of Ethiopian, perhaps in an attempt to preserve a positive image of Ethiopians at the expense of some other, unidentified black ethnic group. Furthermore, the fact that some Ge'ez accounts include racial terminology and others do not attests to the variety of ways that racial categories were received and renegotiated in anti-Chalcedonian literature across cultural contexts.

Daniel goes to Constantinople "diligently seeking the home of Eulogius the Egyptian."[173] The text identifies Eulogius as an Egyptian, thus distinguishing him from his Byzantine neighbors. The Coptic text is missing at this point and the Geʿez does not identify Eulogius's ethnic background here.[174] This is another example of Greek texts identifying Egyptians as the ethnically-distinct Other.[175] It is possible that the author of the Greek *Life* felt a need to emphasize Eulogius's Egyptian ethnicity since the text was written in a *lingua franca*, while Eulogius's Egyptian identity would have been more obvious to a Coptic-speaking audience. However, the Coptic *Life* highlights Egyptian identity in the form of anti-Byzantine/pro-Miaphysite rhetoric.

When Daniel finds Eulogius, the stonecutter ignored him and his escort begins to beat Daniel. Daniel then encounters the empress and asks her to abandon his pledge to Eulogius. The empress declares, "I do not have the authority," and so Daniel tries talking with Eulogius again, only to be beaten by a doorkeeper until his "entire body"[176] is broken. Distressed, Daniel departs for Alexandria and the Lord rebukes him in a vision while at sea, as an angelic figure criticizes Daniel for his over-zealous attempt at saving Eulogius. Daniel sees a vision of the empress arguing with the angelic figure, who orders Daniel to return to his cell in Scetis, and states that Eulogius would return to his simple, monastic way of life. If Justinian was emperor during Eulogius's time in Constantinople in the Coptic *Life*, the negative attitude toward Justinian on the part of the anti-Chalcedonian Coptic community is evident. However, so is the positive view of the Empress Theodora.

Theodora acts as Daniel's advocate here in a manner consistent with anti-Chalcedonian depictions of the empress throughout this period. Indeed, it is likely that Justin I in the Greek became Justinian in the Coptic so that the "empress" could be the well-known ally of the Miaphysites. The *Life* then reports the death of Justinian and states that his successor brought charges against Eulogius, along with two other consuls. When word reaches Eulogius that he has been sentenced to death,[177] he flees to his village in Egypt. He "clothed himself in his former manner"[178] and went back to the cave where he had found the treasure, hoping to find more.

When he finds the cave empty, he declares: "Get yourself up and work! There's nothing like this in Egypt!"[179] In the Greek text, Eulogius declares instead, "for here is Egypt,"[180] expressing his disappointment that, because he is now in Egypt, he will not have the same wealth and status that he had in

Constantinople. The Armenian and Latin versions express this sentiment more directly: "This is Egypt, and not Constantinople."[181] In the text, according to sixth-century Egyptians, Constantinople is the source of wealth and power and Egypt is a place of squalor where material prosperity is limited. Similar strategies of symbolic geography appear in the recension of this story in other language communities. This phrase is entirely absent from the Geʿez text.[182] This may indicate a different view of Egypt on the part of their Ethiopian neighbors. Perhaps from the perspective of the Geʿez translator, Egypt is not the inferior economic society compared to Byzantium that is presented in the Coptic *Life*.

Eulogius returns to his previous way of life, including extending hospitality to foreigners. Daniel visits the village and tells Eulogius about all that has happened to him and the two weep together. In summary, the story of Eulogius does not retain the Miaphysite material present in the larger *Life* but it does indicate ways in which Egyptian ethnicity was evident in the sixth century. First, categories of ethnicity (such as "Egyptian") were distinct from racial categories (such as "black men"). Second, the ethnic category of "Egyptian" encompassed multiple languages (Coptic and Greek), thus demonstrating the ethnic boundary extending beyond the linguistic. Third, theological and social identity appear in the context of a sixth-century Byzantine world where it was common for Egypt and Egyptians to be viewed as inferior to the imperial capital with which they were at odds.

The remainder of the Coptic *Life* deals with Daniel's confrontation with Justinian and the Christological controversy:

> And it was at that time that the impious Justinian became emperor, he who was polluted and terrorized the entire world and the Catholic Church in every place. He endeavored to enforce the accursed faith of the defiled Council of Chalcedon everywhere and scattered the beautiful flocks of Christ. He chased the orthodox bishops and archbishops from their thrones, and the impious Justinian was not satisfied with this, but also disseminated the impious *Tome* of Leo, which the impious Council of Chalcedon had accepted. He propagated it everywhere that lay under his control in order to make everyone subscribe to it. When it was brought to Egypt, a great disturbance occurred among all the orthodox faithful who were in the land of Egypt,[183] and it was brought to the holy mountain of Scetis in order that our holy fathers might subscribe to it.[184]

God warned Daniel of this visit, so he gathered the monastic community of Scetis and led them in a corporate rejection of the *Tome* of Leo and the

Council of Chalcedon. The author of the *Life* leaves nothing to the imagination with regard to the attitude of the community of Scetis toward the *Tome*, the Council of Chalcedon, and Justinian, all of which do not appear without adding a descriptor such as "defiled" or "impious." While the anti-Chalcedonian literature of the late fifth century also repeatedly targets the *Tome* and Chalcedon as the source of heresy and division, the sixth century adds Justinian to this list of Chalcedonian villains.

Later centuries will bring further additions to the ever-expanding dossier of the Egyptian anti-Chalcedonian community's greatest adversaries. Conversely, Egypt and her church appear as the lone defenders of orthodoxy. While Chalcedonian hegemony being imposed throughout the "entire world" by Justinian, Egyptian monastic heroes resist the polluted doctrine. It is true that the foil for this resistance rhetoric—Byzantine imperial authority, in this case, the emperor and his soldiers—is not an ethnic entity. However, this is typical in the formation and reification of ethnic boundaries in a multiethnic state such as the Roman Empire. As an ethnic minority in a multiethnic empire, Egyptians largely asserted their identity through resistance, or "ethnic incorporation."[185] As has been stated, the Egyptian Miaphysites did not seek political autonomy from the Roman Empire nor did they assimilate to its dominant theology. Rather, they resisted (largely) peacefully against the state while galvanizing the Egyptian people around the Miaphysite cause. The *Life* is not contrasting the community of Scetis with an alternative ethnic group but against political authorities. However, the Miaphysite cause embodies Egypt and Egyptian people. After describing Justinian's efforts at theological assimilation throughout all the territory that "lay under his control," the text contrasts this "impiety" with the "faithful, orthodox" people of Egypt. Again, Egyptian identity emerges primarily through faithfulness to Miaphysite doctrine.

Immediately after painting a grim picture of Justinian's imperial policy that affected "every place that lay under his control," Egypt emerges as the only region that reacts to Justinian's intervention with a "great disturbance."[186] Daniel's resistance to the imperial soldiers stands as a model for the monastic community of Scetis and all of Egypt: "As for us, it will never happen that we accept this impious rule of the faith but we will anathematize everyone who accepts it and believes in it." This is an example of how anti-Chalcedonian Egyptian hagiographers fashion the boundaries of Egyptian ethnic identity. Daniel is clearly laying down the requirements for inclusion in the Egyptian Christian community.

As a result of Daniel's "great courage" and the soldiers' "rage," Daniel and the elders of Scetis are subjected to "great tortures so that for a little while he approached death."[187] Daniel then goes "to Egypt" (echēme)[188] and builds a small cell to the west of a village named Tambōk where he briefly lives, while continuing in his ascetic politeia.[189] After the death of "the impious emperor Justinian,"[190] Daniel returns to Scetis and resumes his office as hegoumenos. The Life describes a raid on Scetis led by "barbarians" (nibarbaros) shortly after Daniel's return that results in the destruction of Scetis and many prisoners being taken to "their country" (etouchōra).[191] The closing section of the Coptic Life narrates Daniel's return to Tambōk and his subsequent death.

Daniel emerges as an anti-Chalcedonian role model meant to encourage the audience of the Life to follow his example. The author of the Life galvanizes his congregation around a specific dogmatic position in a manner quite common in early Christian polemic. The ethnic dimension of the conflict is evident in the frequent juxtaposition of Byzantine Chalcedonians and Egyptian monastic figures. The Life of Daniel frames Egyptian ethnicity by equating it with the standard of Miaphysite orthodoxy and setting the Byzantine Other outside the boundaries of Egyptian identity. The Life delineates the boundaries of Egyptian Christianity quite clearly: "We will anathematize everyone who accepts it and believes in" (Chalcedonian doctrine).[192]

FIVE

Identity Formation under Islam

THE ARAB MUSLIM CONQUEST in Egypt created conditions that furthered the ethnic boundary maintenance in anti-Chalcedonian texts that began two centuries earlier in the aftermath of Chalcedon. The majority Miaphysite Egyptian church was a pariah to imperial authorities, experiencing a significant degree of oppression.[1] The schism with Constantinople led the Egyptian ecclesiastical leaders to reconstruct their identity in opposition to their former Christian brethren. Before Chalcedon, it would have been unnecessary for Egypt and Alexandria to make such a point of asserting an individual identity as they could proudly associate themselves with imperially-endorsed Byzantine Christianity. However, the Chalcedonian schism necessitated the renegotiation of identity boundaries governed by their new-found religious identity.

Two centuries later, the Arab Muslim conquest introduced two significant developments in this process of identification. First, the Copts' situation as a double-minority—living as "schismatic" Christians within the wider Christian world and as a minority under Arab Muslim dominance—resulted in increasingly blatant ethnic rhetoric in Coptic texts. Second, Byzantine Chalcedonianism (and the Chalcedonian/Melkite church in Egypt) remained the primary target of Coptic religious polemic despite Arab Muslim hegemony.

The following chapter will focus on the Coptic and Arabic texts concerning the seventh-century figures Benjamin of Alexandria, Samuel of Kalamun, and Isaac of Alexandria. The texts concerning these figures spend more time criticizing their previous Byzantine rulers than their contemporary Muslim ones. This comes about because, unlike the new Muslim authorities, the Byzantines were Christians and held to a higher degree of accountability by

Egyptian Miaphysites. From the perspective of Egyptian Christians, the Arab Muslims were simply barbarians. Byzantine Chalcedonians, however, were heirs to the Christian tradition and were corrupting the faith. It may seem that a lack of Arab Muslim critique by seventh-century Christians could be an attempt to avoid persecution. However, the Byzantine persecution of the sixth century did not stop sixth-century Christians from publicly speaking out against Byzantine Chalcedonians.

Seventh-century Coptic figures continued to distance themselves from Chalcedonians while expressing various attitudes toward their Arab Muslim leaders. Texts related to Benjamin of Alexandria, for example, give the impression that the Muslim conquerors liberated the persecuted Copts from the devious Chalcedonians. The *Chronicle* of John of Nikiu interprets the Arab Muslim conquest as a divine judgment on the Byzantine Empire for the error of Chalcedonian doctrine. The *Apocalypse of Samuel of Kalamun* offers a different perspective several centuries later as it calls the Copts to distance themselves from the Arab language. However, even in one of the few examples of anti-Muslim rhetoric from this period, the point is not to criticize Islam but to call Christians to renewal by rejecting the Arabic language.

The persistence of Chalcedonians as the primary enemy of Egyptian Miaphysites into Islamic times demonstrates the importance of anti-Chalcedonianism for constructing Egyptian identity. The trajectory of Egyptian Christian ethnic boundary maintenance after the Arab Muslim conquest continued along the same path which had begun after Chalcedon. The Copts had to distinguish themselves from fellow Christians who held a different theological position; the difference between Copts and Muslims was obvious. Groups often express greater disapproval toward neighbors with whom they have more familiarity and similarity than toward groups that are distant and unknown.[2]

Yet, the Arab Muslim conquest did increase the ethnic rhetoric in Coptic texts. The reality of Arab Muslim rule and the increasing Muslim population in Egypt following the seventh century engendered concern for the preservation of Coptic identity. This is evident in that the strongest examples of Egyptian ethnic rhetoric come from texts composed in Arabic. When the Coptic language was endangered, the assertion of Egyptian identity among Copts became more strident. The following texts will demonstrate the culmination of anti-Chalcedonian Egyptian identity formation by setting a trajectory for Coptic identity under Muslim rule. Some of the texts included in this chapter focus on Egyptian figures who lived during the seventh century, but were written much later. These texts are still considered in this study along with literature more positively dated to the seventh century for two reasons: these later texts demonstrate continuity with how these figures were received by the Egyptian community during the seventh century and into the medieval period, and they also demonstrate continuity with how Egyptian ethnic identity was constructed in the seventh century into the medieval and modern periods.

BENJAMIN OF ALEXANDRIA

Benjamin served as Alexandria's thirty-eighth patriarch from 622–61 CE, placing him at the crucial turning point when control over Egypt passed from Byzantine to Persian, back to Byzantine, and then to Arab Muslim forces.[3] The political upheaval only heightened the religious tension in Egypt as Chalcedonians, supported by the Byzantine authorities, vied with Miaphysites for adherents. The socio-religious context of seventh-century Egypt is evident in the writings of Benjamin.[4] The *Arabic History of the Patriarchs of Alexandria* is a collection of biographies of Coptic patriarchs which Severus ibn al-Muqaffa edited during the tenth century. It contains a lengthy entry on Benjamin that echoes much of the information presented about him from his own writings and those of his patriarchal successor Agathon. Although written several centuries after the time of Benjamin, several passages demonstrate how the memory of Benjamin in the *History* is consistent with late antique themes in Egyptian ethnic identity formation.

Benjamin came from the village of Barhût in the province of Al-Buhairah, the son of a wealthy family. Strongly desiring the monastic life, Benjamin entered the Monastery of Canopus under the leadership of Theonas, where he quickly achieved monastic excellence.[5] After Benjamin received a vision in which he became patriarch, Theonas took him to Patriarch Andronicus, who ordained Benjamin as a priest. After the death of Andronicus, Benjamin became patriarch during the Persian occupation.[6] After the victory of Heraclius over the Persians and the appointment of Cyrus as Chalcedonian patriarch, Benjamin fled Alexandria, expecting persecution by the authorities.

The medieval Coptic community remembered Benjamin as a restorer of orthodoxy after times of Chalcedonian persecution: "So the Father Benjamin, the confessor, the warrior by the power of our Lord Jesus the Messiah, restored the conditions of the Church and organized it and he ordered the priests and the laity and commanded them to hold firm to the orthodox faith, even unto death. He wrote to the entirety of the bishops of the land of Egypt[7] that they should beware the coming tribulation."[8] Cyrus pursued Benjamin throughout Egypt for ten years until the armies of 'Amr ibn al-Âs conquered Babylon.[9]

Benjamin returned to his patriarchal throne in Alexandria and was granted security by 'Amr, who allegedly instructed the patriarch to maintain "the government of his (Benjamin's) nation."[10] Benjamin's reputation as the savior of Coptic orthodoxy during the medieval period reflected a similar depiction of the patriarch in his own time. The brief mention of Benjamin in the seventh-century *Chronicle* of John of Nikiu also highlights Benjamin's restoration work among the churches of Egypt: "And Abba Benjamin, the patriarch of the Egyptians,[11] arrived at to the city of Alexandria in the thirteenth year after his escape from the Romans[12] and he went to the Churches, and looked over all of them."[13] Now that Egyptians such as John of Nikiu were living under Arab Muslim rule in the mid/late-seventh century, the memory of Chalcedonian imposition in early-seventh-century Egypt appears with the label "Roman." This more totalizing ethnic rhetoric further exacerbates ethnic boundaries along a Egyptian/Miaphysite and Roman/Chalcedonian binary.[14] When Egyptians were themselves Roman citizens during the fifth and sixth centuries, Egyptian identity contrasted with Roman imperial officials rather than Roman identity. This strategy of ethnic boundary maintenance was not a new innovation in early Islamic Egypt but rather an extension of the Egyptian/Roman tension that had been shaping the Egyptian Christian social imagination since the schism at Chalcedon. As will become evident below, the medieval memory of Benjamin echoed such strategies of identification.

After engaging in rigorous religious reform and reestablishing the Miaphysite movement in Egypt, Benjamin fell ill and died on the 8th of Tubah. The medieval *AHPA* reports that Benjamin received a heavenly reception from Athanasius, Severus, and Theodosius of Antioch after he passed.[15] Starting in late antiquity and continuing into the contemporary world, Benjamin received credit for consolidating the Egyptian church under the banner of the Miaphysite confession.[16]

One of the central texts connected to Benjamin is the *Book of the Consecration of the Sanctuary of Benjamin.*[17] This text, attributed to Benjamin's successor Agathon, narrates the events surrounding the consecration of the church of Makarios at Scetis. This was a typical event in the administration of Benjamin as he actively engaged in the reestablishment of churches and monasteries following his reinstatement as patriarch. The Coptic manuscript containing the *Book of the Consecration* comes from the monastery of Makarios of the Wadi El Natrun and this copy is dated to 1348 CE.[18]

Given the high number of Greek loan words and awkward sentence structure differing from typical Bohairic syntax, it is likely that the Coptic *Book of the Consecration* is based on a Greek original.[19] The *Book of the Consecration* identifies its author as a certain Agathon, a priest of Benjamin who succeeded Benjamin as patriarch. There are no other texts identifying Agathon as author; therefore, his authorship cannot be conclusively proven or disproven.[20]

The proemium introduces Abba Benjamin, "patriarch of the great town[21] of Alexandria," and describes the occasion of the homily as "concerning the consecration of the great, catholic and apostolic church of the great *Theophoros* and *Pneumatophoros* our father Abba Makarios of the holy mountain of Scetis."[22] The homily describes the sanctuary of Makarios as "the sanctuary that is greater than every sanctuary in the world."[23] Benjamin receives much praise; the introduction describes him as "the fame of orthodoxy" and "the one who understood the concepts of the Scriptures." Such a description is likely an attempt to depict Benjamin as the champion of orthodoxy (anti-Chalcedonianism) in contrast to Cyrus, a rhetorical move that likely reminded the audience of the theological issues of the seventh century. The descriptor "orthodox" labels the Miaphysite position and is also used for Macarius, who is called "this strong and orthodox ascetic."[24]

While the text does not anachronistically assign Macarius an anti-Chalcedonian position, labeling him "orthodox" during a period when this term is clearly associated with Miaphysitism represents a common strategy among Egyptian anti-Chalcedonians. Pre-Chalcedonian figures exist in an uninterrupted succession of orthodoxy with Miaphysite figures.[25] Throughout this period, Egyptian Miaphysites depicted their leaders as the legitimate heirs who are in theological continuity with the Egyptian forebears who lived before Chalcedon, despite the fact that these leaders (like Macarius) did not have the opportunity to weigh in on this schism.

The author of the *Book of the Consecration* identifies himself as Agathon, "son of my father Abba Benjamin the archbishop. And I myself knew a multitude of establishments[26] of my father."[27] Agathon begins the homily by recounting a vision told to him by Benjamin, which occurred "while finding a little time of peace from the persecution of the heretics."[28] Here, Benjamin is again the suffering shepherd of Egypt who is constantly harassed by the oppression of heretical (Chalcedonian) forces. This indirect method of battling Chalcedonian doctrine also appears later when the text refers to Jesus as "the indivisible Christ,"[29] a refutation of the alleged Chalcedonian division of the natures of Christ.

After Benjamin's consecration of the newly constructed church of Makarios, "some ascetic monks"[30] come to Alexandria during the celebration of the Nativity. A large and diverse crowd gathers at the Church of the Theotokos: "All the clergy gathered unto me with the powerful of the city and all the people; peasants and aristocrats; wealthy and poor; and a multitude of high-ranking, faithful women."[31] Benjamin accepts the monks' invitation to come to Scetis in order to consecrate the Church of Makarios for elderly monks who need to visit a more accessible church. While Benjamin and the monks are traveling to Scetis, they pass by several notable monasteries including those of Isaac of Pernouj, Abba Pishoi, Abba John, and "the community of our Roman fathers Maximus and Dometius."[32] It is unclear if "Roman"—which can alternatively be understood in the sense of "Byzantine" or "Greek"—here refers to linguistic, ethnic, or geographic identity. Typically, in Egyptian anti-Chalcedonian texts, "Roman" referred to the oppressive Chalcedonian emperor. Therefore, regardless of what aspect of social identity functions here in the *Book of the Consecration,* it is important that it is possible to describe pre-Chalcedonian leaders as "Romans" even though later use of the term was negative.

While the reference to "Romans" is often negative in Egyptian Miaphysite literature, it is significant that positive uses of the labels (Byzantine, Roman) moderate any nationalist reading of anti-Chalcedonian literature. Likewise, any attempt at positing a simple Greek-versus-Egyptian conflict in late antique Egypt is mistaken. The highest allegiance of Egyptian Miaphysites was to their faith community, which, especially before Chalcedon, included "Romans" as well as any other people group of the faith understood to be orthodox in Egypt. These monastic figures, Maximus and Dometius, function as kindred spirits of the Miaphysite hero Benjamin and the text highlights their social identity as "Roman," thus indicating a degree of distinction from Egyptians who do not receive such identifiers. This further highlights two fundamental aspects of Egyptian ethnic identity development being advanced here: Egypt and her citizens are the primary focus while outsiders are marked as Other and yet are afforded a degree of insider membership, provided they can be connected to anti-Chalcedonian doctrine. This example of religious "insiders" who are yet ethnic "outsiders" helps to avoid two extremes in assessing Egyptian Christological resistance: reading nationalist sentiment into the literature on the one hand and ignoring the importance of Egyptian identity in the literature on the other.

Upon arrival at the monastic "community" of Makarios, Benjamin is greeted "in the manner of the sons of the Hebrews when they sang to our Lord Jesus Christ when he entered Jerusalem" to the point of "shaking the entire mountain (of Scetis)."[33] Moved by the scene at Scetis, Benjamin proclaims:

> I give you thanks my Lord Jesus Christ for you have saved my soul from the hands of the tyrant, dragon, apostate, the one who chased me on account of the orthodox faith. I give you thanks, my lord Christ, for you have allowed me to see my sons once more as they surround me in your honor, my Lord Jesus.[34]

Benjamin's remarks here resemble those of Dioscorus and Timothy Aelurus who also endured persecution and exile for their stance on Chalcedon. The minority discourse reinforces Egyptian ethnic identity formation, which focused on persecution and martyrdom. Indeed, the tradition of Egyptian patriarchs being exiled for their adherence to a particular concept of orthodoxy goes back to Athanasius and Peter I. Benjamin's pursuer is the Chalcedonian patriarch Cyrus. After leaving "the Romans,"[35] Benjamin calls on his priest Agathon to bring him the necessary books for the consecration of the church and its sanctuary. Benjamin describes Agathon as "my priest, the one who suffered with me because of the faith in the time of the tribulation when he chased me, namely, Cyrus the Caucasian, the enemy of every righteousness."[36]

In anti-Chalcedonian literature of this period, Cyrus is constantly labeled by his ethnic origin in the Caucasus (*pikaukos*), a rhetorical strategy that ascribes the status of Other to the imperially-sanctioned Chalcedonian party in Egypt. The boundaries of Egyptian Miaphysite identity are contrasted with the foreign doctrine of Chalcedon.[37] The text depicts Cyrus as the Chalcedonian oppressor, while the Miaphysites (who were actually the majority party in Egypt) present themselves as an oppressed minority. The text berates Cyrus in a manner consistent with that used for former enemies of Egypt and he is added to the list of most despised adversaries, including Leo, Marcian, and Justinian. Though the *Book of the Consecration* was written during Arab Muslim rule in Egypt, its most despicable figure is the "tyrannical dragon" Cyrus.

This dynamic of Egyptian Christian identity development during times of Arab Muslim rule cannot be overstated. Even after the Roman Chalcedonian government had long left Egypt, Egyptian Christians continued to criticize an entity that no longer had power in Egypt. This demonstrates the degree to which, for Egyptian Miaphysites, the anti-Chalcedonian cause was a central tenet of what it meant to be Egyptian. Another factor is the continued presence of Egyptian citizens who embraced Chalcedonian theology ("Melkites"), whom mainstream Egyptian Miaphysites considered heretical. The fact that the text Otherized Cyrus by his ethnic background further demonstrates how this movement was simultaneously religious and ethnic. Ethnic groups do not form in isolation from the Other but rather depend on an "Other" against which to assert who the group is and who the group is not.[38] In this case, Benjamin defines Egyptian as orthodox (Miaphysite) while Caucasians and Romans are heretics (Chalcedonian).

Yet, Egyptian strategies of identification include a complex pattern of exclusion and inclusivity. At the outset of the consecration, Benjamin received a vision of Makarios described as "father of the peoples."[39] This is another example of the way that Egyptian anti-Chalcedonian texts ascribe universal authority to Egyptian heroes of the faith. Similarly, when Benjamin saw a vision of a cherubim, the angelic figure lauded Makarios as "the father of the patriarchs and the bishops" as well as "all the monks of this entire mountain."[40] Makarios is "father" to Egypt's highest ecclesiastical and political office holder, the Alexandrian patriarch, while also being the father of church leaders around the world.

Indeed, the horizon of this homily reaches beyond Egypt. While praising the benevolence of Makarios, Benjamin refers to certain righteous ones as "the nets that gather together every race to the kingdom of God and do not reject anyone."[41] The vision set forth in the *Book of the Consecration* is one in which "every race" of humanity gathers in the Kingdom of God; it is a global vision that motivates Benjamin and it does not only concern Egypt.[42] The text described the church as "the gathering place of the angels and the port of every soul that takes refuge in God, the Savior of each one."[43]

Benjamin makes it clear in his homily that ethnic identity does not determine having a share in the orthodox community. Rather, those who "love the glory of people more than the glory of God"[44] are the ones whom "the blessed, catholic, and apostolic church excludes."[45] However, Egyptian figures such as Makarios, "the guardian of all,"[46] are those who lead the rallying call for orthodoxy. The text centers Egypt as Benjamin quotes from Isaiah at the consecration of the Church of Makarios: "There will be an altar to the Lord in the land of the Egyptians and a stele to the Lord in its holy districts."[47]

Despite the fact that the context of the biblical passage refers to Jews suffering at the hands of Egyptians, Benjamin appropriates and uses it to depict the Church of Makarios as the fulfillment of biblical prophecy. While Egyptian Christians typically disassociated themselves from the Egypt of the Old Testament, in this passage there is an example of pro-Egyptian rhetoric emerging in the seventh century. The text modifies biblical interpretation to elevate Egyptian, anti-Chalcedonian identity. Perhaps the most significant aspect of Egyptian ethnic rhetoric here is not the hermeneutic revision but instead the alteration of the wording. While Benjamin's quotation refers to Egypt's "districts" (*nefthōs*) as "holy," this positive label is wholly absent from the Septuagint: "In that day there shall be an altar to the Lord in the land of the Egyptians and a pillar to the Lord by its border."[48] The text transforms Egypt from the source of the oppression of the people of God (that is, Israel) to the bulwark of Christian orthodoxy. Such scriptural revisions enhance the pro-Egyptian aspect of anti-Chalcedonian texts. Thus, while Benjamin's vision is of a translocal Christian community open to all, it is also one in which Egypt stands at the center, inviting others to follow its decidedly Egyptian brand of orthodoxy. The homily then describes a vision in which Benjamin sees elderly monks of every rank offering incense that covers the entire church and then receiving the Eucharist.

In another vision, Benjamin sees a celestial figure who implores him to read the canons of the church. The canons include one involving the introduction of "foreign clerics": "Anyone among the clergy who brings a cleric foreign to Egypt or a ruler into this holy sanctuary because of human glory, let him be anathema."[49] While the focus of this canon is the importance of ascetic humility, the emphasis on preventing the intrusion of outsiders adds an ethnic dimension.

After reading the canons to Agathon, Benjamin describes the events surrounding Anatolios, ruler of Pšate, who came to the consecration of the church. The text describes the miraculous healing of Anatolios' son and concludes with praise for Makarios and the monastic community of Scetis. Benjamin concludes the homily with encouraging words that continue the theme of minority discourse:

Now, O my holy fathers, let us pray steadfastly so that our Lord Christ strengthen us in the foundation of his holy Church and that he would be a fence for us in his goodness and that he would allow the orthodox faith to persevere, having received freely a fearlessness in all times. And we, the Christians, are exalted in him at all times. And he saves us from the oppression of those who rule and from the malice of the hunter, the enemy of every truth- the devil. For the kingdom and the power and the authority belong to our Lord and our God and our Savior Jesus Christ.[50]

The oppression (*pišthorter*) of the faithful comes from those who rule (*nnē etmahi*), which further underlines the depiction of the orthodox Egyptian majority as faithful martyrs living under tyrannical Chalcedonian rule. It is important to note that the enemies explicitly named in the homily refer to Byzantine Chalcedonianism, while reference to the new Islamic hegemony is absent. What is clear is Benjamin's use of the rhetoric of the oppressed minority to shape an identity for the Egyptian church that centers anti-Chalcedonian resistance. This same type of rhetoric is characteristic of Benjamin's own writing.

The second core text surrounding Benjamin is his exegesis of John 2:1–11, found in the *Homily on the Wedding at Cana*. While the *Book of the Consecration* identifies Agathon as its author, the *Homily* is likely an authentic work of Benjamin and the only surviving text written by the patriarch.[51] The complete Bohairic text of the *Homily* appears in a tenth-century manuscript and was likely a translation of a Sahidic original.[52] Although the date of composition of the *Homily* is unknown, 13 Tubah is both the date of the liturgical celebration for the miracle at Cana and the death of the monk Isidoros, suggesting that this was the date that the sermon was delivered.[53] The *Homily* is not only important in reconstructing the life of Benjamin, but it is also one of the best literary examples of Coptic preaching.[54] The *Homily* is a source for understanding Benjamin's anti-Chalcedonian and Monoenergist theology.[55]

The *Homily* begins with the same type of minority rhetoric that appears in the *Book of the Consecration,* in this case using imagery of sheep, wolves, and shepherds: "It is the custom of shepherds to tend sheep in pastures that have no bad weeds in them; and not only this, but you find them bearing the burden of (guarding against) the wolf. For they do not allow themselves to sleep so that they (the wolves) do not enter the pen while the sheep are inside and seize one of them."[56] Benjamin described the vulnerability felt by the Copts of the seventh-century through the imagery of innocent sheep at the mercy of the wolves of heresy. Again, it is possible that the Arab Muslim conquerors are also in the background. Benjamin is the shepherd who protects his flock in a manner consistent with that of his patriarchal predecessors: "We also, my fathers and brothers, according to the commandment of our fathers, eagerly beseech God at all times to protect us in the saving faith of our holy fathers, Athanasius, Alexander, and Cyril—the equal, unwavering balance of the dogmas of the faith."[57] The anti-Chalcedonians present their position as being in direct continuity with that of pre-Chalcedonian patriarchs, from whom both sides claim descent. Ancestry (both theological and ethnic) continues to play a role throughout the *Homily*. It is likely not coincidental that the church fathers mentioned by Benjamin are all Egyptian. Egyptian Christians during the seventh century certainly celebrated non-Egyptian figures such as Basil of Caesarea or Clement of Rome. However, the *Homily* especially highlights the native Egyptian leaders.

While warning his congregants against drunkenness (in the context of discussing the presence of wine at the wedding feast), Benjamin asks: "Is there not a man here today who drank, became drunk, went out, committed robbery, was arrested, was killed, died, and his body was not worthy to go to the tomb of his ancestors (*nefioti*)?"[58] Benjamin also rhetorically asks: "Is there anyone today that has not become a foreigner to their hometown[59] because of debts for wine?"[60] Benjamin is warning against drunkenness using the well-known example of people whose drinking habits had caused them to fall into such debt and become "foreigners"[61] to their community. The sense of belonging, of being a part of the in-group, comes from adherence to the behavioral standard of orthodoxy offered here. The *Homily* contrasts the inclusion of the faithful orthodox with the exclusion of those who reject orthodox doctrine. Benjamin's deployment language of "foreignness" and "ancestry" with reference to theological views vividly illustrates the patriarch's continuation of the late antique Egyptian trend of framing Christological allegiance in ethnic terms.

Benjamin begins his exposition of the Gospel passage by introducing each apostle in attendance and explaining his typological role in the miracle. While it may seem odd that a seventh-century Coptic text would introduce Peter as "the first among the apostles," Peter's importance emerges throughout the Coptic tradition.[62] Any attempt to minimize the Apostle's importance in the Egyptian church is a modern phenomenon.[63] The anti-Chalcedonian agenda picks back up when the Apostle Judas appears in order to attack the ever-expanding list of enemies:

> For, I will say that a single Judas gave up his Lord at that time, but I do not know where all these Judases came from. But you will say to me, 'Do you know who they are?' It is I who will tell you about each one of them.

He is Arius, he is Nestorius, he is Macedonius, he is the impious Leo, he is Ibas, he is Theodore, he is Theodoret, he is Leontius, he is the defiled Julian, he is George the Arian, he is Gregory his brother who resembled him in his deeds. He is the one whose name is not worthy to be announced, who brought great evils upon the church, the lawless Cyrus who is polluted in all his deeds. He is Victor, the bishop who bore the sins of his entire city, and behold, he is Melitius in Upper Egypt (*phmarēc*). Are they not all Judases?[64]

Only anti-Chalcedonian Egyptians are in continuity with the orthodox champions of the fourth and early fifth centuries; the Chalcedonians are the direct successors of earlier heretics. This section is a clear example of how communal memory is as an integral component to ethnic identity.[65] Benjamin offers two fundamental trajectories for theological lineage: the anti-Chalcedonians are the faithful heirs to the orthodox teachings of Alexander, Athanasius, and Cyril, while the Chalcedonians are spreading the heretical teachings of Arius, Julian, and Nestorius.

The theological opponent given most negative attention in Benjamin's dossier of heretics is his Chalcedonian nemesis, Cyrus. Cyrus also receives the most attention in the *Book of the Consecration* and the medieval entry on Benjamin in the *AHPA*. Continuing the exposition of the miracle at Cana, the *Homily* addresses other theological positions common to Benjamin's context: "But let it not be that one of the heretics say that Christ ate and drank like a human. Go away, defiled dog! I believe that everything that people do my Savior did except sin alone."[66] Benjamin is commenting on the miracle at Cana and arguing against those who claim that the human actions of Jesus cannot be reconciled with his divinity:[67] "My beloved, let us not trust the heretics, lest they lead us astray and take us to perdition with them."[68] It is significant that this rare example of Coptic preaching includes this strong defense of the full humanity of Jesus, despite centuries of caricatures of Egyptian Christology as minimizing the humanity of Christ.

Benjamin's polemic is directed at Eutychianism, which was part of the larger doctrinal context of seventh-century Egypt. Given the position that Benjamin takes regarding the will and activity of Jesus, his target could also be the monoenergist/monothelite positions that were also being advanced during the seventh century. It is noteworthy that Coptic anti-Chalcedonian literature focuses on other issues beyond Chalcedonian doctrine. While the majority of texts in this period focus on the Chalcedonian controversy, the Miaphysites were also competing with other "heresies." The multi-faceted theological landscape of seventh-century Egypt opposes any interpretation that reduces the concerns of the Copts to Chalcedonianism only.

The *Homily* then shifts to a collection of seemingly unrelated anecdotes that deal with monastic and priestly roles. The first anecdote relates a vision that Benjamin received "when God gave us relief from the suffering and oppression which befell us from the lawless Cyrus (*kuros pparanomos*)."[69] The vision describes the expulsion of a fornicating priest from the White Monastery, due to an apparition of Shenoute accompanied by angelic figures. The priest swore oaths denying charges of sexual impurity. However, the archimandrite Shenoute appeared in a vision and rebuked the priest. The second story concerns Benjamin's encounter with two Manichaeans at an Upper Egyptian chapel who engaged in an unspecified sinful act. Benjamin became aware of this through divine revelation.

The text labels the Manichaeans as "foreigners": "they were foreigners (*hanxenikos*), merchants from Egypt."[70] This outsider label was motivated by a desire to disassociate the "heresy" of Manicheanism from Egyptian identity. They confessed to Benjamin that they faced persecution in "our land"[71] for selling the Eucharistic elements and for engaging in devil worship. Enraged, Benjamin reported them to Shenoute, the magistrate of Antinoë, who had them burned alive until "nothing at all was found of them."[72]

The story ends with an exhortation to Christians of every rank to guard themselves from sin, "especially (from) Manichaeans like these."[73] Yet while it is the Manichaeans who are the victims of terrible violence endorsed by Benjamin, the patriarch represents himself as a member of an oppressed minority. This anecdote begins in a manner similar to the first story: "It happened to me, the insignificant Benjamin, while I ran from the persecution of those who rose up against me."[74] The rhetoric of minority discourse persists despite the majority status in Egypt of the Coptic orthodox or the oppression enacted by this group towards others. The religious violence in late antique Egypt was complex and multidirectional as the Egyptian Miaphysites suffered intense persecution at the hands of Roman Chalcedonian authorities for two centuries and yet engaged in violence against religious communities who were in the minority in Egypt. What is most significant for this study is that, unlike the Monothelite, Eutychian, Manichaean or any other religious communities in Egypt, the Miaphysites were the majority party and the only religious group to go to great lengths to depict their religious views as an extension of Egyptian ethnic identity.

The final section of the *Homily* recounts a meeting between Benjamin and a "perfect monk"[75] named Isidoros who lived at the Enaton monastery. This anecdote chronologically precedes other events described in the *Homily* since Benjamin's first meeting with Isidoros takes place before Benjamin's exile. Isidoros shut himself in his cell for thirty-six years and when the superior of the Enaton knocked at his door, Isidoros declared that no one would see his face except Benjamin, "the father of the faith."[76]

Upon hearing this news, Benjamin visits Isidoros, who recounts the events of his life. His parents and sister died when he was a child and Isidoros then entered the Enaton where he became close to his monastic father, who left Isidoros and went into the desert. When that happened, Isidoros did not leave his cell for over three decades. After narrating these events to Benjamin, Isidoros begins weeping bitterly as he receives a vision of the imminent persecution of Benjamin:

> As for you, O my father, during this year a devil is coming to this city to persecute you. For the Romans will rule over the country of Egypt and they will persecute you until they cast you from your throne.[77] You will flee to Upper Egypt as they persecute you until you go to the monastery of the Archimandrite Abba Shenoute. You will suffer great, evil oppression. As it is written, the shepherd will be struck and the sheep of the flock will scatter. You will spend eleven years persecuted from place to place. But do not fear. No one will be able to subdue you, nor will the evil one conquer you. After this, God will remember you and he will bring you back to your throne joyfully.[78]

The text refers to Cyrus as the "devil" who is the source of persecution. The phrase *kyoči nsōk* appears four times in Isidoros's apocalyptic vision to stress the theme of persecution. The text emphasizes Benjamin's role as a persecuted martyr by the shepherd/sheep imagery, by expulsion from the episcopal throne, and by pursuit from "place to place," reaching as far as the White Monastery.[79] However, the oppressive concepts of persecution (*kyoči nsōk*), expulsion (*šatouhitk*), injury (*cenarōht*), and suffering (*šōp ḥici*) are contrasted with protection (*ntefrōic*), remembrance (*erpekmeui*), and restoration (*ouoč*).

Benjamin addresses the Coptic orthodox community through Isidoros, offering the hope of restoration in the midst of persecution. While Arab Muslim hegemony is the oppressive reality of his audience, it is nonetheless "Roman" persecutors who function as primary targets in Benjamin's polemic. The elusive third person plural "they" who enact the various persecutions endured by Benjamin are identified as *nirōmeos*,[80] and they are contrasted with the "country of Egypt" (*tchōra nchēmi*). The text depicted "Romans" as the source of social oppression and theological heresy in a rhetorical strategy in which Egyptian Miaphysite identity opposes the Chalcedonian, Byzantine Other.

Later in the medieval period, the *AHPA* followed this strategy by portraying the Arab Muslim conquest as a consequence of the "Roman" faith: "The Lord forsook the Roman forces[81] right in front of him (Muhammad), as a result of their putrid beliefs, and because of the curses that were placed upon them, because of the council of Chalcedon, by the forefathers."[82] Likewise, the *AHPA* calls Benjamin a "fugitive from the Romans."[83] The *AHPA* also contains one of the clearest examples of anti-Chalcedonianism shaping the boundaries of Egyptian ethnic identity. After his return to Alexandria, the *AHPA* describes Benjamin's monastic residence:

> And the location in which the patriarch lived was a pure residence without pollution, in a monastery called the Monastery of Metrā—it was the episcopal (residence). And the churches and monasteries which belonged to the virgins and monks were ruined by Heraclius the dissident, when he forced them to accept the doctrine of Chalcedon, with the exception of this sole monastery; for those who were in it were an immensely powerful ethnic group—Egyptians, collectively indigenous—without a foreigner among them.[84] Thus, he was not able to influence their hearts towards him. For this reason, when the Father Benjamin returned from Upper Egypt, he remained with them, because they maintained the orthodox faith, and had never deviated from it.[85]

This passage demonstrates how Miaphysite doctrine was a prerequisite for inclusion in the Egyptian people. The *AHPA* contrasts Egyptian and Miaphysite with Roman and Chalcedonian, going so far as to employ the vocabulary of "purity" and "dilution" with reference to the pure Egyptian (Miaphysite) ethnicity. Indeed, ethnicity and religion were synonymous in late antique Egypt.[86] Just as this passage does not express nationalist sentiment, this statement is likely more than mere "regional chauvinism."[87]

These passages from the *AHPA* reflect traditions in the Egyptian community of how Benjamin and his teachings were received in the tenth century; these excerpts do not directly indicate the sentiment of late antique Egyptians. However, the editor of the *AHPA* endeavored to demonstrate the congruity between the memory of Benjamin during the tenth century and the writings associated with the patriarch during his own lifetime.[88] The medieval Coptic community remembered the Chalcedonian "heresy" as an extension of the "Romans" and their leaders such as "Heraclius the heretic." Conversely, Miaphysitism was the logical consequence of Egyptian ethnic identity. These medieval strategies of identification appeared in the writings that emerged from Benjamin's lifetime and the patriarch's own hand. The *Homily* also elevates Egypt as the source of orthodoxy and labels Chalcedonianism not with a precise theological moniker but simply as "the Romans." This congruity between late antique and medieval Coptic sources on ethnic identity demonstrates the foundational nature of anti-Chalcedonian resistance as a boundary for ethnic identity that took shape in the late antique period and set a trajectory that would continue for centuries to come. That Chalcedon was the shift in the boundaries of Egyptian identity is also demonstrable in the rise in anti-Roman rhetoric. The *Homily* lists Peter as being first among the apostles, a position the Coptic Orthodox church has maintained until the present day. However, this title persisted with the understanding that all bishops, not just those from Rome, are successors to Peter.[89] The veneration of Peter in the presence of anti-Roman rhetoric in the seventh-century *Homily* is a departure from pre-Chalcedonian Egyptian Christians who heralded Rome as the universal head of the Church.[90] While Rome was the "head of all" prior to Chalcedon, Rome became the persecutor of all following the council.

In the *Homily* as in the *AHPA,* ethnicity and theological orthodoxy function as overlapping markers of identity. Benjamin guides his audience to identify with the oppressed Egyptian anti-Chalcedonians who hope for salvation from their theological opponents, who are also given ethnic labels. Benjamin then describes the fulfillment of prophecy, including his persecution and restoration:

> I went to Alexandria. And you all know how great the evil that happened to us was and how much was the danger. I fled from place to place until I went to the Monastery of the Saint Apa Shenoute according to the prophecy of the saint. All the things that he told me happened to me. Afterwards, God the Merciful again had pity on his church. The people (*nilaos*) rejoiced with us, and we went to Alexandria. After we rested for a few days, I arose and went to that saint. While standing outside his door, he cried out from inside, "It is fitting that the Archbishop, the new Dioscorus, has come."[91]

Benjamin emerges from great evil and danger and returns from exile. Like Dioscorus, his episcopal predecessor, he suffered exile due to his Miaphysite convictions. The fact that the patriarch could only find refuge during his exile in the White Monastery federation of Shenoute further demonstrates the significant role this monastic complex played in the anti-Chalcedonian cause. A century after the decline of the Pachomian community during the time of Abraham of Farshut, the Shenoutean community continued to serve as a beacon of Miaphysite support. This ensured its superior role in subsequent Egyptian Christian identity formation compared to that of the Pachomian monastery.[92] While recounting his time at the White Monastery, Benjamin calls on his audience to remember the persecution carried out by the Chalcedonians ("you all know," *tetencōoun*) and draws on collective memory to construct an image of the orthodox as faithful martyrs. Benjamin shares the sense of oppression of his audience and then shares in their hope, due to the resolution of his restoration.

What exactly is meant by the celebratory gathering of "the peoples/nations" (*nilaos*) at Benjamin's return to Alexandria? Is this a reference to the collective Egyptian people, including cultural and administrative factions? Or is Benjamin describing a global gathering of various anti-Chalcedonian groups? In any event, the scene depicts a universal celebration of a return to "orthodoxy" in the episcopal seat of Egypt. As reported in the *AHPA*, "And when this spiritual Patriarch Benjamin sat among his ethnicity[93] once again, by the favor of Christ and His mercy, the whole land of Egypt[94] rejoiced over him."[95] This further demonstrates how the Egyptian memory of Benjamin as a universal authority in orthodoxy began in the seventh century and continued as this tradition served to shape tenth-century accounts of the patriarch.

Benjamin's account of the events of the early seventh century lacks any polemic against the present-day Arab Muslim rulers, in contrast to the decidedly negative portrayal of Byzantine Chalcedonians. As Mikhail notes: "Interestingly, even where it might be expected, there is no reference at all to 'Amr or the Arab conquest in the sermon."[96] While it may be possible that anti-Islamic or anti-Arab polemic was absent due to fear of persecution, it is more likely that the text simply has other interests: namely maintaining an intense anti-Byzantine tone and portraying Coptic life in a positive light, as Benjamin does at the end of the *Homily*. It is also significant that two centuries of persecution did not stop Egyptian Miaphysites from speaking out against Roman imperial and ecclesiastical authorities.

If one were to read the *Homily* with no knowledge of its wider historical context, Arab Muslim dominance in seventh-century Egypt would go unnoticed. This is in contrast to the way John of Nikiu describes the Muslim conquerors and uses pejorative ethnic terminology: "Indeed 'Amr had no mercy on the Egyptians,[97] and he was not faithful to the covenant they had made with him, for he was of a barbaric ethnicity."[98] In the *Homily,* the Coptic orthodox are in a place of peace and self-determination after the tyranny of Cyrus.[99] Such rhetoric was the tradition that formed the foundation of the *AHPA,* which also depicted Benjamin's return as the end of an era of oppression:

> Therefore when the holy Benjamin heard this, he joined Alexandria with great joy, after thirteen years of being gone, ten years of which were because of the unbelieving Roman Heraclius,[100] three years before the Muslims conquered Alexandria, and clothed with the crown of patience and intense warfare which happened to the orthodox people[101] by means of the oppression of the heretics. When he (Benjamin) appeared, the people[102] and the whole city rejoiced, and reported his arrival to Sānutyus, the governor who believed in the Messiah, who had agreed with the emir 'Amr about his (Benjamin's) arrival, and acquired safety for him (Benjamin) from him ('Amr).[103]

The *AHPA* further reports that Benjamin prayed for, prophesied about, and exhorted 'Amr and left the commander's presence after receiving great signs of respect.[104] Roman authorities retained prejudice against Egyptians in the *Chronicle* of John of Nikiu. A certain Menas, who was governor of Lower Egypt by Emperor Heraclius, retained his position under 'Amr. The *Chronicle* reported that Menas was an "arrogant, uneducated man who intensely hated the Egyptians."[105] While Egyptian Christian writings following the Islamic conquest vary in their depiction of Islamic rulers, they consistently reject "Roman" Chalcedonian identity. Benjamin's own writings indicate a positive view of Arab Muslim authorities in Egypt, supporting this later tradition of the patriarch's relationship with the new government. In a shifting political landscape and in the face of political instability, ethnicity and ethnic boundary maintenance were important. As Barth states: "The process whereby ethnic units maintain themselves are thus clearly affected, but not fundamentally changed, by the variable of regional security."[106] The late antique and medieval texts that provide information about Benjamin illustrate this point. Egyptian, anti-Chalcedonian identity took form by using insider/outsider terms for Egyptians versus Byzantines and their Chalcedonian/Melkite allies. This is the primary concern in these texts even after the Arab conquest.

The absence of Islamic critique also could be an effort to protect the Coptic community from a new type of persecution. For it is clear from texts such as the *Chronicle* of John of Nikiu that Egyptian Christians were not entirely in support of Arab Muslim rulers. It seems more plausible, however, that the need to distinguish themselves from their fellow Christians was stronger than any need to distinguish themselves from the Arab conquerors who were clearly of a different faith. The remaining texts that focus on seventh-century Coptic figures will further illustrate the degree to which Byzantine Chalcedonian authority remained the primary target of Miaphysite polemic even under Islamic rule.

SAMUEL OF KALAMUN

During the period following the Arab Muslim conquest, one of the central figures in the anti-Chalcedonian movement was Samuel of Kalamun. Samuel was a monk who suffered at the hands of the Roman Chalcedonian administration for his defense of Miaphysite orthodoxy. Samuel's principal opponent was an imposed Chalcedonian bishop named Cyrus. Cyrus's foreign background—he was from the Caucus region—features prominently in the literature regarding Samuel. Indeed, in all subsequent Egyptian Christian literature where Cyrus is mentioned, he is called "Cyrus the Caucasian," or simply "the Caucasian." This form of ethnic othering is further evidence of how Egyptian Christians framed their ethnic identity along theological boundaries with "Roman" and "Caucasian" heretics as a contrast.

The texts associated with Samuel are the *Life of Samuel of Kalamun* and the *Apocalypse of Samuel of Kalamun*, a text of unknown authorship attributed to Samuel. The two works are "complementary texts springing from the same monastic tradition."[107] For this reason, these texts are integral to an investigation of ethnic identity development in Egyptian Christological resistance in late antiquity. It is likely that the *Life* was written during the seventh century while the *Apocalypse* likely came about much later in the medieval period, perhaps the tenth century. While an earlier date for the *Apocalypse* is possible, it is helpful to consider even if it comes from a later period as it demonstrates continuity with Coptic strategies of ethnic identity between the texts related to Samuel. Samuel of Kalamun joined the ranks of anti-Chalcedonian Egyptian heroes who suffered for the faith at the hands of Roman Chalcedonians. The numerous beatings endured by Samuel throughout the *Life* afford him the title of a martyr even though he did not die for his belief: "O the one who was martyred many times without losing his life!"[108] Most of the information about Samuel is present in his *Life*. While Samuel likely lived c. 597–695, the Sahidic manuscripts of the *Life* may have been written between the seventh and ninth centuries.[109]

The *Life* identifies its author as Samuel's successor Isaac and instructs its audience to read the *Life* publicly on Samuel's feast day, 8 Khoiak.[110] Isaac acknowledges a lack of personal acquaintance with Samuel but says he learned about his life from disciples of Samuel: "Our holy fathers heard from their fathers who were before them, and they heard from their fathers, who were the disciples of that great one, Apa Samuel ... our honored spiritual fathers, who we are under and who told us everything." After customary remarks of self-abasement, Isaac proceeds with relating the life and conduct of "the holy champion, Apa Samuel."[111]

Isaac provides information regarding Samuel's regional identity: "As to the ancestry (*tpatria*) of the holy Apa Samuel, he was a man of the northern region (*techōra etcahēt*), belonging to the neighborhood (*enhōrion*) of the city of Pelhip from the village of Tkello."[112] However, Samuel's local identity is less important than his heavenly citizenship: "However, his true ancestry[113] was the heavenly Jerusalem."[114] This qualification indicates the subordination of regional and/or ethnic identity to religious identity in Coptic anti-Chalcedonian literature. From the perspective of the *Life*, it is Samuel's adherence to orthodoxy that affords him a place in heavenly Jerusalem. That is more significant than his regional affiliation.

However, Egypt and her people dominate the *Life*, which attests to the way that ethnic and religious identity gradually become synonymous. Egyptian Christians of this period display a consistently complex vision of religious and ethnic identity; ideal Christian universalism is present in some instances while ethnic rhetoric appears in the context of theological polemic in other instances. Samuel came from a pious, wealthy family, and his father, Silas, was an elder in the church. After their initial attempts at persuading Samuel to marry failed, his parents allowed him to become a monk. Samuel's father passed away shortly after building a church and seeing Samuel ordained a deacon. Samuel then went to Scetis where he served under Apa Agathou and matured in his ascetic practices. After Agathou's death, Samuel continued his monastic lifestyle and "his fame reached the northern region (*nechōra etcahēt*), even the cities on the coast."[115] The *Life* then reports the first of Samuel's encounters with Chalcedonians. The "lawless Cyrus" comes to Alexandria to kill Benjamin, who flees to Upper Egypt:

After these things, the Caucasian[116] sat on the throne and he was given authority over the populace.[117] Then when he sat on the throne tyrannically, he set forth the *Tome* of Leo. Later he sent a cruel magistrate into the holy mountain of Scetis, as his feet were in a hurry to shed blood. He gave him the polluted *Tome* of Chalcedon[118] and told him, saying, 'Let all the elders subscribe to this *Tome* from the least to the greatest,'—because the entire country of Egypt depended on those elders.[119] 'Make haste and search the cells of the monks and the deserts. Perhaps you will find the one with the great beard, Benjamin,[120] and send him to me that I may take my revenge on him; for while he still lives, my kingdom and archbishopric do not extend throughout the entire country of Egypt.'[121]

Cyrus arrives at Scetis with a show of pomp, while the *hegoumenos* is captured by "barbarians"[122] who take him to their "country" (*chōra*). The encounter reported here contains many of the typical features of ethnic rhetoric common to Egyptian anti-Chalcedonian literature: villainization of Byzantine Chalcedonians,[123] assumption of Miaphysite uniformity among Egyptians, readiness for martyrdom in the cause of orthodoxy, and equating Egyptian identity with rejection of Chalcedonianism. The *Life* depicts the Byzantine-endorsed "Caucasian" magistrate as a snorting, enraged tyrant in contrast to the tranquil, courageous Egyptian monks. Indeed, Cyrus held a prominent place in the social and theological imagination of seventh-century Egyptian Christians, as he features prominently in the texts related to Benjamin as well as Samuel of Kalamun. This scene demonstrates the political and military power accompanying the Chalcedonian imposition in Egypt, as the imposed Patriarch Cyrus had the support of local magistrates. The rhetorical embellishments reinforce the attitude that Egyptians are encouraged to maintain toward themselves and toward the Chalcedonians. Note that Isaac indicated that the entire country of Egypt depends on Miaphysite leaders. This is a striking demonstration of Egyptian ethnic boundary maintenance through Miaphysite confession; not only the Egyptian church, but the "country" of Egypt depends on Miaphysite dominance.

Samuel encounters a magistrate who comes on behalf of the "Caucasian" in order to force the Egyptian monks to adhere to the *Tome*. After the magistrate invoked the "might of kings" on the humble Egyptian ascetics, Samuel appeals to the authority of Benjamin and the Egyptian Christian ancestors:

When it was placed in his hand, he held it out towards the people (*laos*), saying, 'O my fathers, do you accept this *Tome*? Anathema to this *Tome*!

Anathema to the Council of Chalcedon! Anathema to the impious Leo! Anathema to everyone who believes according to it!' He made haste, tore up the *Tome,* and threw it outside the door of the church.[124]

The enraged magistrate orders Samuel beaten and flogged within an inch of his life. When the soldiers accidently whips Samuel's eye, causing it to burst, the magistrate orders the beatings to stop and says: "Your eye which has been destroyed has saved you from death, strange[125] monk." The *Life* uses ethnic competition by claiming strategic motivation on the part of the imperial Chalcedonians, who want to gain the support of the majority Miaphysites. Cyrus tried to convert the monasteries because "the entire country of Egypt depended on those elders." The *Life* also describes the Caucasian's motivation in these terms: "For while he (Benjamin) still lives, my kingdom and archbishopric do not extend throughout the entire country of Egypt." This statement vividly depicts the social imagination of Egyptian Miaphysites— Chalcedonianism is foreign to Egypt and its people, who are loyal to the Miaphysite leader Benjamin. Any would-be leader in Egypt who is disloyal to Miaphysite theology lacks the ability to exercise authority.

In Samuel's second confrontation with the Chalcedonians, Cyrus restates his desire to control the people of Egypt by controlling the monastic communities.[126] It is difficult to overstate the effect on Egyptian collective consciousness when Chalcedonian foreigners are vigorously pursuing control over the unified people of Egypt. The Egyptian Miaphysites depict themselves as the majority of the Egyptian populace opposing the hegemony of the Chalcedonian minority. An anti-Chalcedonian majority in Egypt is assumed, while Chalcedonianism represents the oppressive ruler who Egyptians ostracize by referring to his foreign origins: "the Caucasian." Muslim sources often call Cyrus a "Greek", despite his Arabic moniker "Muqaqas."[127] This Muslim association of Cyrus's identity with "Greek" is due to his connection to Byzantine imperial authority.[128] However, the constant use of his Caucasian origin in Egyptian Christian sources is a powerful method of casting Chalcedonianism as outside the boundaries of Egyptian identity.

After horrific torture, Samuel's disciples take his battered body to a cave outside of Scetis where they make preparations for him to die. An angel appears, heals Samuel, and instructs the monks to settle in the monastic community of Neklone in the Fayyum. After a short period of monastic activities, Samuel's fame again spreads "from the Fayyum district and even reached the districts that surrounded it."[129] As a result, Samuel heals so many that he eventually has to carve out a retreat space a mile from the monastery. After a short time of peace, Samuel again engages in the struggle against the Chalcedonians. This time, Cyrus himself confronts Samuel:

> Then after he (Samuel) spent a full year in complete tranquility in the small cave, Cyrus the Caucasian came south in[130] the land of Egypt, persecuting everywhere and seeking the holy Apa Benjamin. Every monk he came upon, he would make him subscribe to the defiled *Tome* of the impious Leo and receive communion from his hands. After this he came into the district of the Fayyum with a great show (of force), and Victor the Bishop of the Fayyum came out to meet him in great joy and empty glory of this world, glorifying him until he was received into the city of the Fayyum. And it happened after this he announced from the city of the Fayyum the polluted *Tome* of Chalcedon, by the order of Justinian the fraudulent king of the Romans, who ordered that the entire land of Egypt join the defiled *Tome* of Chalcedon.[131] When the orthodox people (*laos*) saw that the Caucasian had endeavored to lead them astray with his erroneous words, they withdrew each to his own cell (*ma*) and left him, in order to ignore him.

The "Caucasian" turns his attention to the monasteries in order to impose "his faith" in Egypt. While the *Life* would have its readers think that the entire Egyptian populace is uniformly Miaphysite, there is mention of Egyptian Chalcedonians. However, the text depicts Egyptian support for Chalcedon as arising from corrupt motivations. The Egyptians who accept Chalcedon are sycophants who attempt to curry imperial favor, as in the case of Victor, bishop of Fayyum. The text presents Victor's position as bishop as the result of the "empty glory" he receives in the company of Cyrus.[132] This is the same method of ethnic identity formation in the case of Abraham of Farshut where Egyptian leaders who accepted Chalcedon were traitors to the Egyptian people and to orthodoxy. Though Heraclius was on the throne during the time of Cyrus, the reference to Justinian attests to the intense Egyptian hatred (at least in Miaphysite circles) for the sixth-century champion of Chalcedonianism. It is interesting that the *Life* mentions that the Chalcedonian imposition came at the order of Justinian, whose reign had ended half a century prior during the time of Abraham of Farshut. This demonstrates the continuity in Egyptian Christian identity development as specific heroes and villains encounter praise and polemic throughout the final centuries of the late antique period. The case of Victor in the *Life of Samuel of Kalamun* is characteristic of how Egyptian Chalcedonians are presented as motivated by imperial favor and not theological orthodoxy. The validity of

Victor's bishopric dissipates because his position rests on apostasy. While the *Life* reports the existence of Chalcedonians in Upper Egypt, the text leaves the impression that Egyptian Chalcedonians are yielding to worldly desire, a chief concern of ascetics.

During his travels throughout Upper Egypt, Cyrus arrives at Samuel's monastery at Neklone. Samuel was concerned about "the destruction that occurred through the deceitful Caucasian," and he prepared the "worldly brothers" to reject Cyrus.[133] Samuel beckoned to the Egyptian monks to reject the "stinking blasphemies of the polluted Council of Chalcedon" and to prepare themselves to "die for the orthodox faith." The Egyptian monks refused to speak to the "Caucasian," whom the text also refers to as the "godless Chalcedonian Jew"—and to accept the "foreign" communion from his hand.[134]

In this second encounter, the orthodox Egyptian people (*nrōme*) again oppose the daunting imperial forces. While Samuel is consistently cool-headed, the *Life* reports numerous instances of Cyrus rampaging and resorting to physical violence. The text underscores the ascetic patience and long-suffering of the Egyptians, while Chalcedonian authorities are raging heretics, lacking in the monastic virtues. As in the case of the *Panegyric on Apollo,* the *Life* of Samuel frames Egyptian identity and Christological resistance through anti-Semitic rhetoric, as the text labels Cyrus a "godless Chalcedonian Jew."[135] Thus, Chalcedonianism is foreign through its association with Roman imperialism, ethnic outsiders such as the Caucasian, and religions such as Judaism that are also distinct from Egyptianness in this context.

The Caucasian[136] finally catches up with Samuel in the Fayyum district and becomes insane with rage when Samuel embraces his destiny to be martyred for the Miaphysite faith. The *Life* juxtaposes the orthodox faith of Samuel with the Caucasian, who refers to his doctrine as "my faith":

> When the Caucasian heard these things, he ordered that Samuel be struck on the mouth, crying out and saying, 'Samuel, the glory that men give you as an ascetic[137] is destroying your mind. But it is I who shall instruct you and teach you to speak well;[138] for this reason you have not honored me as archbishop nor have you honored my authority as I am commander of the citizenry of the land of Egypt.'[139] The holy Apa Samuel answered him and said to the Caucasian, 'Mastema[140] too is a commander:[141] he rules the angels. His arrogance and faithlessness estranged him from God and His angels. But you, O Chalcedonian heretic, your faith is defiled and you are more accursed than the devil and his demons.'[142]

While Cyrus represents oppressive imperial power, the *Life* subverts Byzantine authority through its presentation of the Miaphysite population. The Egyptian people are persecuted, but Cyrus still needs the assent of the monastic communities and the capture of Apa Benjamin: "for this reason you have not honored me as archbishop, nor have you honored my authority as I am commander of the citizenry (*nedemōcion*) of the country of Egypt."[143] The *Life* presents Cyrus as an insecure leader. On the one hand, he childishly asserts his authority; on the other, he wants the lowly Samuel to recognize that authority. The Egypt/Byzantium opposition is an "in-house" debate between divergent Christian factions and it is distinct from the anti-Hellenistic sentiment that sometimes appears in Coptic monastic texts. While giving final exhortations on his deathbed, Samuel comments on the value of prayer: "It is said in the wisdom of the Greeks (*nehellēēn*) that he who desires separation from God, let him neglect prayer and fasting. If the Greeks, who do not know God, commend prayer and fasting as the great principles, then how much more should we, the children of the exalted God."[144] Here, *hellēēn* clearly refers to Greek philosophy and non-Christian, "pagan" culture. This criticism is distinct from the anti-Chalcedonian polemic prevalent in the *Life*. While the Coptic texts view "Greeks"[145] as ignorant of God, Chalcedonians are separated brethren who have strayed from the orthodox faith.

After the second encounter, an angel leads the weakened Samuel to settle with his disciples on the mountain of Takinash.[146] Shortly thereafter, the angel instructs Samuel to leave his disciples at Takinash and to settle in the marsh near a small church,[147] which is the place where Samuel's encounter with the "barbarians" begins. A "godless"[148] raiding band of barbarians seize Samuel, destroy the church, and beat Samuel severely while shouting angrily "in their language."[149]

The "godless" barbarians are ethnically distinguished from the Egyptian people of God, further positioning Samuel and the Copts as the godly influence on both heretics (Chalcedonians) and heathens (barbarians). After the "barbarians" carry Samuel away on a camel, an angel of the Lord possesses the camel and keeps it from moving. Frustrated, the barbarians leave Samuel for dead and he makes his way back to the church.

After a brief respite, the barbarians return to Samuel's village. After raiding the village, the barbarians take Samuel as prisoner to "their country" (*teuchōra*) and sell him as a slave to a "great barbarian"[150] named Sokortes.[151] While living as a slave in the "foreign and idolatrous country"[152] of the barbarians, Samuel reunited with John, *hegoumenos* of Scetis who was sold into slavery after the Chalcedonian incursion into Scetis. Sokortes tries to force Samuel to worship the sun and then savagely tortures Samuel when he refuses. John describes the pagan practice of the Mazices to Samuel:

> For it is the custom that when they see the sun come up, they turn their face to the east and worship it, saying 'Welcome, our lord the Sun, for you have illuminated us as we were in the darkness of the night.' And again, when it comes to set just a little, they turn their face to the west and worship it saying, 'Our lord the Sun, will you go and leave us in the darkness of the night? Come quickly up and illuminate us.' Now this, my holy father, is the custom the barbarians do daily.[153]

After failing to convert Samuel to sun worship, Sokortes attempts to force Samuel to marry. The devil visits Sokortes in the guise of a man and suggests he bind Samuel to a female slave so that he will forgo his monastic vow of celibacy and provide Sokortes with slave heirs. While Samuel is distressed by his situation, an angel informs him that God would use him to heal people. Samuel then indeed heals many people, including a man who could not walk and a deaf child whose mother Samuel calls "the seed of Canaan."[154] When Samuel's fame begins to spread throughout the land of the Mazices, "the elder of the village" fears that Samuel might "do wickedness in our entire country (*chōra*)." He wants to send Samuel "back to his own country" and decides that the Mazices will no longer engage in slave trafficking in Egypt "since their God is greater than all the gods."[155] After Samuel heals Sokortes's wife, the slave-owner similarly exclaims: "Your God is one, and there is no other beside him."[156] Sokortes's wife calls Samuel "a god of the Egyptians."[157] Sokortes swears "by the oath of the Mazices,"[158] that he will return Samuel to Egypt if he heals his wife of barrenness and she gives birth to a son. After complying, Samuel returns to re-establish his monastery at Kalamun where Mary appears to him and assures him that "no barbarian would come to this place again."[159] The Mazices play a significant role in the social imagination of the *Life*. The text contrasts Roman Chalcedonians with Egyptian Miaphysites in a manner similar to the "pagan" tribes along the border and the Egyptian people.[160] Both Romans and the Mazices form the boundary of Egyptian identity as outsiders that reinforce who belongs inside. The primary function of ethnic boundaries is to define a group in opposition to the Other.[161] Egyptian Miaphysites, with Samuel as their representative in the *Life*, "correct" the religious errors among the Roman Empire to the north and the "pagans" to the east.

Indeed, Samuel and his monastery ensure the liberation of the Egyptian people from the marauding "barbarians": "God will put an end to the barbarians by the faith of these saints and they will not come to Egypt and attack it again. And the path to Kalamun has opened up to everyone without any fear."[162] The *Life* celebrates Samuel as the Egyptian champion and victor over the barbarians: "For all the rulers of Egypt heard that the holy Apa Samuel had begun to build a church in the valley of Kalamun.... All men who lived in Egypt said, 'Because of the prayers of the holy Apa Samuel and the sufferings he has undergone, God has withheld the barbarians and not let them enter Egypt to this very day.' So he was to the surrounding districts like an apostle of God."[163]

Another example of the popular Egyptian support of Samuel and his monastery is the financial support Samuel received from leaders such as the bishop of Kois,[164] the eparch of Pelhip, and the bishop of Fayyum who consecrated the church at Kalamun.[165] Samuel spent the remainder of his life as *hegoumenos* of the monastery at Kalamun, performing miracles. Samuel's place in Coptic memory as an ascetic hero who defended Egyptian orthodoxy is evident.

A fragment of a tenth-century homily in praise of Samuel attests to the place of Samuel in Egyptian Christian memory: "For he is a benevolent guardian of the Christian faith; he is a pride for the monks in their monasteries; he is a joy for the ascetics in the desert cells; he is an ambassador of the archimandrites; he is a fellow citizen (*sumpolitēs*) of the kingdom of heaven; and a great leader (*remnēi*) of all the archimandrites."[166] Indeed, the early medieval period produced another text associated with Samuel that further attests to the significant role of this ascetic in the formation of Egyptian identity during both the late antique and medieval periods.

The fame of Samuel in Egypt and the Fayyum is also evident in the medieval *Apocalypse* attributed to him. The *Apocalypse* claims to be the words of Samuel of Kalamun as recorded by his disciple Apollo[167] and Nau describes it as a hybridized text that is part sermon and part apocalypse.[168] While the *Life* does not mention this text, the Ethiopic and Copto-Arabic *Synaxarium* mention the *Apocalypse*.[169] While the Arabic text of the *Apocalypse* is the only extant version, a Coptic original is possible.[170] The Arabic of the *Apocalypse* is awkward and does not conform to typical grammatical conventions, further suggesting a Coptic original. However, the Egyptian-centeredness of the text (its focus on Egyptian names, places, etc.) should not be seen as evidence for a Coptic *vorlage;* one would expect a similar focus on Egypt from Copto-Arabic writers of this period.[171]

On the other hand, the *Apocalypse* may represent an appeal of fully-Arabized Copts to return to the language of their ancestors.[172] While this is certainly possible, it seems more likely that the original of such an anti-Islamic polemic focusing primarily on the use of the Arabic language would be Coptic. It is inaccurate to equate the contemporary attitude of modern Copts with the feelings of the medieval audience of the *Apocalypse*.[173] Unlike the author of the *Apocalypse*, the modern Coptic community does not express a general disapproval of the Arabic language.

The *Apocalypse* likely comes from the early medieval period and thus does not represent how Egyptian ethnicity persisted during the period immediately following the Arab Muslim conquest. However, this text expresses a vision of identity that emerged from a similar community as that of the *Life*.[174] As such, the *Apocalypse* further demonstrates the continuity of ethnic rhetoric that existed in Egypt during the fifth, sixth, and seventh centuries. The *Apocalypse* does not demonstrate the attitude of seventh-century Egyptians but, rather, the prevalent influence of Egyptian views of ethnicity that started during late antiquity.

The *Apocalypse* begins with introductory remarks describing the nature of Egypt during the Islamic conquest. Arab Muslim invaders contrast with the Egyptian people who the text calls the Christian people: "When the Arab immigrants conquered Egypt,[175] they were few, but they have increased privileges to the Christian people."[176] Such a generalization continued a trend common to Egyptian anti-Chalcedonian literature of assuming that Egyptian ethnic identity is tantamount to Christian (Miaphysite) identity. The present study has examined this trend in Egyptian texts from multiple centuries, geographical regions, and various levels of society.

Equating "Egyptian" with "Miaphysite" is not unique to the context of seventh-century Fayyum. As Zaborowski states: "It is regional peculiarities and ambivalence toward the authorities, not anachronistic theories of nationalism, that should be the bases for understanding seventh-century Egyptian Christianity."[177] Zaborowski is correct in rejecting nationalism as an interpretive mechanism; however, the pro-Egyptian/Miaphysite attitude is more than "a localized, religious tradition."[178] While Egyptian ethnic boundary maintenance takes the specific form of anti-Arab xenophobia in the *Apocalypse*, the Egyptocentrism that goes along with this sentiment was evident immediately after Chalcedon.

The anti-Chalcedonian Egyptian movement collapsed religious and ethnic identity and any attempt to neatly separate the two misses the unified identity development in the text: "Even the text's many references to the loss of Coptic language are most clearly in connection with spiritual instruction (*waṣīyah*), and not explicitly connected with ethnic pride or ethnic solidarity. . . . Forgetting Coptic means losing their religious identity, not an ethnically-defined identity."[179] The *Apocalypse* dealt with religious conversion and cultural assimilation simultaneously, which further attests to the complex, interconnected nature of Coptic identity. It is because of these broad themes in the *Apocalypse* that the intended audience was not exclusively monastic but included the urban laity.[180] The exposition of pseudo-Samuel begins with commentary on the role of God in the recent imperial power shift:

> Blessed is God who has established the era and its boundaries; the One who humbles ethnicities (*āmat*) and exalts ethnicities (*āmat*), the One who overthrows kings and installs other kings. You should not hold the opinion, O my children, that this ethnicity (*āmat*) is a friend of God because He has given this land (*ārḍ*) to their hands. Rather, humans are not able to examine the wisdom of God and there is not a soul who can comprehend the actions of the Creator or the abrogation of time.[181]

The author prescribed the attitude that the Copts should maintain toward Islamic hegemony: the current political power was not a godly one, but the change in imperial hegemony was ultimately in God's hands. The *Apocalypse* reminded its readers that such oppression of the orthodox is nothing new: "I am explaining to you, O my children, the many evils that the heretics have committed against the Orthodox in the time of father Dioscorus."[182] The text recounted various periods of oppression endured by the Egyptian orthodox and offered this as the reason for the Islamic Conquest of Egypt: "Therefore God heard the prayers of His dear ones who cried to him and sent to them this people (*āmat*) that wanted gold and not instruction in prayer."[183] This is also the perspective of the *Chronicle* of John of Nikiu: "And every one was saying: 'This persecution and conquest of the Moslem came about by means of the injustice of the emperor Heraclius which was his persecution of the Orthodox by the hand of the patriarch Cyrus. And the destruction of the Romans was for this reason as well as the dominion of Egypt by the Moslem.'"[184] The theological perspective on divine providence over the Arab Muslim conquest is consistent between late antique and medieval sources. The *Apocalypse* further demonstrates how late antique constructions of ethnicity in response to the conquest became normative for medieval sources. While sources such as John's *Chronicle* or the *Apocalypse* see the conquest as permissible by God, Egyptian Miaphysite literature does not endorse Muslim dominance: "Do not let it happen that you promote their legacy among us today, for it is a savage ethnic group[185] that are inappropriate to talk about in the gathering of the saints. Ugh! This name, which is the Hajj-folk[186] whose dominion is opposite to our laws. These tyrannical kings who reign in their time!"[187]

The *Apocalypse* contains extensive anti-Islamic polemic; the text accuses Muslims of adultery, oppression of the poor, fornication, governmental mismanagement, and blasphemy. Indeed, the *Apocalypse* not only condemns conversion to Islam but acting like Muslims in matters of social ethics.[188] Islam is depicted as a disease of the "Arab immigrants"[189] which contaminates the Christian peoples (*āmat*) of the world: "Many other ethnicities (*āmat*) mixed with them: the Georgians, the Hebrews, the Greeks, residents of Urhoy (Edessa), those who are from Amid and the ethnicities[190] of the Chaldeans, the Persians, the Amazigh (*āl-barbar*), the Sindh and the Hindus."[191]

The greatest concern of the *Apocalypse* is the way in which Islam will affect the Christians of Egypt, specifically their use of the Coptic language: "In addition, they will perform a deed that, if I told you about it, your hearts would be in terrible pain. Here is what it is: they will renounce the beautiful Coptic language![192] The one in which the Holy Spirit has spoken on many occasions through the mouths of our spiritual fathers. They will teach their children, from childhood, to speak the Arabic language[193] and to be proud of it."[194]

This passage expresses the union of Coptic orthodox confession with Egyptian ethnic identity. The Coptic language, an extension of Egyptian ethnic identity,[195] is necessary for theological orthodoxy: "Behind this linguistic bias is the perception of the Coptic language as the cultural conduit and authenticating seal of Egyptian Christianity."[196] As Papaconstantinou has indicated, the period preceding the composition of the *Apocalypse* was one in which Greek fell into disuse and Coptic became the distinctive language of the Christians.[197] The primarily linguistic focus of the *Apocalypse* was part of a larger argument against Egyptian assimilation to Arabization.[198] It is in the Egyptian language that the "spiritual fathers" spoke, and loss of this language naturally results in apostasy.

The *Apocalypse* laments the replacement of Coptic by Arabic in the liturgy and the loss of Coptic literature due to the presence of "foreign books."[199] The primary invective of the *Apocalypse* is against the clergy who adopted Arabic for the purpose of upward mobility:[200] "All of them will renounce it (Coptic) and will speak the Arabic language and be proud of it, to the point that we can no longer clearly recognize them as Christians; conversely, we will take them to be Amazigh (*barbar*)."[201] The *Apocalypse* claims that the loss of the "pleasurable language"[202] renders Copts unidentifiable—not as Egyptians (as one might expect), but as *Christians*.

This further demonstrates the merging of religious and ethnic identity that began long before the time of the *Apocalypse*. The *Apocalypse* is less of an accurate description of the linguistic situation of early medieval Egypt than a method of critique between various Christian sects.[203] Again, it does not advance understanding of Coptic identity after the Arab conquest to separate religious and ethnic identity when reading a text in which they clearly overlap. Zaborowski states: "The faith of the monks of Qalamūn is fixed on Egypt for reasons of spiritual heritage, but not for any apparent ethnic nationalist motives."[204] While it is true that the nationalist thesis is an ineffective analytical tool, to dismiss the role of ethnicity is to miss a vital component in Coptic identity formation.

The value of the Egyptian language and ethnicity among the Coptic orthodox (Miaphysite) is evident in the *Apocalypse*.[205] The rejection of the Coptic language is tantamount to exclusion from the heavenly community: "I tell you in truth, my children, that those who renounce the names of saints and name their children foreign names,[206] those who do this will be cut off from the blessing of the saints. And the one who has the audacity to speak the language of the temple of the Hajj-folk, this person will walk away from the commandments of our holy fathers."[207] The message of the *Apocalypse* is clear: preserve Christian orthodoxy through continued use of the Coptic language: "And I humbly implore you with the request that you recommend to those who come after you until the end of the ages, for the guarding of their souls with the utmost protection, that you not allow a Christian to speak Arabic in these places, for that is a massive and severe judgment to have the audacity to speak the language of the Hajj-folk at the altar."[208] The emphasis of the prohibition in Christian holy space exacerbates the conflation of religious and ethnic purity.

The linguistic argument in the medieval *Apocalypse* builds upon the foundations of late antiquity: the *Panegyric on Macarius of Tkôw* went out of its way to emphasize the Coptic language of its title character and the Coptic versions of the *Life of Daniel of Scetis* retained anti-Chalcedonian material not present in the Greek original. The *Apocalypse* is helpful to consider in this study of late antique Egyptian identity as it demonstrates how this period became normative for Coptic ethnicity. Even in the modern period, the

Coptic language is a central component of religious and ethnic identity.[209] The insistence in the *Apocalypse* on maintaining the Coptic language as a defining feature of Egyptian ethnic boundaries challenges Barth's argument that "cultural matter" is not tied to shifting ethnic boundaries: "However, most of the cultural matter that at any time is associated with a human population is not constrained by this boundary; it can vary, be learnt, and change without any critical relation to the boundary maintenance of the ethnic group."[210] Indeed, ethnic boundaries are not static and are social constructs that protect the interests of the in-group. In the case of the *Apocalypse* during the early medieval period, the author has decided on language as an integral component of the ethnic boundary. Even during late antiquity, Copts were a marginalized linguistic community in a Hellenized world. Nonetheless, Coptic was elevated by an ethno-religious community that strongly identified with martyrdom along with a theological position that was equally ostracized throughout the final centuries of late antiquity. The Egyptian ethnic boundary aligned with Miaphysite lines and elevated Coptic, while embracing Greek-speaking Egyptians as well.[211]

Given Egypt's multilingual environment, the *Apocalypse* represents an alternative perspective: insisting on language as an identifying mark for insiders. The *Apocalypse* presents an Egyptian ethnic boundary that is dependent on and most visible through the Coptic language, a defining aspect of "cultural matter." The decline of the Coptic language and the growing use of Arabic support Barth's argument, since the boundaries of Egyptian identity continued even while cultural matter shifted from Coptic to Arabic. Yet the Coptic language stands in high esteem even in the modern period when most Copts speak Arabic in daily life.

It is interesting that the *Apocalypse* focuses less on the dangers of Islamic doctrine and primarily on the use of the Arabic language.[212] The *Apocalypse* cautions Egyptians through "radical alarmist rhetoric"[213] to avoid not only the Muslim religion, but also the Arab ethnic group: "Whoever keeps themselves from the behavior of the Hajj-folk and does not resemble them, that one will be able to have salvation for their soul."[214] The texts calls Egyptian Christians to return to the language, tradition, and practice of the monastic forefathers, "whose prayers cause the land of Egypt to prosper."[215]

The *Apocalypse* pleads with those Egyptians who have "sold out."[216] The Egyptian people must protect the land of Egypt and its monastic dwellings: "Blessed are you, my beloved children! You deserve to live in the monastery of the pure Virgin, our Lady Mary."[217] The conflation of religious and ethnic identity goes both ways in the *Apocalypse*.[218] Just as Egyptian and Christian are synonymous, so too are Arab and Muslim: "How long will this oppression and this domination of that ethnic group on the land of Egypt last?"[219] The *Apocalypse* has as its goal the non-violent ethnic purification of the Egyptian people by the eradication of Arabic in future generations: "Recommend to your children and recommend to those who come after them until the final age that is to come that no one speaks the language of the Hajj-folk inside the altar."[220]

The *Apocalypse* ends with eschatological predictions of the fall of the Arab people at the hands of the Greek and Ethiopian empires: "It will happen that the king of the Habesha will cause tremendous calamity in the land of their (Arabs) ancestors in the Eastern regions. The Hajj-folk will flee to the desert where they were before. They will flee from the East before the king of the Habesha. And the king of the Romans will attack the sons of Ishmael and will inter the relics of their ancestors in the Wadi al-Haffar."[221]

These events would be the beginning of the reign of the anti-Christ and the appearance of the nations of Gog and Magog. The strong concluding eschatological motif underlines the need for the Egyptian church to solidify its commitment to orthodoxy through a re-shaping of ethnic boundaries. The *Apocalypse* represents a desperate attempt at bolstering the Coptic language during a period of Egyptian history in which Arabic was increasingly becoming the language of daily life and the liturgical language of the Coptic community. Regardless of the date and language of composition, the place of the *Apocalypse* in the trajectory of the Egyptian Miaphysite movement is clear. Consideration of medieval texts is helpful in this current study to demonstrate how consistently Egyptian ethnic identity aligns with Miaphysite Christianity and excludes any other religious community as fundamentally anti-Egyptian. Evidence of this in medieval texts attests to the significance of the fifth, sixth and seventh centuries for Egyptian ethnicity. Both the *Life* and the *Apocalypse* define Egyptian ethnic identity by reference to anti-Chalcedonian doctrine and contrast it with the Byzantine and Arab/Muslim Others.

ISAAC OF ALEXANDRIA

Another figure who looms large in Egyptian Christian memory during the early period of Arab Muslim rule is the Patriarch Isaac. Isaac's biography provides further evidence of Egyptian ethnic identity presented through Miaphysite polemic. Even during the earliest period of Arab Muslim rule, Isaac's biographer more harshly criticizes Roman Chalcedonians. Isaac's Egyptian ethnicity emerges at the outset. The Egyptian Christian community serves as a guide for Christian communities in other parts of the African continent.

Most of the available information regarding Isaac during the late seventh century comes from the hagiographical *Life of Isaac of Alexandria*.[222] An entry about Isaac in the medieval *AHPA* will also be considered in this study to fill out the Egyptian tradition regarding this patriarch. As above, the medieval tradition will also demonstrate continuities with seventh-century Egyptian visions of ethnicity. The *AHPA* claims that Isaac was patriarch for only three years.[223] Much scholarship has focused on the question of exactly when Isaac's three-year reign transpired: the *Life* claims that Isaac's consecration took place on Sunday 8 Choiahk (December 4).[224] If December 4 fell on a Sunday, Isaac's reign would have occurred between 684 and 690 CE. However, a beginning date of 690 CE is more likely since 684 CE fell within the lifetime of Isaac's predecessor, John III of Samannud.[225]

While this dating contradicts the claim of the *AHPA* that Isaac reigned from 686–89 CE,[226] it follows the *AHPA* in its claim that Isaac's reign lasted two years and eleven months, thereby agreeing with the date provided in the *Life* for Isaac's death date, 9 Hator (November 5, 693 CE).[227] The dates of 690–93 CE seem most probable. The facts provided by the author of the *Life*, a contemporary, hold greater weight than that of the *AHPA*, written centuries later.[228] However, the *AHPA* still provides useful content that demonstrates the influence of the *Life* on its vision of social and religious identity.

Isaac was likely born sometime in the early seventh century, given the past-tense reference in the *Life* to the persecution of Cyrus and the reestablishment of the Coptic patriarchate in Alexandria (after 644 CE).[229] While Isaac's entry into Scetis occurred after 644 CE, it is unlikely that Isaac was a small child at this point, given his service as archivist. Rather, his birthdate was most likely before the 640s.[230] The *Life* identifies its author in the proemium as Mena, bishop of Pishati (the Greek name of which is Nikiu). A late-seventh/early-eighth-century date of composition for the *Life* is most likely.[231] Mena was likely appointed bishop of Nikiu in the late 690s before Patriarch Simon's death in 700 CE.[232]

The *Life* begins with customary remarks of self-abasement and introduces Isaac by focusing on his most notable feature, his role as patriarch: "He was entrusted with tending the sheep of the Church of the great city of Alexandria, of all of Egypt, and even of those under all of heaven."[233] The *Life* here continued a trend common to anti-Chalcedonian literature of Egypt: the ascription of universal authority to the Alexandrian patriarch. Attention focuses on the land of Egypt, thus highlighting the importance of its people in the universal Church. Patriarchal authority in Egypt is synonymous with universal ecclesiastical authority. At the time of Isaac's ordination as patriarch, the *Life* claims "he illuminated the entire world."[234] Such rhetoric is evidence of the attitude and feelings of seventh-century Egyptian Christians, to some extent.

Egyptian Christian writers—now separated from Byzantine Christianity, with practitioners of traditional religion neighboring immediately to the west, and living under Islamic hegemony—depict themselves as the lone champions of orthodoxy shining the light of sound doctrine on the dark world surrounding them. While the Egyptians have Christian neighbors to the south in Ethiopia and the kingdoms of Nubia, these nations are represented as dependent on the ecclesiastical strength of Egypt. The *Life* vividly depicts this paternalistic relationship with African Christian nations to the south, and the theme of Egypt as the world's guiding light appears throughout the *Life*. The text begins by highlighting the importance of Egyptian ethnic identity in the life of Isaac: "This saint, my brothers, was an Egyptian in his ethnicity[235] and came from a village called Pisho."[236] The *Life* goes on to describe the wealthy Christian family into which Isaac was born, his baptism, and catechetical education during childhood.

It is significant for ethnic boundary maintenance that Isaac's "race" features at the beginning of the *Life*, expressing the text's "thoroughly Egyptian spirit."[237] The word *genos* here should not be translated as "race," according to the working definition of race as outlined above. The reconstruction of ancient concepts of race and ethnicity is not a simple matter of equating these social phenomena with the words *genos* and *ethnos*.[238] Put another way, the definitions of these terms ought to be as interchangeable as the words themselves. These terms and their use in antiquity do not equate with the contemporary understanding of race and ethnicity. Rather, in the analysis of the present study, ethnicity persists through a process of defining the boundaries of a social group through ascription of inclusivity and exclusivity.[239] Although Isaac's *genos* here is *remenchēmi,* this does not refer to inherited physical characteristics that are associated with a "race," meaning a complex of genotypic and phenotypic characteristics.[240] Rather, Egyptianness is a social ideal that is inclusive of multiple languages, skin tones, and geo-political regions, but exclusive when it comes to religion. The exclusive factor among the Egyptian people is Miaphysite confession. In sum, *genos* in this context refers to the social concept of ethnicity. The reason is simple: there is no mention that Isaac's "race" is a reference to his physicality. For this reason, I have chosen to translate this term as "ethnicity" rather than "race."

Understood this way, the *Life* begins by letting the audience know that Isaac identifies with the two most important characteristics for this community: he is orthodox (Miaphysite) and a part of the Egyptian ethnicity. In this way, Isaac appears in the *Life* as an insider due to his doctrine and his ethnicity. After Isaac's schooling, he soon rose to prominence in the service of an archivist (*chaltolarios*) named Meneson who served the prefect (*peparchos*) of Egypt, George.[241] Despite attempts by his parents to have Isaac betrothed, Isaac entered the monastic community at Scetis where he came under the influence of Zacharias, *hegmoumenos* of the monastery of Makarius.[242] Because Isaac did not inform his parents about where he was going, they engaged in a massive search for him, resulting in Isaac's hiding with a priest named Joseph. Joseph had endured persecution at the hands of the Chalcedonian patriarch Cyrus: "A multitude ... testified of him that he was a confessor who had been made to stand before the throne of the impious Cyrus and had been given many blows for the confession of the faith."[243] A negative recollection of the Chalcedonian patriarch places the *Life* in the Egyptian anti-Chalcedonian literary tradition and the reference to Cyrus suggests that the *Life* belongs to the period following the "Muslim liberation."[244] Once again, Cyrus appears with more vehement negativity than even the Muslim conquerors of Egypt, despite the fact that Byzantine Chalcedonians had not controlled Egypt for half a century by the time of the *Life*'s composition. After making inquiries of the archbishop, Zacharias fears Isaac's parents would involve the "ruler" (*tiexoucia*) of Egypt, and orders Isaac to hide with an ascetic named Abraham.[245] Soon after, Isaac confronts his parents, explains his decision to become a monk, and reconciles with them.

Isaac remains under the supervision of Zacharias at Scetis and his fame spreads "in all the country (*tichōra*) of Egypt."[246] As Isaac grows in ascetic fame, an old monk of Scetis prophesies that Isaac would become patriarch of Alexandria: "Behold an Israelite (*ousraēlitēs*) in whom there is no treachery! This one will be archbishop of the city of Alexandria and patriarch. This one will be great before the Lord and his words will reach the end of the world!"[247] It is interesting that the quotation from John 1:47 is applied here to Isaac, who is called "an Israelite," in a manner consistent with Egyptian monastic literature.[248] While the *Life* places Isaac's identity as an Egyptian at the forefront, his orthodoxy affords him citizenship in the heavenly New Jerusalem. This rhetorical flourish represents a contrast to the instances of anti-Semitic language in Egypt Miaphysite literature, illustrating the complex manner in which this community framed its own identity in relationship to Judaism. The positive deployment of the term "Israelite" contrasts with the anti-Semitic manner that the term "Jew" appears in late antique Egyptian Christian literature.

Isaac next restores someone from the party of *akephalai* to the orthodox, Miaphysite faith. This person of the "unblessed" party, whose name was Ianne, is introduced as being of an exalted ethnicity.[249] The *akephalai* claimed that, after Dioscorus, the patriarch of Alexandria did not have legitimate authority and thus, they had "divided the church."[250] What exactly is meant by "exalted ethnicity" is unclear; Bell translates this phrase as "noble lineage."[251] Amélineau also understands the phrase to refer more specifically to a particular family ("from an esteemed family")[252] while the sense in Porcher retains a broader cultural dimension ("who was of a noble ethnicity").[253] While this is lexically possible, it does not bring any further clarity to the description of Ianne. Does this refer to ethnic, phenotypic, governmental, or familial affiliation? The appearance of *genos* here indicates a reference to a broader social identity. What is clear is that members of heterodox (non-Miaphysite) communities are rhetorically differentiated from the Egyptian orthodox by highlighting aspects of social otherness. The text blames non-Miaphysite groups for the division of the churches, while anti-Chalcedonian figures such as Isaac stand as beacons of orthodoxy who restore penitents to the "Christian" faith.[254] Ianne's admission to anti-Chalcedonianism is synonymous with his becoming "Christian," that is, Miaphysite. Isaac emerges in Scetis as the next Egyptian hero of the faith in a long succession of Miaphysite champions.

Isaac's reputation as associate or aide and secretary in Scetis draws the attention of the Alexandrian patriarch, John III of Sammanud.[255] Despite Isaac's attempts to hide his talent as secretary, Archbishop John enlisted his service in composing paschal letters[256] one month a year while spending the rest of the year in solitude at Scetis. Isaac's ascetic fame continues to spread to "everyone in the land of Egypt"[257] and there is pressure for Isaac to be ordained a bishop. After the death of Zacharias, the patriarch John receives a vision indicating that Isaac would be the next patriarch. While describing the death of John, the *Life* also provides information about the relationship between Christians and Muslims in seventh-century Egypt:

> It happened in those days that the king (*pouro*) sent for the archbishop to meet with him. Indeed he did this many times, as he brought the archbishop to him because of the love for him. The name of that king was 'Abd al-'Aziz, and he was also called Al-Emir. And he had secretaries who were two God-loving men—Athanasius and Isaac, and their sons. And the entire *praetorium* was full of Christians. In fact, in his beginning when he first came to Egypt, he endeavored to do evil to the churches. He broke the crosses and did many evil things to the archbishop. But God, who punished Pharaoh of old, He also put fear into this other one in a dream, saying, "Be careful concerning the archbishop." And he loved him as an angel of God.[258]

This excerpt demonstrates the relatively positive attitude of the Copts toward their Muslim rulers in contrast to the decidedly negative presentation of Byzantine Chalcedonians. Indeed, references to "Christians" in the *Life* almost exclusively refers to anti-Chalcedonian Christians.[259] The *AHPA* takes a similar attitude: "And by his (Isaac's) hands the liturgies in the churches of the orthodox were renewed, those which were not able to be celebrated before."[260] Yet Coptic orthodoxy did not exhibit a blind allegiance to all things Egyptian. The text contrasts Pharaoh with the orthodox faithful and there is no attempt to maintain continuity between pharaonic and Coptic Egypt. The "new Pharaoh" of Muslim rule is favorable to Christians and plays an important part in the elevation of Isaac.

During his visit to the Muslim ruler, John falls ill and returns to Alexandria where he soon dies. Although John had indicated his desire for Isaac to succeed him as patriarch, a deacon named George wanted the office. George rallies many bishops to his cause and is almost ordained. One bishop halts the process while other bishops attempt to ordain George in the middle of the week, against the custom of ordination on Sunday. When the rest of the bishops arrive in Alexandria, a sharp division arises as many want to ordain Isaac, following John's wishes, while others want to ordain George. Isaac is presented as the humble ascetic who simply "served George as he was not thinking of things of this sort."[261]

During the deliberation process, the Christian populace discovers that George is married and has "very evil children,"[262] and Isaac becomes patriarch. There is a great feast at the monastery of St. Sergius during which Isaac is "seized" and ordained "against his will" in front of "a multitude of people[263] of Babylon and Alexandria and the entire country."[264] Despite the alleged national support for Isaac, the matter came before 'Abd al-'Aziz ibn Marwan, who presents the two candidates to the multitude in a manner similar to the Gospel story of Pilate, Jesus, and Barabbas.[265] The Egyptians, however, are presented in a more positive light than the crowd at the trial of Jesus, as they cry out for Isaac's ordination, choosing him rather than the priest George.

There is an intentional contrast between Isaac and the caliph's choice that is evident by their clothing. The contrasting clothing illustrates the value of humility and martyrdom in Egyptian Miaphysite ethnic identity construction. 'Abd al-'Aziz is a reverse Pilate as he insists on the ordination of George, who is clad in priestly garments: "He (Isaac) is a feeble man!"[266] Despite 'Abd al-'Aziz's preference for George, the Egyptian people choose Isaac, dressed in the humble monastic habit. The account found in the *AHPA* differs significantly from the *Life;* in the *AHPA,* 'Abd al-'Aziz is said to have discovered John's preference for Isaac and vetoed George's nomination.[267] In the account found in the *Life,* the Egyptians are depicted as a new Israel that knows how to recognize God's anointed, in place of a worldly imposter.[268] It is possible that increasing persecution of Egyptian Christians during the medieval period influenced a more positive depiction of 'Abd al-'Aziz in the *AHPA*. In any case, Isaac's ordination becomes a source for joy of the entire Egyptian people:

> Oh, how great was the joy and gladness that occurred in the entire country of Egypt![269] And the multitude jubilated before him, as each village alternated with one another, on the east and the west of the river, from Babylon to Alexandria. Multitudes of bishops walked with him, those who all gathered unto him for his appointment over the churches. And there was John among them, bishop of Pshati, who was commissioner[270] of the episcopate of Upper Egypt, he being a man perfected in the wisdom of God and of men, along with Gregory, bishop of Kais, he being superintendent of the bishops of Lower Egypt.[271]

The *Life* presents Isaac in the tradition of Athanasius and Cyril—as the pillar of orthodoxy rescuing the Egyptian people from heresy: "When the holy Isaac went into Egypt,[272] he brought back a multitude from their heresies and brought them into the orthodox faith of our Lord Jesus Christ."[273] Isaac further solidifies Miaphysite orthodoxy in Egypt through a certain local council known as the "One Hundred": "And in those days the One Hundred gathered in Alexandria because the archbishops before him were unable to do this because of the enemies of our faith."[274] This reference most likely does not concern the recent Islamic rulers in Egypt but the former Byzantine Chalcedonian hegemony.[275] The *Life* continues to express greater disdain for past Byzantine rulers than for the current Muslim government. The relatively empowering Islamic leadership provides Isaac with the opportunity to align the boundaries of Egyptian identity with the standard of anti-Chalcedonianism ("our faith"). Isaac enjoys great favor from the Muslim governor: "And God kept him safe before the king of the Saracens,[276] for he was greatly honored by him (Isaac) as he ('Abd al-'Aziz) also honored him. He ('Abd al-'Aziz) summoned him many times and they sat together and they socialized for the king had seen many healings by his (Isaac's) hands."[277]

The use of the ethnic term "Saracens" in reference to Muslims continued during the medieval period. The thirteenth-century Coptic *Martyrdom of John of Phanijōit* frequently refers to Muslims as "Saracens" and was written during a period of intense Christian persecution, unlike the late seventh century.[278] In the *Martyrdom of John of Phanijōit*, conversion to Islam was seen as a result of ethnic mixing with foreigners such as the Arabs and "Saracens." It is not surprising that, when Islamic persecution of Christians in Egypt intensified during the medieval period, the close association of theological orthodoxy and Egyptian ethnicity which emerged in late antiquity framed religious conversion as the result of ethnic mixing.[279]

Isaac exerts great spiritual influence on the Muslim governor. One day, 'Abd al-'Aziz sees an awesome fiery presence surrounding Isaac as he stands at the altar, which causes the governor great fear. When Isaac explains that the divine presence accompanies him every time he was at the altar, 'Abd al-'Aziz exclaims: "Your faith is a great (one), you Christians! And I thought until today that Abba John[280] who was before you was great before God. But now I know that you are a father to that one and you are higher before God."[281] The *Life* claims that 'Abd al-'Aziz called Isaac "Patriarch" and that his attachment to Isaac extended to the whole of the Egyptian church: "The king built churches and monasteries for monks around his city, for he loved the Christians."[282]

Tensions later arise between Isaac and 'Abd al-'Aziz. First, some "Saracens who hated our faith" accuse Isaac, saying he "abominates (*fji boti*) us and our faith."[283] These officials suggest that 'Abd al-'Aziz invite Isaac to dinner and kill him if he made the sign of the cross over the food. Several of the governor's Christian secretaries, however, warn him that Isaac would certainly make the sign of the cross. Many Christians held high office in the government, which is evidence that Arab Muslim conquerors were a numerical minority in the seventh-century. The *Life* also depicts these Christians as positioned to influence Muslim authorities by voicing their sense of special knowledge. When Isaac comes to dinner, he craftily makes the sign of the cross as he picks up a basket of dates and points his hands in either direction under the guise of asking the governor where he wants Isaac to sit. When the Christian secretaries later inform 'Abd al-'Aziz of Isaac's cunning, he becomes all the more enthralled: "Truly, I have not found a wise man like this one!"[284] The importance of these Christian-Muslim encounters for this present study is the way that ethnicity frames the inter-religious dialogue. Late antique Egyptian sources such as the *Life* form the practice of ethnically distinguishing the Muslims as "Saracens," which would continue through the medieval period. Christians—defined by Miaphysite Christology—are associated with the Egyptian ethnicity. Egyptian Christians still formed most of the population and Isaac was their chief leader. For this reason, the *Life* frequently mentions the great power the patriarch exerted in Egypt and beyond—a reality that led to complications.

The *Life* concludes with a final anecdote further attesting to the influence Isaac exerted as patriarch during Umayyad rule in Egypt and provides fascinating insight into international relations along the Nile Valley:

> Listen, and I will tell you of this other marvelous deed! It happened at that time that the king of Makouria (*timakouria*) sent messengers to the archbishop with letters telling him how the bishops in his country (*tefchōra*) were few because of the length of the journey and the time. For they were not able to pass through by (order of) the king of Mauritania (*timaurōtania*) until he had made peace with him.[285] Although the two kings established in these countries were both Christians, they were not at peace with each other. Since one of them was at peace with the king of the Saracens, this was the king of Mauritania. But the other who was of the great country (*tiništi nchōra*) of Makouria was not at peace with the king of the Saracens. It happened that when the archbishop read the king's letters, he knew what was in them. He was grieved much for the sake of the churches, and he immediately wrote letters to the king of Mauritania, giving him counsel and instruction through the words of the holy Scripture as he also said, "You are both Christians!" He wrote many words to him to establish his soul in the orthodox faith of the Son of God. Afterwards he wrote to him,[286] "Do not prevent the men of the upper kingdom from passing through his country when they were going for the sake of their bishop so that the churches would not be deserted lest you will find great guiltiness before God!"[287] When the enemies of our faith knew of these things, they slandered the archbishop before the king,

saying, 'We tell you, O king, that the king of Makouria has sent messengers with letters to Abba Isaac the archbishop so that he will appoint a bishop for them who they will take to their country. Not only this, but he sent another one to the king of Mauritania counselling him to make peace with the king of Makouria, our enemy. If this happens, O king, they will be of one single mind, and will rise up against us and make war with us."[288]

The Muslim governor 'Abd al-'Aziz is enraged and has Isaac brought to the provincial capital at Babylon to be executed. When Isaac is brought before 'Abd al-'Aziz, however, he is accompanied by the luminous presence of Peter and Mark. The governor, terrified at their presence, asks Isaac who these figures are. Isaac replies: "These two men you saw were disciples of Christ, the King of kings, the one by whom kings are kings. Moreover, those whom you saw walk with me at all times. Because of this, O king, be careful concerning the Church. Do not oppress it! For truly, he who oppresses the Church has oppressed God!"[289] The Muslim governor, terrified at these words, orders Isaac to build a church at Halban. The medieval *AHPA* provides a strikingly different account of the governor's reaction to Isaac:

> Then he commanded to destroy all the crosses, which were in the land of Egypt,[290] even the crosses of gold and silver. So the Christians in the land of Egypt were disturbed. Furthermore, he wrote many letters and placed them on the doors of the churches in Egypt and in the Delta,[291] saying in them: 'Muhammad is the great Apostle who is of God. So too is Jesus is the Apostle of God. But, God indeed is not begotten and does not beget.'[292]

The *AHPA* abruptly turns to Isaac's death and says nothing about 'Abd al-'Aziz's changed attitude toward Isaac and the Copts. The different account of the *AHPA* is likely a product of the relatively hostile environment experienced by the Copts centuries later. However, the positive depiction of 'Abd al-'Aziz and Islamic rulers in general during the seventh century indicates not so much an absence of interreligious tension as a preference on the part of the Copts for Islamic hegemony in comparison to Byzantine Chalcedonian rule. This difference between seventh-century and medieval Egyptian Christian texts indicates a rigorous anti-Chalcedonian attitude among the Copts in the decades immediately following the Arab Muslim conquest that eventually subsided after centuries of Byzantine absence and an increase in Islamic persecution. While there are certainly significant differences between the seventh-century sources and those of the medieval period, there was still a common understanding of religious and ethnic identity that persisted between the periods. This vision of identity was extant in the centuries between Chalcedon and the conquest.

After the Nubian incident in the *Life*, Isaac soon falls ill and dies in the presence of all the bishops, clerics, and monks. However, this incident testifies to the influence exerted by the Alexandrian patriarch over the kingdoms of the Nile Valley. The above narrative provides a fascinating example of Egyptian ethnic boundary maintenance. While under Islamic rule, Coptic Egypt is presented as the pillar of orthodoxy that provides doctrinal guidance to the neighboring Christian kingdoms of Nubia. That 'Abd al-'Aziz was enraged at this Coptic intervention in translocal affairs is no surprise. The *Life* boldly depicts Isaac, and by extension the Egyptian church, as the true authority that commands greater respect than political rulers from outside of Egypt. In this, the *Life* illustrates resistance to the polyethnic stratification that entails the maintenance of "a categorically different distribution of assets"[293] between the Egyptian Christians and their Arab Muslim rulers. Under Islamic hegemony, Isaac is the symbol of Egyptian religious superiority. The *Life* represents a final phase of Egyptian ethnic boundary maintenance in anti-Chalcedonian literature that would influence later periods of Egyptian Christian identity formation. Under Islamic rule, the Copts fashioned an identity distinct from that of Muslim Egyptians. Their identity continued to be defined by the Miaphysite faith.

SIX

Egyptian Identity from Outside Perspectives

IT IS CLEAR THAT EGYPTIAN anti-Chalcedonians established adherence to Miaphysite doctrine as the requirement for inclusion in the Egyptian community. It is necessary, therefore, to balance this internal process of ethnic boundary maintenance with the perspectives of anti-Chalcedonian ethnic "outsiders." Ethnic boundaries are formed by insiders through negotiating difference with outsiders. Sources that emerge from the outsiders also help to clarify who the insiders of a particular group are.[1] Identity and boundaries are constantly re-negotiated interdependently by those within and their neighbors. This was certainly the case for late antique Egyptian Miaphysites, where Egyptian ethnicity and Miaphysite faith were seen as one and the same.

This social imagination anticipates the question: how can one equate anti-Chalcedonianism with the faith of the Egyptian people given that it also had a presence beyond Egypt in Palestine, Syria, and still other regions? How does ethnic identity continue to frame dialogue between various groups in which Miaphysite theology took root (especially groups in Egypt and Syria)?[2] There was a high degree of transregional contact in the anti-Chalcedonian community and the best example of this is when exiled Miaphysite leaders live among their Miaphysite brethren of different ethnic backgrounds. This final chapter will demonstrate that, while Miaphysitism was by no means unique to Egypt, non-Egyptian Miaphysites confirmed the Egyptian perception that Egypt was the center of the anti-Chalcedonian movement.

One of the most prominent such examples was the exile of the Miaphysite Patriarch Severus of Antioch (465–538 CE). Severus was born in the Pisidian region of southwest Asia Minor, educated in Alexandria, and ordained patriarch in 512 CE. However, following the accession of Emperor Justin I in 518

CE, Patriarch Severus avoided imprisonment by fleeing to Egypt, where he lived the last twenty years of his life in exile. Severus was welcomed by the patriarch of Alexandria and he lived in the famous Enaton Monastery near Alexandria. Though condemned by the Byzantine government, the citizens of Antioch revered Severus as the true patriarch, much in the same way that Egyptians held the exiled Dioscorus and Timothy Aelurus to be the true patriarch during their exile. Indeed, the arrival of Severus of Antioch in Egypt is still celebrated by the modern Coptic Church on 2 Baba. In the various letters that survive in Syriac translation,[3] Severus provides much insight into the Egyptian community from the perspective of a non-Egyptian fellow Miaphysite. Severus claims that he engaged in a "sojourn in a foreign land"[4] which he also calls "the Christ-loving city of the Alexandrines."[5]

The portrait of Alexandria is similarly positive in the *Life of Severus:* "I will be baptized in Alexandria where there is orthodoxy all the time."[6] The *Life* reports that Severus's first act as patriarch was to "reestablish the union with the Egyptians"[7] that had been dissolved by his predecessor. Severus frequently holds Egypt and the East together as equal safeguards of orthodoxy: "I find the present state of the holy churches in the East and in Egypt to be more pure than the conditions of those previous ones."[8]

Severus displays the utmost respect and admiration for his Miaphysite colleagues in Alexandria, "the city renowned for its orthodox faith of the city of the Alexandrines."[9] Understanding the immense reverence felt by Egyptians for Cyril of Alexandria, Severus refers to the patriarch as "Cyril the chief warrior of orthodoxy."[10] In a manner similar to anti-Chalcedonian literature in Coptic, Severus refers to the Miaphysite confession of "all of Egypt" as he praises the Egyptians' readiness to forgo their own safety and comfort for the anti-Chalcedonian cause: "This is not only in the men, but also in all the women, and it is to be seen in every age. Thus, those who are in all of Egypt are also ready to forgo themselves for such struggles if the time calls for it."[11]

Egyptians themselves, as well as foreigners, saw Egypt as the home of a thoroughly anti-Chalcedonian people. Despite the evidence for religious diversity in sixth-century Egypt, Miaphysitism emerges as the favored belief of the Egyptian people. Severus depicts Syria, along with Egypt, as purely Miaphysite, in contrast to the Byzantine "heretics." His home region of the East is presented as a beacon of orthodoxy and leading example for other regions. In recounting the oppression of Eastern Miaphysites at the hands of Byzantine Chalcedonians, Severus claims:

For I have not wept for you—it is unnecessary to weep for you—but for the countries[12] that are deprived of you and for those who are God-fearing who dwell in them, and generally speaking for that entire district.[13] If there were not universal wrath, and the face of God were not rejected, you by all means would have endured, as pillars of the great house who would have prevented the fall that was threatening it.[14]

Egyptian Miaphysites also describe themselves as a source of orthodoxy shining light into the darkness prevailing in the regions around them. During his time as a prisoner among the "barbarians," Samuel of Kalamun demonstrates the power of God to the Mazices, leading to the conversion of many.[15] While Severus portrays his own people as a guiding light, he also understands Eastern Miaphysites to be part of the broader community of orthodox believers:

> We were set forth as ridicule by those who are zealous for the Chalcedonian ungodliness; and in Palestine, as I have learned, and in other provinces[16] they were going all around, high and low, opening and extending their big mouth and saying: 'Those who pride themselves on being orthodox, behold—they have been manifestly seen to be obedient to the teaching of Eutyches, which is the error of the house of Mani.'[17]

In a letter addressed to Dioscorus II of Alexandria, Severus frequently speaks of the union between the two Sees as "our communion."[18] Severus then refers to those "outside"[19] the communion who will recognize God's presence among the Egyptian-Eastern party because of the great faith of its members. Miaphysite confession is again the primary standard for membership in this multiethnic community. The anti-Chalcedonian community was a diverse community from the beginning and its greatest champion, Severus, expresses the desire for the "outsiders" to be included.

Severus later mentions the *Tome* of Leo, the "king of the church of the Romans."[20] This contrast sets Romans against Egyptians and Easterners in a manner similar to that of Egyptian anti-Chalcedonian texts.[21] This rhetorical strategy also contradicts the view that Chalcedonianism slowly became associated with the Roman Empire.[22] Egypt, in particular, through some leaders, expressed an immediate and vehement opposition to Byzantine Chalcedonianism. Also for theologians representing Syria, Chalcedonianism became synonymous with Byzantium in the sixth century. In the writings of John of Ephesus, there seems to be an accepted understanding of a visible and physical difference between Near Eastern people and "Romans." In his

Ecclesiastical History, John narrates the consecration of Paul as patriarch of Alexandria and reports that, before his consecration, he was living in Libya "disguised as a Roman."[23] This phenomenon explains Egypt's altered relationship with Byzantium following Chalcedon, which included a degree of isolation. The Chalcedonian schism resulted in the "appeal" of Egyptian monasticism being significantly diminished among Chalcedonian Christian communities.[24]

In another letter addressed to Dioscorus II of Alexandria, Severus refers to "our people,"[25] including the orthodox of Syria and Egypt in contrast to "all strangers."[26] In the same letter, the "evil Leo" is the "head of the church of the Romans,"[27] not the leader of the orthodox communities. It is likely that the "outsiders" Severus speaks of refers principally to Byzantine Chalcedonians. The letters of Severus clearly demonstrate that the anti-Chalcedonian movement extends beyond Egypt and seeks expansion.

Severus's diplomatic attitude is evident in the way he blames the previous tension between Egypt and the East on the Syrians. The patriarch claims that the association of some Syrians with Nestorius brought division between the two regions. Severus credits the "unity" between the churches in Egypt and the East, to the latter's eventual condemnation of Nestorius.[28] Severus's genius as an ecumenical ambassador is evident: as an exile living among Egyptians, denouncing Nestorius and accepting responsibility for previous tension solidifies unity between Syrians and Egyptians. The affinity between Egypt and the East is also evident in how Egyptian Miaphysite texts praise Severus, such as the *Panegyric on Apollo*[29] and the *Life of Isaac of Alexandria*.[30] Arietta Papaconstantinou points out that the *Life of Samuel of Kalamun* names the predecessors of the Fayyumic monk as not only the expected Egyptian figures of Antony, Pachomius, Macarius, and Shenoute, but also Severus.[31]

The *History of Dioscorus* presents the patriarch Dioscorus as promoting a universalized Christianity that cuts across ethnic boundaries. In one episode, an Egyptian merchant has a chance encounter with Dioscorus and some of his disciples while they are in exile at Gangra. Dioscorus sends his disciples (including, according to the narrator, the author of the text, Theopistus) to beg for alms from the merchant. The disciples come to the Egyptian merchant's ship and ask for alms: "I did this not knowing that the man was from our city.[32] Since I didn't know, I would rather die of starvation than ask him."[33] The merchant, however, responds: "'My lord deacon, do not be ashamed, for I know that you are in a foreign (place).'[34] For he didn't know that we were in exile but he thought that we made an error at sea."[35] When the disciples bring him to Dioscorus, the merchant pleads with the exile to accept financial aid. However, the patriarch replies: "My son, we are not in a foreign (place);[36] God is the one who created the entire world, who gives us strength to do battle for the sake of the true faith, and who empowers and doesn't make us foreigners[37] in every place that we go to."

Despite the patriarch's initial refusal to accept charity, the merchant insists until Dioscorus accepts. The incident with the merchant inspires Dioscorus to begin giving all his money away to those in need in Gangra. What is significant in this scenario, however, is the universalizing rhetoric attributed to Dioscorus. Dioscorus and Severus—mirror images as patriarchs exiled in another's country—were both champions of the ethnic inclusivity of the Miaphysite faith. The two patriarchs were praised by their foreign brethren in similar terms. Just as Severus enjoyed fame among the Egyptians, the citizens of Gangra celebrated Dioscorus: "The fame of the holy Dioscorus spread throughout the entire island of Gangra as they said, 'God has sent us a protector and savior.'"[38] Despite the universalizing rhetoric that ultimately prescribes multiethnic unity within orthodoxy, the *History* nonetheless betrays the existence of ethnocentrism among Egyptian Miaphysites. Theopistus declares that he "would rather die" than ask a foreigner for help. Likewise, the merchant extends sympathies to Dioscorus, assuming that the patriarch loathes being in a foreign country. The patriarch, however, rebukes these expressions of Egypt-centrism and admonishes the merchant that "we are not in a foreign place." This text promotes a universal unity among the orthodox. Yet, the need for this message implicates a sense of ethnic and cultural dissonance felt between Egyptians and those from the Syrian East, a reality that will become more evident below.

The patriarch's biography also expresses a sense of solidarity between Egyptian and Eastern Miaphysites. After his death, the remaining anti-Chalcedonian community of Gangra receives consolation. The text reports that after the time of the exiles at Gangra, there will be universal devastation for orthodox Christians: "But only we who are in Egypt and Syria of the East are the remnant of the true faith. But the remnant of the nations[39] is filled with the teaching of the Devil."[40]

A fifteenth-century homily attributed to a bishop of Assiut commemorated Severus: "We remember him on the holy altars for he is worthy to be remembered in all the Orthodox churches, not only in his jurisdiction of

Antioch but also throughout all the jurisdiction of the great city of Alexandria."[41] This homily expresses the profound reverence for Severus among the Copts. Egyptian pride is also present as attention constantly focuses on the benefit of Severus for the Egyptian people: "Your benefits will not be confined to Antioch but will extend to the whole land of Egypt and the land of Upper Egypt, for you will wander around it preaching like our masters, the apostles."[42] Indeed, the *Homily* describes Severus's flight from Antioch as intended for the benefit of the Egyptian church:

His escape was made, not out of fear of death, but rather God did not yet wish to give him rest but instead wished him preserved for the benefit of many people and especially for the land of Egypt and that of Upper Egypt, for (this land) was seized by false teachings and the Lord desired that the holy Abba Severus should be (the land's) physician.[43]

The *Life of Severus* articulates a similar statement, as the patriarch is said to have been born for the edification of all peoples: "The great Severus was Pisidian in his ethnicity.[44] The city of Sozopolis brought him forth. The name was attested by his deeds, especially because he was not only the savior of one city, but of all the faithful of the entire world,[45] as his tribulation demonstrates."[46] Severus is remembered both in Syria and in Egypt as God's gift to the world. The bishop in Assiut delivered the *Homily* in the Monastery of Saint Severus: "Your name will be placed in this monastery forever to commemorate your presence in the land of Egypt and as a sign of your coming to the land of Upper Egypt."[47] This monastery attests to the important role Severus played in Egyptian Christian memory a millennium after his death. While this *Homily* does not indicate the social vision of late antique Egypt, it helps to illustrate how Egyptian and non-Egyptian leaders from the period between the Council and the Conquest were formational for Egyptian identity in subsequent periods of Egyptian history. Before his death, Severus receives consolation from the Virgin that stresses his importance for the Egyptian people:

Do not be sad O Severus, for my beloved Son wanted the land of Egypt to receive the benefits of your teachings and your sayings and the words, which He delivers by your mouth. Do not be sad, O Severus, and do not let your heart be distressed by your death in a foreign country, for all the earth is for the Lord and we are foreigners in it, as the prophet said: 'I am a foreigner in the earth, hide not from me Your commandments.[48]

While there is a universal understanding of orthodox identity, the medieval *Homily* nonetheless assumes that ethnic and regional identity is important to its audience. The Lord's admonishment to Severus to not worry about dying in a foreign land is evidence of this. The homilist links his see in Assiut to that of Severus: "What shall I say about you, O city of Assiut, which is worthy of all honors? If I compare you to the city of Antioch, I find you her inheritor, just as the daughter inherits from her mother."[49] The author of the *Homily* demonstrates the extent to which Egyptian Christians stand in the tradition of Severus. The text illustrates this by claiming that Egyptian Christian communities are the progeny of the Syrian center of Antioch. Severus is a foundational pillar of Egyptian Christianity in later centuries, which demonstrates the extent to which participation in the Miaphysite community transcends ethnicity. The medieval homily echoes the themes that emerged in late antiquity, as demonstrated through leaders such as Severus and Dioscorus.

Both Egyptian and non-Egyptian Miaphysites assume an ecumenical unity that prioritizes doctrine over ethnicity. Even when tensions rose between Egypt and Syria in the later sixth century, the belief in unity of doctrine persisted. Despite intense theological debate between Peter of Callinicum and Damian of Alexandria, the former still expressed respect for "the great and Christ-loving city Alexandria."[50] In appealing for unity to Damian, Peter encourages the "peace and concord of the holy churches of Egypt and the East."[51] Peter maintains his desire for unity despite his having been "banished from the country of Egypt like evil-doers."[52] He distances himself from Apollinarianism and Arianism by appealing to the "all-wise Cyril, the renowned teacher, and by Saint Severus, his exact stamp and seal." Peter venerates Cyril as "the light of the Christ-loving Alexandrians, and even of the whole world."[53] Though his writing expresses contempt for the position of Damian, Peter nonetheless articulates a desire for unity and a respect for the Egyptian church.[54]

As has been pointed out throughout this study and in much of modern scholarship, ethnic identity is subordinate to religious confession in the Christian Near East and Egypt in particular.[55] Jason Zaborowski argues that individual ethnic identity was not a significant factor in the medieval Christian Near East but that a larger Christian identity was the primary identifier for Egyptian Christians.[56] As evidence, Zaborowski points to Egyptian refugees in Syria, such as John of Phanijōit, as well as to prominent leaders in the Egyptian Church who were of Syrian origin, such as Patriarch Mark III (r. 1163–89) and the historian al-Makīn Ibn al-'Amīd (1205–73).[57]

Indeed, Coptic hagiographies strongly emphasize the presence of foreign, non-Egyptian saints.[58] The early Christian world was composed of various *ethnie* who belonged to the group not by ancestry but by following a superior way of life.[59] Christianity's ultimate goal was to include all ethnic groups by appealing to the universality of the Gospel. This Christian practice finds resonance with Greek philosophy.[60] Porphyry similarly depicted various ethnic groups as having various degrees of compatibility with the philosophical values of Hellenism.[61] However, Egyptian ethnic boundaries distinguished themselves from the wider anti-Chalcedonian community. This happened through patterns of inclusion and exclusion that were adopted from neighboring communities.

Late antique and early medieval Copts found inspiration from Hellenism as well as from their fellow anti-Chalcedonians. Egyptian communities also drew upon Palestinian traditions of resistance, such as the *Plerophoria* and the *Life of Peter the Iberian,* which circulated widely in Egypt.[62] Egyptian sources express support for the position of Palestinian Miaphysites: "How many thousands have been killed for Christ because of this (Chalcedon); in Alexandria and in Egypt and in Jerusalem because they would not bow to the golden idol nor submit to communion with the Council of Chalcedon."[63] From the "foreign" side, the *Life of Peter the Iberian* depicted Egyptian Miaphysites as fellow participants in the anti-Chalcedonian struggle:

> But it thus happened that when the news of the death of Marcian, that head, cause, and patron of evils such as these, arrived at the city of the Alexandrians, those believing people who already started grieving from the many sufferings and persecutions that had come upon them, as has been said, and their hands were weak, while they acquired time to breathe, were revived again.[64]

The *Life of Peter the Iberian* attributed the strength of anti-Chalcedonianism in Gaza during the time of Peter to Egyptian influence.[65] In the above passage from the *Life,* ethnic distinctions persisted as the text referred to Alexandrians/Egyptians as "those believing people," giving the reader the sense that the Egyptian orthodox are a distinct group, apart from the broader community addressed by the *Life.*

Despite the ecumenical unity between Egypt, Palestine, and Syria, ethnic distinctions continued to appear in Miaphysite writings. Severus displayed awareness of the distinction between the Greek vocabulary of the "Byzantines" and Greco-Coptic vernacular: "But the Egyptians call a male child *malakion,* whereas the Byzantines (say) *philikarion.*"[66] It is interesting that Severus, a Greek-speaking representative of Syria, did not include Antiochenes in this comparison.

The significance of local custom is also present in the *Life of Severus*. The *Life* claims that, before his baptism, Severus went to Alexandria to study grammar and rhetoric "since the custom[67] has taken root in his country, as people say, that they should approach holy baptism as adults."[68] Ethnic difference or local custom also influenced liturgical traditions. In a letter to Caesaria, Severus discussed liturgical differences among various ethnic groups within the orthodox community:

> But I want your God-loving excellence to know that the order of hymns and psalms have been handed down differently[69] for the Egyptians, differently for the Palestinians and Phoenicians, and differently for the Syrians; according to the custom it has been preserved from the beginning in each of the districts.[70]

And when the *Panegyric on Apollo* introduced Severus into the story, the patriarch's ethnic difference is noted: "The patriarch Severus came and the saint Apa Apollo was in another district (*hnketōs*). So then this man prayed in a foreign monastic habit and went his way."[71] Linguistic and cultural differences exacerbated the Tritheist conflict involving Damian and Peter of Callinicum.[72]

The inclusion of ethnic foreigners in Coptic artwork depended upon adherence to anti-Chalcedonian doctrine, such as the presence of Barsuma at the Monastery of St. Antony.[73] There were even foreign leaders in Egypt who drew many Egyptians to the opposing sides of theological debates that were smaller in scope than the Chalcedonian schism. Severus of Antioch and Julian of Halicarnassus were both exiled in Egypt and argued about the corruptibility of the flesh of Jesus. Severus wrote about Julian after his death, stating that he "pointlessly became wicked" and despite "kind and brotherly" admonishments, was not "converted to virtue" regarding the question of the incorruptibility of Christ's body.[74] However, unlike the Chalcedonian schism, the Severan/Julianist debate in sixth-century Egypt did not take on ethnic rhetoric framing the boundaries of identity. This is of note given that this sixth-century debate raged largely in Egypt but was led on both sides by exiled foreigners.

Coptic art from this period also illustrates the co-existence of Christian universalism and Egypt-centrism. Coptic Christian art is open to persons who denounced Chalcedon, as this was the primary boundary of Egyptian identity. However, while open to anti-Chalcedonians from other territories, the art of the monastery strongly exhibits Egyptian pride. The primacy of Egyptian identity over other possible identities in the Monastery of Antony is also evident in the graffiti of the monastery. The formal inscriptions of the upper walls of the monastery are all in Coptic while the graffiti written on the lower walls is in the vernacular of various pilgrims.[75] The image of Coptic inscriptions dominating graffiti in various languages is consistent with the role of Egyptian ethnicity in multicultural contact in the centuries after Chalcedon. While Egyptian Christianity embraced all ethnic groups who confess Miaphysite doctrine, the role of the Egyptian people stands over that of non-Egyptians.

In addition to mentioning cultural differences between Egyptians, Syrians, and others, one of Severus's central concerns in his letters is celebrating the Eucharist across ethnic lines. Severus tirelessly champions Egyptian-Syrian unity, but many people on both sides were not enthusiastic about shared communion. Severus assures a presbyter of the doctrinal purity (i.e. Miaphysite confession) of the Egyptian church: "He should not be disturbed as to the condition that prevails in the holy churches in Alexandria and in Egypt, in that it is purified from comingling and communion[76] with heretics now, to speak with God's assured confidence now."[77] The assurance Severus offers the presbyter indicates that there was doubt on the part of Syrian Christians regarding the orthodoxy of Egyptians. Severus constantly addresses the "bishops from Syria in Alexandria,"[78] many of whom have caused tension between foreign exiles and native Egyptians:

> Our entire argument with you concerns those who are residing in Alexandria and are of divisions that are superfluous and intolerable[79] because they have damaged many. This has become manifest. Therefore do not cease giving, in the right time and to those in need, the grace that is never-ending; that which, as it is written, was given without expense[80] and without expense is being asked for.[81]

In a different letter, Severus recommended the ordination of a presbyter named Thomas to an archimandrite named Theodore, who was in doubt as to the qualifications of Thomas. Given the context of the letter, it is clear that Theodore's hesitation is rooted in ethnic tension. Severus admonishes:

> All of you who are held in communion to us must not conceive of one single distinction between those who are exiled from the East, and are glorified by

the struggle of confessorship, and the holy bishops in Egypt. And you must reckon to be one church[82] which is united[83] in the orthodox faith, thanksgiving, and communion; and is well purified and clean from the lack of comingling with the heretics. And you must not be divided meaninglessly over ordinations; but that the fear of God that is in you and the God-fearing archimandrites of the rest of the holy monasteries who were exiled from Palestine on account of true doctrine ought to present, with discernment, the familial brethren[84] to the God-loving bishops in Egypt so that they will perform ordinations for elders and deacons for you and they will satisfy the deficiency of your need. . . . Therefore for one to attempt to separate[85] by vain thinking those things which are so clearly united,[86] and to divide[87] those things that are so indivisible[88] through the inspiration of grace from above is filled with every reproach and accusation.[89] Of this, we admonish your love of God as well as all who share communion with us to flee from, and to throw such stumbling blocks out of the Lord's paths as it is written.[90] And that you should reckon as one the ordination, as we said before, of the holy Eastern and Egyptian bishops, and that you shall conceive of not one difference[91] between them.[92]

Severus told fellow refugees not to hesitate to share communion with Egyptians. He explained that their shared anti-Chalcedonian faith is the foundation for the shared communion between the two ethnic groups: "For as one and the same faith prevails in the holy churches in the East and those in Egypt, one ought to reckon the communion also to be of the same value, since priests are not able, whatever they be in their conduct, to improve or diminish the sacrament."[93]

This letter is the first in the third "section" (*títlos*) of Severus' letters and the colophon reads as follows: "Third section: That one not doubt on account of the conduct (*polítya'*) as well as the customs (*dubara'*) of priests, but only ask if they are orthodox as well as of the proper doctrine."[94] The main concerns exiled Syrians have regarding Egyptian bishops is their conduct (*polítya'*) and customs (*dubara'*). While the broader context reveals that *polítya'* refers to moral character, it is unclear what *dubara'* means here. It is likely that *dubara'* refers to cultural differences that, while not affecting the moral or doctrinal correctness of the bishops, nonetheless created barriers in the minds of Syrians in Egypt. This tension demonstrates the degree to which ethnic boundaries persisted among fellow Miaphysites—despite the attempt of Severus and others to promote unity. Severus constantly emphasizes that the standard for accepting Egyptian communion is anti-Chalcedonian doctrine, or "so long as they are of one and the same orthodox faith."[95]

He also claims that it is an offense "against the laws of the Spirit" and "a superfluous and very oppressive thing"[96] for Syrian exiles to refuse Egyptian communion and request it from "beyond the borders." Severus denounces the prejudice of exiled Syrian priests in Egypt by highlighting the plight of other exiled priests: "For to those the offering is of necessity[97] sent who, while living in countries outside of the borders and being orthodox, are devoid of priests to offer the edifying and heavenly sacrifice."[98] Unlike the Syrians in Egypt, these exiled Syrians required communion to be sent to them due to a lack of orthodox priests. Those in Egypt had no excuse for refusing communion simply due to prejudice. Severus mentioned a certain John and Sergius who hesitated to receive communion with Egyptians: "For one could hear them reciting various dreams and prophecies; indeed, on account of them they hesitated to share communion with the holy churches in Egypt."[99] It is likely that the tensions referred to by Severus were not doctrinal but cultural differences that existed among the Egyptian and foreign, exiled anti-Chalcedonians.[100] Severus argues instead for unity among "the persecuted church[101] of the East and in all the Egyptian church," which "is pure in the proclamation of the faith, and in the rejection of the evil Chalcedonian ungodliness, and in purification and no commingling with heretics."[102]

Severus appeals to his prejudiced Syrian brethren by pointing to the strength of numbers found in the Egyptian-Syrian unity: "We gained besides the East the whole of Egypt also supporting us and equipped with purity along with us, and not bound in a yoke[103] with unbelievers."[104] Severus applies the minority discourse so common to Egyptian Miaphysite literature in a manner inclusive of Egypt and the East. The Christians of Egypt, Palestine, and Syria are, for Severus, "the persecuted church." In framing this multiethnic community as both orthodox and persecuted, Severus added to the framing of international Miaphysite identity in contrast to the powerful and "heretical" Roman Church. Severus expressed a similar attitude of unity toward the Palestinian church. Although "Palestine was subject to the apostolic seat of Antioch in previous times," Severus claims that he and the "God-loving bishop Isidore are one person together."[105]

It is significant that before describing the unity of Syria and Palestine, Severus mentions the latter's prior subordination to the former. For the Church of Jerusalem and its environs were indeed under the jurisdiction of the Patriarchate of Antioch, in accordance with the ordinances of the Council of Nicaea. However, Jerusalem became a patriarchate after the

Council of Chalcedon.[106] Therefore, Severus's call for a return to Jerusalem's subordination to Antioch is part of his anti-Chalcedonian resistance.

Despite the multiethnic Miaphysite unity, Severus also indicated tensions along ethnic lines. Egyptian culture caused many exiled Syrian Christians to avoid communion in Egyptian churches. Syrians raised questions about ecclesiastical rank and moral quality in ways that displayed prejudice:

> The same grace of adoption is received from the cleansing of regeneration both by one who has been made worthy of baptism from a priest resplendent in virtues, and by one (person) from one (priest) who is abased and despicable in his lifestyle; both one (who receives) from an archbishop, and one (who receives) from an elder who holds the lowest rank. For both confer one and the same seal at the time they symbolize and believe one orthodox faith that is the same in every matter and soundness. . . . The difference of the character of those who offer sacrifice makes no difference whatsoever in the mysteries that are celebrated, as long as both of them confess one orthodox faith, and are not stained by the mark of any heresy.[107]

Severus encourages unity by declaring his equal concern for Egypt and Syria: "For do not reckon me as anything but equal in my concern for the church of the Antiochenes and that of the Alexandrines; but I am not lying even if I say it is much greater."[108]

Severus claims to care equally for the orthodox of Egypt and Syria equally and his tireless striving for unity demonstrates this concern. However, his writings are a strong indication of ethnic tension that persisted nonetheless. Furthermore, Severus makes critical statements towards the Egyptians. It is likely that, while he worked for unity, Severus sometimes sided with his frustrated, exiled, non-Egyptian community in their perspective on Egyptians. Severus claims that he had greater success than the Alexandrian patriarch in converting Hellenistic philosophers, "those who for a very long time had not shared communion as you know, but were satisfied by the acts of the records made by the blessed Dioscorus."[109] Despite the respect paid to Dioscorus, Severus clearly depicts himself as the orthodox savior rescuing Egypt from heresy. Severus goes on to describe the incompetence of the presbyter Theodore:

> Even while I was living in the city of Antiochus, I used to hear concerning the memory of the saintly bishop, father Theodore, that he would answer and say publicly to many who came to Egypt asking him whether or not they should receive communion, 'If you have been made fully assured, receive

communion,' and other things that resemble these things and approximate them. And I endured because it was a time of endurance, and because none of those bishops in the East heard anything like this. But as the reports were yours and confined to you, not much harm befell.[110]

Though Severus worked to establish unity, statements such as this reveal an underlying sense of superiority to Egyptian Christians. Ironically, Severus critiqued Egyptian leaders for not being as good as him at building unity between Egyptians and Easterners. Other Syrian sources expressed condescending attitudes towards Egypt more blatantly; John of Ephesus calls Alexandrians "a horde of barbarians."[111] The existence of anti-Palestinian sentiment among extreme Egyptian anti-Chalcedonians attests to the ethnic division among Miaphysites. Severus illustrates such tension as he offered a critique of Christian Egypt. An interesting example is a comment about how the ethnocentricity of some Egyptian Christians led them to deny communion to fellow Miaphysites of a different ethnic background:

> I do not know how, while you have abandoned the letters and advice that are from within that time, you say to us that we shouldn't pay attention to those that are from Cappadocia, the useless country,[112] but to despise the divine laws I just now mentioned. Rather, attention is due to one soul and to many. Furthermore, how can we call the two Cappadocias and Armenia useless? But in this you thought or spoke rather like the natives of the country[113]—grant me your pardon to say- and not truly. For it is the habit of the Alexandrians to think that the sun rises for them only, and towards them only the lamp shines, so that they even jokingly nickname outside cities 'lampless.'[114] For if it were that one could weigh the population of a people[115] for an accurate judgment, as in the case of weights that are distinguished by the tipping of the surface of a scale, the inhabitants of all these countries will produce no less than the entire city of the Alexandrians.[116]

This statement is perhaps the most poignant in all of Severus's writings as well as other non-Egyptian residents of Egypt with regard to Egyptian identity. In another ironic statement, Severus argued for unity and condemned ethnocentric prejudice by claiming that Egyptians think they are better than other people, that the "sun rises only for them." Severus judges Egyptians while critiquing other exiles for separating from Egyptians. Moreover, Severus's judgment of Egyptians is that they think themselves superior to others. While the amount of available evidence does not permit one to gain a complete picture of how late antique Egyptians articulated and defined their identity (a task I would say is impossible for any ethnic group), these statements are a strong indication of ethnic distinctions even among Miaphysites of other ethnicities. What is more, the Egyptian pride that has been amply demonstrated here and that characterized much of late antique Egypt even led to divisions among their orthodox kindred.

These visions of Egyptianness from the perspective of outsiders are crucial in understanding late antique Egyptian ethnic identity. Since ethnic identity is by definition a product of interaction with other groups—against a primordialist vision of a pure, untouched ethnic group—ethnicity is formed just as much by the insiders as the outsiders.[117] Egyptian identity is the creation of the Egyptian people and their Palestinian, Syrian, and Pisidian neighbors—and these groups that lived in Egypt would have a more intimate perspective of the Egyptian people. What is more, the insider and outsider perspectives on Egyptian Miaphysite identity coalesce significantly. This study has demonstrated copious evidence where late antique Egyptian sources set a vision of ethnic identity that continued in medieval and modern periods where Egypt emerged as the champion of Christian orthodoxy in the ancient world. It is not surprising, then, that non-Egyptian residents would comment that the Egyptians had a chip on their shoulder. Insider and outsider perspectives on Egyptian ethnicity agreed on one thing: Egyptians thought they were the most orthodox ethnic group in the world.

While the nationalist thesis is unhelpful here, ethnic differences clearly played a role in the theological schisms of late antiquity. This is not merely a modern interjection into antiquity. Rather, ethnic difference was understood to play a role in the divisions of the Church by figures of this time period. Peter of Callinicum blames the Chalcedonian schism on linguistic and cultural factors: "The Westerners, not from heretical intention but rather from simplicity[118] and the constraints[119] of their language, were not a little bit hindered over the phrase 'three hypostases of the Father, Son and Holy Ghost.'"[120] There were also examples of Egyptian animosity towards foreigners. The *Life of Severus* recounted an uprising led by an Alexandrian monk named Nephalius in whom "jealousy was suddenly aroused against all those in Palestine who were of the communion with the fathers in Egypt and Alexandria."[121] Nephalius "disturbed the people of his country"[122] and "was the cause of a myriad of seditions and killings in his country"[123] because he resented the union between Peter Mongus and emperor Zeno. Nephalius apparently led a force of thirty thousand Egyptians as he continued "perverting the peace and order of his country."[124] While Nephalius was a nuisance to his own people, his animosity targeted Palestinians, although they were not the only ethnic group whose majority supported Zeno. Thus, ethnic tensions exacerbated theological divisions.

Severus defended the position of the moderate anti-Chalcedonians and gained the favor of the emperor who ordered that the exiled monks return to their monasteries.[125] This instance is one of the few in anti-Chalcedonian literature in which the Byzantine emperor stands in a positive light, but it also undermines any sense of anti-Byzantine nationalism at work in Egypt. Severus's assessment of Egyptian pride also reveals his own persistent ethnic prejudices despite his attempts to foster unity.[126] However, Severus's critique of Egyptian ethnocentricity accurately reflects the situation, for Coptic anti-Chalcedonian texts do express this attitude. In the *Life of Isaac,* a "Saracen" Christian woman who comes to Egypt is unable to recognize heresy and must receive instruction from the wise Egyptians.[127]

In various passages from Severus, as well as throughout Egyptian anti-Chalcedonian literature, Egypt is the source of orthodoxy, shining its light on nations darkened by heresy. Modern anthropologists have noted how Egyptian Christians assert ethnic pride in the present day, in contrast to the stance of the Maronites, who display more solidarity with the national government.[128] Ethnic tension also persists between Egyptian and Syrian Christians despite their shared Miaphysite confession. This phenomenon is a constraint on inter-ethnic contact resulting from the threat of violence toward a particular community:

> In this situation, many forms of interaction between members of different ethnic groups may fail to develop, even though a potential complementarity of interest obtains. Forms of interaction may be blocked because of a lack of trust or a lack of opportunities to consummate transactions. What is more, there are also internal sanctions in such communities which tend to enhance overt conformity within and cultural differences between communities. If a person is dependent for his security on the voluntary and spontaneous support of his own community, self-identification as a member of this community needs to be explicitly expressed and confirmed; and any behavior which is deviant from the standard may be interpreted as a weakening of the identity, and thereby of the bases of security.[129]

The available sources certainly speak of a lack of trust between the various Miaphysite communities in the fifth, sixth, and seventh centuries. Despite many expressions of inter-ethnic unity among anti-Chalcedonians by the movement's greatest leaders, many of these communities wanted to elevate their own group over other groups, despite the "complementarity of interests." Chalcedonian Byzantine hegemony represented a threat to Miaphysite identity and this contributed to persistent ethnic tension among the various groups in this international movement. Preoccupied with survival, Egyptian Christians reacted by elevating their own status as those for whom "only the lamp shines."[130]

Conclusion

MIAPHYSITE CHRISTOLOGY AS
IDENTITY BOUNDARY

THE COUNCIL OF CHALCEDON is an identifiable turning point for assertions of Egyptian identity. Before Chalcedon, most of Egypt was in theological agreement with the mainstream Christianity of the Byzantine Empire. Indeed, one of the most revered figures in Egypt, Athanasius, is remembered across the Christian tradition as the champion of Nicene orthodoxy. Although he experienced exile and persecution at the hands of imperial authorities, there was no ongoing Egyptian resistance or lasting schism. Likewise, most Christian groups in the Roman Empire supported the victory of Cyril over Nestorius at the Council of Ephesus. Egypt agreed doctrinally with the other important regions of the empire before Chalcedon, and assertions of Egyptian pride were infrequent.

This is not to say that manifestations of Egyptian pride only came into existence at the time of Chalcedon; Egyptian Christians were certainly aware of and took pride in their Egyptian identity in the fourth and early fifth centuries, as is evident in parts of the *Life of Anthony* and the *Apophthegmata Patrum*. These early texts emphasize a native Egyptian, Coptic-speaking identity. Therefore, it would be partially inaccurate to speak of the ethnic boundary maintenance in anti-Chalcedonian texts in terms of ethnogenesis. Used to describe the emerging Gothic communities of the fifth-century, ethnogenesis refers more broadly to new collective identities that could support independent communities.[1]

Egyptian ethnic identity already had a well-established history. However, Chalcedon represented a turning point in Egyptian identity development wherein ethnic rhetoric came to the fore in a new way that expanded beyond the focus on Coptic language and culture. In this sense, there was a new collective identity.[2] The social significance of Egyptian Christological developments is a product of the outcome of the process, more than the beginning.

Miaphysite doctrine provided Egyptian Christians with a frame to assert identity in an unprecedented manner.[3] Even in Shenoute, who wrote before Chalcedon and became the greatest Coptic writer in the history of the language, ethnic rhetoric was strikingly absent. Shenoute interpreted his social world through categories such as barbarian, Hellene, Jew, Christian, and heretic.[4] While Shenoute lived in a world in which some Coptic-speaking Egyptians retained ethnic consciousness, the assertion of any kind of Egyptian identity was not a priority for the leader of the White Monastery Federation. Such ethnic rhetoric was common in the anti-Chalcedonian literature produced in Egypt in the fifth, sixth, and seventh centuries. Furthermore, the same ethnic rhetoric that was absent before the fifth century was still normative for Copts throughout the medieval period. In making the case against nationalism by noting the Greek-Coptic unity of Egypt, there has been a tendency to downplay the growth of anti-Byzantine/pro-Egyptian rhetoric following Chalcedon.[5]

While there was no Egyptian anti-Hellenism in fourth-century Egypt, pro-Egyptian rhetoric in anti-Chalcedonian literature cannot be subsumed into a "pan-Hellenic cultural model."[6] Dismissing Egyptian ethnic boundary maintenance as a function of Roman provincialism is an insufficient explanation. Anti-Chalcedonian polemic was modified in Egypt to enhance the Egyptian people's role, distinguishing it within a "pan-Hellenic" strategy of identification. The anti-Chalcedonian writers surveyed above took the doctrines of patriarchs such as Cyril, Dioscorus, and Timothy, and narrated stories of monks who suffered for anti-Chalcedonian doctrine in a way that especially highlighted the land, people and language of Egypt.[7] Anti-Chalcedonian identity in Egypt was framed by ascribing "otherness" to the Chalcedonian Roman Empire. The rise of the Miaphysite movement included expressions of intense hatred for the Byzantine Empire, as represented by Egyptian anti-Chalcedonians. Indeed, Egyptian ethnic pride does not entail a hatred of Greek culture; but the late fifth century saw an emerging anti-Byzantine Egyptian identity that does not fit the nationalist thesis.

"Egypt" and "Egyptian" are late antique categories of ethnicity that are framed, to a significant extent, through categories of language, geography, and imperial politics. The Roman Empire, once Egypt's ally in the fight for orthodoxy in the times of Athanasius and Shenoute, was now the principal source of heresy against which Egyptian identity emerged. Beginning with

Timothy Aelurus, one of Chalcedon's initial resisters, the theological schism was framed through geographical and political terms; the "heresy" of Chalcedon was the cause of the fall of the Roman Empire and was the cause of division between the Westerners and Easterners. Timothy's contemporaries echoed the conflation of Chalcedonianism with the Roman Empire while presenting Egyptians as completely Miaphysite. Longinus resisted and even won over many Roman soldiers and magistrates while Macarius of Tkôw—the "Egyptian elder"—died defending the Miaphysite faith and was a proud Egyptian-speaker. Therefore, the paradigm for constructing Egyptian Christian ethnicity formed long before the Islamic conquest but in ways that were unprecedented in the earliest centuries of Christian Egypt.

Assertions of Egyptian identity along the boundary of anti-Chalcedonianism continued throughout the sixth century, especially in reaction to the heavy-handed tactics of Justinian. The followers of Apollo claimed that "almost the entire land of Egypt" rejected the "insane" Justinian and the "defiled" *Tome* of Leo. Those who commemorated Abraham of Farshut were known, at least by some, as "hating the Roman emperor" and "all who live under the authority of the Roman Empire." Likewise, the Coptic versions of the biography of Daniel of Scetis emphasize how Justinian "terrorized the entire world" with the *Tome* and how the "faithful of Egypt" resisted it. Even after the Arab Muslim conquest of Egypt, the "Roman heretics" were continuously criticized by Benjamin of Alexandria, especially the "Caucasian devil" Cyrus as well as Emperor Heraclius. The labels "Roman," "Chalcedonian," "Egyptian," and "orthodox" litter the biography of Samuel of Kalamun in the same way: Justinian is the "fraudulent king of the Romans" and Cyrus is the "deceitful Caucasian" who attempts to impose the "defiled *Tome*" upon the "faithful orthodox of Egypt," whom Cyrus desires to control. Even after Arab Muslim control was absolute during the late seventh century, the biography of Isaac of Alexandria—he who was "Egyptian in his ethnicity"—still expresses contempt for the "impious Cyrus." Indeed, the coalescence of Egyptian and Miaphysite identity was so extensive that other Miaphysites—notably Severus of Antioch—often felt that Egyptians believed that the "lamp shines only on them."

Furthermore, the assertion of a separate Egyptian identity did not develop in the medieval redactions of the *AHPA*.[8] While Pharaonism in its modern form may have many connections to anachronistic and prejudiced depictions of Egypt in nineteenth-century scholarship, the highly ethnicized polemic of pre-Islamic Egypt demonstrates the existence of Egyptian ethnic boundary maintenance in late antiquity. As has been demonstrated above, the ethnic strategies of identification in medieval Egypt reflect rhetoric that developed in the late antique period. Moreover, the renunciation of nationalism, or Pharaonism, still leaves no helpful alternative with which to understand the role of Egyptian-ness in late antique religious life.

Accepting Egyptian-centered rhetoric as evidence for the development of Egyptian ethnicity through the assertion of Miaphysite boundaries leads to a more clear understanding of late antique Egyptian identity. The fifth century witnessed the expansion of themes of ethnicity that were already present in Egyptian Christianity. Following Chalcedon, however, Egyptians had to construct an identity in opposition to some of their fellow Christians. The seventh century saw the rapid and complete subjugation of the Egyptian Christians to Arab Muslim rule. This led to the acceleration of the process of Egyptian anti-Chalcedonian ethnic boundary maintenance, a process that had been underway since the council's conclusion. With the passage of time, concern increased for the preservation of the Coptic (that is, Egyptian Christian) heritage in the face of increasing oppression.

However, the anti-Byzantine/anti-Chalcedonian polemic was harsher than any anti-Islamic sentiments expressed in seventh-century Coptic litera-ture. It is likely that Copts expressed greater hostility toward Byzantine Chalcedonians than toward Muslims because the former were considered heretics, while the latter were barbarians or pagans. As Foat has pointed out, for Shenoute heretics are "supremely dangerous."[9] Shenoute's thought became foundational for the Coptic community for all subsequent generations of the Egyptian people; it is reasonable to see his social vision continuing through influential Egyptian ascetics following his lifetime. If Shenoute saw Christian "heretics" as more dangerous than "barbarians," it is likely that seventh-century Egyptian Christians thought similarly. For the Copts of the seventh century and following, Arab Muslims were simply "barbarians," while Byzantine Chalcedonians were heretics.

The social, ecclesiastical, and political subjugation of Egypt to Constantinople in the fifth century necessitated the "continuing dichotomi-zation between members and outsiders."[10] This dichotomization is the pri-mary vehicle through which ethnic identity can be asserted and understood. Assertions of ethnicity are discernible in the heightened rhetoric that calls attention to the land and people of Egypt. Instead of relying on a pre-existing, fixed definition of ethnicity, the theological divisions of Chalcedon led Egyptian Christians to reify those divisions through ethnic rhetoric. Despite the multiregional constituency of the Miaphysite movement, Egyptian anti-Chalcedonians expressed a localized form of this doctrine, specific to and primarily concerned with the people of Egypt. The characteristic hero of (Miaphysite) orthodoxy was most often "Egyptian in his ethnicity."[11] As prescribed in the *AHPA*, the program for the promotion of orthodox Christianity depends on a community of the "immensely powerful ethnic group—Egyptians, collectively indigenous—without a foreigner among them."[12] As outsiders in Egypt attested, Egyptian Miaphysite Christians tended to view themselves as "those for whom the lamp shines."[13]

NOTES

ABBREVIATIONS

AA	*American Anthropologist*
ANES	*Ancient Near Eastern Studies*
ARA	*Annual Review of Anthropology*
CCR	*Coptic Church Review*
CE	*Coptic Encyclopedia*
CPG	*Clavid Patrum Graecorum*
CS	*Critical Sociology*
CSCO	*Corpus Scriptorum Cristianorum Orientalium*
CSEL	*Corpus Scriptorum Ecclesiasticorum Latinorum*
DOP	Dumbarton Oaks Papers
JA	*Journal Asiatique*
JECS	*Journal of Early Christian Studies*
JTS	*Journal of Theological Studies*
ME	*Medieval Encounters*
OC	*Oriens Christianus*
OCA	*Orientalia Christiana Analecta*
PG	*Patrologiæ Græcæ*
PL	*Patrologiæ Latina*
PO	*Patrologia Orientalia*
REB	*Revue des études byzantines*
ROC	*Revue de l'Orient chrétien*
VetChr	*Vetera Christianorum*

1. James Baldwin, "Faulkner and Desegregation," *The Partisan Review,* 568–73 (1956): 568.

2. David Olster, "From Periphery to Center: The Transformation of Late Roman Self-Definition in the Seventh Century," in *Shifting Frontiers in Late Antiquity,* ed. Ralph W. Mathisen and Hagith S. Sivan (Aldershot: Variorum, 1996), 96.

3. The view that the Arab Muslim conquest ignited the Egyptian church's ethnic identity is articulated in studies such as Arietta Papaconstantinou, "Historiography, Hagiography, and the Making of the Coptic 'Church of the Martyrs' in Early Islamic Egypt," *DOP* 60 (2006): 67. Given the argument of this book that religious and ethnic identity are intricately intertwined in the late antique Near East, I refer to the conquests of the Islamic states following Muhammad as "Arab Muslim." See Robert G. Hoyland, *In God's Path: The Arab Conquests and the Creation of an Islamic* Empire (Oxford: Oxford University Press, 2015), 5.

4. Dietmar Winkler originally proposed this term as a more theologically correct and respectful term: "The refusal of the term Monophysites by the Oriental Orthodox should be taken seriously." See "Miaphysitism: A New Term for Use in the History of Dogma and in Ecumenical Theology," *The Harp* 10 (1997); 40. Fergus Millar has proposed the more general term "orthodox." See "The Evolution of the Syrian Orthodox Church in the Pre-Islamic Period: From Greek to Syriac?" *JECS* 21 (2013): 44.

5. Volker L. Menze, *Justinian and the Making of the Syrian Orthodox Church* (Oxford: Oxford University Press, 2008), 2.

6. David W. Johnson, "Anti-Chalcedonian Polemics in Coptic Texts," in *Roots of Egyptian Christianity,* eds. B. A. Pearson and James Goehring (Philadelphia, PA: Fortress, 1986), 218.

7. The schism following Chalcedon was intensified by the episcopal maneuvering of Juvenal of Jerusalem as well; Mary K. Farag, *What Makes a Church Sacred? Legal and Ritual Perspectives from Late Antiquity* (Berkeley, CA: The University of California Press, 2021), 167.

8. In contrast to, for example, the argument of Papaconstantinou, "Historiography," 69.

9. Stephen J. Davis, *The Early Coptic Papacy* (Cairo: American University in Cairo Press, 2004), 42.

10. For examples of scholarship that pinpoints the emergence of Egyptian ethnic rhetoric at the Arab Muslim conquest, see W. H. C. Frend, "Heresy and Schism as Social and National Movements," in *Studies in Church History Vol. 9: Schism, Heresy and Religious Protest,* ed. Derek Baker (Cambridge, UK: Cambridge University Press, 1972), 51.

11. *Vite Longino,* 86.

12. Papaconstantinou, "Historiography," 72; Timothy Aelurus, "Extraits de Timothée Aelure," ed. François Nau, PO 13, 202–18 (1919): 215–16; *Histoire de Dioscore,* ed. F. Nau, *JA* 10: 55.

13. Davis, *The Early Coptic Papacy*, 90.

14. Averil Cameron, *Byzantine Matters* (Princeton, NJ: Princeton University Press, 2014), 60.

15. Richard Price, "The Development of a Chalcedonian Identity in Byzantium (451–553)," in *Religious Origins of Nations? The Christian Communities of the Middle East*, ed. Bas ter Haar Romeny (Leiden: Brill, 2010), 307.

16. Peter Sarris, *Economy and Society in the Age of Justinian* (Cambridge, UK: Cambridge University Press, 2006), 8.

17. Roger Bagnall, *Egypt in the Byzantine World* (New York: Cambridge University Press, 2007), 16.

18. Leslie S. B. MacCoull, "The Apa Apollos Monastery of Pharoou (Aphrodito) and its Papyrus Archive," in *Documenting Christianity in Egypt, Sixth to Fourteenth Centuries* (Burlington, VT: Ashgate, 2011), 58–59.

19. Émile Amélineau, *Résumé de l'histoire de l'Égypte depuis les temps les plus reculés jusqu'a nos jours* (Paris: Ernest Leroux, 1894), 63. Amélineau supplied the persistence of the practice of the preservation of corpses to support his thesis (211); Egyptian monasticism, the most unique feature of Egyptian Christianity in Amélineau's estimation, was also rooted in ancient Egyptian religious practice (215). Following this analysis is Alfred J. Butler, *Arab Conquest of Egypt and the Last Thirty Years of the Roman Dominion*, ed. P. M. Fraser, 2nd ed. (Oxford: Clarendon Press, 1978), 491.

20. Johannes Leipoldt, *Schenute von Atripe und die Entstehung des national ägyptischen Christentums* (Leipzig: J. C. Hinrichs'sche Buchhandlung, 1903), 26.

21. E. L. Woodward, *Christianity and Nationalism in the Later Roman Empire* (London: Longmans, Green, 1916), vi.

22. Jean Maspero, "Horapollon et la fin du paganisme égyptien," *BIFAO* 11 (1914): 180.

23. Maspero, "Horapollon," 182.

24. Maspero, "Horapollon," 3. Maspero's prejudice is directed specifically at Christian Egypt: "The extensive theological literature of the Copts does not contain a single work of value or even of simple mediocrity" (17); "Because the Orientals, especially the Egyptians, are barely capable of abstract speculations" (18).

25. Harold I. Bell, *Egypt from Alexander the Great to the Arab Conquest: A Study in the Diffusion and Decay of Hellenism* (Oxford: Clarendon Press, 1948), 113. Condescending statements like these are frequent throughout Bell's analysis: "The Monophysites or Jacobites, supported by the ignorant monks, who were hostile to Hellenic culture in all its forms, were quite incapable of making any important contribution to the thought of the age" (116).

26. Bell, *Egypt from Alexander*, 116.

27. A. H. M. Jones, "Were Ancient Heresies National or Social Movements in Disguise?," *JTS* 10 (1959): 289. R. Y. Ebied and L. R. Wickham also caution against dismissing the validity of religious conviction in favor of viewing theological controversy as purely political: Timothy Aelurus, "A Collection of Unpublished Syriac Letters of Timothy Aelurus," *JTS* 21 (1970): 328. See also Johnson, "Anti-Chalcedonian Polemics in Coptic Texts," 219–20.

28. Further iterations of the nationalism thesis: W. H. C. Frend, *The Rise of the Monophysite Movement: Chapters in the History of the Church in the Fifth and Sixth Centuries* (Cambridge, UK: Cambridge University Press, 1972), xi; Tito Orlandi, "Literature, Coptic," *CE* 5 (1991): 1454. For opposition to the nationalism thesis see David W. Johnson, "A Coptic Source for the *History of Patriarchs of Alexandria*" (PhD diss., The Catholic University of America, 1973), 81.

29. Ewa Wipszycka, "Le nationalisme a-t-il existé en Égypte byzantine?," in *Études sur le Christianisme dans l'Égypte de l'Antiquité tardive* (Roma: Institutum Patristicum Augustinianum, 1996), 18.

30. Peter Brown, *Poverty and Leadership in the Later Roman Empire* (Hanover, NH: University Press of New England, 2001), 107.

31. Ernest Gellner, *Nations and Nationalism* (Ithaca, NY: Cornell University Press, 1983), 1. See also Benedict Anderson, *Imagined Communities: Reflections on the Origin and Spread of Nationalism* (New York: Verso, 1983), 4; Anthony D. Smith, *Theories of Nationalism* (New York: Harper & Row, 1971), 3.

32. Stephen Davis has proposed the terminology "national culture" in describing the "minority discourse" at play in Egyptian ethnic rhetoric (*The Early Coptic Papacy,* 121). Likewise, Tito Orlandi has referred to Egyptian ethnic rhetoric as the development of an "Egyptian national Christian consciousness"; see "The Coptic Ecclesiastical History: A Survey," in *The World of Early Egyptian Christianity: Language, Literature, and Social Context,* ed. James E. Goehring and Janet A. Timbie (Washington, DC: The Catholic University of America Press, 2007), 5.

33. Jason R. Zaborowski, *The Coptic Martyrdom of John of Phanijōit: Assimilation and Conversion to Islam in Thirteenth-Century Egypt* (Leiden: Brill, 2005), 176–77. Likewise, Volker Menze suggests that "an issue beyond the Christological question caused the final break" (*Justinian,* 59).

34. Bagnall, *Egypt in the Byzantine World,* 16.

35. This perspective is formed significantly by the work of Siniša Malešević, *The Sociology of Ethnicity* (London: Sage Publications, 2004), 4.

36. Smith, *Theories of Nationalism,* 23.

37. Thomas Hylland Eriksen, *Ethnicity and Nationalism: Anthropological Perspectives,* 2nd ed. (London: Pluto Press, 2002), 105; Smith, *Theories of Nationalism,* 16.

38. Ron Suny, "Making Minorities: The Politics of National Boundaries in the Soviet Experience," in *The Construction of Minorities: Cases for Comparison Across Time and Around the World,* ed. André Burguière and Raymond Grew (Ann Arbor: The University of Michigan Press, 2001), 247.

39. Zaborowski, *John of Phanijōit,* 175.

40. Pieternella Van Doorn-Harder, "Copts: Fully Egyptian, but for a Tattoo?," in *Nationalism and Minority Identities in Islamic Societies,* ed. Maya Shatzmiller, 22–57 (Montreal: McGill-Queen's University Press, 2005), 25, draws heavily upon the theories advanced by Anthony Smith in analyzing modern Coptic nationalism (49). On modern Coptic nationalism, see Jacques van der Vliet, "The Copts: 'Modern Sons of the Pharaohs?,'" in *Religious Origins of Nations? The Christian Communities of the Middle East,* ed. Bas ter Haar Romeny (Leiden: Brill, 2010), 279–80.

41. Max Weber, *Economy and Society: An Outline of Interpretive Sociology*, 4th ed. (New York: Bedminster Press, 1968), 389.

42. Stephen Cornell and Douglas Hartmann, *Ethnicity and Race: Making Identities in a Changing World* (Thousand Oaks, CA: Pine Forge Press, 2007), 17.

43. Fredrik Barth, *Ethnic Groups and Boundaries: The Social Organization of Culture Difference* (Oslo: Universitetsforlaget, 1969), 9–10.

44. Barth, *Ethnic Groups*, 15. This view is reflected in Smith: "Ethnicity is a matter of myths, memories, values and symbols, and not of material possessions or political power" (*Theories of Nationalism*, 28). For further support of Barth, see Cornell and Hartmann, *Ethnicity and Race*, 81. For an updated articulation of Barthian theory, see Fredrik Barth, "Boundaries and Connections," in *Signifying Identities: Anthropological Perspectives on Boundaries and Contested Values*, ed. Anthony P. Cohen (New York: Routledge, 2000), 17–36.

45. Hans Vermeulen and Cora Govers, *The Anthropology of Ethnicity: Beyond 'Ethnic Groups and Boundaries'* (Amsterdam: Het Spinhuis, 1994), 1; Iain Prattis, "Barthing up the Wrong Tree," *AA* 85 (1983): 103; Ronald Cohen, "Ethnicity: Problem and Focus in Anthropology," *ARA* 7 (1978): 383; Anna De Fina, "Code-Switching and the Construction of Ethnic Identity in a Community of Practice," *Language in Society* 36 (2007): 373.

46. George De Vos, "Ethnic Pluralism: Conflict and Accommodation," in *Ethnic Identity: Creation, Conflict, and Accommodation*, ed. George De Vos and Lola Romanucci-Ross, 3rd ed. (London: Altamira Press, 1995), 16. The work of Montserrat Guibernau and John Rex is also strongly rooted in Barth's methodology; see *The Ethnicity Reader: Nationalism, Multiculturalism and Migration* (Cambridge, UK: Polity Press, 1997), 7. See also Cornell and Hartmann, *Ethnicity and Race*, 72; Richard Jenkins, *Rethinking Ethnicity*, 2nd ed. (London: Sage Publications, 2008), 12. Critics of Barth still recognize the profound impact of *Ethnic Groups* and operate under its influence. See Rogers Brubaker, "Ethnicity Without Groups," in *Ethnicity, Nationalism, and Minority Rights*, eds. Stephen May, Tariq Modood, and Judith Squires (Cambridge, UK: Cambridge University Press, 2004), 69; Leo A. Despres, *Ethnicity and Resource Competition in Plural Societies* (The Hague: Mouton, 1975), 3.

47. Jonathan M. Hall, *Ethnic Identity in Greek Antiquity* (Cambridge, UK: Cambridge University Press, 1997), 1. For an example of scholarly reluctance to utilize modern methodology in analyzing ancient sources, see Maged Mikhail, *From Byzantine to Islamic Egypt: Religion, Identity and Politics after the Arab Conquest* (London: I. B. Tauris, 2014), 17.

48. Smith, *Ethnic Origins of Nations*, 46; Ton Derks and Nico Roymans, *Ethnic Constructs in Antiquity: The Role of Power and Tradition* (Amsterdam: Amsterdam University Press, 2009), 1–4; Stephen Mitchell and Geoffrey Greatrex, *Ethnicity and Culture in Late Antiquity* (London: Duckworth, 2000), xiv. Greatrex finds the term "ethnicity" unhelpful in analyzing late Roman identity (278). This objection, though frequent, is unnecessary as it is based on an attempt to understand ethnicity in late antiquity simply by equating the modern concept of ethnicity to the use of *ethnos* in ancient texts. See also Philip Wood, *History and Identity in the Late Antique Near*

East (Oxford: Oxford University Press, 2013); Ralph W. Mathisen and Hagith S. Sivan, *Shifting Frontiers in Late Antiquity* (Aldershot: Variorum, 1996); Aaron P. Johnson, *Ethnicity and Argument in Eusebius' Praeparatio Evangelica* (Oxford: Oxford University Press, 2006); Nathanael Andrade, *Syrian Identity in the Greco-Roman World* (Cambridge, UK: Cambridge University Press, 2013); Averil Cameron, *Christianity and the Rhetoric of Empire: The Development of Christian Discourse* (Berkeley: University of California Press, 1991), 2; Andrew S. Jacobs, *Remains of the Jews: The Holy Land and Christian Empire in Late Antiquity* (Stanford, CA: Stanford University Press, 2004), 23. In his analysis of early Jewish/Christian relations, Daniel Boyarin also draws on the work of Foucault: "Semantic Differences; or 'Judaism/Christianity'," in *The Ways that Never Parted: Jews and Christians in Late Antiquity and the Early Middle Ages,* ed. Adam H. Becker and Annette Yoshiko Reed (Tübingen: Mohr Siebeck, 2003), 65. Walter Pohl and Gerda Heydemann, eds., *Strategies of Identification: Ethnicity and Religion in Early Medieval Europe* (Turnhout: Brepols, 2013), 2. This volume explores the concept of "ethnogenesis" in the emergence of Western European ethnic groups during the early medieval period. Bas ter Haar Romeny relies on Geertz for his analysis of Syrian Christian identity, *Religious Origins of Nations? The Christian Communities of the Middle East* (Leiden: Brill, 2010), 8. Some scholars have argued that modern concepts of race and racism have roots in Greco-Roman antiquity; see Benjamin Isaac, *The Invention of Racism in Classical Antiquity* (Princeton, NJ: Princeton University Press, 2004), 17; Denise K. Buell, *Why This New Race: Ethnic Reasoning in Early Christianity* (New York, NY: Columbia University Press, 2008), 2. Buell's use of the term "race" as a social construct operative in antiquity stands in contrast to more conservative scholars; see Jonathan M. Hall, *Hellenicity: Between Ethnicity and Culture* (Chicago, IL: University of Chicago Press, 2002), 15.

49. For example, see a response to Sarah Bond's argument regarding polychromy in classical artwork: Jon Street, "College Professor Says White Marble Statues Promote Racism," *Blaze Media,* June 8, 2017, https://www.theblaze.com/news/2017/06/08/college-professor-says-white-marble-statues-promote-racism. For the original article, see Sarah E. Bond, "Why We Need to Start Seeing the Classical World in Color," *Hyperallergic,* June 7, 2017, https://hyperallergic.com/383776/why-we-need-to-start-seeing-the-classical-world-in-color.

50. Rebecca Futo Kennedy, "Why I Teach About Race and Ethnicity in the Classical World," *Eidolon,* 2017, https://eidolon.pub/why-i-teach-about-race-and-ethnicity-in-the-classical-world-abe379722170.

51. Gay L. Byron, *Symbolic Blackness and Ethnic Difference in Early Christian Literature* (New York: Routledge, 2002), 5–6. Of note is how Byron describes ethnicity as "a relationship between two contrasting individuals or groups of people" (2) while race is described as an "external factor" (5).

52. Buell, *Why This New Race,* 176–77n42.

53. W. E. B. Du Bois called race a "vast family of human beings" comprised of a multitude of cultures and ethnicities; see "The Conservation of Races," in *The Oxford W. E. B. Du Bois Reader,* ed. Eric Sundquist (New York: Oxford University

Press, 1996), 38–47. Stuart Hall builds on Du Bois's idea of race as "the physical bond," and understands race as a "sliding signifier" that is a distinct network of meaning from ethnicity in *The Fateful Triangle, Race, Ethnicity, Nation* (Cambridge, MA: Harvard University Press, 2017), 39.

54. Denise Eileen McCoskey, *Race: Antiquity and Its Legacy* (Oxford: Oxford University Press, 2012), 2.

55. Byron, *Symbolic Blackness,* 117–18.

56. Ausonius, *Parentalia,* ed. Hugh G. Evelyn White (Cambridge, MA: Harvard University Press, 1919), 66.

57. Erich S. Gruen, *Rethinking the Other in Antiquity* (Princeton, NJ: Princeton University Press, 2011), 198.

58. Gruen, *Rethinking the Other,* 197.

59. Frank M. Snowden, Jr., *Blacks in Antiquity* (Cambridge, MA: Belknap Press, 1970), 126.

60. For additional social scientists who make similar distinctions between race and ethnicity, see Neil J. Smelser, William Julius Wilson and Faith Mitchell, *America Becoming: Racial Trends and Their Consequences,* vol. 1 (Washington, DC: National Academy Press, 2001), 3.

61. Isaac, *The Invention of Racism,* 24.

62. Rebecca F. Kennedy, C. Sydnor Roy and Max L. Goldman, eds., *Race and Ethnicity in the Classical World: An Anthology of Primary Sources in Translation* (Indianapolis, IN: Hackett Publishing Company, 2013), xiii.

63. ܐܦܪ and ⲣⲙ-, respectively.

CHAPTER 2. EGYPTIAN CHRISTIANS AND ETHNICITY PRIOR TO CHALCEDON

1. Christian universalism depended upon, rather than negating, extant concepts of ethnicity, such as "Egyptian" (Buell, *Why this New Race,* 138).

2. Athanasius, *Life of Antony,* ed. G. J. M. Bartelink (Paris: Les Éditions du Cerf, 2011), 332.

3. Athanasius, *Life of Antony,* 202. Athanasius viewed the Church as a diverse and unified body, with heretics existing outside the Church; see David Brakke, *Athanasius and Asceticism* (Baltimore, MD: The Johns Hopkins University Press, 1995), 161. For more on how Chalcedon was an unprecedented theological schism that was largely geographical, see Farag, *What Makes a Church Sacred,* 158.

4. Athanasius, *Life of Antony,* 174. Cf. Phil. 3:20. Claudia Rapp demonstrates how the *Life,* among many early Christian texts, deploys citizenship language in order to frame Christian identity, in "Monastic Jargon and Citizenship Language in Late Antiquity," *Al-Masāq: Journal of the Medieval Mediterranean* 32, no. 1 (2020): 58.

5. "Race of humanity," ἀνθρώπινον γένος. See Athanasius, *Against the Greeks,* ed. Jacques-Paul Migne, *PG* 25 (Paris: Imprimerie Catholique, 1857), 5.

6. Athanasius, *Life of Antony*, 260.

7. ἐθνικῶν.

8. Athanasius, *Life of Antony*, 204. Cf. 2 Cor. 6:14; 1 Jn. 1:5; Rom. 1:25. Again, Christians and the "Greeks" (or pagans) are contrasted in a spiritual cleasning episode (*Life of Antony*, 318).

9. Athanasius, *Life of Antony*, 356–58.

10. *Life of Pachomius* in Bohairic, ed. L. Lefort in *S. Pachomii Vita, Bohairice Scripta*, CSCO Scriptores Coptici 89.7 (Louvain: Secrétariat du SCO, 1953), 23, ꞴⲈⲚⲠⲒⲔⲀⲂⲒ ⲦⲎⲢϤ ⲚⲦⲈⲬⲎⲘⲒ ("the entire land of Egypt"). Hereafter *Bohairic Life of Pachomius*.

11. *Bohairic Life of Pachomius*, 101–2. Cf. 1 Th. 2:7.

12. Athanasius, *Life of Antony*, 362. The *Life* goes on to highlight how Antony "was heard about in Gaul and in Spain and in Rome and in Africa while he sat hidden on a mountain" (374).

13. *Life of Pachomius* in Greek, Apostolos N. Athanassakis, *Vita Prima Graeca* (Missoula, MT: Scholars Press, 1975), 118. Hereafter *Vita Prima Graeca*.

14. *Bohairic Life of Pachomius*, 104.

15. Just as in the *Apophthegmata Patrum*, Alexandria is often represented as a context for sin and temptation; another ascetic who visited Pbow was reported to have lived a life of sin beforehand in Alexandria (*Bohairic Life of Pachomius*, 148).

16. ⲢⲈⲘⲈⲚⲎⲒ ⲈⲀⲈⲚⲐⲀⲚⲀⲈⲚⲒⲔⲞⲤ.

17. *Bohairic Life of Pachomius*, 105–6. The Greek *Life* says that Theodore was "host (οἰκιακὸν) of the Alex andrians and foreigners (ξενικῶν) who came to him" (*Vita Prima Graeca*, 134).

18. ϮⲘⲈⲦⲢⲈⲘⲚⲬⲎⲘⲒ.

19. *Bohairic Life of Pachomius*, 108. The Greek *Life* says that Pachomius "put him in a house with an elder brother who knew the Greek language, to encourage him, until he also learned and comphrended the Theban (θηβαϊκήν)" (*Vita Prima Graeca*, 134). The language is later referred to as "Egyptian" (αἰγυπτιστί) (136).

20. *Paralipomena on Saints Pachomius and Theodore*, ed. André-Jean Festugière, in *Le Corpus Athénien de Saint Pachome*, 73- 93 (Geneva: Patrick Cramer, 1982), 89.

21. ⲘⲘⲈⲦⲠⲢⲈⲘⲚⲬⲎⲘⲒ.

22. *Bohairic Life of Pachomius*, 177–78. The inclusive attitude in the *Life* betrays a vision of Egypt as a people that "absorbed and enhanced a variety of races and cultures" (Philip Rousseau, *Pachomius: The Making of a Community in Fourth-Century Egypt* [Berkeley: University of California Press, 1985], 1).

23. ⲠⲒⲠⲞⲖⲒⲦⲒⲔⲞⲤ ⲠⲒⲢⲈⲘⲚⲎⲒ ⲚⲦⲈⲚⲒⲞⲨⲈⲒⲚⲒⲚ (*Bohairic Life of Pachomius*, 205).

24. For examples of increased marginalizing language in Greek Egyptian texts in the post-Chalcedonian period, see the discussion on ethnic and racial categories in the stories on Eulogius in the *Life of Daniel of Scetis*, below.

25. Jacques van der Vliet, "Coptic as a Nubian Literary Language: Four Theses for Discussion," in *The Christian Epigraphy of Egypt and Nubia* (New York: Routledge, 2018), 272.

26. πάτριον σχῆμα.

27. Athanasius, *Apologia ad Constantinum,* ed. Jacques-Paul Migne, *PG* 25, 593–642 (Paris: Imprimerie Catholique, 1857), 632–33. Early Christian claims of universalism were influenced significantly by Roman concepts of *humanitas* ("civilization") (Buell, *Why This New Race,* 152). It is not surprising, therefore, that a schism with the Roman Empire and its dominant Church would engender new strategies of Egyptian identity. For late antique strategies of shaping ethnic identity within the Roman Empire, see Nico Roymans, *Ethnic Identity and Imperial Power: The Batavians in the Early Roman Empire* (Amsterdam: Amsterdam University Press, 2004), 253.

28. μετρίοις (*Vita Prima Graeca,* 38). The Greek *Life* also refers to Pachomius's second monastic settlement, Pbow, as a "desolate village," a descriptor that is absent in the Bohairic (80).

29. *Bohairic Life of Pachomius,* 18.

30. *Vita Prima Graeca,* 114.

31. *Bohairic Life of Pachomius,* 24.

32. Jerome, *Preface to the Pachomian Rules,* ed. Jacques-Paul Migne, *PL* 23, 65–68 (Paris: Imprimerie Catholique, 1883), 67: "et qua simplicitatem Ægyptii sermonis imitate sumus, interpretationis fides est." The assignment and resistance of stereotypes is a fundamental component of ethnic boundary maintenance in polyethnic socieites such as the Roman Empire (Barth, *Ethnic Groups and Boundaries,* 17).

33. *Vita Prima Graeca,* 162.

34. ΘΕΟΔⲰΡΟⲤ ⲠⲒⲠⲠⲞⲖⲒⲦⲒⲔⲞⲤ.

35. *Bohairic Life of Pachomius,* 108. Note that the Greek *Life* counts "Alexandrians" among the foreigners at Pbow, along with Romans and Armenians, further demonstrating the social distinctions between Alexandrians and Upper Egyptians (*Vita Prima Graeca,* 136).

36. ⲘⲈⲦⲢⲈⲘⲚ̄ⲬⲎⲘⲒ.

37. *Bohairic Life of Pachomius,* 191.

38. Ⲛ̄ⲄⲈⲚⲞⲤ ⲚⲒⲘ Ⲛ̄ⲢⲰⲘⲈ.

39. Mark Moussa, "I Have Been Reading the Holy Gospels by Shenoute of Atripe (Discourses 8, Work 1): Coptic Text, Translation, and Commentary" (PhD diss., The Catholic University of America, 2010), 52. Shenoute's identity maintenance for his monks relied upon extant categories of identity in the broader world; see Bentley Layton, *The Canons of Our Fathers: Monastic Rules of Shenoute* (Oxford: Oxford University Press, 2014), 85.

40. ⲖⲀⲞⲤ.

41. ⲤⲈⲐⲚⲞⲤ Ⲛ̄ⲀⲦⲚⲞⲨⲦⲈ; Moussa, "I Have Been Reading," 52. Shenoute frequently critiqued groups that he framed in ethnic and religious categories (Greeks, Jews, heretics, pagans). However, his foil against his enemies was always "Christian," never "Egyptian." See Michael Foat, "I Myself Have Seen: The Representation of Humanity in the Writings of Apa Shenoute of Atripe" (PhD diss., Brown University, 1996), 94. In the post-Chalcedonian period, "Egyptian" and "orthodox" become synonymous categories in religious polemic.

42. οὐκ ἔστιν ἔθνος ὑπὸ τὸν οὐρανὸν ὡς τὸ τῶν χριστιανῶν, *Apophthegmata Patrum*, 252.

43. Αἰγυπτίων πατέρων.

44. Ἑλλήνων, *Apophthegmata Patrum*, ed. John Wortley (Cambridge, UK: Cambridge University Press, 2013), 492.

45. ἔθνος.

46. πάντα τὰ ἔθνη.

47. Athanasius, *Oration against the Arians*, ed. Jacques-Paul Migne, *PG* 26, 12–524 (Paris: Imprimerie Catholique, 1857), 1, 100. Cf. Is. 49:6.

48. *Ex gentibus sumus.*

49. Theophilus of Alexandria, *On Isaiah 6:1–7*, ed. D. Germani Morin, in *Sancti Hieronymi Presbyteri: Tractatus Siue Homiliae, Anaecdota Maredsolana*, 3.3, 103–128 (Maredsoli, 1903), 116. For an argument on Theophilus's argument of this work attributed in the edition to Jerome, see Norman Russell, *Theophilus of Alexandria* (New York: Routledge, 2007), 91.

50. ⲘⲠⲄⲈⲚⲞⲤ ⲚⲚⲒⲢⲰⲘⲒ.

51. *Bohairic Life of Pachomius*, 22.

52. ⲚⲄⲈⲚⲞⲤ ⲚⲒⲘ ⲚⲢⲰⲘⲈ ⲈⲂⲞⲗ ⲌⲚⲞⲩⲁ.

53. *Life of Pachomius*, Sahidic, L. Lefort in *S. Pachomii Vitae*, CSCO Scriptores Coptici, Sahidice Scriptae 3.8 (Paris: E Typographeo Reipublicae, 1933), 114–15. Hereafter *Sahidic Life of Pachomius*. The followers of Pachomius embraced a universalizing concept of a "Christian people;" see Phillip Rousseau, "The Successors of Pachomius and the Nag Hammadi Codices: Exegetical Themes and Literary Structures," in *The World of Early Egyptian Christianity: Language, Literature, and Social Context: Essays in Honor of David W. Johnson*, ed. David W. Johnson, James E. Goehring, and Janet A. Timbie (Washington, DC: The Catholic University of America Press, 2007), 151.

54. The Greek *Life* admonishes: "Do not call him Horsiesios, but Israelite" (*Vita Prima Graeca*, 164). Cf. Jn. 1:47. This language also appears many times in the letters of Antony; see Pamela Bright, "The Church as 'The House of Truth' in the Letters of Antony of Egypt," in *Origeniana Octava: Origen and the Alexandrian Tradition*, ed. L. Perrone (Leuven: Leuven University Press, 2003), 2:981. Buell describes this type of racial/ethnic reasoning as an "aggregative" process of forming the Christian *genos* by merging existing ethnic categories together (*Why This New Race*, 140). This type of universalism is rare post-Chalcedon.

55. σάρκα γένους.

56. πνεῦμα γένους.

57. λαοῦ.

58. ἔθνος ἅγιον.

59. Cyril of Alexandria, *Commentary on John*, 10, ed. Jacques-Paul Migne, *PG* 74, 9–757 (Paris: Imprimerie Catholique, 1863), 388. Cf. 1 Pt. 2:9.

60. ⲢⲰⲘⲒ.

61. Cyril of Alexandria, *Memra 11 on the Commentary on the Gospel of Luke by Holy Cyril Archbishop of Alexandria concerning the Appearance of Our Lord*, ed.

Jean-Baptiste Chabot, CSCO Scriptores Syri 4.1 (Paris: E Typographeo Reipublicae, 1922), 28.

62. Late antique ethnic groups within the Roman Empire shaped their identity through a process of integration and assimilation into the Empire as both a political and ethnic "Other" against which to shape and assimilate specific identities; see Roymans, *Ethnic Identity and Imperial Power,* 251. For a similar argument with specific regard to Egypt, see Samuel Moawad, "The Role of the Church in Establishing Coptic Identity," *Coptica* 13 (2014): 11.

63. Gen. 12:2–3.

64. Mt. 28:19. The close affiliation of the Pachomian community and the imperial authorities continued even after the Chalcedonian schism; see James E. Goehring, *Ascetics, Society, and the Desert: Studies in Early Egyptian Monasticism* (Harrisburg, PA: Trinity Press International. 1999), 254. This situation changed in the sixth century during the tenure of Abraham of Farshut, as discussed below.

65. εἰς πᾶσαν τὴν γῆν.

66. *Vita Prima Graeca,* 2. The newfound religious unity across the Roman Empire contrasted with the early Roman sentiment of Egyptian religious practices being incompatible with Roman religion, Emma Dench, *From Barbarians to New Men: Greek, Roman, and Modern Perceptions of Peoples from the Central Apennines* (Oxford: Clarendon Press, 1995), 170. Dench also frames "Egyptians" as an ethnicity.

67. πάσῃ χώρᾳ καὶ νήσῳ.

68. The Greek *Life* has "the first of the Christian Roman Emperors" (*Vita Prima Graeca,* 6).

69. ϩⲉⲛⲡⲓⲕⲟⲥⲙⲟⲥ ⲧⲏⲣϥ ⲛ̄ⲧⲉⲧⲉϥⲙⲉⲧⲟⲩⲣⲟ.

70. *Bohairic Life of Pachomius,* 4. The reforms of Constantine gave Egyptian Christian leaders the opportunity to exercise leadership that extended beyond the region of Egypt (Rousseau, *Pachomius,* 6).

71. ⲡⲟⲩⲣⲟ ⲙ̄ⲙⲁⲓⲛⲟⲩϯ ⲕⲱⲥⲧⲁⲛⲧⲓⲛⲟⲥ.

72. *Bohairic Life of Pachomius,* 5.

73. Athanasius, *Apologia ad Constantinum,* 608.

74. Athanasius, *Apologia ad Constantinum,* 609. Athanasius's attitude toward imperial authorities does not appear "ambivalent" (Brakke, *Athanasius and Asceticism,* 203). Fourth and early-fifth-century Egyptian Christians display a consistently supportive attitude towards the emperor as the standard-bearer for Christianity, a tone that inverts following Chalcedon.

75. γένος.

76. Athanasius, *Apologia ad Constantinum,* 636.

77. Athanasius, *Versio Sahidica,* 87. This direct statement is in the Coptic version, whereas the Greek mentions the Christian identity of the emperors in a less emphatic manner: "However, he was convinced by all the monks that the emperors were Christians" (*Life of Anthony,* 342).

78. τὸν λαὸν Θεοῦ.

79. *Vita Prima Graeca,* 156. The documentary testimony corroborates the pre-Chalcedonian view of Egypt as an integral part of the Empire, without marked distinction; see Joëlle Beaucamp, "Byzantine Egypt and Imperial Law," in *Egypt in the Byzantine World, 300–700,* ed. Roger S. Bagnall (Cambridge, UK: Cambridge University Press, 2007), 285. While Egypt remained similar in economic and legislative matters after Chalcedon, there was a new view of Egypt's distinction fromt the empire from religious sources.

80. Athanasius of Alexandria, *Letter on the Nicene Decrees,* ed. Jacques-Paul Migne, *PG* 25, 411–476 (Paris: Imprimerie Catholique, 1857), 449.

81. Athanasius of Alexandria, *Letter to Marcellinus on the Interpretation of the Psalms,* ed. Jacques-Paul Migne, *PG* 27, 11–58 (Paris: Imprimerie Catholique, 1857), 33.

82. ⲚⲄⲈⲚⲞⳟ ⲚⲓⲘ ⲚⲢⲱⲘⲈ.

· 83. Shenoute, *I Have Been Reading the Holy Gospels,* ed. Johannes Leipoldt, in *Sinuthii Archimandritae Vita et Opera Omnia,* vol. III, 218–224 (Paris: E Typographeo Reipublicae, 1931), 219. Shenoute's interpretation of politics and imperial ecumenics are a fine example of what Foat calls "memory distortion," that is, the appropriation of the past that frames who people-groups are in Shenoute's world ("I Myself Have Seen," 25).

84. ἐτισήμου λαοῦ.

85. Justinian, *Against Origen,* ed. Jacques-Paul Migne, *PG* 86 916–993 (Paris: Imprimerie Catholique, 1865), 967.

86. It should also be pointed out that Athanasius himself was accused of significant persecution of the Arians; see Carlos R. Galvao-Sobrinho, *Doctrine and Power: Theological Controversy and Chrisitan Leadership in the Later Roman Empire* (Oakland: University of California Press, 2021), 117.

87. ⳟⲓⲚⲓⲔⲞⳟ.

88. *Bohairic Life of Pachomius,* 166– 67. The Greek *Life* names the emperor as Constantius (*Vita Prima Graeca,* 180). The Armenian monk, Domnius, is introduced as being "Armenian in his ethnicity" (ⲆⲞⲘⲚⲓⲞⳟ ⲈⲞⲩⲀⲢⲘⲈⲚⲓⲞⳟⲠⲈ ⳹ⲈⲚⲠⲈⳝⲄⲈⲚⲞⳟ).

89. The Greek *Life* reports that there was an Arian bishop among the imperial cadre. Furthermore, Artemios decided to pray by himself anyway which resulted in him falling asleep and waking with a bloody nose in a "distressed" state (*Vita Prima Graeca,* 182).

90. Athanasius, *Letter to Serapion concerning the Death of Arius,* ed. Jacques-Paul Migne, *PG* 25, 679–690 (Paris: Imprimerie Catholique, 1857), 685–88.

91. Athanasius, *Letter to Serapion concerning the Death of Arius,* 689.

92. προγόνων φιλόθεον.

93. Athanasius, *Apologia ad Constantinum,* 597.

94. Athanasius, *Apologia ad Constantinum,* 608.

95. Athanasius, *Apologia ad Constantinum,* 640.

96. λαῶν.

97. Cyril of Alexandria, *Letter* 17, ed. Jacques-Paul Migne, *PG* 77, 105–122 (Paris: Imprimerie Catholique, 1859), 108.

98. Cyril of Alexandria, *Letter to John of Antioch,* ed. P. E. Pusey, in *The Three Epistles of S. Cyril,* 40–53 (Oxford: James Parker and Co., 1872), 42.

99. *Apohthegmata Patrum,* 260–62.

100. *Apophthegmata Patrum,* 440–44.

101. "Egypt" is used as an allegory for returning to worldly lifestyles in the *Apophthegmata Patrum* (494). For the sake of the allegory, the text here compares a return to a sinful lifestyle to the desire on the part of some biblical Hebrews to return to Egypt, the land of slavery.

102. *Apophthegmata Patrum,* 538. Cf. Ex. 2:12.

103. Samuel Moawad, "John of Shmoun and Coptic Identity," in *Christianity and Monasticism in Middle Egypt: Al-Minya and Asyut,* ed. Gawdat Gabra and Hany N. Takla (Cairo: The American University in Cairo Press, 2015), 92.

104. Athanasius, *Life of Antony,* 336. Cf. Ex. 7:11, 22. The Coptic *Life* adds a redundant sentence, emphasizing the futility of Egyptian traditional religion: "Where are the illusions by which the Egyptians work magic?" (*Versio Sahidica,* 84).

105. Jennifer Taylor Westerfield, *Egyptian Hieroglyphs in the Late Antique Imagination* (Philadelphia: University of Pennsylvania Press, 2019), 5. See also David Frankfurter, *Christianizing Egypt: Syncretism and Local Worlds in Late Antiquity (*Princeton, NJ: Princeton University Press, 2018), 44.

106. Athanasius, *On the Incarnation,* ed. Jacques-Paul Migne, *PG* 25, 85–196 (Paris: Imprimerie Catholique, 1857), 176–77.

107. Athanasius, *Life of Antony,* 366. During his final speech, Antony directed that his body be taken "to Egypt" to prevent anyone from mummifying his body, 370. "Egypt" here likely refers to the countryside apart from Alexandria, specifically his mountain dwelling.

108. Athanasius, *On the Incarnation,* 177.

109. Theophilus of Alexandria, *Letter to Emperor Theodosius,* ed. Bruno Krusch, in *Studien zur Christlich-Mittelalterlichen,* 220–21 (Leipzig: Verlag von Veit, 1880), 220. Theophilus assumed universal doctrinal unity that could become naturalized by the solar year and Paschal celebration; see Peter Van Nuffelen, "What Happened after Eusebius? Chronicles and Narrative Identities in the Fourth Century," in Richard Lower and Morwenna Ludlow, *Rhetoric and Religious Identity in Late Antiquity* (Oxford: Oxford University Press, 2020), 176.

110. Cyril of Alexandria, *Against Julian,* ed. Jacques-Paul Migne, *PG* 76, 490–1065 (Paris: Imprimerie Catholique, 1859), 505. Cf. Ps. 24:7–8; Pro. 8:15. The late-fourth/early-fifth century was a time of unprecedented hegemony for the Egyptian Church, which also entailed an increased connection to the broader Roman world; see Zsolt Kiss, "Alexandria in the Fourth to Seventh Centuries," in *Egypt in the Byzantine World, 300–700,* ed. Roger S. Bagnall, 187–206 (Cambridge: Cambridge University Press, 2007), 193; Moawad, "Role of the Church," 24.

111. Cyril participated in a practice common to early Christians in the Roman Empire of viewing the emperor as an extension of God's rule on earth; see Susan Wessel, *Cyril of Alexandria and the Nestorian Controversy: The Making of a Saint and of a Heretic* (Oxford: Oxford University Press, 2004), 92. This view would shift for Egyptian Christians following Chalcedon.

112. *Apophthegmata Patrum,* 108. On Christian legitimization of violence encouraged by imperial religious policies, see Michael Gaddis, *There is No Crime for Those who Have Christ: Religious Violence in the Christian Roman Empire* (Berkeley: University of California Press, 2005), 70.

113. ⲚⲐⲈ ⲞⲚ Ⲛ̄ⲦⲀⲠⲈⲨⲄⲈⲚⲞⲤ̄ ⲈⲦⲦⲀⲒⲎⲨ Ⲛ̄ⲢⲢⲰⲞⲨ ⲦⲈⲚⲞⲨ Ⲛ̄ⲀⲒⲔⲒⲞⲤ̄ ⲈⲦⲀⲢⲭⲈⲒ ⲈⲀⲙ̄ ⲠⲔⲀⲈ ⲦⲎⲢϤ.

114. Shenoute of Atripe, *Let Our Eyes,* ed. Stephen Emmel, in "Shenoute of Atripe and the Christian Destruction of Temples in Egypt: Rhetoric and Reality," in *From Temple to Church: Destruction and Renewal of Local Cultic Topography in Late Antiquity,* ed. Johannes Hahn Stephen Emmel and Ulrich Gotter (Leiden: Brill, 2008), 190.

115. Shenoute, *Let Our Eyes,* 197. Shenoute's competition with wealthy landowners and acknowledgment of the emperor's divinely-instituted authority fall into the schema of Roman Christian hierarchy of power as laid out by Foat, "I Myself Have Seen," 88. Foat illustrates how the emperor was at the top of the late antique Roman hierarchy. When that authority was removed from the Egyptian vision of community following Chalcedon, the Patriarch became the principal leader for Egyptian Christians.

116. Shenoute of Atripe, *Not Because a Fox Barks,* ed. Emile Chassinat, in *Le Quartrième Livre des Entretiens et Épîtres de Shenouti: Mémoires publiés par les membres de l'Institut français d'archéologie orientale 23,* 204–216 (Cairo: Institut Français d'Archéologie Orientale du Caire, 1911), 205–6. Shenoute's defense of his own violent actions against the "wrong leaders" are undergirded by a sense of loyalty to the "right leaders" (Gaddis, *There is No Crime,* 297). Indeed, Egyptian Christians' resistance to leadership deemed to be heretical formed a significant foundation for Chalcedonian resistance.

117. While beyond the scope of this study, it should be noted that such anti-"pagan" constructions of a universally-Christian Egypt was part of the rhetorical strategy of Christian leaders and does not reflect the persistence of traditional Egyptian practice along with religious blending with Christianity among the populace (Frankfurter, *Christianizing Egypt,* 21). Frankfurter notes that such examples of religious blending form a minority of how religious life is presented in the extant documents.

118. Theological disunity later necessitated modified identity boundaries which relied principally on the limits of inclusion and exclusion from the ethnic group (Barth, *Ethnic Groups and Boundaries,* 15).

119. The constant reframing of ethnicity within polyethnic societies (or "nations") is an example of what Paul Gilroy called "the changing same" (cited in Hall, *The Fateful Triangle,* 133). Hall's analysis on the intersection of ethnicity and

nation are a helpful comparison for how the category "Egyptian" shifted when the Egyptian Church became opposed to the Roman Empire. Here are also echoes of the argument that ethnicity has, from its inception, negotiated its boundaries within the context of imperial or national tensions; see Azar Gat and Alexander Yakobson, *Nations: The Long History and Deep Roots of Political Ethnicity and Nationalism* (Cambridge, UK: Cambridge University Press, 2013), 19.

120. ξένης (*Apophthegmata Patrum*, 352). Similarly, non-Egyptian ethnic outsiders such as Libyans (Λιβυκὸς) are so labelled (378); monks from Syria (Συρίᾳ) are also thus identified (398).

121. γένος μὲν ἦν Αἰγύπτιος (Athanasius, *Life of Antony*, 130). English translation in Gregg, *Athanasius: The Life of Antony and The Letter to Marcellinus*, 30. The Sahidic version reads ογρμ̄νκημεπε καταπεγγενος, "an Egyptian according to his ethnicity" (*Versio Sahidica*, 3). Tim Vivian provides a translation that diminishes the racial and ethnic sense intended by Athanasius: "Antony was an Egyptian by birth" (Tim Vivian and Apostolos N. Athanassakis, *The Life of Antony: The Coptic Life and The Greek Life* [Kalamazoo, MI: Cistercian Publications, 2003], 57). While this translation is certainly plausible, *genos* is best understood in this context as an ethnic identity. This is because "Egyptian" is paired with *genos,* indicating the broader ethnic group to which Antony is connected, rather than simply his family geneology or the location of his birth. Gregg's use of "race" is closer to the original intent. However, understanding "Egyptian" as ethnicity is preferable in this context given the understanding of ethnicity and race explained above.

122. The sixth-century anti-Chalcedonian John of Shmoun embellishes the pro-Egyptian language far beyond that present in the pre-Chalcedonian biography of Athanasius; see Moawad, "John of Shmoun," 93.

123. μέλας αὐτῷ φαίνεται ταῖς (Athanasius, *Life of Antony,* 146). Antony responds to the devil by saying that his "heart is black." Such negative depictions of Black people were common to Egyptian Christian literature due to Greco-Roman influence; see Aaron P. Johnson, "The Blackness of Ethiopians: Classical Ethnography and Eusebius's Commentary on the Psalms," in *The Harvard Theological Review* 99, no. 2 (2006): 169–70; Brakke, *Athanasius and Asceticism,* 229.

124. ὁ μέλας.

125. ογεϭωϣ.

126. *The Life of Apa Aphou,* ed. Lincoln H. Blumell and Thomas A. Wayment, in *Christian Oxyrhynchus: Texts, Documents, and Sources,* 638–657 (Waco, TX: Baylor University Press, 2015), 646. For background on the anthropomorphite controversy surrounding Aphou and Theophilus, see Paul A. Patterson, *Visions of Christ: The Anthropomorphite Controversy of 399 CE* (Tübingen: Mohr Siebeck, 2012), 54.

127. *Versio Sahidica,* 93. The Greek *Life* says that Anthony was "like a physician" while the Coptic simply says "he was a physician" (*Life of Anthony,* 358). Vivian and Athanassakis suggest a more direct tone present in the Coptic (*The Coptic Life and the Greek Life,* 243) against the suggestion of Garitte. This reading is correct and illustrates the stronger endorsement of Antony in the Coptic than in the Greek.

128. Athanasius, *Life of Antony,* 176.

129. Stanley M. Burstein, *Graeco-Africana: Studies in the History of Greek Relations with Egypt and Nubia* (New Rochelle, NY: Aristide D. Caratzas, 1995), 5. Burstein narrates the origins of Greek exoticization of Egypt as a cultural Other whose degree of "civilization" was measured against a Hellenistic standard.

130. Athanasius, *Against the Greeks,* 48–49.

131. Athanasius, *Life of Antony,* 188. Indeed, Athanasius cautioned against the elevation of any particular ethnic group as part of his invective against Jewish people; see David Frankfurter, *Pilgrimage and Holy Space in Late Antique Egypt* (Leiden: Brill, 1998), 451. Pro-Egyptian rhetoric yet creeps into his writings and forms a foundation for a time when Egyptianness came to the fore prominently.

132. Athanasius, *Oration against the Arians,* 17. Athanasius later says that denying the full omniscience of Jesus is "not from Christians but of Greeks" (Athanasius, *Oration against the Arians* 2, 208).

133. While it is true that a complete Greek/Coptic division did not exist in ancient Egyptian Christianity, the complex ways that Hellenistic attitudes disparaged Egyptianness also must factor into an analysis of late antique Egyptian identity. See Bas ter Haar Romeny, "Ethnicity, Ethnogenesis and the Identity of the Syriac Orthodox Christians," in *Visions of Community in the Post-Roman World: The West, Byzantium and the Islamic World, 300–1100,* ed. Walter Pohl, Clemens Gantner, and Richard Payne (New York: Routledge, 2012), 203.

134. Athanasius, *Against the Greeks,* 45–48. Indeed, the differences and contradicitons between the various "pagans" bolstered Athanasius's argument about their fallibility. For the use of "Christian" as a racial/ethnic group, see Buell, *Why this New Race,* 8.

135. Cyril of Alexandria, *Against Julian,* 564. Here Cyril uses both the terms δεισιδαιμονίαν and θρησκείας with reference to religion—both Christian and Greek. What is of note is how "Greek" is an ethnic modifier for religion, highlighting the contrast between Christians and Greeks.

136. Athanasius, *Life of Antony,* 196. Athanasius makes similar distinctions between "Greeks" and Christians in *On the Incarnation,* 168.

137. Athanasius, *Life of Antony,* 320–22. This common Christian rejection of Greek identity inverted the early Roman tendency to ascribe to Hellenistic identity; see Emma Dench, *From Barbarians to New Men: Greek, Roman, and Modern Perceptions of Peoples from the Central Apennines* (Oxford: Clarendon Press, 1995), 46.

138. Athanasius, *Life of Antony,* 322. As Roymans points out, ethnic groups within the Roman Empire should be understood by how these groups framed their own identity with regard to extant contructions of these communities from the Roman center (*Ethnic Identity and Imperial Power,* 4).

139. Athanasius, *Life of Antony,* 332.

140. *Apophthegmata Patrum,* 286.

141. Greg Woolf, "Becoming Roman, Staying Greek: Culture, Identity and the Civilizing Process in the Roman East," *Proceedings of the Cambridge Philological Society* 40 (1994): 119. Woolf gives examples from classical writers such as Cicero

who presented *humanitas*—the status of a community being "civilized"—as a gift that the Romans learned from the Greeks and were now called to "give" to the rest of the "barbarians."

142. *Vita Prima Graeca*, 122–24.

143. *Apophthegmata Patrum*, 168. "Egypt" is distinguished from Scetis again, in a neutral way without criticism (224–26). Also, an "Egyptian" comes to visit an elder at Scetis (362). Scetis is said to have its own "custom" (ἔθος) of dress (454). This might refer to monastic habits to distinguish between monastic communities. However, there may also be an underlying geoethnic meaning that adds to the cultural distinctions between various regions of Egypt.

144. *Apophthegmata Patrum*, 372. "Egypt" is sometimes contrasted with the Red Sea coastal region (400); at another point, a monk comes "from Scetis to the Thebaid," i.e. Upper Egypt (372); Daniel "the Scetan" goes "to Egypt" (428). The letter about Pachomius from Bishop Ammon referred to the Pachomian monks as "Tabennesiotes from Thebes" (τῶν παρὰ Θηβαίοις καλοθμένων Ταβεννησίων); see Ammon, *Letter of Ammon*, ed. James E. Goehring (Berlin: Walter de Gruyter, 1986), 124.

145. *Apophthegmata Patrum*, 550.

146. Denise McCoskey argues that, even toward the end of Ptolemaic rule in Egypt, the categories of "Greek" and "Egyptian" were still distinct groups that were differentiated and stratified. Specifically, papyrological evidence demonstrates that "Greeks" were receiving tax breaks unavailable to those classified as "Egyptian." See "Race Before 'Whiteness': Studying Identity in Ptolemaic Egypt," *CS* 28.1–2 (2002): 29. McCoskey is correct that "Egyptian" represented the colonized in Ptolemaic Egypt while "Greek" represented the colonizer, and "Roman" is equally represented as the colonizer in Roman Egypt, especially during the anti-Chalcedonian period. However, it is not necessary to understand "Egyptian" and "Greek" as racial terms, nor is it necessary to posit that ethnicity lessens the degree to which Egyptians were marginalized under Ptolemaic and Roman rule. While "Egyptian" is best understood as an ethnic category, this does not minimize the social stratification this label carried with respect to "Greek" or "Roman."

147. Ammon, *Letter of Ammon*, 149. Goehring translates Ἑλληνιστῶν as "Greek-speaking" (176). However, the specific reference to linguistic affinity is not highlighted in the text. Bishop Ammon simply calls himself and his companions "Greeks." The social and cultural distinctions between Alexandrians and Upper Egyptians should not be minimized by reducing the distinction here to linguistic capacity only.

148. αἰγυπτιστί (*Apophthegmata Patrum* 456).

149. For example, the *Apophthegmata Patrum* celebrates the ascetic humility of the "Scetan" (300).

150. *Sahidic Life of Pachomius*, 176.

151. *Apophthegmata Patrum*, 204–6.

152. *Apophthegmata Patrum*, 612.

153. Other stories in the text include Roman emperors learning from and financially supporting the ministry of some of the Scetan ascetics, further illustrating the

positive relationship between Egyptian Christians and Roman impierial authorities in the fourth and early-fifth centuries (*Apophthegmata Patrum*, 252).

154. *Apophthegmata Patrum*, 262.

155. Theophilus, *Letter to Emperor Theodosius*, 221. In another letter regarding Paschal date celebrations, Theophilus praises the Egyptians as the originators of the solar calendar; see Theophilus of Alexandria, *Chronicon Paschale*, ed. Bruno Krusch in *Studien zur Christlich-Mittelalterlichen*, 221–226 (Leipzig: Verlag von Veit, 1880), 222.

156. Jerome, *Preface to the Pachomian Rules*, 66.

157. *History of the Monks of Egypt*, ed. André-Jean Festugière (Bruxelles: Société des Bollandistes, 1971), 6. I follow the argument of Andrew Cain that there does not currently exist a compelling argument for the text's authorship. See *The Greek Historia Monachorum in Aegytpo: Monastic Hagiography in the Late Fourth Century* (Oxford: Oxford University Press, 2016), 57. Claudia Rapp demonstrates how this text deploys Hellenistic citizenship (*politeuma*) language in order to articulate universal Christian identity ("Monastic Jargon," 56–57).

158. *Apophthegmata Patrum*, 616–18. The critique here is notable, given the common desire among Upper Egyptian peasantry to enter the social circles of urban Alexandrian elites (Rousseau, *Pachomius*, 9).

159. See the warnings of Eulogius to the Scetan monks not to delay when running errands in Alexandria, lest they be drawn into all manner of sin (*Apophthegmata Patrum*, 628).

160. Athanasius, *Life of Antony*, 316. Athanasius's own life and tenure as patriarch were characterized by persecution due to his critique of the emperor. The role of Egyptian patriarch as the persecuted prophet to the Empire was an archetype formed by Athanasius that would influence generations of his successors. See Davis, *Early Coptic Papacy*, 57.

161. *Apophthegmata Patrum*, 630–40. The ascetic superiority that is sometimes present even with respect to Alexandria may have been bolstered by the increasing authority of desert monastic leaders (Goehring, *Ascetics, Society and the Desert*, 256).

162. ⲚⲦⲔⲞⲨⲢⲘ̄ ⲦⲰⲚ ⲈⲘ̄ ⲠⲈⲔⲄⲈⲚⲞⲤ.

163. *Life of Apa Aphou*, 648. This text also contains none of the Egyptian-centered rhetoric that characterizes post-Chalcedonian Egyptian texts. It represents one of the rare examples of the Egyptian Church being divided between the patriarchate and monastic communities, in addition to international conflict with Constantinople; see Davis, *Early Coptic Papacy*, 69.

164. Athanasius of Alexandria, *History of the Arians*, ed. Jacques-Paul Migne, PG 25, 695–796 (Paris: Imprimerie Catholique, 1857), 784.

165. Athanasius, *History of the Arians*, 788.

166. A pre-Chalcedonian example is Theophilus's claim that "the whole of Egypt" (*tota paene Aegypto*) was against "Origenist" teaching and had collectively burned the writings of Origen. See Theophilus of Alexandria, *Second Synodal Letter to the Bishops of Palestine and Cyprus*, ed. Isidor Hilberg, CSEL 55, 147–155 (Leipzig: Temksy, 1912), 148.

167. *Vita Prima Graeca*, 180.

168. Monks travelling to Alexandria often used the opportunity to inquire about the state of the "holy, catholic Church" (*Bohairic Life of Pachomius,* 140).

169. Αἰγυπτιακῆς διοικήσεως.

170. Cyril of Alexandria, *Letter* 17, 105. Cyril followed Theophilus's strategy of creating a unified Egyptian Christian identity that would claim dominance over non-Christian territory in Egypt (Davis, *Early Coptic Papacy,* 74).

CHAPTER 3. AFTERMATH OF CHALCEDON

1. Johnson, "Anti-Chalcedonian Polemics in Coptic Texts, 223.

2. Papaconstantinou, "Historiography," 72.

3. Samuel Moawad identifies the Diocletianic persecutions, the Chalcedonian schism and the Arab Muslim conquest as the three most pivotal eras in forming Egyptian Christian identity ("Some Features of Coptic Identity," *ANES* 53 [2016]: 243).

4. The fact that no pro-Chalcedonian literature survives in Coptic and that the Melkites of Egypt were concentrated in a few urban centers attests to the lasting assimilation of Miaphysite and Egyptian/Coptic identity (Mikhail, *From Byzantine to Islamic Egypt,* 82).

5. W. Bright, "Timotheus," in *Dictionary of Christian Biography* (London: John Murray, 1887), 4:1031. See also H. J. Quentin, *Jean-Dominique Mansi et les grandes collections conciliaires* (Whitefish, MT: Kessinger Publishing, 1900); Aloys Grill-meier, *Christ in Christian Tradition Volume Two, Part One: From the Council of Chalcedon (451) to Gregory the Great (590–604): Reception and Contradiction the Development of the Discussion about Chalcedon from 451 to the Beginning of the Reign of Justinian* (Atlanta, GA: John Knox Press, 1996).

6. Translation from David Johnson, "Pope Timothy II Aelurus: His Life and His Importance for the Development of Christianity in Egypt," *Coptica* 1 (2002): 78.

7. For αἴλουρος as a sneaky "Weasel" see Bright, "Timotheus," 1031; for αἴλουρος referring to Timothy's physique, see Johnson, "Pope Timothy II Aelurus," 78–79; Timothy Aelurus, "Against the Definition of the Council of Chalcedon," ed. R. Y. Ebied and L. R. Wickham, in *After Chalcedon: Studies in Theology and Church History Offered to Professor Albert van Roey,* ed. and trans. C. Laga, J. A. Munitiz, and L. Van Rompay (Leuven: Peeters, 1985), 115.

8. Edward Watts, "John Rufus, Timothy Aelurus, and the Fall of the Western Roman Empire," in *Romans, Barbarians, and the Transformation of the Roman World: Cultural Interaction and the Creation of Identity in Late Antiquity,* eds. Ralph W. Mathisen and Danuta Shanzer (Burlington, VT: Ashgate, 2011), 102.

9. Edward J. Watts, *Riot in Alexandria: Tradition and Group Dynamics in Late Antique Pagan and Christian Communities* (Berkeley: University of California Press, 2010), 153.

10. Zacharias of Mytilene, *Chronicle,* in *The Chronicle of Pseudo-Zachariah Rhetor: Church and War in Late Antiquity,* ed. Geoffrey Greatrex (Liverpool: Liverpool University Press, 2011), 134.

11. *Life of Timothy Aelurus,* ed. Hugh G. Evelyn White, in *New Texts from the Monastery of Saint Macarius: The Monasteries of Wadi 'n Natrûn* (New York: Arno 1996), 1:165. Evelyn White explains how the *Life,* though influenced heavily by the *Life of Peter the Iberian* and John of Maiuma's *Plerophoria,* is a distinct Coptic composition that most likely consulted the Syriac version of the aforementioned texts (164).

12. *Vite dei monaci Phif e Longino,* ed. Tim Vivian, in *Words to Live By: Journeys in Ancient and Modern Egyptian Monasticism* (Kalamazoo, MI: Cistercian Publications, 2005), 268.

13. Zacharias of Mytilene explains how Dionysius enlisted the aid of Apa Longinus to protect Timothy (*Chronicle,* 135).

14. Zacharias of Mytilene, *Chronicle,* 136.

15. Zacharias of Mytilene, *Chronicle,* 147.

16. Zacharias of Mytilene, *Chronicle,* 151. See also John of Maiuma, *Plerophoria,* ed. F. Nau. PO 8.1 (1911): 63.

17. *Life of Timothy Aelurus,* 166.

18. *Life of Timothy Aelurus,* 166. There is confusion in the *Life* with Timothy's second banishment occurring in 475 CE at his return during the reign of Zeno.

19. *Life of Timothy Aelurus,* 184.

20. Bright, "Timotheus," 1033; Watts provides the date of July, 477 CE (*Riot in Alexandria,* 229).

21. Frend, *Rise of the Monophysite Movement,* 173.

22. Watts, *Riot in Alexandria,* 228.

23. There are also several texts attributed to Timothy preserved in Armenian. However, the Timothean corpus was almost certainly originally composed in Greek; see Joseph Lebon, "Version arménienne et version syriaque de Timothée Elure," *Handes Amsorya: Zeitschrift für armenische Philologie* 41 (1927): 718.

24. Timothy Aeulurus, "Against Chalcedon," 117.

25. Johnson, "Pope Timothy II Aelurus," 82.

26. Alberto Camplani, "A Syriac Fragment from the *Liber Historiarum* by Timothy Aelurus (*CPG* 5486), the Coptic Church History, and the Archives of the Bishopric of Alexandria," in *Christianity in Egypt: Literary Production and Intellectual Trends Studies in Honor of Tito Orlandi,* eds. Paola Buzi and Alberto Camplani (Roma: Instituta Patristicum Augustinianum, 2011), 214. Timothy has been argued to be one of the composers of the *Coptic Church History (CCH);* see Walter E. Crum, "Eusebius and Coptic Church Histories," *Society of Biblical Archeology* 24 (1902): 71–72. See also Orlandi, "The Coptic Ecclesiastical History," 6. Timothy's participation in the *CCH,* however, is unlikely; see Johnson, "A Coptic Source," 53–55.

27. Timothy Aelurus, "A Collection of Unpublished Syriac Letters."

28. Johnson, "Pope Timothy II Aelurus," 83. These letters stand in contrast to the collection of florilegia contained in *Against Chalcedon* in which Timothy's distinctive voice is more absent as he relies heavily on the doctrinal statements of previous Church fathers; see Watts, *Riot in Alexandria,* 225.

29. Grillmeier, *Christ in Christian Tradition* 2.1, 64.

30. R. V. Sellers, *The Council of Chalcedon: A Historical and Doctrinal Survey* (London: SPCK, 1953), 262; Joseph Lebon, "La christologie de Timothée Ailure, archevêque monophysite d'Alexandrie, d'aprés les sources syriaques," *RHE* 9 (1908): 685. For example, Lebon demonstrates how Timothy's understanding of Eutychian theology denied the unity of the flesh of Christ and humanity (686).

31. Timothy Aeulurus, "Against Chalcedon," 115.

32. Liberatus, *Brevarium,* ed. Edward Schwartz, ACO 2.5 (1932), 124.

33. Timothy Aelurus, *Letter to Egypt, the Thebaid, and Pentopolis,* in "A Collection of Unpublished Syriac Letters of Timothy Aelurus," 341.

34. ܪܒܘܬܐ .

35. ܟܝܢܐ ܕܝܠܢܝܐ.

36. *Histoire de Dioscore,* ed. F. Nau, *JA* 10: 25.

37. John of Maiuma, *Plerophoria,* 20. John of Maiuma later claims that the coronation of Marcian brought to the entire empire the same "darkness that had seized Egypt" (25). John interestingly associates Dioscorus' adherence to Miaphysitism with Simon of Cyrene, claiming that "Cyrene is a part of Egypt" (31).

38. Timothy Aelurus, *Letter to Egypt, the Thebaid, and Pentopolis,* in "A Collection of Unpublished Syriac Letters of Timothy Aelurus," 341.

39. Lebon, "La christologie de Timothée Ailure," 701.

40. Philippe Blaudeau, "Timothée Aelure et la direction ecclésiale de l'Empire post-chalcédonien," *REB* 54 (1996): 107.

41. Zacharias of Mytilene, *Chronicle,* 136. Timothy often equates Chalcedonian ("Diophysite") doctrine to Nestorianism; see François Nau, "Sur la christologie de Timothée Aelure," *ROC* 2nd ser. 4.14 (1909): 99. Compare to the negative portrayal of Maximus the Confessor in his Syriac *Life*; see Sebastian Brock, "An Early Syriac Life of Maximus the Confessor," *Analecta Bollandiana* 91 (1975): 299–346.

42. ܢܘܟܪܝܐ ܐܘܡܢܘܬܐ

43. Timothy Aelurus, *Letter to Egypt, the Thebaid, and Pentopolis,* in "A Collection of Unpublished Syriac Letters of Timothy Aelurus," 341. Ebied and Wickham rightfully render this phrase as "foreign religious." However, the Syriac word that would more likely be behind "religious" (i.e. a devout Christian of an unspecific rank) would more likely be ܚܣܝܐ. That Timothy takes up the theme of how to deal with converted priests later in his letter further supports the idea that he is specifically talking about traveling monks here. The populist fashion in which monks tended to be drawn to various theological camps is likely behind Timothy's caveat "even if it has escaped their notice."

44. Timothy Aelurus, *Letter to Egypt, the Thebaid, and Pentopolis,* in "A Collection of Unpublished Syriac Letters of Timothy Aelurus."

45. ܬܘܒ ܠܟܐ

46. Timothy Aelurus, *Letter to Egypt, the Thebaid, and Pentopolis,* in "A Collection of Unpublished Syriac Letters of Timothy Aelurus."

47. Frend, *Rise of the Monophysite Movement,* 227.

48. Johnson, "Pope Timothy II Aelurus," 86.

49. Timothy Aelurus, *Letter to Egypt, the Thebaid, and Pentopolis,* in "A Collection of Unpublished Syriac Letters of Timothy Aelurus," 342.

50. Timothy Aelurus, *Letter to Egypt, the Thebaid, and Pentopolis,* in "A Collection of Unpublished Syriac Letters of Timothy Aelurus," 342.

51. ܐܬܘܪܐ ܡܘܪܒܚܐ, Timothy Aelurus, "Extraits de Timothée Aelure," 208; see also p. 211.

52. Timothy Aelurus, "Extraits de Timothée Aelure," 208.

53. Timothy Aelurus, *Letter to Egypt, the Thebaid, and Pentopolis,* in "A Collection of Unpublished Syriac Letters of Timothy Aelurus," 342–43. ܒܗܪܐ appears as "faction" in the translation of Ebied and Wickham.

54. For an analysis of Egyptian resistance rhetoric utilizing postcolonial theory, see Davis, *The Early Coptic Papacy,* 85–128; Haldon, *Byzantium,* 287.

55. See Frend, *Rise of the Monophysite Movement,* 70–71.

56. Timothy Aelurus, *Letter to Egypt, the Thebaid, and Pentopolis,* in "A Collection of Unpublished Syriac Letters of Timothy Aelurus," 341 (emphasis mine).

57. Timothy Aelurus, *Letter to Egypt, the Thebaid, and Pentopolis,* in "A Collection of Unpublished Syriac Letters of Timothy Aelurus," 342 (emphasis mine).

58. Timothy Aelurus, *Letter to Egypt, the Thebaid, and Pentopolis,* in "A Collection of Unpublished Syriac Letters of Timothy Aelurus," 343 (emphasis mine).

59. Timothy Aelurus, "Against Chalcedon," 138.

60. Timothy Aelurus, "Against Chalcedon," 134.

61. ܟܬܠ.

62. ܟܣܝܐ.

63. Timothy Aelurus, *Another Letter Written by the Same to the Priest and Abbot Claudianus from Exile at Chersonesus,* in "A Collection of Unpublished Syriac Letters of Timothy Aelurus," 346.

64. Timothy Aelurus, "Against Chalcedon," 141.

65. Johnson, "A Coptic Source," 113–14. This passage appears in a parallel manuscript published by David W. Johnson, "Further Fragments of a Coptic History of the Church: Cambridge OR. 1699 R," in *Enchoria: Zeitschrift für Demotistik und Koptologie* 6 (1976): 7–17. The *CCH* depicts Egyptian Chalcedonians as the result of political sycophancy or persecution: "Those who subscribed to the *Tome* of Chalcedon destroyed this (the orthodox faith) as they were *forced* (Ϩⲙⲡⲧⲣⲉⲩⲕⲁⲧⲉⲭⲉ) to say that Christ functions in natures," 117.

66. ܪܒܝ ܟܣܝܐ ܐܘܪܒܚܐ ܡܠܒܐ ܟܣܝܢ, *Histoire de Dioscore,* 55.

67. Blaudeau, "Timothée Aelure," 125.

68. Timothy Aelurus, *Another Letter Written by the Same to the Priest and Abbot Claudianus from Exile at Chersonesus,* in "A Collection of Unpublished Syriac Letters of Timothy Aelurus," 346.

69. Timothy Aelurus, *Another Letter Written by the Same to the Priest and Abbot Claudianus from Exile at Chersonesus,* in "A Collection of Unpublished Syriac Letters of Timothy Aelurus," 344.

70. Timothy Aelurus, *The Letter Written to Alexandria from Gangra Concerning the Excommunication of Isaiah and Theophilus,* in "A Collection of Unpublished Syriac Letters of Timothy Aelurus," 341.

71. Frend, *Rise of the Monophysite Movement,* 308.

72. "In Egypt, however, the Chalcedonian cause was lost" (Frend, *Rise of the Monophysite Movement,* 154); see also Watts, *Riot in Alexandria,* 226; Davis, *The Early Coptic Papacy,* 90. The anaphoras of Timothy were included alongside Cyril, Basil and Gregory in the *Great Euchologion* of the White Monastery, attesting to the way anti-Chalcedonianism became embedded in all areas of Coptic Christianity, including liturgy; see Stephen J. Davis, *Coptic Christology in Practice: Incarnation and Divine Participation in Late Antique and Medieval Egypt* (Oxford: Oxford University Press, 2008), 104.

73. Timothy Aelurus, "A Collection of Unpublished Syriac Letters of Timothy Aelurus," 328.

74. Malešević, *Sociology of Ethnicity,* 4.

75. L. Abramowski, "Ein Text des Johannes Chrysostomus über die Auferstehung in den Belegsammlungen des Timotheus Älurus," in *After Chalcedon: Studies in Theology and Church History Offered to Profesor Albert van Roey,* eds. C. Laga, J. A. Munitiz and L. Van Rompay (Leuven: Departement Oriëntalistiek, 1985), 9.

76. Frend, *Rise of the Monophysite Movement,* x–xi.

77. ܟܢܘܫܝܐ ܕܐܓܪ̈ܬܐ, John of Maiuma, *Plerophoria,* 130.

78. ܐܠܟܣܐ.

79. Timothy Aelurus, "Extraits de Timothée Aelure," 215–216.

80. ܐܝܪܐ ; Timothy Aelurus, "Extraits de Timothée Aelure," 216.

81. Timothy Aelurus, "Extraits de Timothée Aelure," 216–217.

82. Timothy Salofaciolus, the Chalcedonian patriarch who is often called Pshoi in the *CCH* to distinguish him from Timothy Aelurus; see David Johnson, "A Coptic Source," 181.

83. ⲡⲀⲎⲘⲞⲤ ⲦⲎⲢϥ.

84. Johnson's edition has ⲦⲈⲔⲔⲖⲎⲤⲓⲀ [ⲩⲱⲡⲉ ⲈⲘⲠⲈⲤ ⲕ]ⲤⲞⲡ which he has translated "and it (the church) was again at rest (?)" ("A Coptic Source," 119; trans. 139). Orlandi's edition has ⲦⲈⲔⲔⲖⲎⲤⲓⲀ [ⲘⲠⲈ ⲈⲘ ⲠⲈⲤ] ⲔⲈⲤⲞⲡ which does not appear in his translation; see *Storia della Chiesa di Alexxandria: Testo Copto, Traduzione e Commento: Vol. II: Da Teofilo a Timoteo II* (Milano: Istituto Editoriale Cisalpino, 1967), 57. Because of the discrepancies in the editions, the apparent uncertainties of both modern translators, and the gaps that are present in both, I have chosen to include a lacuna indicating the inability of rendering a sensible translation at this point.

85. ⲚⲖⲀⲞⲤ ⲦⲎⲢⲞⲨ.

86. Johnson, "A Coptic Source," 119. Note the editor of the *CCH* and the use of the Greco-Coptic loan-word ⲚⲖⲀⲞⲤ, "peoples." Given that the "peoples" who resisted Chalcedon were not united by common political or phenotypical characteristics, it is most helpful to understand the use of "peoples" here to correspond to the modern understanding of ethnic groups.

87. Blaudeau, "Timothée Aelure," 128.

88. *Vite dei monaci Phif e Longino,* 42.

89. *Vite dei monaci Phif e Longino,* 44. For example, six of the eighteen sayings attributed to Longinus in the *Apophthegmata Patrum* appear in the *Life*; see *Life of Longinus,* ed. Tim Vivian, in *Words to Live By: Journeys in Ancient and Modern Egyptian Monasticism* (Kalamazoo, MI: Cistercian Publications, 2005), 242.

90. *Vite dei monaci Phif e Longino,* 45. Vivian argues that the sections focusing on Longinus's humility and miraculous deeds make up the earliest recension while the anti-Chalcedonian section was added by a later editor; see *Life of Longinus,* 243.

91. *Life of Longinus,* 239.

92. *Life of Longinus,* 242. Though much later, the Arabic *Synaxarium* of Alexandria places Longinus at the Enaton monastery, referring to it by its Arabic name Ez-Zedjâdj; see *Synaxarium,* ed. Réne Basset. PO 11 (1915): 764.

93. Evagrius Scholasticus, *Ecclesiastical History,* ed. J. Bidez and L. Parmentier (Amsterdam: Hakkert, 1964), 56. The account provided by Zacharias of Mytilene reports that Proterius only suffered exile in accordance with the *Life* (Zacharias of Mytilene, *Chronicle,* 64–66).

94. Davis, *The Early Coptic Papacy,* 91.

95. See also John Wortley, *The Spiritual Meadow by John Moschos* (Collegeville, MN: Cistercian Publishing, 1992).

96. John of Maiuma, *Life of Peter the Iberian,* ed. Cornelia B. Horn and Robert R. Phoenix Jr. (Atlanta, GA: SBL, 2008), 137.

97. *Vite dei monaci Phif e Longino,* 46.

98. *Vite dei monaci Phif e Longino,* 48–50.

99. Barth, *Ethnic Groups and Boundaries,* 11.

100. ΠΕϤΓΕΝΟC.

101. Vivian translates ΓΕΝΟC as "birth," thus losing the ethno-cultural sense of ΓΕΝΟC in this context (*Life of Longinus,* 249).

102. Phil. 3:20.

103. *Vite dei monaci Phif e Longino,* 50.

104. Buell, *Why This New Race,* 19. Buell here notes the interchangeability of race and ethnicity in antiquity and their incongruity with contemporary concepts of race and ethnicity. Yet, she cautions against seeing this incongruity as cause for failing to interpret ancient sociological phenomena through modern categories.

105. ΝΜΜΟΝΑΧΟC ΝϨΕΝΙΚΟC.

106. *Vite dei monaci Phif e Longino,* 60.

107. ΟΥϢΗΡΕ ϢΗΜ ΝϨΕΝΙΚΟC, *Vite Longino,* 62.

108. *Vite dei monaci Phif e Longino,* 64.

109. *Vite dei monaci Phif e Longino,* 64.

110. *Vite dei monaci Phif e Longino,* 66.

111. *Vite dei monaci Phif e Longino,* 70. Vivian renders ΚΗΜΕ ΤΗΡϤ as "the surrounding countryside" (*Life of Longinus,* 261). However, such a translation would be more fitting for the reference to "Alexandria and its region" (ΡΑΚΟΤΕ ΜΝ ΝΕCΤΟϢ) (*Vite dei monaci Phif e Longino,* 70).

112. Peter van Minnen, "The Other Cities in Later Roman Egypt," in *Egypt in the Byzantine World 300–700*, ed. Roger S. Bagnall (Cambridge: Cambridge University Press, 2007), 207.

113. Frend, *Rise of the Monophysite Movement*, 155; *Vite dei monaci*, 44; Tim Vivian, "Humility and Resistance in Late Antique Egypt: The Life of Longinus," *CCR* 20 (1999): 243.

114. *Vite dei monaci Phif e Longino*, 78.

115. *Vite dei monaci Phif e Longino*, 80.

116. *Vite dei monaci Phif e Longino*, 80. Vivian expands ⲡⲁⲩⲅⲟⲩⲥⲧⲁⲗⲓⲟⲥ as "the prefect *of Egypt*" ("Humility and Resistance," 268).

117. *Vite dei monaci Phif e Longino*, 82. This juxtaposition occurs just a few lines before the monks declare their refusal as based in their obedience to "the Almighty" (ⲡⲁⲛⲧⲱⲕⲣⲁⲧⲱⲣ). Interestingly, this stands in contrast to the emperor who is referred to as "your authority" (ⲧⲉⲕⲉⲍⲟⲩⲥⲓⲁ), insinuating a lack of recognition of Marcian as a legitimate authority over the orthodox community.

118. *Vite dei monaci Phif e Longino*, 82.

119. *Vite dei monaci Phif e Longino*, 82. Cf. Ps. 32:10.

120. *Vite dei monaci Phif e Longino*, 84. Orlandi identifies the biblical citation as Psalm 10:1–3 (85). However, Vivian notes that it is a conflated citation including elements from 10:1–3 and 11:1–2 ("Humility and Resistance," 270). Vivian's citation follows the LXX while the Coptic Psalms combine Psalms 9 and 10; see Wallis E. A. Budge, *The Earliest Known Coptic Psalter: The Text, in the Dialect of Upper Egypt, Edited from the Unique Papyrus Codex Oriental 5000 in the British Museum* (London: Kegan Paul, Trench, Trübner & Co. Ltd., 1898), 9–11. The above citation therefore, draws from Psalm 10:2 and 9:22 as it is numbered in the Coptic Psalms. The difference between the above citation and the Coptic Psalm 9:22 is of interest: ⲉⲙ ⲡⲧⲣⲉ ⲡⲁⲥⲉⲃⲏⲥ ⲁⲓⲥⲉ ⲙⲙⲟⲩ ϣⲁⲣⲉ ⲡⲏⲕⲉ ⲁⲉⲣⲟ̄ "While the wicked are puffed up, the poor burn." The word ⲟⲩⲉⲃⲓⲏⲛ is not present in the Coptic nor its equivalent in the LXX: ἐν τῷ ὑπερηφανεύεσθαι τὸν ἀσεβῆ, ἐμπυρίζεται ὁ πτωχός. The addition of ⲟⲩⲉⲃⲓⲏⲛ by the encomiast of the *Life*, amplifying the already present ⲟⲩⲑⲏⲕⲉ, can only serve to emphasize the meek position of the monks of the Enaton in comparison to the Byzantine soldiers. This edition emphasizes the ongoing contrast of the meek Egyptian orthodox with the impious Byzantine Chalcedonians prevalent in the *Life*.

121. *Vite dei monaci Phif e Longino*, 86.

122. ⲁⲡⲟⲧⲁⲥⲥⲉ, the encomiast uses the same word often used to describe the monastic renunciation of worldly possessions characteristic of the ascetic life, thus linking anti-Chalcedonian confession with ascetic piety.

123. *Vite dei monaci Phif e Longino*, 86–88.

124. *Synaxarium*, 766–67.

125. *Vite dei monaci Phif e Longino*, 88. Psalm 11:6 (Coptic Psalm 10:6), again, a variant reading of the Coptic Psalm 10: ϥⲛⲁϩⲱⲟⲩ ⲉⲍⲛ ⲛ̄ⲣⲉϥⲣⲛⲟⲃⲉ ⲛ̄ⲟⲩⲕⲱϩⲧ̄ ⲙⲛ̄ ⲟⲩⲡⲛⲁⲑⲥⲁⲧⲏⲩ ⲡⲉⲧⲙⲉⲣⲓⲥ ⲙ̄ⲡⲉⲩϫⲱ. Perhaps the "scorching wind" is removed in the above citation and emphasis is placed upon "fire and sulfur" because of the nature of the assassination of Acacius.

126. *Vite dei monaci Phife Longino,* 88.

127. *Vite dei monaci Phife Longino,* 90.

128. *Vite dei monaci Phife Longino,* 88.

129. *Vite dei monaci Phife Longino,* 90.

130. *Vite dei monaci Phife Longino,* 90.

131. Vivian, "Humility and Resistance," 281n119. For the presence of Chalcedo-nians/Melkites in predominately urban areas, see Mikhail, *From Byzantine to Islamic Egypt,* 82.

132. The fifth-century *Life of Zenobius* offers no critique against the Council of Chalcedon or the *Tome* of Leo but, however, takes serious issue with the Nestorian movement that has maintained popularity in the region of Akhmîm in the late fifth century. See, David W. Johnson, "The Dossier of Aba Zenobius," in *Orientalia* 58 (1989), 193–212; Walter Till, "Koptishe Heiligen- Und Martyrerlegenden: Texte, Übersetzungen und Indices Herausgegeben und Bearbeitet," in *OCA* 102 (Roma: Pont. Institutum Orientalium Studiorum, 1935), 126–33. The silence on Chalcedo-nianism in Upper Egypt in contrast to the frequent critique of Nestorianism found in the *Life* offers a more variegated picture of the concerns of orthodox Egyptian Christians during the late fifth century.

133. Johnson, "Anti-Chalcedonian Polemics," 219.

134. Watts, *Riot in Alexandria,* 136.

135. ⲘⲠⲉⲓϩⲗ̅ⲗⲟ Ⲛⲉⲕⲩⲡⲧⲓⲟⲥ.

136. Pseudo-Dioscorus, *Panegyric on Macarius of Tkôw,* ed. David W. Johnson, CSCO 416 (Louvain: Secrétariat du Corpus SCO, 1980), 16. Morgan 609 does not have Ⲛⲉⲕⲩⲡⲧⲓⲟⲥ. The reference to Macarius as the "Egyptian elder" is quite frequent throughout the *Panegyric.* While the Sahidic typically has this as Ⲡⲉⲓϩⲗ̅ⲗⲟ Ⲛⲉⲕⲩⲡⲧⲓⲟⲥ, the Boharic, as in the case above, often has ⲠⲀⲓϨⲉⲗⲗⲟ ⲚⲢⲉⲘⲚⲬⲎⲘⲓ; see *Panégyrique de Macaire de Tkoou,* ed. Émile Amélineau, in *Monuments pour servir à l'histoire de l'Égypte chrétienne aux 4. et 5. Siècles* (Paris, Leroux, 1895), 100.

137. Stephen Emmel, "Immer erst das Kleingedruckte lesen: 'Die Pointe verste-hen' in dem koptischen Panegyrikos auf Makarios von Tkōou," in *Ägypten- Mün-ster. kulturwissenschaftliche Studien zu Ägypten, dem Vorderen Orient und ver-wandten Gebieten,* eds. Erhart Graefe, Anke I. Blöbaum, Jochem Kahl and Simon D. Schweitzer (Wiesbaden: Harrassowitz Verlag, 2003), 96.

138. Emmel, "Immer erst das Kleingedruckte lesen," 92.

139. Pseudo-Dioscorus, *Panegyric on Macarius of Tkôw,* 8.

140. Pseudo-Dioscorus, *Panegyric on Macarius of Tkôw,* 12. This is also the date suggested by Michael Gaddis (*There is No Crime,* 188n144).

141. Nau has argued for the dependence of the *Panegyric* on the biographical *History of Dioscorus,* of which Theopistus may have been the author (*Histoire de Dioscore,* 16).

142. ⲨⲉⲚⲚϦ̅ⲚⲟⲓⲀⲚ ⲉⲨϢⲀⲨⲉ Ⲙ̅ⲘⲚ̅ⲦⲟⲨⲀ̄ⲦⲚ̄ⲓ̄Ⲛ (Pseudo-Dioscorus, *Panegyric on Macarius of Tkôw,* 3). The Bohairic manuscript from which Amélineau made his edition differs significantly from the two Sahidic manuscripts found in Johnson. For example, for the above citation, Amélineau has ⲉϤⲉⲘⲓ ⲚⲤⲀⲨⲓ ⲀⲚ ϨⲉⲚ ⳁⲀⲤⲠⲓ

ⲛϨⲉⲗⲗⲏⲛⲓⲕⲏ (Pseudo-Dioscorus, *Panégyrique de Macaire de Tkoou,* 93). The Bohairic manuscript Amélineau edited was incomplete; see Pseudo-Dioscorus, *Panegyrikos auf Makarios von Tkōōu,* ed. Samuel Moawad (Wiesbaden: Reichert Verlag, 2010), 47. Moawad's edition, translation and commentary is of the Arabic translation of the *Panegyric,* to which he assigns a *terminus a quo* of the thirteenth century (53).

143. ⲁⲗⲗⲁ ⲙⲡⲉϥϭⲱ ⲛ̄ⲟⲩⲉϣⲉⲧ̄ ⲛⲙ̄ⲙⲁⲛ ⲉⲡⲡⲟⲗⲩⲙⲟⲥ ⲛ̄ⲕⲁⲗⲭⲏⲁⲱⲛ (Pseudo-Dioscorus, *Macarius of Tkôw,* 3). Moawad points out in his commentary that Dioscorus's ability to speak Greek is what affords him status as "der vorne das Heer" (*Panegyrikos auf Makarios von Tkōōu,* 158).

144. Pseudo-Dioscorus, *Panegyric on Macarius of Tkôw,* 4.

145. ⲛ̄ϣⲁⲭⲉ ⲛⲉⲕⲩⲡⲧⲓⲟⲥ. The Bohairic has ⲉϥⲉⲣϨⲉⲣⲙⲏⲛⲉⲩⲉⲓⲏ ⲛⲏⲓ ⲭⲉ ⲉϥⲉⲙⲓ ⲉⲧⲗⲁⲗⲓ ⲥⲛⲟⲩϯ "he translated because he knew the two languages" (Pseudo-Dioscorus, *Macaire de Tkoou,* 95–96).

146. Pseudo-Dioscorus, *Panegyric on Macarius of Tkôw,* 4–7.

147. Pseudo-Dioscorus, *Panegyric on Macarius of Tkôw,* 41.

148. For example: "Egypt is—unlike Syria—geographically enclosed by natural boundaries, has constant scenic and climatic characteristics through the centuries, and consequently is largely homogenous, imprinting a certain manner of the country's population" (C. D. G. Müller, *Die Kirche in ihrer Geschicte: Geschicte der orientalischen Nationalkirchen* [Göttingen: Vandenhoeck & Ruprecht, 1981], 320).

149. During these early centuries of Byzantine ascendance, Greek enjoyed a prized position above other "barbarian" languages across the Empire; see Guglielmo Cavallo, *The Byzantines* (Chicago: The University of Chicago Press, 1997), 4. Late antique Hellenistic philosophers such as Porphyry expressed specific contempt for the Egyptian language which they viewed as theologically inferior in religious matters; see Ilinca Tanaseanu-Döbler, *Theurgy in Late Antiquity: The Invention of a Ritual Tradition* (Beiträge zur Europäischen Religionsgeschichte (BERG) (Göttingen: Vandenhoeck & Ruprecht, 2013), 1:78–79.

150. Carmen Fought, *Language and Ethnicity* (Cambridge, UK: Cambridge University Press, 2006), 20.

151. ⲛ̄ⲛⲉⲉⲡⲓ̈ⲥⲕⲟⲡⲟⲥ ⲧⲏⲣⲟⲩⲙ̄ⲡ̄ⲕⲁⲧⲁⲭⲱⲣⲁ, Pseudo-Dioscorus, *Panegyric on Macarius of Tkôw,* 11.

152. Pseudo-Dioscorus, *Panegyric on Macarius of Tkôw,* 20. Identifying Tkôw as "humble" or "small" further amplifies the contrast between the humility of both Macarius and the Egyptian people and the insolence of Byzantine Chalcedonians.

153. Eriksen, *Ethnicity and Nationalism,* 175.

154. ⲡⲉⲭⲉⲉⲡ̄ⲛⲉⲉⲃ ⲁⲉ ⲛⲁϥ ⲙ̄ⲙⲉⲧⲉⲕⲩⲡⲧⲓⲟⲥ.

155. ⲭⲉⲛⲉⲟⲩⲉⲕⲩⲡⲧⲓⲟⲥ Ϩⲱⲱϥⲡⲉ (Pseudo-Dioscorus, *Panegyric on Macarius of Tkôw,* 15). The above citation is from the Morgan 609 manuscript. The Cairo Hamouli B has: ⲡⲉⲭⲁϥ ⲛⲁϥ ⲛⲉⲕⲩⲡⲧⲓⲟⲥ. The identification of the sailor as Egyptian is wholly absent from the edition of Amélineau; see Pseudo-Dioscorus, *Macaire de Tkoou,* 101.

156. ⲙ̄ⲡⲉⲓ̈ Ϩⲗ̄ⲗⲟ ⲛⲉⲕⲩⲡⲧⲓⲟⲥ.

157. Pseudo-Dioscorus, *Panegyric on Macarius of Tkôw*, 16. Morgan 609 does not have ⲛⲉⲕⲩⲡⲧⲓ̈ⲟⲥ. The reference to Macarius as the "Egyptian elder" is quite frequent throughout the *Panegyric*. While the Sahidic typically has this as ⲡⲉⲓ̈Ϩⲗⲗⲟ ⲛⲉⲕⲩⲡⲧⲓ̈ⲟⲥ, the Boharic, as in the case above, often has ⲡⲁⲓ϶ⲉⲗⲗⲟ ⲛⲣⲉⲙⲛⲭⲏⲙⲓ (Pseudo-Dioscorus, *Macaire de Tkoou*, 100).

158. The word "language" does not appear here; the Coptic prefix ⲙⲛⲧ/ⲙⲉⲧ indicates an abstraction. Therefore, the Coptic here literally says: "the sailor spoke to him in Egyptianness for he himself was an Egyptian."

159. Philip Riley, *Language, Culture and Identity: An Ethnolinguistic Perspective* (London: Continuum, 2007), 70. Language and geography were ways that hierarchy and marginalization occurred in late antique Roman Egypt; just as Coptic was often subordinated to Greek (as were many other non-imperial languages), so too was "Egypt" often disparaged in favor of Alexandria. See John M. G. Barclay, "'Ἰουδαῖος: Ethnicity and Translation," in *Ethnicity, Race, Religion: Identities and Ideologies in Early Jewish and Christian Texts, and in Modern Biblical Interpretation*, ed. David G. Horrell and Katherine M. Hockey (London: Bloomsbury Publishing, 2018), 46.

160. Macarius' deacon, Pinution, claims: "The primary quality of my father is this: nothing is ever hidden from him" (Pseudo-Dioscorus, *Panegyric on Macarius of Tkôw*, 22).

161. ⲛⲉⲕⲩⲡⲧⲓ̈ⲟⲥ ⲧⲏⲣⲟⲩ Ϩⲛ̄ⲣⲉϥϫⲓ̈ϭⲟⲗⲛⲉ Ϩⲛ̄ⲣⲉϥϭⲱⲣⲕ̄ ⲛ̄ⲛⲟⲩⲅⲛⲉ (Pseudo-Dioscorus, *Panegyric on Macarius of Tkôw*, 17). Cairo Hamouli B has only Ϩⲛ̄ⲣⲉϥϫⲓ̈ϭⲟⲗⲛⲉ, without Ϩⲛ̄ⲣⲉϥϭⲱⲣⲕ̄ ⲛ̄ⲛⲟⲩⲅⲛⲉ while the Bohairic has only ⲣⲉϥϫⲉ ⲙⲉⲑⲛⲟⲩⲅ: *Macaire de Tkoou*, 103. Perhaps this expression is an adaptation of Titus 1:12. Moawad translates from the Arabic: "Alle Kopten sind Lügner" (110).

162. Pseudo-Dioscorus, *Panegyric on Macarius of Tkôw*, 18.

163. See Abdul Jan Mohamed and David Lloyd, "Introduction: Toward a Theory of Minority Discourse," *Cultural Critique* 6 (1987): 5–12.

164. Pseudo-Dioscorus, *Panegyric on Macarius of Tkôw*, 12. Johnson argues against the presence of "national pride." He further argues against Coptic authorship of the *Panegyric* in light of the writer's disassociation with the "barbaric south" of Egypt (Pseudo-Dioscorus, *Panegyric on Macarius of Tkôw*, 60). This argument, however, is problematic ,as it depends upon the antequated view that the Coptic language ought to be associated with Upper Egypt and Greek with Lower Egypt.

165. Gay L. Byron, *Symbolic Blackness and Ethnic Difference in Early Christian Literature* (New York: Routledge, 2002), 120.

166. ⲉⲕⲉⲡⲓ̈ⲥⲧⲓⲥ ⲛ̄ϣⲙⲙⲟ.

167. ⲛ̄ⲧⲩⲫⲩⲥⲓⲧⲏⲥ (Pseudo-Dioscorus, *Panegyric on Macarius of Tkôw*, 47). The pejorative term used by the anti-Chalcedonian party to refer to the adherents of Chalcedon. While the adherents of Chalcedon did indeed believe in two natures, this name was not used by this community, but in a polemic fashion by their opponents. From the perspective of the *Panegyric*, the Chalcedonian faith created a God-head of four persons: "You have made the Trinity a quaternity by dividing his body into four pieces" (ⲁⲕⲉⲣⲧⲉⲧⲣⲓⲁⲥ ⲛ̄ⲧⲉⲧⲣⲁⲥ ⲉⲩⲉⲉⲣⲡⲉⲕⲥⲱⲙⲁ ⲛ̄ϥ̄ⲧⲟⲟⲩ ⲛ̄ⲕⲟⲙ̄ⲙ̄ⲁ) (48).

168. *Plerophoria,* 104. See also B. Flusin, "L'Hagiographie palestinienne et la reception du concile de chalcédoine," in *LEIMWN: Studies Presented to Lennart Rydén on His Sixty-Fifth Birthday,* ed. J. O. Rosenqvist (Uppsala, 1996), 25–47.

169. Jerusalem was a contentious location because of its spiritual significance for global Christians. Therefore, Juvenal's alliance with Chalcedon was especially berated in Miaphysite literature (Farag, *What Makes a Church Sacred,* 166).

170. ⲡⲗⲁⲟⲥ ⲇⲉ ⲧⲏⲣϥ (Pseudo-Dioscorus, *Panegyric on Macarius of Tkôw,* 49). Cairo Hamouli B has "the entire city" (ⲧⲡⲟⲗⲓⲥ ⲇⲉ ⲧⲏⲣⲥ).

171. ⲭⲉⲁⲅⲓⲟⲥ ⲑⲥ: ⲉⲧⲉⲡⲁⲓⲡⲉ ⲭⲉⲕⲟⲩⲁⲁⲃ ⲡⲛⲟⲩⲧⲉ· ⲁⲅⲓⲟⲥ ⲉⲓⲥⲭⲩⲣⲟⲥ· ⲉⲧⲉⲡⲁⲓⲡⲉ ⲭⲉⲕⲟⲩⲁⲁⲃ ⲡⲁⲧⲙⲟⲩ ⲟ ⲥⲧⲁⲩⲣⲟⲑⲉⲓⲥ ⲇⲓⲏⲙⲁⲥ ⲉⲗⲉⲏⲥⲟⲛ ⲏⲙⲁⲥ· ⲉⲧⲉⲡⲁⲓⲡⲉ ⲭⲉⲡⲉⲧⲧⲁⲩⲥⲧⲟⲩ ⲙⲙⲟϥ ϩⲁⲣⲟⲛ ⲛⲁ ⲛⲁⲛ (Pseudo-Dioscorus, *Panegyric on Macarius of Tkôw,* 50). The Panegyric decision to include the Coptic translation of the Trisagion further amplifies the focus of the *Panegyric* on the significance of the Coptic language as it is the primary language of its hero. The wording is almost identical in the Bohairic, likely a result of the significance of this declaration of Miaphysite identity across dialectical boundaries (*Macaire de Tkoou,* 125). The inclusion of the Miaphysite Trisagion, usually attributed to Peter the Fuller in 470 CE, is further evidence negating Dioscoran authorship of the *Panegyric* (Pseudo-Dioscorus, *Panegyric on Macarius of Tkôw,* 10).

172. Pseudo-Dioscorus, *Panegyric on Macarius of Tkôw,* 51. Morgan 609 has "the transgressing emperor" (ⲙⲡⲛⲕⲉⲉⲣⲣⲟ ⲙⲡⲁⲣⲁⲃⲁⲧⲏⲥ).

173. ⲛⲛⲉⲕⲭⲉⲡⲉⲑⲟⲟⲩ ⲉⲡⲁⲣⲭⲱⲛ ⲙⲡⲉⲕⲗⲁⲟⲥ (Pseudo-Dioscorus, *Panegyric on Macarius of Tkôw,* 58). The panegyrist is closely following the vocabulary found in Exodus 22:28, from which Acts 23:5 quotes: see *Der Pentateuch Koptisch,* ed. Paul de Lagarde (Leipzig: B. G. Teubner, 1867), 181.

174. ⲁⲡⲁ ϣⲉⲛⲟⲩⲧⲉ ⲡⲉⲕⲩⲡϯⲟⲥ· ⲡⲉⲧⲏⲡ ⲉⲡⲧⲟϣ ⲙⲡⲃⲁⲣⲃⲁⲣⲓⲕⲟⲛ ⲛⲧⲉⲕⲏⲙⲉ (Pseudo-Dioscorus, *Panegyric on Macarius of Tkôw,* 60). It is interesting that the *Panegyric* uses ⲕⲏⲙⲉ for the first time here in contrast to the frequent use of ⲉⲕⲩⲡϯⲟⲥ. While ⲕⲏⲙⲉ is used here to designate the land of Egypt, ⲉⲕⲩⲡϯⲟⲥ is most often used in this text to refer to an Egyptian's ethnic identity. ⲕⲏⲙⲉ is used again with the connotation "barbarian": "he (Cyril) caused him (Nestorius) to be exiled to Egypt's barbaric south" (ϣⲁⲣⲏⲥ ⲙⲡⲃⲁⲣⲃⲁⲣⲓⲕⲟⲛ ⲛⲧⲉⲕⲏⲙⲉ) (107). This indicates that ⲕⲏⲙⲉ likely refers to Southern Egypt or the majority of Egyptian territory outside of Alexandria.

175. Karim Mata, "Of Barbarians and Boundaries: The Making and Remaking of Transcultural Discourse," in *Romans and Barbarians Beyond the Frontiers: Archaeology, Ideology and Identities in the North,* ed. Sergio González Sánchez and Alexandra Guglielmi (Philadelphia, PA: Oxbow, 2017), 22.

176. Pseudo-Dioscorus, *Panegyric on Macarius of Tkôw,* 63.

177. Pseudo-Dioscorus, *Panegyric on Macarius of Tkôw,* 64.

178. Pseudo-Dioscorus, *Panegyric on Macarius of Tkôw,* 71. Morgan 609 claims that the soldiers came to a monastery in Lycia while Cairo Hamouli B claims that "they came to the city of Alexandria (ⲣⲁⲕⲟⲧⲉ) by the command of the lawless emperor. They came to the monasteries which are in the ninth district

(ⲉⲧⲥⲙ̄ ⲛ̄ⲋⲉⲛⲁⲧⲟⲛ)." David Johnson notes that Hamouli B conforms more closely to the Coptic tradition of Longinus's tenure as *hegoumenos* of the monastery at Enaton while the association of Longinus with Lycia in Morgan 609 most likely arises from Lycia being Longinus' birthplace (Pseudo-Dioscorus, *Panegyric on Macarius of Tkôw*, 54n92). This is highly likely and the relative distance from Jerusalem to Lycia, as compared to Alexandria, makes a visit from Juvenal more probable to have occurred in Alexandria.

179. Pseudo-Dioscorus, *Panegyric on Macarius of Tkôw*, 72. On the relationship between the Alexandrian patriarchate and the monastic communities of Egypt see Brakke, *Athanasius and Asceticism*, 83–110.

180. ⲛⲃⲁⲣⲃⲁⲣⲟⲥ ⲉⲧⲟⲩⲙⲟⲩⲧⲉ ⲉⲣⲟⲟⲩ ⲭⲉⲁⲣⲁⲃⲟⲥ (Pseudo-Dioscorus, *Panegyric on Macarius of Tkôw*, 78). The *Apophthegmata Patrum* also uses the term "barbarian" in reference to Persian conquerors of Jerusalem (622).

181. ⲛ̄ϣⲏⲣⲉ ⲛⲟⲣⲑⲟⲇⲟⲝⲟⲥ (Pseudo-Dioscorus, *Panegyric on Macarius of Tkôw*, 90). The second part of this exclamation is only present in Morgan 609. The sense here could be ethnic as well as religious; the wording is literally "the orthodox children."

182. Papconstantinou, "Historiography," 72.

183. Pseudo-Dioscorus, *Panegyric on Macarius of Tkôw*, 94. The pejorative use of "Manichaean" in theological controversy is a common way to insult an opponent and should not be taken literally. See also Johnson's comment at 73n133.

184. The suggestion that Dioscorus represents the beginning of a movement of Egyptian independence from Byzantium does not accurately express the tone of the *Panegyric* (Pseudo-Dioscorus, *Panegyrikos auf Makarios von Tkôou*, 38).

185. It is helpful to compare studies analyzing the way that Jewish Romans struggled to assert their identity within the larger imperial network. In areas where ethnic and/or religious minorities experience dissonance with the empire, identity will be asserted through expressions of tension. This comparison is also useful in that Jewish Romans, like Egyptian Miaphysites, represent an alternative community within the Roman Empire that is simultaneously ethnic and religious; see Anna Collar, *Religious Networks in the Roman Empire: The Spread of New Ideas* (Cambridge, UK: Cambridge University Press, 2013), 149. The difference, however, is that the Egyptian Miaphysites did not engage in widescale acts of political rebellion.

186. ⲟⲩⲋⲉⲑⲛⲟⲥ ⲛⲁⲧⲥⲟⲟⲩⲛ (Pseudo-Dioscorus, *Panegyric on Macarius of Tkôw*, 113; Genesis 20:4). The wording found in the Bohairic Gen. 20:4 is quite different: "My Lord, will you destroy an unknowing and just people?" ⲡⲁϭⲟⲓⲥ ⲟⲩⲙ̄ϣⲗⲟⲗ ⲛⲁⲧⲉⲙⲓ ⲟⲩⲟϩ ⲛⲉⲙⲏⲓ ⲭⲛⲁⲧⲁⲕⲟϥ: see *Der Pentateuch Koptisch*, 40–41. This wording more closely follows the LXX: "Lord, will you destroy an unknowing and righteous nation?" Κύριε, ἔθνος ἀγνοοῦν καὶ δίκαιον ἀπολεῖς. This also varies from the Hebrew: "My Lord, will you destroy a just nation?" אדני הגוי גם צדיק תהרג. While the biblical account of Abimelek reports the king of Geras understanding his kingdom as "just," Sabinus is depicted less righteously as "ignorant." While "ignorant" can have a meaning approximating "innocent" as in the LXX and Bohairic OT, the

absence of the quality of "just" in the *Panegyric* is likely an intentional omission by the panegyrist as a critique of Sabinus.

187. ⲡⲉⲓⲥ̅ⲗ̅ⲗⲟ ⲛⲉⲕⲩⲡⲧⲓⲟⲥ (Pseudo-Dioscorus, *Panegyric on Macarius of Tkôw*, 97); again, notice how the text refers to Dioscorus, a Greek-speaker, as Egyptian in the same way as it does Macarius, who only speaks Coptic. This underscores the reality that while the Egyptian language is a marker of celebrating Egyptian ethnicity, Egyptian identity is celebrated in a way that includes Greek-speakers.

188. Pseudo-Dioscorus, *Panegyric on Macarius of Tkôw*, 98–99.

189. ⲡⲃⲉⲗⲉⲧⲁⲣ̄ⲧⲟⲥ (Pseudo-Dioscorus, *Panegyric on Macarius of Tkôw*, 120). Morgan 609 has ⲡⲃⲉⲣⲉⲧⲁⲣⲓⲟⲥ (119).

190. More often spelled Salophaciolus.

191. Pseudo-Dioscorus, *Panegyric on Macarius of Tkôw*, 121. This phrase is absent from Cairo Hamouli B.

192. Pseudo-Dioscorus, *Panegyrikos auf Makarios von Tkôôu*, 4; this demonstrates the potential for a political movement of Egyptian independence if that had been the desire of the Egyptian church.

193. Pseudo-Dioscorus, *Panegyric on Macarius of Tkôw*, 122.

194. *Plerophoria*, 19.

195. *Synaxarium*, ed. Jacques Forget (Louvain: Secrétariat du corpus SCO Scriptores Arabici 18 (text & Latin translation) (Rome: Excudebat Karolus de Luigi, 1921), 9.

196. Barth, *Ethnic Groups and Boundaries*, 14.

197. Pseudo-Dioscorus, *Panegyric on Macarius of Tkôw*, 123. The *Synaxarium* also reports Macarius' death occurring after returning with Dioscorus; however, it claims Macarius accompanied Dioscorus to Chalcedon (Forget, 10).

198. ⲡⲁⲩⲙⲟⲥ ⲛⲉⲛⲣⲉⲙⲣⲁⲕⲟⲧⲉ.

199. ⲡⲉⲓ̄ⲉⲕⲩⲡⲧⲓⲟⲥ ⲛⲁⲕⲁⲑⲁⲣⲧⲟⲥ.

200. Pseudo-Dioscorus, *Panegyric on Macarius of Tkôw*, 124.

201. This event is clearly fictitious, as Timothy Salofaciolus became Patriarch of Alexandria after the exile of Timothy Aelurus.

202. This indicates the degree to which the theological controversy also included cultural dynamics (Pseudo-Dioscorus, *Panegyrikos auf Makarios von Tkôôu*, 6).

203. ⲡⲉⲓⲥ̄ⲗ̅ⲗⲟ ⲛⲉⲕⲩⲡⲧⲓⲟⲥ (Pseudo-Dioscorus, *Panegyric on Macarius of Tkôw*, 125).

204. Pseudo-Dioscorus, *Panegyric on Macarius of Tkôw*, 127.

205. ⲛⲉⲕⲩⲡⲧⲓⲟⲥ ⲧⲏⲣⲟⲩ.

206. Pseudo-Dioscorus, *Panegyric on Macarius of Tkôw*, 128. Cairo Hamouli B has: "For truly Macarius has become more blessed than all Egyptians of this time. Macarius died a single time. But you, my lord father, have died many times." In the context of the narrative, the panegyrist is addressing Antony the Great. Cairo Hamouli B adds material not present in Morgan 609 which indicates the purpose of this statement: the victory of Macarius is on the shoulders of the greater sufferings endured by Antony, the father of all Egyptian monastic figures.

1. Menze, *Justinian*, 276.

2. Bagnall, *Egypt in the Byzantine World*, 13; Brakke, *Athanasius and Ascetisism*, 10.

3. Mikhail, *From Byzantine to Islamic Egypt*, 91.

4. Barth, "Boundaries and Connections," 70.

5. ⲈⲚⲎⲤ. The only other text attributed to the same Stephen is a panegyric on the martyr Elijah. Isaiah 30:4 refers to the city as Τάνει. The late antique name, Heracleopolis Magna, refers to its status as the capital of the *nome* Heracleopolis, just south of the Fayyum Oasis.

6. Stephen of Hnēs, *Panegyric on Apollo*, ed. K. H. Kuhn, CSCO 394–395 (Louvain: Secrétariat du Corpus SCO, 1978), x.

7. E. A. E. Reymond and J. W. B. Barnes, *Four Martyrdoms from the Pierpont Morgan Coptic Codices* (Oxford: Clarendon Press, 1973), 18.

8. Stephen of Hnēs, *Panegyric on Apollo*, xi. The frequent occurrence of relatively complex Greek-like constructions gives the *Panegyric* a rather awkward flow in Coptic, as opposed to Orlandi's praise of Stephen's work as being "written in very elegant Coptic," (*Vite di Monaci Copti* [Roma: Città Nuova Editrice, 1984], 186).

9. Stephen of Hnēs, *Panegyric on Apollo*, xi-xii.

10. Wipszycka, "Le nationalisme," 38.

11. Michel Bert and James Costa describe how languages can co-exist within a regional or ethnic community in a common sense of belonging; see "What Counts as a Linguistic Border, for Whom and What Implications? Exploring Occitan and Francoprovençal in Rhône-Aples, France," in *Language, Borders and Identity*, ed. Dominic Watt and Carmen Llamas (Edinburgh: Edinburgh University Press, 2014), 187. Greek and Egyptian languages had co-existed, overlapped and influenced one another since Ptolemaic times to the extent that the ethnic and linguistic background of various texts remains unclear; see Trevor Evans, "Complaints of the Natives in a Greek Dress: The Zenon Archive and the Problem of Egyptian Interference," in *Multilingualism in the Graeco-Roman Worlds*, ed. Alex Mullen and Patrick James (Cambridge, UK: Cambridge University Press, 2012), 116.

12. Stephen of Hnēs, *Panegyric on Apollo*, xii. Orlandi also concurs that the *Panegyric* must have been composed before the Arab Conquest (*Vite di Monaci Copti*, 186). The manuscript from which Kuhn made his edition is dated to 822–23 CE (*Panegyric on Apollo*, xii).

13. Stephen of Hnēs, *Panegyric on Apollo*, 34.

14. Stephen of Hnēs, *Panegyric on Apollo*, 1–2.

15. ⲠⲖⲀⲞⲤ ⲘⲘⲀⲒⲦⲈⲬⲤ̄; Stephen of Hnēs, *Panegyric on Apollo*, 2.

16. Buell, *Why This New Race*, 2. In another anti-Chalcedonian Coptic text composed in the sixth century, Jesus is referred to as the "pride of our race" (ⲠϢⲞⲨϢⲞⲨ ⲘⲠⲈⲚⲅⲈⲚⲞⲤ). See Constantine of Siout, *Encomia in Athanasium duo*, ed. Tito Orlandi, CSCO 349–350 (Louvain: Secrétariat du Corpus SCO, 1974), 37.

17. Stephen of Hnēs, *Panegyric on Apollo*, 22. This section can also be found in the additional manuscripts edited by Karl H. Kuhn, "Two Further Fragments of a Panegyric on Apollo," *Le Muséon* 95 (1982): 264–65.

18. Stephen of Hnēs, *Panegyric on Apollo*, 20.

19. ⲡⲉϥⲕⲁϩ ⲙⲛⲧⲉϥⲥⲩⲅⲅⲉⲛⲓⲁ ⲙⲛⲡⲏⲓ ⲙⲡⲉϥⲉⲓⲱⲧ.

20. Stephen of Hnēs, *Panegyric on Apollo*, 3.

21. Gen. 22.

22. ⲡⲉⲓⲧⲟϣ.

23. Stephen of Hnēs, *Panegyric on Apollo*, 3–4.

24. ⲁϥⲕⲱ ⲛⲥⲱϥ ⲙⲡⲉϥⲕⲁϩ.

25. Stephen of Hnēs, *Panegyric on Apollo*, 3.

26. Stephen of Hnēs, *Panegyric on Apollo*, 3. For similar dynamics in the eighth-century recollection of the Pachomian disciple Mar Awgen in fourth-century Nisibis, see Paul Bedjan, *Liber superiorum seu Historia Monastica auctore Thoma, Episcopa Margensi' Dicta de Sévres* (Leipzig: Harrassowitz, 1901).

27. The Coptic word the appears most often for "country/region" is ⲕⲁϩ which also mean "land" or "soil," denoting a stronger connection to the land of Egypt in assertions of ethnicity compared to the Greek πατριά which connects more to ancestry and citizenship.

28. For Pachomius's birthplace, see his *Life*: Armand Veilleux, *Pachomian Koinonia I: The Life of Saint Pachomius and His Disciples* (Collegeville, MN: Cistercian Publications, 1980).

29. ⲕⲁϩ often refers to the whole earth. For an example of such a use in this text, see *Panegyric on Apollo*, 18. Its lexical range also refers to specific lands or countries: see, Walter E. Crum, *A Coptic Dictionary* (Oxford: Oxford University Press, 1939), 131a-b. Orlandi translates ⲕⲁϩ using the Italian word "terra," which would equate more closely with the English "land" (*Vite di Monaci Copti*, 189). Likewise, Orlandi later uses "terra" to translate the Greco-Coptic word ⲭⲱⲣⲁ (199).

30. Stephen of Hnēs, *Panegyric on Apollo*, 3.

31. Stephen of Hnēs, *Panegyric on Apollo*, 9.

32. Stephen of Hnēs, *Panegyric on Apollo*, 10.

33. Stephen of Hnēs, *Panegyric on Apollo*, 11.

34. Stephen of Hnēs, *Panegyric on Apollo*, 12.

35. Stephen of Hnēs, *Panegyric on Apollo*, 12.

36. Davis, *The Early Coptic Papacy*, 42.

37. I follow Kuhn's emendation of ⲛⲟⲓ found here to the Coptic word ⲛⲟⲓⲉⲛ (*Panegyric on Apollo*, 14).

38. Stephen of Hnēs, *Panegyric on Apollo*, 14.

39. Zacharias of Mytilene, *The Chronicle of Pseudo-Zachariah Rhetor*.

40. Zacharias of Mytilene, *The Chronicle of Pseudo-Zachariah Rhetor*, 9.26.

41. Even today, it is common for modern Copts to refer to Egyptian Chalcedonians (or "Melkites") as "Romans" in Arabic.

42. ⲟⲩⲟⲓ ⲛⲛⲉⲗⲁⲟⲥ (Stephen of Hnēs, *Panegyric on Apollo*, 15). This is Stephen's paraphrase of Nah. 3:18–19.

43. Stephen of Hnēs, *Panegyric on Apollo,* 15.

44. Stephen of Hnēs, *Panegyric on Apollo,* 15–16. This section of the *Panegyric* is also in Kuhn, "Two Further Fragments," 266–68. Instead of Kuhn's rendering ⲙⲛⲧⲓⲟⲩⲇⲁⲓ as "the Jews' religion," I have rendered a more literal translation in an attempt to allow the text to evoke a religious as well as ethnic sense of ⲙⲛⲧⲓⲟⲩⲇⲁⲓ in order to demonstrate the way in which ethnic and religious boundaries cannot be so neatly delineated. Orlandi also translates more closely to the text: "Essi divisero in una concezione giudaica ('they divided by means of Jewish thought')" (*Vite de Monaci Copti,* 199). For an example of reading anti-Jewish rhetoric as purely theological, see Christina Shepardson, *Anti-Judaism and Christian Orthodoxy: Ephrem's Hymns in Fourth-Century Syria* (Washington, DC: The Catholic University of America Press, 2008), 20.

45. ⲧⲉⲭⲱⲣⲁ ⲧⲏⲣⲥ̄ ⲥⲭⲉⲇⲱⲛ ⲛⲕⲏⲙⲉ.

46. Kuhn speculates a scribal error in ⲛⲉⲕⲗⲅⲣⲓⲕⲟⲥ and mentions the possibility of reading instead ⲛⲉⲕⲕⲗⲅⲣⲓⲕⲟⲥ (Stephen of Hnēs, *Panegyric on Apollo,* 17n133). If the addition of both kappas is not a scribal error, however, the emphasis on "*your* clerics" serves to enhance the minority discourse at play in the *Panegyric.*

47. ⲡⲉⲍⲟⲩⲟ ⲛⲛⲉⲉⲡⲓⲥⲕⲟⲡⲟⲥ ⲛⲛⲟⲑⲟⲇⲟⲍⲟⲥ, again, reinforcing the Egyptian Miaphysite self-perception as a faithful minority.

48. ⲡⲭ̄ⲱ ⲛⲧⲙⲛⲧⲓⲟⲩⲇⲁⲓ: For further evidence of anti-Jewish rhetoric in Egyptian anti-Chalcedonian texts: "The light and the sweet fragrance remained in the place of the saints (Scetis) effecting the salvation of everyone for a long time—until the Jewish council (ⲡⲓⲥⲩⲛⲉⲇⲣⲓⲟⲛ ⲛⲓⲟⲩⲇⲁⲓⲕⲟⲛ) gathered, which occurred in Chalcedon where they divided (ⲫⲱⲣⲭ) the Holy Church by their impiety, placing a blindness filled with obstacles (ⲛⲋⲣⲟⲡ) and stumbling blocks (ⲛⲥⲕⲁⲇⲁⲗⲟⲛ) on the entire world." See Zacharias of Sakha, *Vie de Jean Kolobos,* ed. Émile Amélineau (Paris: Annales du Musée Guimet 25, 1894), 389. The translation is from Tim Vivian and Maged Mikhail, *CCR* 18 (1997): 3–64.

49. Kuhn translates ⲉⲩⲧⲙⲟⲩⲱϣ as having a circumstantial converter ("if"), which would be more appropriate in the presence of the conditional conjugation base ⲉⲩϣⲁⲛ. The conversion taking place in ⲉⲩⲧⲙⲟⲩⲱϣ could be either focalizing or circumstantial; in either case, beginning the clause with "if" is not as appropriate as something like "for," "because," "as," or "while." The significance lies in the fact that the *Panegyric* is communicating the unwavering faith of the orthodox in the face of Chalcedonian persecution. From the perspective of Stephen of Hnēs, their desire not to transgress the faith of the Lord was reality, not hypothetical.

50. Stephen of Hnēs, *Panegyric on Apollo,* 16–17.

51. Cf. Mt. 5:13–16.

52. Note here the use of the Coptic word ⲕⲏⲙⲉ here in contrast to the Greco-Coptic word ⲉⲕⲩⲡⲧⲓⲟⲥ which appeared more often in the earlier years of Egyptian Christological resistance.

53. Constructing Christian identity through ethnic reasoning was common to early Christianity in the Roman Empire. It is lamentable that this often occurred through anti-Semitic rhetoric. See Judith M. Lieu, "Identity Games in Early Christian

Texts: The Letter to Diognetus," in *Ethnicity, Race, Religion: Identities and Ideologies in Early Jewish and Christian Texts, and in Modern Biblical Interpretation,* ed. David G. Horrell and Katherine M. Hockey (London: Bloomsbury Publishing, 2018), 70.

54. There will be more discussion about Severus and the degree to which, even among Miaphsyites, ethnic tension still existed.

55. Ethncity is often defined as an "additional characteristic" of identity that forms over existing layers that correspond to more specific forms of attachment such as language, religion, politics or race (phenotype); see John Rex, "The Fundamentals of the Theory of Ethncty," in *Making Sense of Collectivity: Ethnicity, Nationalism and Globalization,* ed. Siniša Malešević and Mark Haugaard (London: Pluto Press, 2002), 93.

56. ΠΑΡΑΒΑΤΗC (Stephen of Hnēs, *Panegyric on Apollo,* 17).

57. For more, see the following section on Abraham of Farshut.

58. Stephen of Hnēs, *Panegyric on Apollo,* 18. The same phrase is repeated on p. 19.

59. ΝΑλλΟΤΡΙΟC.

60. Stephen of Hnēs, *Panegyric on Apollo,* 18. The full lexical range of ἀλλότριος, denoting idolatry and adultery (i.e. belonging to another god or person) as well as ethnic foreignness, could be operative here. The sin of apostasy (i.e. adherence to Chalcedon) evokes the imagery of violating both one's faith as well as ethnic group.

61. ЄϤΟ ΝΡΜΝϬΟΙλЄ ƧΝΟΥΤΟϢ ÑϢ̄ΜΜΟ (Stephen of Hnēs, *Panegyric on Apollo,* 18).

62. Stephen of Hnēs, *Panegyric on Apollo,* 18.

63. Stephen of Hnēs, *Panegyric on Apollo,* 20.

64. However, the Panegyric serves as an indication of ongoing Melitian presence (Orlandi, *Vite de Monaci Copti,* 186). Goehring argues that the absence of details on Melitian activity in Pbow is because the majority of textual evidence that survives comes from the Pachomian camp, and from times much later than the events they describe. However, Goehring does provide helpful documentary evidence that provides information on the Melitian presence in Pbow (*Ascetics, Society, and the Desert,* 187–95).

65. Stephen of Hnēs, *Panegyric on Apollo,* 26.

66. Stephen of Hnēs, *Panegyric on Apollo,* 27–28.

67. ƧΝΟΥCΧΗΜΑ ΜΜΟΝΑΧΟC ΝϢΜΜΟ.

68. Stephen of Hnēs, *Panegyric on Apollo,* 31–32.

69. Orlandi therefore translates it with the Italian term "straniero," which also has an ethnic sense (*Vite de Monaci Copti,* 212).

70. Stephen of Hnēs, *Panegyric on Apollo,* 35.

71. Stephen of Hnēs, *Panegyric on Apollo,* 35.

72. ΝΤЄΚCΥΝΑΓΩΓΗ.

73. Stephen of Hnēs, *Panegyric on Apollo,* 38.

74. ΠЄΙλΑΟC ΔЄ ƧΩΩϤ ΤЄΝΟΥ ΝΝΟΡΘΟΔΟΧΟC ΑΥΩ ΝƧΟΜΟΔΟΧΟC (Stephen of Hnēs, *Panegyric on Apollo,* 38).

75. Advanced largely by sociologist Maurice Halbwachs, collective memory is constructed within specific social frameworks through cultural institutions and

shaped by changing political circumstances; see Jeffrey K. Olick, Vered Vinitzky-Seroussi and Daniel Levy, *The Collective Memory Reader* (Oxford: Oxford University Press, 2011), 37.

76. The following analysis of the literature relating the life of Abraham is the author's translation based on the Coptic text as edited by Goehring: *Panegyric on Abraham of Farshut*, ed. James E. Goehring, in *Politics, Monasticism, and Miracles in Sixth Century Upper Egypt: A Critical Edition and Translation of the Coptic Texts on Abraham of Farshut*, Studien und Texte zu Antike und Christentum (Tübingen: Mohr Siebeck, 2012), 98.

77. *Panegyric on Abraham of Farshut*, 72.

78. ⲧⲟⲩ ⲛ̄ⲧⲟⲥⲧⲡⲟⲗⲓⲥ, *Panegyric on Abraham of Farshut*, 72.

79. Émile Amélineau, *Geographie de l'Égypte à l'époque copte* (Paris: Imprimerie nationale, 1893), 178–79.

80. ⲛ̄ϩⲉⲛⲣⲱⲙⲉ ⲛ̄ⲛⲟϭ.

81. *Panegyric on Abraham of Farshut*, 72.

82. E.g. Rom. 9:3; 16:7; Josephus, *Antiquities of the Jews*, 12:338; *Wars of the Jews*, 7:262.

83. ⲙ̄ⲙⲛ̄ⲧⲣ̄ⲙⲛ̄ⲕⲏⲙⲉ, *Panegyric on Abraham of Farshut*, 74.

84. *Panegyric on Abraham of Farshut*, 74.

85. *Panegyric on Abraham of Farshut*, 74. Goehring notes that ⲛ̄ⲧⲣⲟⲙⲡⲉ ⲛ̄ⲛⲉϥⲉⲓⲟⲧⲉ refers to a "year of mourning for his parents" (75n29).

86. *Panegyric on Abraham of Farshut*, 76.

87. Perhaps a reference to Manicheans whose doctrine are commonly referred to as *mania*, a polemical word-play on the name of the founder of the movement, Mani; see John Kevin Coyle, *Manichaeism and Its Legacy* (Leiden: Koninklijke Brill, 2009), 10–12. Indirectly associating Justinian with Mani would be consistent with the other names listed in the *Panegyric on Abraham of Farshut* with whom Chalcedonian doctrine is inappropriately connected.

88. ⲉⲧⲉⲭⲱⲣⲁ ⲧⲏⲣⲥ̄ ⲛ̄ⲕⲏⲙⲉ.

89. ⲉⲧⲡⲟⲗⲓⲥ ⲛ̄ⲧⲙⲛ̄ⲧⲉⲣⲟ.

90. *Panegyric on Abraham of Farshut*, 78. The Bohairic manuscript has ⲛ̄ϩⲩⲅⲟⲩⲙⲉⲛⲟⲥ ⲙ̄ⲡⲃⲟⲟⲩ as opposed to the Sahidic ⲛ̄ϩⲩⲅⲟⲩⲙⲉⲛⲟⲥ ⲉⲡⲃⲟⲟⲩ. For an edition of the Bohairic manuscript see Émile Amélineau, *Monuments pour servir a l'histoire de l'Égypte chrétienne aux 4., 5., 6., et 7. siècles*. Mèmoires publiés par les membres de la mission archéologique français au Caire 4/2, 742–753 (Paris: Leroux), 1895.

91. Goehring, *Politics, Monasticism and Miracles*, 51. See also A. Cameron, *Christianity and the Rhetoric of Empire*, 7.

92. *Panegyric on Abraham of Farshut*, 78.

93. *Panegyric on Abraham of Farshut*, 78.

94. Paul van Cauwenbergh, *Étude sur les moines d'Égypte depuis le concile le Concile de Chalcédoine (451) jusqu'à l'invasion arabe (640)* (Paris: Imprimerie Nationale, 1914), 153–54. Van Cauwenbergh claims that the conflict between Justinian and Abraham "introduced" anti-Chalcedonianism into Pbow (159). Van Lant-

schoot and Goehring argue in favor an anti-Chalcedonian predominance at Pbow; see Arnold van Lantschoot, "Allocution de Timothée d'Alexandrie prononcée a l'occasion de la dédicace de l'église de Pachome a Pboou," *Le Muséon* 47 (1934): 21–22; James E. Goehring, "Remembering Abraham of Farshut: History, Hagiography, and the Fate of the Pachomian Tradition," *JECS 14* (2006): 16. See also James E. Goehring, "Chalcedonian Power Politics and the Demise of Pachomian Monasticism," Occasional Paper 15 (Claremont, CA: Institute for Antiquity and Christianity, 1989), 13.

95. *Panegyric on Abraham of Farshut,* 80.

96. ⲟⲩⲛⲟϭ. Cf. Heb. 13:7.

97. ⲚⲚⲉⲚⲉⲓⲟⲧⲉ ⲚⲀⲢⲬⲀⲒⲟⲚ Ⲁⲅⲱ ⲘⲠⲢⲟⲠⲀⲧⲱⲢ.

98. ⲚⲈⲒⲟⲧⲉ ⲘⲠⲔⲟⲤⲘⲟⲤ, *Panegyric on Abraham of Farshut,* 98.

99. Sebastian Garman, "Ethnosymbolism in the Ancient Mediterranean World," in *Nationalism and Ethnosymbolism: History, Culture and Ethnicity in the Formation of Nations,* ed. Athena S. Leoussi and Steven Grosby, 113–125 (Edinburgh: Edinburgh University Press, 2007), 118; Garman points out how the literary genre of the panegyric was a significant "ethnosymbol" in the Hellenistic world that was used to assert ethnic identity through a curated collective memory.

100. *Panegyric on Abraham of Farshut,* 86.

101. ⲟⲩⲠⲢⲟⲧⲉⲔⲧⲱⲢ ⲠⲉⲚⲢⲘⲘⲀⲟ ⲈⲘⲀⲧⲉ, *Panegyric on Abraham of Farshut,* 92.

102. ⲈⲘ ⲠⲔⲀϨ ⲦⲎⲢⲞⲨ ⲚⲔⲎⲘⲉ ⲘⲚ Ⲛⲉϭⲟⲟϣⲉ, *Panegyric on Abraham of Farshut,* 102; this reference to "Ethiopia" likely refers collectively to the various Nile Valley kingdoms south of Egypt, as the word "Ethiopian" simply means "burnt-face one" and often referred interchangeably to dark-skinned people groups in Africa, Arabia, and India. The sixth century was significant in the Nile Valley as this is the time period commonly understood to be when the kingdoms of Nubia embraced Christianity. The Nubian kingdoms embraced the Miaphysite faith of Egypt and rejected attempts on the part of Justinian to spread Chalcedonian faith there. This exacerbated the Christological tension in Africa and also served to unite the Christian communities along the Nile Valley; see Artur Obłuski, *The Rise of Nobadia: Social Changes in Northern Nubia in Late Antiquity* (Warsaw: University of Warsaw Institute of Archaeology/Department of Papyrology, 2014), 169–72.

103. ⲔⲀⲧⲀ ⲠⲈⲐⲟⲤ ⲚⲚⲉⲧⲚⲈⲒⲟⲧⲉ; *On Abraham of Farshut,* ed. James E. Goehring, *Politics, Monasticism, and Miracles in Sixth Century Upper Egypt: A Critical Edition and Translation of the Coptic Texts on Abraham of Farshut,* Studien und Texte zu Antike und Christentum (Tübingen: Mohr Siebeck, 2012), 102.

104. ⲔⲀⲧⲀ ⲠⲈⲐⲟⲤ ⲚⲚⲉⲔⲉⲒⲟⲧⲉ. The change from plural ⲚⲚⲉⲧⲚⲈⲒⲟⲧⲉ to ⲚⲚⲉⲔⲉⲒⲟⲧⲉ indicates that while the initial confrontation with the imperial secretary included Abraham's entourage, the present scene with Justinian includes only Abraham.

105. *On Abraham of Farshut,* 104. In a forthcoming translation, Mary Farag interprets Justinian's statement as a jussive command: "Your faith shall be likened to that of all," intensifying the assimilationist tactics of the emperor as presented in the text (cited with permission).

106. ⲉⲑⲟⲥ.

107. Goehring, "Chalcedonian Power Politics," 7.

108. Sarris, *Economy and Society,* 15–16; Sarris highlights the broader societal context in which Egypt began to wane in influence in the Byzantine Empire due to its divergent Christology and suspicion for involvement in the Nika Revolt in 532 CE.

109. ⲉⲩⲡⲓⲥⲧⲓⲥ ⲛ̄ⲩⲙⲙⲟ (*On Abraham of Farshut,* 104).

110. *On Abraham of Farshut,* 104.

111. ⲧⲡⲓⲥⲧⲓⲥ ⲉⲧⲥⲟⲩⲧⲱⲛ (*On Abraham of Farshut,* 106).

112. *On Abraham of Farshut,* 108.

113. *On Abraham of Farshut,* 106.

114. ⲧⲁⲡⲓⲗⲏ (*On Abraham of Farshut,* 106).

115. ⲧⲉϥⲙⲁⲛⲓⲁ. Perhaps a further insult by associating Justinian with Mani.

116. *On Abraham of Farshut,* 108.

117. ⲉⲩⲙⲟⲛⲁⲭⲟⲥ ⲡⲉⲛ̄ⲣⲙ̄ⲧⲥⲩⲣⲓⲁ.

118. ⲉⲩⲟⲣⲑⲟⲇⲟⲭⲟⲥ ϩⲱⲱϥ ⲡⲉ (*On Abraham of Farshut,* 108); as shown above, when figures associated with "Syria" appear in Egyptian Miaphysite texts—such as Severus of Antioch in the Panegyric on Apollo—they are often portrayed as fellow orthodox along with the Egyptians. This increase in Syrian solidarity in the sixth century is likely due to the fact that the Syrian Miaphysites became divided from Byzantine imperial authority and Chalcedonianism during this time period, whereas there wasn't as much resistance immediately following Chalcedon in the fifth century.

119. ⲁⲡⲟⲧⲁⲥⲥⲉ (*On Abraham of Farshut,* 108).

120. ⲁⲩⲣⲁϣⲉ ⲉⲙⲁⲧⲉ ⲛ̄ⲑⲉ ⲙ̄ⲡⲇⲓⲁⲃⲟⲗⲟⲥ ⲉⲁⲩϭⲉⲙϭⲙ̄ ⲛ̄ⲑⲉ ⲛ̄ⲛⲉⲓⲙⲟⲩⲓ ⲙⲛ̄ ⲛⲉⲓⲟⲩⲱⲛⲩ̄ ⲛ̄ⲧⲉ ⲧⲁⲣⲁⲃⲓⲁ (*On Abraham of Farshut,* 108). Chalcedonian oppressors are also referred to as "wolves" (ⲟⲩⲱⲛⲩ̄) in the *Panegyric on Apollo,* 17. Cf. Zeph. 3:3.

121. *Panegyric on Manasseh,* ed. James E. Goehring, *Politics, Monasticism, and Miracles in Sixth Century Upper Egypt: A Critical Edition and Translation of the Coptic Texts on Abraham of Farshut,* Studien und Texte zu Antike und Christentum (Tübingen: Mohr Siebeck, 2012), 110.

122. *Panegyric on Manasseh,* 110.

123. ⲛⲉⲧϣⲟⲟⲡ ⲧⲏⲣⲟⲩ ϩⲁ ⲡⲉⲕⲣⲁⲧⲟⲥ ⲛ̄ⲧⲙⲛ̄ⲧⲉⲣⲟ ⲛ̄ⲛⲉϩⲣⲱⲙⲁⲓⲟⲥ.

124. ⲛ̄ⲧⲙⲛ̄ⲧⲛⲟϭ, Goehring highlights Crum's gloss of ⲧⲙⲛ̄ⲧⲛⲟϭ as referring to monastic authority (*Panegyric on Manasseh,* 113n182). See also Crum, *A Coptic Dictionary,* 251b.

125. ⲟⲩⲕⲉⲗⲉⲩⲥⲓⲥ ⲛⲁⲩⲑⲉⲛⲧⲓⲁ ⲛ̄ⲃⲁⲥⲓⲗⲓⲕⲟⲛ, *Panegyric on Manasseh,* 112.

126. James E. Goehring, "Keeping the Monastery Clean: A Cleansing Episode from an Excerpt on Abraham of Farshut and Shenoute's Discourse on Purity," in *The World of Early Egyptian Christianity: Language, Literature, and Social Context,* ed. James E. Goehring and Janet Timbie (Washington, DC: The Catholic University of America Press, 2007), 162.

127. *Panegyric on Manasseh,* 175.

128. *Panegyric on Manasseh,* 112.

129. *Panegyric on Manasseh,* 112.

130. Antonella Campagnano, "Monaci egiziani fra V e VI secolo," *VetChr* 15 (1978): 243.

131. See the remaks of Dionysius of Halicarnassus to this effect in Kennedy, Roy and Goldman, *Race and Ethnicity,* 23.

132. Barth, "Boundaries and Connections," 29; Barth describes how ethnic boundaries can function as a means of separation rather than conjunction, as is evidenced here in *Panegyric on Manasseh.*

133. ⲡⲟⲩ\ⲭⲁ ⲉⲛⲕⲏⲙⲉ ⲧⲏⲣϥ (*Panegyric on Manasseh,* 114).

134. Goehring notes the similarity in wording here to Mark 14:1, probably an intentional effort on the part of the panegyrist to liken the arrest of Abraham to that of Christ (115n194).

135. *Panegyric on Manasseh,* 114.

136. ⲃ̄ⲛ̄ⲧⲃ̄ⲛⲟⲟⲩⲉ, i.e. by land, not by sea.

137. ⲛ̄ⲃⲉⲛⲙⲁⲧⲟⲓ ⲛⲁⲅⲣⲓⲟⲛ (*Panegyric on Manasseh,* 114); the term "savage" is also frequently used in an ethnic sense, referring to people Romans would have considered "barbarians." See Fiona K. Nicks, "Literary Culture in the Reign of Anastaius I," in *Ethnicity and Culture in Late Antiqiuty,* ed. Stephen Mithcell and Geoffrey Greatrex (London: Duckworth, 2000), 191. It is ironic that, in this context, the Egyptians are now using this common Roman epithet against the Byzantine authorities.

138. *Panegyric on Manasseh,* 116.

139. *Panegyric on Manasseh,* 116.

140. *Panegyric on Manasseh,* 116.

141. *Panegyric on Manasseh,* 118.

142. *Synaxarium,* 402. For a comparison with the rules of Moses, see Coquin, "La "Règle" de Moïse D'Abydos," 103–10.

143. *Synaxarium,* 403.

144. Goehring, "Remembering Abraham of Farshut," 1.

145. Goehring, "Chalcedonian Power Politics," 20.

146. Goehring, "Keeping the Monastery Clean," 162. See also Tito Orlandi, "Un Projet Milanais Concernant les Manuscrits Coptes du Monastère Blanc," *Le Muséon* 85 (1972): 403. In a different work, Goehring demonstrates that while the Greek versions of the *Vita* emerge throughout Byzantium and the West through Alexandria, the Coptic versions, with numerous anti-Chalcedonian additions, survive only in the White Monastery; see "Pachomius' Vision of Heresy: The Development of a Pachomian Tradition," *Le Muséon* 95 (1982): 260. The survival of the anti-Chalcedonian *vitae* exclusively in Coptic further attests to the prominence of Miaphysite doctrine in Egyptian identity.

147. Tim Vivian, *Witness to Holiness: Abba Daniel of Scetis* (Kalamazoo, MI: Cistercian Publications, 2008), 241, 251.

148. Hugh G. Evelyn White, *The Monasteries of the Wadi 'N Natrun,* vol. 2, *The History of the Monasteries of Nitria and Scetis* (New York, NY: Arno Press, 1973), 241.

149. Vivian, *Witness to Holiness*, 10; Tim Vivian, "Witness to Holiness: Abba Daniel of Scetis." *Coptic Church Review* 24 (2003): 2–52. Vivian provides the dates 485–570/80 for Daniel's life ("Witness to Holiness," 10). Britt Dahlman assigns a late-fifth/early-sixth century birth date and claims his death would have been after 576 CE; see *Saint Daniel of Sketis: A Group of Hagiographic Texts with Introduction, Translation, and Commentary.* Studia Byzantina Upsaliensia 10 (Uppsala: Acta Universitatis Upsaliensis, 2007), 64.

150. Vivian, *Witness to Holiness*, 4.

151. Vivian, *Witness to Holiness*, 5.

152. van Cauwenbergh, *Étude sur les moines d'Égypte*, 14.

153. Evelyn White, *The Monasteries of the Wadi ʾN Natrun*, 246.

154. Vivian, *Witness to Holiness*, 98n7. Also see Isaac the Presbyter, *The Life of Samuel of Kalamun*, ed. Anthony Alcock (Warminster: Aris & Phillips Ltd, 1983), 6–7.

155. van Cauwenbergh, *Étude sur les moines d'Égypte*, 27.

156. Vivian, *Witness to Holiness*, 100.

157. Dahlman, *Saint Daniel of Sketis*, 58.

158. *Vie et récits de l'Abbé Daniel le Scété (VI Siècle)*, ed. Ignazio Guidi. *ROC* 5 (1900): 535–64; *ROC* 6 (1901): 51–53, see p. 535. It is interesting to find ⲭⲓⲛⲱⲛϩ as opposed to the more frequent ⲡⲟⲗⲓⲧⲉⲓⲁ. Perhaps this represents an increasing Coptization of traditionally Greco-Coptic terms in the Bohairic dialect.

159. ⲛⲉ ⲟⲩⲉⲑⲟⲥ ⲡⲉ ⲫⲁⲓ ⲉⲑⲣⲉ ⲡⲓⲛⲓϣϯ ⲛⲓⲱⲧ ⲛⲧⲉ ϣⲏⲧ ⲓ ⲉⲣⲁⲕⲟϯ ⲙⲡⲓⲛⲓϣϯ ⲛϣⲁⲓ ⲉⲑⲣⲉϥⲉⲣⲁⲡⲁⲛⲧⲁⲛ ⲉⲡⲓⲁⲣⲭⲏⲉⲡⲓⲥⲕⲟⲡⲟⲥ (*Vie de Daniel*, 536).

160. The Greek and Armenian versions claim that the monastic communities of Nitria and Kellia also participated in the funeral proceedings: Dahlman, *Saint Daniel of Sketis*, 123; Vivian, *Witness to Holiness*, 211.

161. The *Life* claims that Daniel was "in Egypt" (ϩⲉⲛ ⲭⲏⲙⲓ) and "sailing on the river (i.e. the Nile)" (ⲛⲁⲩϣⲟⲏⲣ ⲅⲁⲣ ϩⲉⲛ ⲫⲓⲁⲣⲟ ⲡⲉ), indicating an Upper Egyptian location (*Vie de Daniel*, 538). ⲭⲏⲙⲓ often refers to Upper Egypt as a geo-cultural region distinct from Alexandria and Scetis. The Ethiopic text identifies the town as "the City of Egypt," which Vivian suggests could have been Memphis (*Witness to Holiness*, 135n4). The Ethiopic version indicates the location as Kift; see Lazarus Goldschmidt and F. M. Esteves Pereira, *Vida do Abba Daniel do Mosteiro de Sceté: Versão Ethiopica* (Lisbon: Imprensa Nacional, 1897) 39n1. The Syriac version indicates the location as Thebes; see Christa Müller-Kessler and Michael Sokoloff, *The Forty Martyrs of the Sinai Desert, Eulogios the Stone-Cutter, and Anastasia.* A Corpus of Christian Palestinian Aramaic III (Groningen: Styx, 1996), 69. Thebes is also the location in the Armenian and Latin versions (Vivian, *Witness to Holiness*, 235; 245). The story of Eulogius also appears in the *Apophthegmata Patrum*, 462–474, where Daniel met Eulogius in the Thebaid.

162. ϩⲱⲥ ϣⲉⲙⲙⲟ ⲛⲣⲱⲙⲓ, or "stranger." See Crum, *A Coptic Dictionary*, 565b-566a. The term "stranger" in modern parlance typically refers to someone with whom an individual has no acquaintance. Unlike the time of Crum, the word "stranger" today does not carry a sense of social difference, which is clearly what is

meant here in the *Life*. Although in modern use, the word "foreigner" typically refers to someone from another nation (which is not the case here in the *Life*); ϣⲙⲙⲟ is also used in Coptic literature to refer to people from other regions of Egypt.

163. ⲉϥⲕⲱϯ ϫⲉⲛ ⲛⲓϑⲓⲣ ⲉⲑⲃⲉ ⲛⲓϣⲉⲙⲙⲱⲟⲩ (*Vie de Daniel*, 539).

164. *Vie de Daniel*, 541. The Greek text has "Israelites" (Dahlman, *Saint Daniel of Sketis*, 154). The Syriac follows the Greek here: ܐܝܣܪܝܠ ܒܢܝ (Müller-Kessler and Sokoloff, *The Forty Martyrs* 80). Vivian speculates that the Coptic translator may have introduced a tenth-century anachronism given the context of Muslim ("Ishmaelite") hegemony (*Witness to Holiness*, 109n79). The Ethiopic also says "Ishmaelites" (Vivian, *Witness to Holiness*, 136).

165. Dahlman, *Saint Daniel of Sketis*, 154. The Armenian, Latin, and Syriac follow the Greek; see Vivian, *Witness to Holiness*, 235; 248; Müller-Kessler and Sokoloff, *The Forty Martyrs*, 81.

166. Vivian, *Witness to Holiness*, 137–38.

167. *Apophthegmata Patrum*, 443–44.

168. ⲟⲩⲙⲉⲧϭⲁⲥⲓϩⲏⲧ ⲟⲩⲟϩ ⲛⲁⲑⲛⲁⲓ (*Vie de Daniel*, 541).

169. λέγεται τὰ Αἰγύπτου μέχρι τῆς σήμερον (Dahlman, *Saint Daniel of Sketis*, 154). While neither the Coptic nor Ethiopic retain this detail, the Armenian, Latin and Syriac follow the Greek here (Vivian, *Witness to Holiness*, 238; 248; Müller-Kessler and Sokoloff, *The Forty Martyrs*, 81; see also *Apophthegmata Patrum*, 466).

170. ἑνὸς Αἰθίοπος ἑνὸς Αἰθίοπος (Dahlman, *Saint Daniel of Sketis*, 154). The Syriac follows the Greek in identifying the person as Ethiopian (Müller-Kessler and Sokoloff, 82). The Armenian claims that Eulogius was dragged away by "black demons" (Vivian, *Witness to Holiness*, 238). The *Apophthegmata Patrum* also calls the figure an "Ethiopian" (Αἰθίοπος) (466). See also Byron, *Symbolic Blackness*, 37.

171. *Vie de Daniel*, 541. Likewise, the Copto-Arabic *Synaxarium* does not identify any person dragging Eulogius away, but merely narrates a vision of Jesus sitting as celestial judge (Vivian, *Witness to Holiness*, 124). This could indicate that the *Synaxarium* follows the Coptic version of Eulogius and not the Greek. For anti-black "Othering" in early Christian literature, see Byron, *Symbolic Blackness*, 122–29.

172. Vivian, *Witness to Holiness*, 174. However, the Geʿez *Life*, following the Coptic, also includes no ethnic or racial modifiers for the arrestors of Eulogius; *Vida do Abba Daniel do Mosteiro de Sceté*, ed. F. M. Esteves Pereira (Lisbon: Imprensa Nacional, 1897), 11.

173. περιεργασάμενος τὴν οἰκίαν Εὐλογίου τοῦ Αἰγυπτίου (Dahlman, *Saint Daniel of Sketis*, 156). Following Vivian, I have also consulted the Greek due to a lacuna in the Coptic text at this point; see *Witness to Holiness*, 110n83.

174. Pereira, *Vida do Abba Daniel*, 12.

175. Byron, *Symbolic Blackness*, 2.

176. Dahlman, *Saint Daniel of Sketis*, 158.

177. The Syriac here refers to Eulogius as "Eulogius the Egyptian" (Müller-Kessler and Sokoloff, *The Forty Martyrs*, 90–91).

178. *Vie de Daniel,* 543.

179. ⲘⲘⲞⲚ ⲪⲀⲒ ⲠⲈ ⲬⲎⲘⲒ (*Vie de Daniel,* 544).

180. ὧδε Αἴγυπτός ἐστι (Dahlman, *Saint Daniel of Sketis,* 162). This same statement appears in the *Apophthegmata Patrum,* 472.

181. Vivian, *Witness to Holiness,* 241; 251.

182. Vivian, *Witness to Holiness,* 139; also, Pereira, *Vida do Abba Daniel,* 14.

183. ⲚⲚⲒⲠⲒⲤⲦⲞⲤ ⲦⲎⲢⲞⲨ ⲚⲞⲢⲐⲞⲆⲞⳀⲞⲤ ⲈⲦϢⲞⲠ ⳅⲈⲚ ⳦ⲬⲰⲢⲀ ⲚⲦⲈ ⲬⲎⲘⲒ.

184. *Vie de Daniel,* 547–49.

185. Eriksen outlines the three strategies of minority ethnic identity in multiethnic states as assimilation, resistance, or secession (*Ethnicity and Nationalism,* 150). Eriksen also notes that minority studies is an area that, like the work of Barth, requires further clarification on the role of minority status in ethnic identity formation (147).

186. *Vie de Daniel,* 548.

187. *Vie de Daniel,* 549.

188. Vivian identifies "Egypt" here as any more densely-populated region outside of Scetis, including Alexandria (*Witness to Holiness,* 116n104). Against this view, "Egypt" more often designates Upper Egypt in hagiographical literature and contrasts with Alexandria (*Macarius of Tkôw,* 60).

189. *Vie de Daniel,* 549.

190. Not surprisingly, the *Life* attributes the death of Justinian to the wrath of the Lord.

191. *Vie de Daniel,* 550.

192. *Vie de Daniel,* 548.

CHAPTER 5. IDENTITY FORMATION UNDER ISLAM

1. Davis, *Early Coptic Papacy,* 87.

2. Eriksen, *Ethnicity and Nationalism,* 23. Eriksen is following Barth on this point in that, because ethnicity is constructed through contact with "Others," it follows that the ethnic Other with which a particular group will clash is the ones with which they share the most proximity.

3. For a comprehensive summary of the life of Benjamin, see C. D. G. Müller, "Benjamin I: 38. Patriarch von Alexandrien," *Le Muséon* 69 (1956): 313–40.

4. Henri De Vis, *Sermon de Benjamin sur les Noces de Cana* (Hauniae: Glyendalske Boghandel-Nordisk Forlag, 1922), 54.

5. Severus ibn al-Muqaffa, *Arabic History of the Patriarchs of Alexandria,* vols. I, ed. B. Evetts. PO 1.4, 381–519 (1904): 487.

6. *AHPA* I, 489.

7. كورة مصر.

8. *AHPA* I, 490.

9. *AHPA* I, 492.

10. *AHPA* I, 496. Following the dating of Jülicher, Müller places the date of Benjamin's return between the end of 643 and the beginning of 644 CE ("Benjamin I," 330).

11. ምስራውያን.

12. ጐይቶተ እግርዝም.

13. John of Nikiu, *Chronicle*, ed. H. Zotenberg (Paris: Imprimerie Nationale, 1888), 219–20.

14. "Egyptian" in this context is an ethnic label of a minority group within a multiethnic empire while "Roman" is the foil that is the State against which the Egyptian ethnic boundary formed. Such strategies are common to minority identities whose contrast is the larger political entity with which the minority group has observable differences. This is vastly different from a nationalist movement; see Thomas W. Simon, *Ethnic Identity and Minority Protection: Designation, Discrimination, and Brutalization* (Lanham, MD: Lexington Books, 2012), 71.

15. *AHPA* I, 502.

16. Tito Orlandi, *Omelie Copte* (Torino: Società Editrice Internazionale, 1981), 267.

17. Also referred to as the "Vision of Benjamin;" Heinzgerd Brakmann, "Zum Pariser Fragment Angeblich des Koptischen Patriarchen Agathon: Ein Neues Blatt der Vita Benjamins I," in *Le Muséon* 93 (1980): 300.

18. Agathon, *Livre de la consécration du sanctuaire de Benjamin*, ed. René-Georges Coquin (Paris: IFAO, 1975), 72. 10. Coquin takes this date to be accurate as this period witnessed great prosperity in the monastery of Makarios (12). The Arabic version of the *Book of the Consecration* is also recorded in the *AHPA* I, 503–18.

19. Agathon, *Livre de la consécration*, 35.

20. Agathon, *Livre de la consécration*, 46. Brakmann favors the possibility of the name Agathon being used as a pseudonym as he holds the authorship of Agathon in greater doubt than Coquin (Brakmann, "Zum Pariser Fragment," 306–7).

21. ϯⲛⲓϣϯ ⲙⲃⲁⲕⲓ a "city" or "town," the Bohairic equivalent of ⲡⲟⲗⲓⲥ which most often describes Alexandria in Sahidic texts (Crum, *A Coptic Dictionary*, 30b).

22. Agathon, *Livre de la consécration*, 72.

23. Agathon, *Livre de la consécration*, 80.

24. Agathon, *Livre de la consécration*, 94.

25. As outlined above, the strategy of imposing Miaphysite beliefs on deceased, pre-Chalcedonian leaders was common in Egyptian literature, as in the case of the *Life of Longinus*.

26. Coquin renders ⲛⲧⲁϭⲟ ⲉⲣⲁⲧϥ as "dispositions," evoking the idea of Agathon enjoying material provisions at the benevolence of Benjamin. The following context, however, reveals the likelihood of ⲛⲧⲁϭⲟ ⲉⲣⲁⲧϥ referring to other "establishments" of other monasteries and churches that Agathon has witnessed (Crum, *A Coptic Dictionary*, 456a).

27. Agathon, *Livre de la consecration*, 78.

28. Agathon, *Livre de la consécration*, 80–82.

29. ⲘⲠⲒⲀⲦⲪⲰⲢⲆ ⲠⲬⲤ (Agathon, *Livre de la consécration*, 84, lines 13 and 25–6).

30. ⲊⲀⲚⲘⲞⲚⲀⲬⲞⲤ ⲘⲠⲞⲗⲒⲦⲉⲩⲞⲘⲉⲚⲞⲤ (Agathon, *Livre de la consécration*, 86).

31. ⲈⲢⲈ ⲠⲒⲔⲗⲎⲢⲞⲤ ⲦⲎⲢϤ ⲐⲞⲨⲚⲦ ⲈⲢⲞⲒ ⲚⲈⲘ ⲚⲒⲊⲞⲨⲀϤ ⲚⲦⲈ ϮⲠⲞⲗⲒⲤ ⲚⲈⲘ ⲠⲒⲗⲀⲞⲤ ⲦⲎⲢϤ ⲚⲒⲔⲞⲨⲆⲒ ⲚⲈⲘ ⲚⲒⲚⲒϢϮ ⲚⲒⲢⲀⲘⲀⲞⲒ ⲚⲈⲘ ⲚⲒⲊⲎⲔⲒ ⲚⲈⲘ ⲊⲀⲚⲔⲈⲘⲎϢ ⲘⲠⲒⲤⲦⲎ ⲚⲦⲈ ⲚⲒⲊⲒⲞⲘⲒ ⲚⲤⲨⲚⲔⲗⲨⲦⲒⲔⲞⲤ (Agathon, *Livre de la consécration*, 82).

32. ⲞⲨⲞⲊ ⲀⲚϢⲀ ⲚⲤⲰⲞⲨⲦⲈⲚ ⲈⲐⲢⲀⲞⲨⲎ ⲚⲚⲈⲚⲒⲞϮ ⲚⲢⲰⲘⲈⲞⲤ ⲘⲀⲌⲒⲘⲞⲤ ⲚⲈⲘ ⲆⲞⲨⲘⲈⲦⲒⲞⲤ (Agathon, *Livre de la consécration*, 100). Coquin emended ⲈⲐⲢⲀⲞⲨⲎ, as it appears in the manuscript to ⲈⲐⲢⲀⲞⲨⲱ given his assessment of the text being "certainly faulty" (101n27). In his French translation however, Coquin follows the Arabic manuscripts that replace ⲈⲐⲢⲀⲞⲨⲎ with what Coquin translates "au couvent" (convent). His emendation is unnecessary as ⲈⲐⲢⲀⲞⲨⲎ is an expected Bohairic spelling for ⲢⲀⲨⲎ and agrees with the Arabic text (Crum, *A Coptic Dictionary*, 306a).

33. Agathon, *Livre de la consécration*, 104.

34. Agathon, *Livre de la consécration*, 106–8.

35. ⲚⲒⲢⲰⲘⲈⲞⲤ (Agathon, *Livre de la consécration*, 110.)

36. ⲚⲆⲈ ⲔⲨⲢⲞⲤ ⲠⲒⲔⲀⲨⲔⲞⲤ ⲠⲒⲆⲀⲆⲒ ⲚⲦⲈ ⲘⲈⲐⲘⲎⲒ ⲚⲒⲂⲈⲚ (Agathon, *Livre de la consécration*, 110–12). The *AHPA* also constantly refers to Cyrus as "the Colchian," even omitting his actual name (*AHPA* I, 491).

37. Davis, *The Early Coptic Papacy*, 120.

38. Barth, *Ethnic Groups and Boundaries*, 10. Studies on Othering have also demonstrated the necessity of an Other for an ethnic group to assert its own identity; see Marissa Sonnis-Bell, "Introduction: Arbitrary Constructions and Real Consequences of the Self and Others," in *Strangers, Aliens, Foreigners: The Politics of Othering from Migrants to Corporations*, ed. Marissa Sonnis-Bell, David Elijah Bell, and Michelle Ryan (Leiden: Brill, 2019), 3. Sonnis-Bell clarifies that, while Othering is often thought of as a process enacted by a hegemonic majority, that even in minority communities Othering is an essential component of asserting group identity (4).

39. ⲞⲨⲒⲰⲦ ⲚⲦⲈ ⲊⲀⲚⲖⲀⲞⲤ (Agathon, *Livre de la consecration*, 114).

40. ⲚⲚⲒⲘⲞⲚⲀⲬⲞⲤ ⲦⲎⲢⲞⲨ ⲚⲦⲈ ⲠⲀⲒⲦⲰⲞⲨ ⲦⲎⲢϤ (Agathon, *Livre de la consécration*, 116). This appears again on p. 138, at which point Benjamin adds "and (the father of) all the doctors (ⲚⲒⲤⲀϦ) of orthodoxy." The universal authority ascribed to Makarios continues throughout the homily as he is later called "the consolation (ⲠⲤⲞⲖⲤⲈⲖ) of all the monks and the bishops and all the great doctors of the entire universe (ϮⲞⲒⲔⲞⲨⲘⲈⲚⲎ ⲦⲎⲢⲤ)" (172). This is likely for the purpose of establishing the hegemony of the Makarian monastery in the Scetis region during periods following the life of Benjamin.

41. ⲚⲒⲤⲀⲄⲎⲒⲚⲒ ⲈⲦⲐⲰⲞⲨϮ ⲈϦⲞⲨⲚ ⲚⲄⲈⲚⲞⲤ ⲚⲒⲂⲈⲚ ⲈϤⲘⲈⲦⲞⲨⲢⲞ ⲚⲦⲈ ⲪϮ ⲈⲨⲦⲀⲤⲐⲞ ⲊⲖⲒ ⲈⲂⲞⲖ ⲀⲚ (Agathon, *Livre de la consécration*, 124).

42. The use of "races" here demonstrates how the word sometimes referred to Christians as a distinct *genos* and other times as a collective of various *genoi*, as in this case. See Buell, *Why This New Race*, 3. The appearance of the word "race" here

is not problematic since, as has been pointed out, race often differs from ethnicity as a broader category referring to physical characteristics. Therefore, Benjamin's universal inclusion of all "races" also includes ethnic groups. Since ethnicity and race appeared interchangeably in ancient texts, this reference to "race" here is still applicable to a study on Egyptian ethnicity.

43. Agathon, *Livre de la consécration*, 146. Likewise, Makarios is described as "the port of health for the entire world (ⲙⲡⲓⲕⲟⲥⲙⲟⲥ ⲧⲏⲣϥ), curing every infirmity" (182).

44. Agathon, *Livre de la consécration*, 150; it should be noted, though, that the "orthodox Church" for Benjamin is the church centered in Alexandria.

45. Agathon, *Livre de la consécration*, 154.

46. Agathon, *Livre de la consécration*, 126.

47. ⲉϥⲉϣⲱⲡⲓ ⲛⲇⲉ ⲟⲩⲙⲁ ⲛⲉⲣϣⲱⲟⲩϣⲓ ⲙⲡⳓⲥ̅ ϧⲉⲛ ⲧⲭⲱⲣⲁ ⲛ̀ⲧⲉ ⲛⲓⲣⲉⲙⲛ̄ⲭⲏⲙⲓ ⲛⲉⲙ ⲟⲩⲥⲧⲩⲗⲏ ⲙ̄.ⲡⳓⲥ̅ ϧⲉⲛ ⲛⲉϥϑⲱϣ ⲉ̀ϑⲟⲩⲁⲃ (Agathon, *Livre de la consécration*, 138–40). From Isaiah 19:19.

48. τὸ ὅριον αὐτῆς.

49. ϩⲗⲓ ϧⲉⲛ ⲡⲓⲕⲗⲏⲣⲟⲥ ⲉⲑⲛⲁⲓⲛⲓ ⲛ̀ⲟⲩⲕⲗⲏⲣⲓⲕⲟⲥ ⲛ̀ϣⲉⲙⲙⲟ ⲛ̀ⲧⲉ ⲭⲏⲙⲓ ⲓⲉ ⲟⲩⲁⲣⲭⲱⲛ ⲉ̀ϧⲟⲩⲛ ⲉ̀ⲧⲁⲓⲥⲕⲩⲛⲏ ⲉ̀ϑⲟⲩⲁⲃ ⲑⲁⲓ ⲉⲑⲃⲉ ⲟⲩⲱⲟⲩ ⲛ̀ⲣⲱⲙⲓ ⲙⲁⲣⲉϥϣⲱⲡⲓ ⲛ̀ⲟⲩⲁⲛⲁⲑⲏⲙⲁ (Agathon, *Livre de la consécration*, 158).

50. Agathon, *Livre de la consécration*, 188–90.

51. Müller, "Benjamin I," 338.

52. Benjamin of Alexandria, *On Cana of Galilee: A Sermon by the Coptic Patriarch Benjamin I*, ed. Maged Mikhail, *CCR* 23.3, 66–93 (2002), at 69. See also the same sermon edited in French and Gemran: *Sermon de Benjamin sur les Noces de Cana,* ed. Henri De Vis (Hauniae: Glydendalske Boghandel-Nordisk Forlag), 1922, 53; C. D. G. Müller, *Die Homilie über die Hochzeit zu Kana* (Heidelberg: Carl Winter Universitätsverlag, 1968), 11–12.

53. Benjamin of Alexandria, *On Cana of Galilee,* 68–69.

54. Benjamin of Alexandria, *Die Homilie über die Hochzeit zu Kana,* 9; Benjamin of Alexandria, *On Cana of Galilee,* 66.

55. Cyril Hovorun, *Will, Action, and Freedom: Christological Controversies in the Seventh Century* (Leiden: Brill, 2008), 51. It is inaccurate to label, as Hovorun does, the anti-Chalcedonian theology of Benjamin as being "Severan" (51). Benjamin, rather, stands in the anti-Chalcedonian tradition of Egypt begun by Dioscorus and Timothy Aelurus, almost a century before Severus.

56. Benjamin of Alexandria, *Die Homilie über die Hochzeit zu Kana,* 54.

57. Benjamin, *Die Homilie über die Hochzeit zu Kana,* 56.

58. Benjamin, *Die Homilie über die Hochzeit zu Kana,* 124–26.

59. ⲉⲧⲁⲩⲉⲣϣⲉⲙⲙⲟ ⲙ̄ⲡⲟⲩⲅ̄ⲙⲁⲛⲙⲓⲥⲓ.

60. Benjamin, *Die Homilie über die Hochzeit zu Kana,* 128. Mikhail translates: "Are there not men today who are evicted from their hometowns on account of their drinking debts?" (*On Cana of Galilee,* 82). Mikhail explains that Benjamin is warning against drunkenness using well-known examples of people whose drinking habits caused them to lose their property because of debts. However, translating

ⲉⲧⲁⲩⲣϣⲉⲙⲙⲟ ⲙ̄ⲡⲟⲩⲙⲁⲛⲙⲓⲥⲓ as "evicted from their hometowns" is a bit far from the Coptic. It is more helpful to retain the sense communicated here, that drinking and financial irresponsibility can cause one to become estranged from their hometown and "become a stranger/foreigner."

61. Or "strangers."

62. Benjamin of Alexandria, *Die Homilie über die Hochzeit zu Kana*, 68.

63. Benjamin of Alexandria, *On Cana of Galilee*, 75n46.

64. Benjamin of Alexandria, *Die Homilie über die Hochzeit zu Kana*, 80–84.

65. G. Mitchell Reyes, *Public Memory, Race, and Ethnicity* (Newcastle upon Tyne: Cambridge Scholars Publishing, 2010), 2.

66. Benjamin of Alexandria, *Die Homilie über die Hochzeit zu Kana*, 118.

67. Mikhail identifies these heretics as Eutychians (*On Cana of Galilee*, 81n90).

68. Benjamin of Alexandria, *Die Homilie über die Hochzeit zu Kana*, 120.

69. Benjamin of Alexandria, *Die Homilie über die Hochzeit zu Kana*, 132. This story is also narrated in a Sahidic fragment published along with a fragment attributed to Benjamin's successor Agathon: C. D. G. Müller, "Neues Über Benjamin I, 38. und Agathon, 39. Patriarchen von Alexandrien," *Le Muséon* 72 (1959): 337–39.

70. Benjamin of Alexandria, *Die Homilie über die Hochzeit zu Kana*, 152. That ⲝⲉⲛⲓⲕⲟⲥ is used in place of the more common Coptic descriptor ϣⲉⲙⲙⲟ could indicate a desire to unambiguously highlight the priests ethnic, outsider status as ϣⲉⲙⲙⲟ can also refer simply to a "stranger" (Crum, *A Coptic Dictionary*, 565b).

71. ⲧⲉⲛⲭⲱⲣⲁ (Benjamin of Alexandria, *Die Homilie über die Hochzeit zu Kana*, 162).

72. Benjamin of Alexandria, *Die Homilie über die Hochzeit zu Kana*, 186.

73. Benjamin of Alexandria, *Die Homilie über die Hochzeit zu Kana*, 190.

74. Benjamin of Alexandria, *Die Homilie über die Hochzeit zu Kana*, 150. Mikhail simply translates "while I fled from persecution" (*On Cana of Galilee*, 84). Müller and De Vis give a more literal translation. The presentation of Benjamin and the Coptic orthodox as persecuted is a frequent theme throughout Benjamin's corpus and the exaggeration of the original text should be reflected in translation (Müller, *Benjamin I*, 150; De Vis, *Sermon de Benjamin*, 79).

75. Benjamin of Alexandria, *Die Homilie über die Hochzeit zu Kana*, 196.

76. Benjamin of Alexandria, *Die Homilie über die Hochzeit zu Kana*, 200.

77. ⲛ̄ⲓⲣⲱⲙⲉⲟⲥ ⲅⲁⲣ ⲥⲉⲛⲁⲣⲃⲧ̄ ⲉⲧⲭⲱⲣⲁ ⲛ̄ⲭⲏⲙⲓ ⲛ̄ⲧⲟⲩⲃⲟⲝⲓ ⲛ̄ⲥⲱⲕ ϣⲁⲧⲟⲩⲉⲓⲧⲕ ⲉⲃⲟⲗ ⲥⲓⲝⲉⲛ ⲡⲉⲕⲑⲣⲟⲛⲟⲥ.

78. Benjamin of Alexandria, *Die Homilie über die Hochzeit zu Kana*, 232–36.

79. Mikhail takes the mention of Shenoute's monastery here as an indication of this being the furthest south Benjamin traveled during his exile (*On Cana of Galilee*, 91n158), a supposition that leads him to doubt the Coptic text claiming that Benjamin traveled north (ⲉ̄ⲏⲧ) to the White Monastery before encountering the fornicating priest (82n101). For the Coptic, see Müller, *Die Homilie über die Hochzeit zu Kana*, 134; De Vis, 75, as Müller and De Vis both follow the Coptic.

80. Mikhail translates ⲛ̄ⲓⲣⲱⲙⲉⲟⲥ literally as "the Romans" (*On Cana of Galilee*, 91), while Müller and De Vis give a more interpretive gloss: "Die Byzantiner"

(Müller, *Die Homilie über die Hochzeit zu Kana*, 232); "Les Grecs" (De Vis, *Sermon de Benjamin*, 98).

81. جيش الروم.

82. *AHPA* I, 492–93. The word امته is used in reference to the "people" or "ethnicity" of Muhammad. Names such as "Egyptian," "Roman" and "Arab" that fill this narrative refer to the concept of ethnic identity framed by امته.

83. هالرب من الروم. *AHPA* I, 495. The text here also calls Benjamin the "freedom fighting Apa" (الاب المجاهد).

84. فان الذين فيه اقوام اقوياء كثيلر أ مصلريون وجميعهم اهل ليس بيهم غريب.

85. *AHPA* I, 498.

86. W. H. C. Frend, "Nationalism as a Factor in Anti-Chalcedonian Feeling in Egypt," in *Studies in Church History vol. 18: Religion and National Identity*, ed. Stuart Mews (Oxford: Blackwell, 1982), 21.

87. Mikhail, *From Byzantine to Islamic Egypt*, 22. Mikhail goes on to present the above statement as expressing "regional sentiment," a watered-down interpretation of the text wth regard to social identity. A specific region is not highlighted, as has been the case in many of the texts surveyed in the present study, but the people of Egypt.

88. It is also important that the material on Benjamin in the *AHPA* was directly borrowed from seventh-century texts (Coquin, *Livre de la consécration*, 24–25).

89. Benjamin of Alexandria, "On Cana of Galilee," 75n46.

90. *Apophthegmata Patrum*, 218.

91. Benjamin of Alexandria, *Die Homilie über die Hochzeit zu Kana*, 236–40.

92. Goehring, "Remembering Abraham of Farshut," 1; Goehring, "Chalcedonian Power Politics," 20.

93. شعبه.

94. كورة مصر كلها.

95. *AHPA* I, 497.

96. Benjamin of Alexandria, *On Cana of Galilee*, 68.

97. ምስራውየን.

98. ውእቱ ኮነ እግምሖመይ በርበር (John of Nikiu, *Chronicle*, 195). Again, I use the term "ethnicity" when matters of genotype and phenotype are not explicit. The Ge'ez word ሐመይ often appears in contexts denoting lingeage, family and species, as well as social grouping.

99. Benjamin of Alexandria, *Sermon de Benjamin*, 55.

100. هرقل الرومى الكافر.

101. الشلعب الارثدكسى.

102. الشعب.

103. *AHPA* I, 496.

104. *AHPA* I, 497.

105. ይጻልአሙ ጥፉ ለምስራውየን (John of Nikiu, *Chronicle*, 214).

106. Barth, *Ethnic Groups and Boundaries*, 37.

107. Jason R. Zaborowski, "Egyptian Christians Implicating Chalcedonians in the Arab Takeover of Egypt: The Arabic Apocalypse of Samuel of Qalamūn," *OC* 87 (2003): 108.

108. Isaac the Presbyter, *Life of Samuel of Kalamun*, ed. Alcock, 16.

109. Isaac, *Life of Samuel of Kalamun*, ed. Alcock, vii-ix. Pereira argues for a Coptic vorlage of the *Life* (Isaac, *Vida do Abba Samuel do mosteiro do Kalamon*, ed. F. M. Esteves Pereira [Lisbon: Imprensa Nacional, 1894], 60). Butler and Hoyland argue for a seventh-century composition; see Butler, *Arab Conquest of Egypt*, 185; Robert G. Hoyland, *Seeing Islam as Others Saw It: A Survey and Evaluation of Christian, Jewish and Zoroastrian Writings on Early Islam* (Princeton, NJ: Darwin Press, 1997), 286.

110. December 4.

111. Isaac, *Life of Samuel of Kalamun*, ed. Alcock, 1.

112. Isaac, *Life of Samuel of Kalamun*, ed. Alcock, 2. The village of Tkello, just outside the city of Pelhip, lies in the northeast Delta region (2n16).

113. ⲦⲈϤⲠⲀⲦⲢⲒⲤ.

114. Isaac, *Life of Samuel of Kalamun*, ed. Alcock, 2. The theme of citizenship in Jerusalem is frequent in the *Life*. Samuel is called the "seed of Zion" and a "relative (ⲞⲨⲢⲘ̄ⲚⲎⲒ) of heavenly Jerusalem" (3). Apa Agathou is "counted among heavenly Jerusalem" (4_. Samuel is also referred to as a "citizen of the Kingdom of Heaven" (17).

115. Isaac, *Life of Samuel of Kalamun*, ed. Alcock, 5.

116. ⲠⲬⲀⲨⲔⲒⲀⲚⲞⲤ.

117. ⲦⲀⲢⲬⲎ Ⲛ̄ⲚⲈⲚⲀⲨⲘⲰⲤⲒⲞⲚ. Alcock translates this portion as follows: "he was given civil authority" (Isaac, *Life of Samuel of Kalamun*, 79). Alcock indicates the Bohairic influence here with the plural article ⲚⲈⲚ, in addition to the text's Fayyumic influence (viii). Orlandi/Campagnano follow this reading: "he was given the administration of the public"; see *Vita di Samuele di Kalamon*, ed. Tito Orlandi and Antonella Campagnano, in *Vite de Monaci Copti* (Rome: Città Nuova Editrice, 1984), 232. The Ethiopic version leaves this detail out and simply claims that "while they are alive (Benjamin and Samuel), he (Cyrus) has no authority in Egypt" (ኢይከውን ፡ ሥምዓ ፡ በብሔረ ፡ ግብጽ) (Isaac, *Vida do Abba Samuel*, 88).

118. ⲠⲦⲞⲘⲞⲤ ⲈⲦⲀⲀ2Ⲙ̄ ⲚⲬⲀⲖⲬⲎⲀⲰⲚ. It is interesting that the *Tome* here is referred to as the "*Tome* of Chalcedon" in addition to its usual name, the "*Tome* of Leo." This demonstrates the way in which Coptic Miaphysites hold the *Tome* and the council as equally despicable enemies of orthodoxy, despite the *Tome*'s composition having preceded the council.

119. ⲚⲈⲢⲈⲦⲈⲬⲰⲢⲀ ⲦⲎⲢⲤ Ⲛ̄ⲔⲎⲘⲈ ⲀⲨϢⲈ Ⲛ̄ⲤⲀⲚⲈ2Ⲗ̄ⲖⲞ Ⲉ̄ⲦⲘ̄ⲘⲀⲨ.

120. Alcock's translation does not include Benjamin's name here, although it is present in the Coptic text (Isaac, *Life of Samuel of Kalamun*, 80).

121. ⲘⲈⲤⲤⲞⲞⲨⲦⲚ̄ Ⲛ̄6ⲒⲦⲀⲘⲚⲦⲢ̄ⲢⲞ ⲘⲚ̄ⲦⲀⲘⲚⲦⲀⲢⲬⲎⲈ̄ⲠⲒⲤⲔⲞⲠⲞⲤ 2Ⲛ̄ⲦⲈⲬⲰⲢⲀ ⲦⲎⲢⲤ̄ Ⲛ̄ⲔⲎⲘⲈ.

122. Alcock translates ⲂⲀⲢⲂⲀⲢⲞⲤ as "Berbers" throughout his translation of the *Life*. This is likely because the *Life* later reports that these "barbarians" came from the West (Isaac, *Life of Samuel of Kalamun*, 13).

123. Although there were Chalcedonians that were Egyptian (thus not associated with Constantinople/Byzantium), Egyptian Chalcedonians are not the primary target of anti-Chalcedonian polemic in Coptic Miaphysite literature. This is

evidenced in the frequent attacks on Leo, Justinian, the *Tome,* and the council itself. In seventh-century Coptic literature, Cyrus is also attacked and his foreign background is highlighted.

124. Isaac, *Life of Samuel of Kalamun,* 6–7.

125. ⲐⲀⲨⲤⲒⲀⲚⲞⲤ. Alcock suggests ⲐⲀⲨⲤⲒⲀⲚⲞⲤ is a corruption of θαυμασιανος, used here in an ironic way (Isaac, *Life of Samuel of Kalamun,* 7n81). Given the ironic sense employed here, I have gone with a more negative gloss provided in Henry G. Liddell and Robert Scott, *Greek-English Lexicon* (Oxford: Oxford University Press, 1843), 786a. The Copto-Arabic *Syanxarion* reports that both Samuel's eyes leaked out (*Vida do Abba Samuel,* 184).

126. Isaac, *Life of Samuel of Kalamun,* ed. Alcock, 9.

127. Isaac, *Vida do Abba Samuel,* 42.

128. Isaac, *Vida do Abba Samuel,* 53.

129. Isaac, *Life of Samuel of Kalamun,* 8. Alcock translates ⲤⲬⲎⲀⲰⲚ as 'almost' as he does on p. 5n57. In this instance, Alcock takes the meaning provided by Liddell-Scott "used to soften a positive assertion with a sense of modesty" (*Greek-English Lexicon,* 1744a-b). Here, the *Life* is depicting the extent of Samuel's renown. It is unlikely that the *Life* would seek to depict the extents to which Samuel's notoriety "almost" spread. Likewise, Orlandi and Campagnano translate ⲤⲬⲎⲀⲰⲚ as "fino a" ("up to") (Isaac, *Vita di Samuele,* 236).

130. ⲞⲘ here more likely means "in" given that Cyrus came from the north in Alexandria to the Fayyum district, against Alcock's reading ⲞⲘ as "from" (Isaac, *Life of Samuel of Kalamun,* 83). It is unlikely that Cyrus is coming from ⲔⲎⲘⲈ (i.e. Upper Egypt) but rather that he comes south from Alexandria into "Egypt," since ⲔⲎⲘⲈ is often associated with ⲢⲎⲤ in contrast to Alexandria. Orlandi/Campagnano's reading concurs: "Cyrus the Caucasian went to the South in the land of Egypt" (Isaac, *Vita di Samuele,* 237).

131. ⲂⲒⲦⲚ̄ ⲦⲈⲔⲈⲖⲈⲨⲤⲒⲤ Ⲛ̄ⲦⲒⲞⲨⲤⲦⲒⲚⲒⲀⲚⲞⲤ ⲠⲈϤⲈⲨⲤⲦⲞⲈⲢⲞⲚ̄ⲦⲈⲚⲈⲞⲢⲰⲘⲀⲒⲞⲤ ⲈϤⲔⲈⲖⲈⲨⲈ̄ ⲈⲦⲠⲢⲈⲦⲈⲬⲰⲢⲀ ⲦⲎⲢⲤ̄ Ⲛ̄ⲔⲎⲘⲈ ⲔⲞⲒⲚⲞⲚⲈⲒ ⲈⲠⲦⲞⲘⲞⲤ ⲈⲦⲨⲀⲞⲘ̄ Ⲛ̄ⲬⲀⲖⲬⲎⲀⲰⲚ. The form ⲠⲈϤⲈⲨⲤⲦⲞⲈⲢⲞⲚ̄ⲦⲈⲚⲈⲞⲢⲰⲘⲀⲒⲞⲤ is problematic. Alcock translates this bound group as "the false-king of the Romans" (Isaac, *Life of Samuel of Kalamun,* 83). Orlandi/Campagnano translate similarly: "the false emperor of the Romans" (Isaac, *Vita di Samuele,* 237). Alcock's Greek index identifies this Greek root as ψευστης. I have avoided the translation of ψευστης as "false" as found in Alcock and Orlandi/Campagnano to avoid association with ψευδο, which appears later in the *Life.*

132. Isaac, *Life of Samuel of Kalamun,* ed. Alcock, 9.

133. Neither Alcock nor Orlandi/Campagnano have been able to identify more precisely what is meant by Ⲛ̄ⲤⲞⲚ Ⲛ̄ⲔⲞⲤⲘⲒⲔⲞⲚ (Isaac, *Life of Samuel of Kalamun,* 84n72; *Vita di Samuele,* 238). Given the elusive nature of this term, I have rendered it more literally. It may also refer to ascetic novices in the monastic community.

134. ⲆⲈⲔⲰ Ⲛ̄ⳛⲘⲘⲞ Ⲛ̄ⲤⲨⲚⲀⲄⲈ Ⲛ̄ⲦⲞⲞⲦⲔ̄. Alcock's translation ignores Ⲛ̄ⳛⲘⲘⲞ and thus loses the ethnic dimension of the text: "we were not to celebrate the mass with you" (Isaac, *Life of Samuel of Kalamun,* 84). Orlandi/Campagnano stick closer

to the *Life*: "you allow foreigners (stranieri) participate in your communion" (Isaac, *Vita di Samuele*, 239). Their reading of ⲧⲉⲕⲱ entails a second-person singular subject prefix not present in Alcock's translation even though both editions come from the same manuscript. This phrase is absent from the Geʿez version: "you are impious and a Jew and have no law" (ⲟⲁⲱ ⲁ7ϯ ⲱⲁⲉⲩⲉⲫ ⲁ7ϯ ⲱⲁⲁⲧⲏ ⲣ7) (Isaac, *Vida do Abba Samuel*, 92). The manuscript from which Amélineau made his edition does not contain ⲇⲉⲕⲱ ⲛ̄ⲩⲙⲙⲟ; see Isaac, *Vie de Samuel de Qalamoun*, ed. Émile Amélineau, in *Monuments pour servir à l'histoire de l'Égypte chrétienne: Mémoires de la mission archéologique française* 4.2. Paris: Ernest Leroux, 1895), 774.

135. Stephen of Hnēs, *Panegyric on Apollo*, 15–17. As "Jewish" should be understood both as an ethnic and religious boundary, calling Cyrus a "Jew" further exacerbates the ethno-religious nature of the Egyptian boundary; see Barclay, "Ἰουδαῖος: Ethnicity and Translation," 47.

136. Alcock's translation leaves out ⲡⲕⲁⲩⲭⲓⲟⲥ with no explanation (Isaac, *Life of Samuel of Kalamun*, 84). Orlandi/Campagnano's translation as well as the manuscript edited by Amélineau retain this epithet in their translations (Isaac, *Vita di Samuele*, 239; *Vie de Samuel de Qalamoun*, 775).

137. Alcock's translation does not have "as an ascetic" (ⲍⲱⲥ ⲁⲥⲕⲏⲧⲏⲥ) although it is in the Coptic (Isaac, *Life of Samuel of Kalamun*, 85). The translations of Orlandi/Campagnano and Amélineau retain this phrase (Isaac, *Vita di Samuele*, 240; *Vie de Samuel de Qalamoun*, 776).

138. Codex B, from which Amélineau made his edition, has ⲕⲁⲕⲱⲥ, whereas Codex A has ⲕⲁⲗⲟⲥ (Isaac, *Vie de Samuel de Qalamoun*, 776). Orlandi/Campagnano's translation follows Codex A: "ma io ti darò una lezione e t'insegnerò a parlar bene" (Isaac, *Vita di Samuele*, 240). While Alcock's translation also follows Codex A (Isaac, *Life of Samuel of Kalamun*, 85), he prefers the reading found in Codex B: "Codex B reads 'badly', which I think is perhaps better: the sense would be 'I will teach you about speaking badly'" (85n77). I follow Orlandi/Campagnano in translating from Codex A; it seems more likely that Cyrus would want to instruct Samuel how to speak well (i.e. to espouse Chalcedonian doctrine).

139. ⲉⲓⲟ ⲛⲧⲁⳅⲓⲁⲣⲭⲏⲥ ⲉ̄ⳍⲉⲛ̄ ⲛⲉⲇⲉⲙⲱⲥⲓⲟⲛ ⲛ̄ⲧⲉⲭⲱⲣⲁ ⲛ̄ⲕⲏⲙⲉ. For translating ⲁⳅⲓⲁⲣⲭⲏⲥ ⲉ̄ⳍⲉⲛ̄ ⲛⲉⲇⲉⲙⲱⲥⲓⲟⲛ, I stick closer to Alcock's translation of "civil ruler" as opposed to the more fiscal sense of the term presented in the translations of Amélineau ("attendant of income") and Orlandi/Campagnano ("commander of tribute"). See Isaac, *Life of Samuel of Kalamun*, 85; *Vie de Samuel de Qalamoun*, 776; *Vita di Samuele*, 240.

140. An alternative name for Satan which Alcock identifies as being mentioned in the *Book of Jubilees* (Isaac, *Life of Samuel of Kalamun*, 11n112). Amélineau identifies this name in a Coptic text contemporary with the *Life* (Isaac, *Vie de Samuel de Qalamoun*, 776n10).

141. ⲧⲁⳅⲏⲥⲁⲣⲭⲏⲥ.

142. Isaac, *Life of Samuel of Kalamun*, ed. Alcock, 10.

143. Isaac, *Life of Samuel of Kalamun*, ed. Alcock, 10.

144. Isaac, *Life of Samuel of Kalamun*, ed. Alcock, 35.

145. I.e. "pagans." For a helpful overview of the problematic nature of the term "pagan" with respect ot practitioners of traditional religious practices, see Wester-field, *Egyptian Hieroglyphs*, 13.

146. Pereira identifies attestation to a monastery and church at Takinash in Coptic documentary papyri (Isaac, *Vida do Abba Samuel*, 40).

147. Isaac, *Life of Samuel of Kalamun*, ed. Alcock, 11.

148. Isaac, *Life of Samuel of Kalamun*, ed. Alcock, 13. Later in the *Life* while Samuel is practicing extreme asceticism alone in the desert, he is attacked by demons who "terrify in the manner of the barbarians" (31).

149. Isaac, *Life of Samuel of Kalamun*, ed. Alcock, 13.

150. ογΝΟϬ ⲚϐⲀⲣϐⲀⲣⲟⲥ (Isaac, *Life of Samuel of Kalamun*, ed. Alcock, 15). The ethnic group of Sokortes is identified as the "country of the Mazices" (ⲧⲉⲭⲱⲣⲀ ⲚⲚⲉⲙⲀⲥⲅϨ) (15). This name also appears in the *Apophthegmata Patrum* in reference to an ethnic group that live in the desert oases away from Scetis. They are referred to as the "race of the Maziks" (τῶν Μαζίκων γένος), *Apophthegmata Patrum*, 86. Alcock translates ϐⲀⲣϐⲀⲣⲟⲥ as "Berbers" throughout his translation. The Geʿez version calls Samuel's captors ሐፀል "barbarians" or "field-people" (Isaac, *Vida do Abba Samuel*, 108). The name ⲙⲀⲥⲅϨ is spelled the same in the *CCH* as in the *Life*; see D. Johnson, "A Coptic Source," 105. Zaborowski suggests the possibility of the "barbarians" referring to Arab conquerors, thus explaining the surprising silence on the Arab Conquest in the *Life* ("Egyptian Christians Implicating Chalcedoni-ans," 115).

151. Isaac, *Life of Samuel of Kalamun*, ed. Alcock, 19.

152. ⲟγⲭⲱⲣⲀ ⲚϢⲙⲙⲟ Ⲁγⲱ ⲚⲣⲉϥϣⲙϣⲉⲉⲓⲆⲱⲗⲟⲛ (Isaac, *Life of Samuel of Kalamun*, ed. Alcock, 15). The *Life* claims that sun-worship was the state religion of the Mazices. When Sokortes' wife desires healing from Samuel, Sokortes expresses his reluctance: "I am afraid of the laws of the Mazices, even more so our lord the Sun" (20).

153. Isaac, *Life of Samuel of Kalamun*, 15.

154. ⲡⲉⲥⲡⲉⲣⲙⲀ ⲚⲭⲀⲛⲀⲀⲛ (Isaac, *Life of Samuel of Kalamun*, ed. Alcock, 20). Alcock sees this as a reference to Mt. 15:22, 180. While this is possible, the wording is not present in the Gospel. Alternatively, this could be an ethnic epithet for neigh-boring barbarians from the perspective of late antique Egyptians.

155. Isaac, *Life of Samuel of Kalamun*, ed. Alcock, 20.

156. ⲟγⲀⲡⲉ ⲡⲉⲕⲛⲟγⲧⲉ (Isaac, *Life of Samuel of Kalamun*, ed. Alcock, 21).

157. Isaac, *Life of Samuel of Kalamun*, ed. Alcock, 21.

158. Isaac, *Life of Samuel of Kalamun*, ed. Alcock, 21.

159. Isaac, *Life of Samuel of Kalamun*, ed. Alcock, 24.

160. The view of "barbarians" in the Life was likely influenced by Roman atti-tudes towards foreign neighbors; see Mata, "Of Barbarians and Boundaries," 21. However, the Egyptian sense of superiority towards other people groups was present in pharaonic times; see Mu-Chou Poo, *Enemies of Civilization: Attitudes Toward Foreigners in Ancient Mesopotamia, Egypt, and China* (Albany, NY: State University of New York Press, 2005), 133.

161. Inge E. Boer, *Uncertain Territories: Boundaries in Cultural Analysis* (Amsterdam: Rodopi, 2006), 6.

162. Isaac, *Life of Samuel of Kalamun*, ed. Alcock, 24. Precisely what is meant by "Egypt" in this context is confusing given that Egypt is presented in this paragraph as a region distinct from Kalamun: "They spent two whole years living on their small fruits, so that they never went to Egypt for anything" (24). Also, one of Samuel's monks traveled "to Egypt" to sell merchandise (25). For another reference to travelling to Egypt for the purpose of commerce, see (30).

163. Isaac, *Life of Samuel of Kalamun,* ed. Alcock, 26.

164. Isaac, *Life of Samuel of Kalamun,* ed. Alcock, 25.

165. Isaac, *Life of Samuel of Kalamun,* ed. Alcock, 26.

166. *Homélie en l'Honneur de Samuel de Kalamon,* ed. Jean Simon; "Fragment d'une Homélie Copte en l'Honneur de Samuel de Kalamon," in *Miscellanea Biblica,* vol. 2 (Rome: Ex Schola Typographica Pio X, 1934), 174.

167. *Apocalypse,* 391. Here the author claims that there was further content regarding a secret conversation between Samuel and Gregorios that Samuel desired not to appear in any recordings

168. *Apocalypse,* 405. Likewise, Arietta Papaconstantiou identifies the *Apocalypse* with a group of Egyptian texts from this period she calls "prophetic homilies," in "'They Shall Speak the Arabic Language and Take Pride In It': Reconsidering the Fate of Coptic After the Arab Conquest," in *Le Muséon* 120 (2007): 281.

169. The Ethiopic *Synaxarion* identifies the subject of the *Apocalypse* as the Muslims; see Isaac, *Vida do Abba Samuel,* 176. The Copto-Arabic *Synaxarion,* however, refers to (185 المهاجرين). The Muhajirun refer more specifically to the earliest companions of Muhammad (188n2). Indeed, the Geʿez word that appears in the Ethiopic Synaxarion, ተንባላት, can refer to the earliest companions of Muhammad as well as to Muslims more generally.

170. *Apocalypse,* 406. Papaconstantinou also presupposes a Coptic composition ("They Shall Speak," 274). She pushes the date back to the tenth century and suggests the *Apocalypse* may have been a reaction to the rise in Arabic use among Copts due to Arabic-speaking figures such as Severus ibn al-Muqqafa' (292). Jos van Lent has argued for a ninth-century composition ("The Nineteen Muslim Kings in Coptic Apocalypses," *Parole de l'Orient* 25 [2000]: 664). John Iskander argues for an eleventh-century provenance in "Islamization in Medieval Egypt: The Copto-Arabic 'Apocalypse of Samuel' as a Source for the Social and Religious History of Medieval Copts," *Medieval Encounters* 4 (1998): 221. Maged Mikhail has argued for a late tenth century composition because of the rise in Arabic names among Christians as well as its use in liturgy during the tenth century (*From Byzantine to Islamic Egypt,* 99).

171. *Apocalypse,* 374–75.

172. Jason Zaborowski, "From Coptic to Arabic in Medieval Egypt," *Medieval Encounters* 14 (2008): 17.

173. Zaborowski, "From Coptic to Arabic," 36.

174. Zaborowski, "Egyptian Christians Implicating Chalcedonians," 108.

175. ملك الهجرة العربية على ارض مصر.

176. شعب النصارى (*Apocalypse*, 376).

177. Zaborowski, "Egyptian Christians Implicating Chalcedonians," 102.

178. Zaborowski, "Egyptian Christians Implicating Chalcedonians," 115. While central to Zaborowski's treatment of the *Apocalypse* is the thesis that its tone represents a localized phenomenon, other statements seem to indicate otherwise: "The *ASQ*'s references to the loss of Coptic certainly signal a provincialism, or regionalism, that reflects the local colors of Christians in Qalamūn, and Egypt in general" (113). This last statement is more accurate in placing the *Apocalypse* in a broader trajectory of pro-Egyptian Miaphysite literature.

179. Zaborowski, "Egyptian Christians Implicating Chalceodnians," 112.

180. Mikhail, *From Byzantine to Islamic Egypt*, 8.

181. *Apocalypse*, 376.

182. *Apocalypse*, 376.

183. *Apocalypse*, 377. Again on 382: "And everyone can see that what they (Muslims) did was indeed because of the sins of my people (شعبي), for they rejected my decrees and my commandments to resemble this people (امة)."

184. ወነለቀ ርኅም በዝንቱ ምክንያት ወተሠለጡ እስላም ላዕለ ምስር (John of Nikiu, *Chronicle*, 220).

185. امة صعبة المراس.

186. الهجرة.

187. *Apocalypse*, 377. الهجرة refers to the Hajj/Hegira; however, the sense here can also be referring to the Arabs as "immigrants."

188. Iskander, "Islamization in Medieval Egypt," 225.

189. الهجرة الاعراب, *Apocalypse*, 382. Or, "Arab Hajj-folk."

190. الاميين.

191. *Apocalypse*, 378.

192. لغة الحسنة القبطلية.

193. لغة الاعراب.

194. *Apocalypse*, 379. Coptic even represented the language of Christian monasticism in its adopted use in Christian Nubia; see van der Vliet, "Coptic as Nubian Literary Langauge," 271.

195. Zaborowski, "From Coptic to Arabic," 16. See also his later comment: "The Coptic language increasingly served as an indexical symbol of Coptic Christian identity, similar to the ways other minority communities have been served by their languages" (36).

196. Mikhail, *From Byzantine to Islamic Egypt*, 100.

197. Papconstantinou, "They Shall Speak Arabic," 273.

198. Papaconstantinou, "They Shall Speak Arabic," 298.

199. الكتب الغريبة, *Apocalypse*, 380. Papaconstantinou suggests the reading "Arabic books" ("They Shall Speak Arabic," 275).

200. Papaconstantinou, "They Shall Speak Arabic," 295.

201. *Apocalypse*, 380. Papaconstantinou disagrees with Ziadeh's identification of the "barbarians" here specifically as Amazigh ("Berbers"); she argues rather that the

Apocalypse refers to the Arab conquerors as "Berbers." She contrasts this with the use of ⲃⲁⲣⲃⲁⲣⲟⲥ in the *Life,* which she identifies with Amazigh along with Alcock ("They Shall Speak Arabic," 276n13).

202. لغتهم الحلوة (*Apocalypse,* 380).

203. Papaconstantinou, "They Shall Speak Arabic," 278.

204. Zaborowski, "Egyptian Christians Implicating Chalcedonians," 111.

205. Iskander, "Islamization in Medieval Egypt," 225.

206. الاسماء الخريبة.

207. *Apocalypse,* 380–81.

208. لخة الهجرة (*Apocalypse,* 384).

209. Van der Vliet, "The Copts," 280. However, the presence of Copto-centric rhetoric in the late antique and medieval periods complicates the common assumption that such Egyptian attitudes are unique to the modern world.

210. Barth, *Ethnic Groups and Boundaries,* 38. However, ethnic studies has also advanced the idea that ethnicity is not dependent on language; see Derks and Roymans, *Ethnic Constructs in Antiquity,* 2.

211. Language can often function as a marker of an ethnic boundary (Fought, *Language and Ethnicity,* 20).

212. Papaconstantinou, "They Shall Speak Arabic," 281.

213. Papaconstantinou, "They Shall Speak Arabic," 286.

214. *Apocalypse,* 384.

215. ارض مصر (*Apocalypse,* 386).

216. Hoyland, *Seeing Islam as Others Saw It,* 258.

217. *Apocalypse,* 387. This is a reference to the consecration of the church at Kalamun to Mary.

218. The ethnic and religious elements of identity are at play here together; see Moawad, "Some Features of Coptic Identity," 247.

219. حتى متى تدوم هذه الصعوبة وهذه الامة مالكة على ارض مصر (*Apocalypse,* 389). Here Apa Gregorius laments and inquires of Samuel as to the duration of the Islamic oppression.

220. *Apocalypse,* 388.

221. *Apocalypse,* 390. It is possible that the reference here to Ethiopia conquering the Arabs may have been influenced by the memory of the sixth-century invasion of Southern Arabia by the Axumite King Caleb which resulted in the dissolution of the Himyarite Kingdom and the short-lived reign of Ethiopia in Southern Arabia; see Glen W. Bowersock, *The Throne of Adulis: Red Sea Wars on the Eve of Islam* (Oxford: Oxford University Press, 2013), 93. The story of Ethiopia's defense of the Christian martyrs of Najran would have been well-known among medieval Egyptian Christians who had close ecclesiastical ties with the Ethiopian Church since the fourth century.

222. The Bohairic text has been edited three times with two French translations and a more recent English translation. See Émile Amélineau, *Histoire du Patriarche Copte Isaac: Étude Critique, Texte et Traduction* (Paris: Leroux, 1890); *Vie d'Isaac Patriarche d'Alexandrie,* ed. E. Porcher, PO 11 (1915); David N. Bell, *Mena of Nikiou: The Life*

of Isaac of Alexandria and *The Martyrdom of Saint Macrobius* (Kalamazoo, MI: Cistercian Publications, 1988). David Johnson notes the similarity between the accounts found in the *Life* and the *AHPA* and argues for a relationship in their transmission ("A Coptic Source," 71). The following study will follow Porcher's edition of the *Life*.

223. Severus ibn al-Muqaffa, *Arabic History of the Patriarchs of Alexandria* vol. III, ed. B. Evetts, in PO 5.1 (Paris: Firmin-Didot, 1947), 24.

224. Mena of Nikiou, *Vie d'Isaac*, 354. M. Chaîne shifts the date of 8 Choiahk to 9 Choiahk; see "La durée du patriarcat d'Isaac, XLIe Patriarche d'Alexandrie," *ROC* 23 (1922–23): 216.

225. Butler, *Arab Conquest of Egypt*, 549.

226. *AHPA* III, 21. Amélineau follows the *AHPA* for Isaac's date of consecration, but claims 688 CE as his death date (*Histoire du Patriarche*, x-xi). A similar date is given by E. Porcher, "Les dates du patriarcat d'Isaac," *ROC* 24 (1924): 219–22. For an earlier date of 684–687 CE, see F. Nau, "Vie d'Isaac, Patriarche d'Alexandrie de 686 à 689", ed. E. Porcher, PO 11 (1915); E. Tisserant and G. Wiet, "La liste des patriarches d'Alexandrie dans Qalqachandi," *ROC* 23 (1922–23): 123–43. A shorter date for Isaac's patriarchate of 690–692 CE has been argued by A. Jülicher, "Die Liste der alexandrinischen Patirachen im 6. und 7. Jahrhundert," in *Festgabe von Fachgenossen und Freunden Karl Müller* (Tübingen, 1922), 13.

227. Butler, *Arab Conquest of Egypt*, 549. For the date provided in the *Life*, see p. 386.

228. Bell, *Egypt from Alexander*, 24.

229. Butler, *Arab Conquest of Egypt*, 550. For the reference to Cyrus see Mena of Nikiou, *Vie d'Isaac*, 315.

230. Bell, *Egypt from Alexander*, 25.

231. Amélineau, *Histoire du Patriarche*, v.

232. Bell, *Egypt from Alexander*, 27.

233. Mena of Nikiou, *Vie d'Isaac*, 304.

234. Mena of Nikiou, *Vie d'Isaac*, 355.

235. ογρεμενχημιπε ϫεν πεϥгενος.

236. Mena of Nikiou, *Vie d'Isaac*, 304–5. The *AHPA* provides the name "Shubra" for Isaac's hometown: *AHPA* III, 23. Note slight translation differences in the various editions: "he was a man of Egypt by race," in Amélineau, *Histoire du Patriarche*, 2; "he was of the Egyptian race," in Porcher, *Vie d'Isaac*, 304; "was an Egyptian by race," in Bell, *Arab Conquest of Egypt*, 43.

237. G. M. Lee, "Coptic Christianity in a Changing World," *Studies in Church History vol. 18: Religion and National Identity* (Oxford: Oxford University Press, 1982), 45.

238. See Isaac, *The Invention of Racism*, 34; Buell, *Why This New Race*, 21.

239. Barth, *Ethnic Groups and Boundaries*, 14.

240. Byron, *Symbolic Blackness*, 5–6; McCoskey, *Race*, 2; Gruen, *Rethinking the Other*, 197–8.

241. Mena of Nikiou, *Vie d'Isaac*, 307. I follow Amélineau and Porcher's emendation of χαλτωλαριος to χαρτολαριος: Amélineau, *Histoire du Patriarche*, 5n1;

Porcher, *Vie d'Isaac,* 307n1. Bell also notes the persistence of Latin and Byzantine government titles, despite the lack of insight into exactly what these titles meant during Islamic rule in Egypt (*Egypt from Alexander,* 44n6).

242. This is the same monastery that was re-consecrated by Apa Benjamin a few decades before the patriarchate of Isaac (see above on Benjamin), testifying to the importance of this monastery for the Egyptian Miaphysite community.

243. Mena of Nikiou, *Vie d'Isaac,* 315.

244. Bell, *Egypt from Alexander,* 47n26.

245. Mena of Nikiou, *Vie d'Isaac,* 317. Bell argues that the patriarch referred to here is Benjamin (*Egypt from Alexander,* 48n28). This is certainly possible, as Isaac's youth most likely fell before the end of Benjamin's reign in 661 CE.

246. Mena of Nikiou, *Vie d'Isaac,* 327.

247. Mena of Nikiou, *Vie d'Isaac,* 327.

248. E.g. *Life of Pachomius,* ed. Armand Veilleux (Kalamazoo, MI: Cistercian Publications, 1980), 189; Anthony, *Letter 5,* ed. Samuel Rubenson (Peabody, MA: Trinity Press International, 1998), 212.

249. ϥⲁⲓ Ⲇⲉ ⲟⲩⲅⲉⲛⲟⲥ ⲉϥϭⲟⲥⲓⲡⲉ.

250. Mena of Nikiou, *Vie d'Isaac,* 328. Amélineau suggests that the "unblessed" group to which Ianne belonged were Chalcedonians (*Histoire du Patriarche,* xxvii-xxviii). Amélineau takes this group to be Chalcedonians. Bell, however, identifies them with the *akepholai* who followed neither the anti-Chalcedonian nor Chalcedonian patriarchs during the time of Peter Mongus (*Egypt from Alexander,* 53n48). This view is more likely as it would be unlikely for Chalcedonians to define themselves as having no patriarch since there was often a rival Chalcedonian patriarch in Alexandria. The *akepholai* (ⲛⲓⲁⲧⲁϥⲉ) was the heresy of a local bishop during a healing story later in the *Life* (370). Mikhail also suggests Ianne belonged to the *akepholai* and highlights this event as part of Isaac's policy of ecumenism (*From Byzantine to Islamic Egypt,* 63).

251. Bell, *Egypt from Alexander,* 53; the use of *genos* in late antique literature can often refer to familial lineage (Buell, *Why This New Race,* 2).

252. Amélineau, *Histoire du Patriarche,* 24.

253. Mena of Nikiou, *Vie d'Isaac,* 328.

254. Crum's dictionary suggests that ⲁⲧⲥⲙⲟⲩ here indicates those who have been forbidden to take communion, lending greater credibility to the argument that this group are *akepholai,* not Chalcedonians (*A Coptic Dictionary,* 336a).

255. Mena of Nikiou, *Vie d'Isaac* 331.

256. ⲛⲛⲓⲟⲣⲧⲁⲥⲧⲓⲕⲏ (Mena of Nikiou, *Vie d'Isaac,* 334).

257. Mena of Nikiou, *Vie d'Isaac,* 339.

258. Mena of Nikiou, *Vie d'Isaac,* 347–48.

259. Mikhail, *From Byzantine to Islamic Egypt,* 43.

260. *AHPA* III, 24.

261. Mena of Nikiou, *Vie d'Isaac,* 350.

262. Mena of Nikiou, *Vie d'Isaac,* 350.

263. ⲟⲩⲙⲏϣ ⲛⲗⲁⲟⲥ.

264. ⲭⲱⲣⲁ ⲛⲓⲃⲉⲛ (Mena of Nikiou, *Vie d'Isaac*, 351–52).

265. Mt. 27:11–26; Mk. 15:1–15; Lk. 23:1–25; Jn. 18:28–40. This is the first attested incident of Islamic governmental involvement in the Coptic patriarchal electoral process (Mikhail, *From Byzantine to Islamic Egypt*, 184).

266. Mena of Nikiou, *Vie d'Isaac*, 352.

267. *AHPA* III, 23.

268. Although the *Life* does not quote from the Gospel story, the similarities between the two accounts indicate a high likelihood of the familiar story being in the mind of the writer.

269. ⲧⲭⲱⲣⲁ ⲧⲏⲣⲥ ⲛⲧⲉ ⲭⲏⲙⲓ.

270. Porcher identified ⲛⲁⲡⲟⲧⲣⲓⲧⲏⲥ as the Greek τοποτηρητής (Mena of Nikiou, *Vie d'Isaac*, 354n2). I follow the suggestion of Amélineau who emends ⲛⲁⲡⲟⲧⲣⲓⲧⲏⲥ to ⲛⲁⲡⲟⲕⲣⲓⲧⲏⲥ as this edition only requires the shifting of one letter (*Histoire du Patriarche*, 49n.e). For an in-depth discussion see Amélineau's comments on xxiv-xxv. Bell does not express a preference for either option but notes that regardless of the loan word used here, the importance of the bishoprics of Nikiou and Kais is evident (*Egypt from Alexander*, 89n96).

271. Mena of Nikiou, *Vie d'Isaac*, 354.

272. A clear understanding of Egypt as a rhetorically-constructed space remains elusive in the *Life;* "Egypt" refers to the entire nation while it also is conceived as a region distinct from Alexandria and Scetis, as in the above excerpt.

273. Mena of Nikiou, *Vie d'Isaac*, 357.

274. Mena of Nikou, *Vie d'Isaac*, 363.

275. This is also the opinion of Bell, *Egypt from Alexander*, 67n119). Bell also notes the enigmatic nature of the reference to this otherwise unknown Alexandrian synod.

276. Mena of Nikiou, *Vie d'Isaac*, 363. The relationship between Isaac and the Muslim governor is an example of the way in which many seventh-century Muslims, often themselves former Christians, paid great respect to Christian leaders; see Jack B. V. Tannous, "Syria Between Byzantium and Islam: Making Incommensurables Speak" (Ph.D. diss., Princeton University, 2010), 472.

277. ⲛⲛⲓⲥⲁⲣⲁⲕⲏⲛⲟⲥ.

278. Zaborowski, *The Coptic Martyrdom of John of Phanijōit*, 30.

279. A similar attitude was evident with regard to language adoption by the author of the *Apocalypse of the Samuel of Kalamun*.

280. Patriarch John III of Samannud, 677–686 CE.

281. Mena of Nikiou, *Vie d'Isaac*, 366.

282. Mena of Nikiou, *Vie d'Isaac*, 368.

283. Mena of Nikiou, *Vie d'Isaac*, 372.

284. Mena of Nikiou, *Vie d'Isaac*, 376.

285. The Roman province Mauretania (modern Morocco) is unlikely (Mikhail, *From Byzantine to Islamic Egypt*, 356n121). The *AHPA* provides different locations for the two disputant nations: "In those days the patriarch addressed letters to the king of the Abyssinians and the king of the Nubians" (*AHPA* III, 24). Amélineau

differs from the *AHPA* as he identifies the nation of "Mauritania" as the territory of the Blemmyes (*Histoire du Patriarche,* xxxv). Rather than identifying "Makouria" with Ethiopia as in the *AHPA,* Amélineau indicates this region encompassing the bishoprics of Dongola, Korti, Ibrim, Bucaras, Saï, Termus, and Suenkur (xxxiv). Porcher suggests, rather, that Mauritania is correct and that the scribe may have confused "Makouria" for Morocco (*Vie d'Isaac,* 377n1). This is less likely and requires a greater deviance from the text. Bell follows the suggestion of Amélineau, stating that "Maurotania" is also associated with the land of the Blemmyes in the *Life of Shenoute* (*Egypt from Alexander,* 94n132). The suggestion of Amélineau and Bell is more likely, especially in light of the frequent conflict between the Blemmyes/Beja and Makouria. See William Y. Adams, *Nubia: Corridor to Africa* (Princeton, NJ: Princeton University Press, 1977), 451–52; George Hatke, *Aksum and Nubia: Warfare, Commerce, and Political Fictions in Ancient Northeast Africa* (New York: New York University Press, 2013), 157.

286. The text here does not supply an indication of a quote (e.g. ϫⲉ). Bell begins the quote much later while Porcher puts nothing in quotes here; see Bell, *Egypt from Alexander,* 73; Porcher, *Vie d'Isaac,* 378. Amélineau also does not provide quotation marks (*Histoire du Patriarche,* 72). I agree with Bell that this should be a quote given the presence of a second-person address (ⲛⲧⲉⲕϫⲉⲙ), but this would work better if the quote begins at the beginning of Isaac's final instructions to the king of Mauritania.

287. The *AHPA* adds that the episcopal secretaries replaced Isaac's letters with their own in an attempt to quell the governor's rage (*AHPA* III, 24).

288. Mena of Nikiou, *Vie d'Isaac,* 377–79.

289. Mena of Nikiou, *Vie d'Isaac,* 384.

290. كورة مصر.

291. الريف.

292. *AHPA* III, 25. The difference likely reflects the different situation of Egyptian Christians under Islamic rule between the period of the *Life* and that of the *AHPA.*

293. Barth, *Ethnic Groups and Boundaries,* 28. Moreover, the self-determination of ethnic minorities such as the Copts under Arab Muslim rule is not without interdepence with other groups; see Iris Marion Young, "Two Concepts of Self-Determination," in *Ethnicity, Nationalism and Minority Rights,* ed. Stephen May, Tariq Modood and Judith Squires (Cambridge, UK: Cambridge University Press, 2004), 177. In the case of the *Life,* Egypt asserts its self-determination among Arab Muslim rule while leveraging its international relations to the South.

CHAPTER 6. EGYPTIAN IDENTITY FROM
OUTSIDE PERSPECTIVES

1. Janette H. Ok, *Constructing Ethnic Identity in 1 Peter* (London: T&T Clark, 2021), 9. Ok also deploys the methodology of Barth in her assessment of Christian

ethnic identity in New Testament literature. Eric D. Barreto also indicates the necessity to balance emic ("insider") and etic ("outsider") perspectives in understanding ethnic identity; see *Ethnic Negotiations: The Function of Race and Ethnicity in Acts 16* (Tübingen: Mohr Siebeck, 2010), 15.

2. Mary Farag's work shows how Egypt became a place of refuge and solidarity for Palestinian Miaphysites (*What Makes a Church Sacred,* 175).

3. It has been suggested that Severus's original works in Greek do not survive due to the posthumous condemnation of his works; see Pauline Allen and C. T. R. Hayward, *Severus of Antioch* (New York: Routledge, 2004), 31. If this is true, it is a further indication of the strength of Miaphysitism among minority language groups within the Byzantine Empire, such as Coptic and Syriac. On the other hand, texts written in the imperial language that support theologies against the dominant imperial doctrine are minimized or erased; see the discussion above on the *Life of Daniel of Scetis.*

4. ܟܬܒܘܢܐ ܐܪܒܥܐ.

5. Severus of Antioch, *The Sixth Book of the Select Letters of Severus, Patriarch of Antioch: In the Syriac Version of Athanasius of Nisibus,* vol. 1, ed. E. W. Brooks (London: Williams & Norgate, 1904), 362.

6. ܣܘܥܪܢܐ ܓܝܪ ܟܕܒܐ, Zacharias of Mytilene, *The Life of Severus,* ed. Lena Ambjörn (Piscataway, NJ: Gorgias Press, 2008), 71. Ambjörn supposes a Greek original for the *Life* to have been written between 538 and 543 CE in response to allegations of the patriarch's involvement in pagan activities (20). See also Zacharius of Mytilene, *Two Early Lives of Severos, Patriarch of Antioch,* ed. Sebastian Brock and Brian FitzGerald (Liverpool: Liverpool University Press, 2013).

7. Zacharias, *Life,* 113.

8. Severus, *Sixth Book,* 56–57.

9. Severus, *Sixth Book,* 237.

10. Severus, *Sixth Book,* 173.

11. Severus of Antioch, *A Collection of Letters of Severus of Antioch from Numerous Syriac Manuscripts,* ed. E. W. Brooks, PO 12 (1916): 371.

12. ܐܬܘܬܐ.

13. ܟܝܢܐ.

14. Severus, *A Collection of Letters,* 279–80.

15. Isaac, *Life of Samuel of Kalamun,* 20.

16. ܣܘܥܪܢܐ.

17. Severus, *A Collection of Letters,* 290.

18. Severus, *Sixth Book,* 291.

19. Severus, *Sixth Book,* 291.

20. ܟܐܒ ܚܫܐ ܗܘ ܕܡܘܬܐ (Severus, *Sixth Book,* 291). Severus follows this with saying, "Oh that he never had been (king)!"

21. For example, the *Life of Timothy Aelurus,* 166; *Vie de Daniel,* 547–9; Isaac, *Life of Samuel of Kalamun,* 6–11.

22. For example, Price, "The Development of a Chalcedonian Identity in Byzantium," 307. If Severus is not considered "immediately," surely the writings of

Timothy Aelurus represent an "immediate" reaction against Chalcedon that simultaneously connects the doctrine with Byzantine imperial authority. From the perspective of its opponents, Chalcedonianism was associated with Byzantium from the beginning.

23. John of Ephesus, *Ecclesiastical History*, ed. Robert Payne Smith, in *The Third Part of the Ecclesiastical History of John Bishop of Ephesus* (Oxford: Oxford University Press, 1860), 261. As noted above, Severus is not ethnically Syrian as he was originally from Pisidia. However, as Patriarch of Antioch, Severus spoke on behalf of the Syrian people and was seen as a representative of the Syrian people by writers like John. While the role of non-Syrians in the formation of Syrian identity is beyond the scope of this study, it should be noted that Severus's statements are prized by the Syrian community as definitive for Syrian theology and identity.

24. William Harmless, *Desert Christians: An Introduction to the Literature of Early Monasticism* (Oxford: Oxford University Press, 2004), 43.

25. ܗܕܐ ܗܘ.

26. ܐܬܚܙܝ ܠܗܘܢ (Severus, *A Collection of Letters*, 323).

27. Severus, *A Collection of Letters*, 324.

28. Severus, *Sixth Book*, 338–39.

29. Stephen of Hnēs, *Panegyric on Apollo*, 31–32.

30. Mena of Nikiou, *Life of Isaac*, 66; Porcher, *Vie d'Isaac*, 366.

31. Papaconstantinou, "Historiography," 82. Severus's importance for Egypt is also evident in his final resting place being the Enaton monastery, also the location of subsequent Coptic papal coronations. See Scott F. Johnson, *Languages and Cultures of Eastern Christianity: Greek* (Burlington, VT: Ashgate Publishing, 2015), 44–47.

32. ܡܪܝܡ, that is, Alexandria.

33. *History of Dioscorus (Histoire de Dioscore)*, 79.

34. ܐܠܟܣܢܕܪ

35. *History of Dioscorus*, 79.

36. ܐܠܟܣܢܕܪ.

37. ܐܠܟܣܢܕܪ.

38. *History of Dioscorus*, 94–5.

39. ܐܠܗܘܬܐ.

40. *History of Dioscorus*, 103.

41. *A Homily on Severus of Antioch by a Bishop of Assiut*, ed. Youhanna Nessim Youssef (Leuven: Brepols, 2006), 23. This homily does not represent the perspective on ethnic and religious identity in sixth-century Egypt as it was written in the late medieval period. It is considered in this context to demonstrate the important role that Severus continued to play in the Egyptian Christian community throughout the medieval and modern periods.

42. *Homily on Severus*, 29–31.

43. *Homily on Severus*, 33. A similar picture is given in the Ethiopic *Life of Severus*; see Athanasius of Antioch, *The Conflict of Severus, Patriarch of Antioch by Athanasius*, ed. E. J. Goodspeed, PO 4 (1907): 712.

44. ‎ܙܟܪܝܐ‎.

45. ‎ܚܝܠܐ‎.

46. Zacharias of Mytilene, *Vie de Sévère par Zacharie le Scholastique*, ed. M. A. Kugener, PO 2 (1907): 211. As in the case of the *Life of Isaac*, I have chosen to translate‎ܓܢܣܐ‎ here as "ethnicity" rather than "race." See Mena of Nikiou, *Life*, 304–5. Again, there is no indication in the text of Severus's phenotypical description. Rather, the *Life* here is simply indicating the region that Severus is originally from.

47. *Homily on Severus*, 55.

48. *Homily on Severus*, 53.

49. *Homily on Severus*, 83.

50. Peter of Callinicum, *Anti-Tritheist Dossier*, ed. R. Y. Ebied, A. Van Roey, and L. R. Wickham. (Leuven: Departement Oriëntalistiek, 1981), 89.

51. Peter, *Anti-Tritheist Dossier*, 92.

52. Peter, *Anti-Tritheist Dossier*, 96.

53. Peter, *Anti-Tritheist Dossier*, 96–97.

54. Ebied and Wickham explain that the *Dossier* represents an earlier, more amiable tone from Peter before composing his principal work; see *Against Damian* in Peter of Callinicum, *Petri Callinicensis Patriarchae Antiocheni Tractatus contra Damianum*, vol. 1, ed. R. Y. Ebied, A. Van Roey, and L. R. Wickham, CSCO Series Graeca 29 (Louvain: Peeters, 1994), xiii. However, in *Against Damian* Peter also exhibits reverence for the orthodoxy of "the great Christian city of the Alexandrians" (2:157). This is not because ethnicized polemic is absent from Peter's writing, for his anti-Sabellian polemic is laced with ethnic rhetoric. Peter frequently refers to Sabellius as "the Libyan" and speaks of Libyan culture as "Jewish" and "atheist" throughout *Against Damian* (for example, 1:272).

55. Wipszycka, "Le nationalisme," 14.

56. Zaborowski, *Martyrdom of John of Phanijōit*, 177.

57. Zaborowski, *Martyrdom of John of Phanijōit*, 177–8.

58. Reymond and Barnes, *Four Martyrdoms*, 5.

59. A. Johnson, *Ethnicity and Argument*, 23.

60. Aaron Johnson, *Religion and Identity in Porphyry of Tyre: The Limits of Hellenism in Late Antiquity* (Cambridge, UK: Cambridge University Press, 2013), 213.

61. A. Johnson, *Religion and Identity*, 298.

62. Watts, *Riot in Alexandria*, 136.

63. Timothy Aelurus, "Extraits," 215.

64. John Rufus, *Life of Peter the Iberian*, 134.

65. John Rufus, *Life of Peter the Iberian*, xlix.

66. Severus, *Collection of Letters*, 334.

67. ‎ܥܡܐ‎.

68. Zacharias, *The Life of Severus*, 9.

69. ‎ܐܚܪܢܝܐܝܬ‎. Brooks has "in one form" for each group. While this is certainly acceptable, the more literal sense of ‎ܐܚܪܢܝܐܝܬ‎ brings out the ethnic distinction present among liturgical tradition more clearly.

70. ܟܠܝܡܐ (Severus, *Collection of Letters*, 332). "Districts" here is the Greek loan word κλίμα.

71. ϨⲚⲞⲨⲤⲬⲎⲘⲀ ⲘⲘⲞⲚⲀⲬⲞⲤ ⲚϢⲘⲘⲞ (Stephen of Hnēs, *Panegyric on Apollo*, 31).

72. C.D.G. Müller, "Damian, Papst und Patriarch von Alexandrien," *OC* 70 (1986): 131.

73. Elizabeth Bolman, *Monastic Visions: Wall Paintings in the Monastery of St. Anthony at the Red Sea* (New Haven: Yale University and the American Research Center in Egypt, 2002), 53.

74. Severus, *Sixth Book*, 393.

75. Sidney Griffith, "The Handwriting on the Wall: Graffiti in the Church of St. Antony," in *Monastic Visions: Wall Paintings in the Monastery of St. Antony at the Red Sea*, ed. Elizabeth Bolman (New Haven, CT: American Research Center in Egypt/Yale University Press, 2002), 185.

76. ܟܕܐܒܕܐܙܐ ܟܠܒܠܐܘ.

77. Severus, *Sixth Book*, 158.

78. Severus, *Sixth Book*, 167.

79. ܟܕܘܝܙܒܕܡܥ ܟܠܐ ܐܪܐܕܝ ܥܙܝ.

80. Mt. 10:8.

81. Severus, *Sixth Book*, 159.

82. ܟܕܝܒ ܟܙܘ.

83. ܟܙܘܠܒܐ.

84. ܟܕܝܒ ܟܘܟܐ.

85. ܐܝܡܥܠ.

86. ܝܝܝܒ ܕܘܟܝܐܥ.

87. ܐܠܥܠܝܠ.

88. ܕܘܟܠܐܥ ܟܠܐ.

89. The polarized language of "division," "indivisibility," "unity," and "separation" is particularly potent given the anti-Chalcedonian context from which Severus operated. It is likely that Severus's warning against "dividing that which is united," while directly referring to the unity between Egyptians and foreign exiles in this context, has a secondary application to Severus's Chalcedonian opponents.

90. Romans 14:13.

91. ܟܠܘܐܥ.

92. Severus, *Sixth Book*, 182–84.

93. Severus, *Sixth Book*, 261.

94. ܟܘܒܐܥ ܝܘܝܕ ܕܐܒܐܟ ܟܡܒܐܝܐܕܝܐܟ (Severus, *Sixth Book*, 261).

95. Severus, *Sixth Book*, 262.

96. ܟܕܝܐܒܐ ܒܠ ܝܡ ܟܕܝܒܕܝ.

97. ܕܘܟܝܠܟ.

98. ܟܕܘܝܒܐܙܐ ܟܕܠܒܠܒ ܝܡ ܟܕܘܙܒ (Severus, *Sixth Book*, 268).

99. Severus, *Sixth Book*, 369.

100. Menze, *Justinian*, 152.

101. ܟܕܐܝܙܝ ܟܕܝܒ.

102. Severus, *Sixth Book*, 370.

103. 2 Cor. 6:14.

104. Severus, *Sixth Book*, 370.

105. Severus, *Sixth Book*, 154.

106. Farag, *What Makes a Church Sacred*, 166.

107. Severus, *Sixth Book*, 271–72.

108. Severus, *Sixth Book*, 147.

109. Severus, *Sixth Book*, 147.

110. Severus, *Sixth Book*, 149.

111. Wipszycka, "Le nationalisme," 22.

112. ܪܘܚܐ ܩܕܝܫܐ.

113. ܚܫ ܐܚܝܕ.

114. ܘܗܘ ܚܣܝܘܬܐ ܕܝܠ ܩܫܝܫ ܒܢܘܣ.

115. ܠܒܐ.

116. Severus, *Collection of Letters*, 317–8.

117. Stuart Tyson Smith, *Wretched Kush: Ethnic Identities and Boundaries in Egypt's Nubian Empire* (New York: Routledge, 2003), 6. Smith's work examines Nubian ethnic identity as it is constructed from Egyptian sources in phaoronic times. Considered alongside this study, Egypt both constructed images of other identities while its own identity was constructed by others.

118. ܟܬܒܘܬܐ.

119. ܐܠܗܘܬܐ.

120. Peter of Callinicum, *Contra Damianum*, 121.

121. Zacharias, *Life of Severus*, 105.

122. ܠܒܐ ܕܒ ܐܚܝܕ ܡܫ ܥܠܝ.

123. Zacharias, *Life of Severus*, 105.

124. Zacharias, *Life of Severus*, 107.

125. Zacharias, *Life of Severus*, 109.

126. In his analysis of the above passage of Severus, Frend notes that the patriarch's influence on religious life or anti-imperial sentiment in Egypt was minimal (*The Rise of the Monophysite Movement*, 31).

127. Mena of Nikiou, *Life of Isaac*, 368–72.

128. Paul S. Rowe, "The Sheep and the Goats? Christian Groups in Lebanon and Egypt in Comparative Perspective," in *Nationalism and Minority Identities in Islamic Societies*, ed. Maya Shatzmiller (Montreal: McGill-Queen's University Press, 2005), 102.

129. Barth, *Ethnic Groups and Boundaries*, 36–37.

130. Severus, *Collection of Letters*, 318.

CONCLUSION

1. Helmut Reimitz, "Ethnogenesis," in *The Encyclopedia of Ancient History*, ed. Roger Bagnall, et al. (Hoboken, NJ: Wiley-Blackwell, 2012), 2528.

2. Lucas Van Rompay, "Society and Community in the Christian East," in *The Cambridge Companion to the Age of Justinian,* ed. Michael Maas (Cambridge, UK: Cambridge University Press, 2005), 254.

3. Recent scholarship on Near Eastern Christianity has demonstrated the way late antique Christian communities used intersecting aspects of identity to continuously reshape and redefine cultural categories; see Andrade, *Syrian Identity,* 31.

4. Foat, "I Myself Have Seen," 26.

5. Ewa Wipszycka, "La christianisation de l'Égypte aux IVe-Vie siècles. Aspects sociaux et ethniques," *Aegyptus* 68 (1988): 161.

6. Wipszycka, "La christianisation de l'Égypte," 161.

7. David Johnson, "Anti-Chalcedonian Polemics," 223.

8. Van der Vliet, "The Copts," 288.

9. Foat, "I Myself Have Seen," 59.

10. Barth, *Ethnic Groups and Boundaries,* 14.

11. Athanasius, *Life of Antony,* 130; Mena of Nikiou, *Life of Isaac,* 304–5.

12. *AHPA* I, 498.

13. Severus of Antioch, *A Collection of Letters,* 318.

BIBLIOGRAPHY

PRIMARY SOURCES

Ammon. *Letter of Ammon,* ed. James E. Goehring. Berlin: Walter de Gruyter, 1986.

Anthony. *Letter 5,* ed. Samuel Rubenson. Peabody, MA: Trinity Press International, 1998.

Apophthegmata Patrum, ed. John Wortley. Cambridge, UK: Cambridge University Press, 2013; Jean-Claude Guy, in *Les Apophtegmes des Pères, Collectio Systématique: Chapitres X-XVI.* Paris: Les Éditions du Cerf, 2003.

Athanasius of Alexandria. *Against the Greeks,* ed. Jacques-Paul Migne, *PG* 25, 1–94. Paris: Imprimerie Catholique, 1857.

———. *Apologia ad Constantinum,* ed. Jacques-Paul Migne, *PG* 25, 593–642. Paris: Imprimerie Catholique, 1857.

———. *History of the Arians,* ed. Jacques-Paul Migne, *PG* 25, 695–796. Paris: Imprimerie Catholique, 1857.

———. *Letter on the Nicene Decrees,* ed. Jacques-Paul Migne, *PG* 25, 411–476. Paris: Imprimerie Catholique, 1857.

———. *Letter to Marcellinus on the Interpretation of the Psalms,* ed. Jacques-Paul Migne, *PG* 27, 11–58. Paris: Imprimerie Catholique, 1857.

———. *Letter to Serapion concerning the Death of Arius,* ed. Jacques-Paul Migne, *PG* 25, 679–690. Paris: Imprimerie Catholique, 1857.

———. *Life of Antony,* ed. G. J. M. Bartelink, Paris: Les Éditions du Cerf, 2011; Coptic edition: G. Garitte, *S. Antonii Vitae Versio Sahidica,* CSCO Scriptores Coptici 4.1. Paris, E Typographeo Republicae, 1949; English translations: Robert C. Gregg, *Athanasius: The Life of Antony and The Letter to Marcellinus.* New York, NY: Paulist Press, 1980; Tim Vivian and Apostolos N. Athanassakis, *The Life of Antony: The Coptic Life and The Greek Life.* Kalamazoo, MI: Cistercian Publications, 2003.

———. *On the Incarnation,* ed. Jacques-Paul Migne, *PG* 25, 85–196. Paris: Imprimerie Catholique, 1857.

————. *Oration against the Arians* 1–4, ed. Jacques-Paul Migne, *PG* 26, 12–524. Paris: Imprimerie Catholique, 1857.

Athanasius of Antioch. *The Conflict of Severus, Patriarch of Antioch by Athanasius,* ed. E. J. Goodspeed, PO 4 (1907): 569–726.

L'Apocalypse de Samuel, Supérieur de Deir-el-Qalamoun, ed. J. Ziadeh. *ROC* 10 (1915–1917): 374–404.

Ausonius. *Parentalia.* Edited by Hugh G. Evelyn White. Cambridge, MA: Harvard University Press, 1919.

Benjamin of Alexandria. *Livre de la consécration du sanctuaire de Benjamin,* ed. René-Georges Coquin. Paris: IFAO, 1975.

————. *Sermon de Benjamin sur les Noces de Cana,* ed. Henri De Vis. Hauniae: Glydendalske Boghandel-Nordisk Forlag, 1922.

————. *Die Homilie über die Hochzeit zu Kana,* ed. C. D. G. Müller. Heidelberg: Carl Winter Universitätsverlag, 1968.

————. *Miracolo delle Nozze di Cana,* ed. Tito Orlandi. In *Omelie Copte.* Torino: Società Editrice Internazionale, 1981.

————. *On Cana of Galilee: A Sermon by the Coptic Patriarch Benjamin I,* ed. Maged Mikhail. *CCR* 23.3 (2002): 66–93.

Constantine of Siout. *Encomia in Athanasium duo,* ed. Tito Orlandi, CSCO 349–350. Louvain: Secrétariat du Corpus SCO, 1974.

Cyril of Alexandria. *Against Julian,* ed. Jacques-Paul Migne, *PG* 76, 490–1065. Paris: Imprimerie Catholique, 1859.

————. *Commentary on John,* 10, ed. Jacques-Paul Migne, *PG* 74, 9–757. Paris: Imprimerie Catholique, 1863.

————. *Letter* 17, ed. Jacques-Paul Migne, *PG* 77, 105–122. Paris: Imprimerie Catholique, 1859.

————. *Letter to John of Antioch,* P. E. Pusey. In *The Three Epistles of S. Cyril,* 40–53. Oxford: James Parker and Co., 1872.

————. *Memra 11 on the Commentary on the Gospel of Luke by Holy Cyril Archbishop of Alexandria concerning the Appearance of Our Lord,* ed. Jean-Baptiste Chabot, CSCO Scriptores Syri 4.1. Paris: E Typographeo Reipublicae, 1922.

Eudoxia and the Holy Sepulchre, ed. Harold A. Drake, Birger A. Pearson, and Tito Orlandi. Milan: Cisalpino, 1980.

Evagrius Scholasticus. *Ecclesiastical History,* ed. J. Bidez and L. Parmentier. Amsterdam: Hakkert, 1964.

Histoire de Dioscore, ed. F. Nau. *JA* 10 (1903): text 21–108; trans. 241–310.

History of the Monks of Egypt, ed. André-Jean Festugière. Bruxelles: Société des Bollandistes, 1971.

History of the Patriarchs of the Coptic Church of Alexandria, ed. B. Evetts. PO 1, (1904): 105–211; 383–518; 5 (1910): 2–215.

Homélie en l'honneur de Samuel de Kalamon, ed. Jean Simon. "Fragment d'une homélie copte en l'honneur de Samuel de Kalamon." In *Miscellanea Biblica,* vol. 2. Rome: Ex Schola Typographica Pio X, 1934, 161–178.

A Homily on Severus of Antioch by a Bishop of Assiut, ed. Youhanna Nessim Youssef. Leuven: Brepols, 2006.

Isaac the Presbyter, *Life of Samuel of Kalamun,* ed. Émile Amélineau. *In Monuments pour servir à l'histoire de l'Égypte chrétienne: Mémoires de la mission archéologique française* 4.2. Paris: Ernest Leroux, 1895.

———, *Vida do Abba Samuel do mosteiro do Kalamon,* ed. F.M. Esteves Pereira. Lisbon: Imprensa Nacional, 1894.

———. *Life of Samuel of Kalamun,* ed. Anthony Alcock. Warminster: Aris & Phillips Ltd, 1983.

———, *Vita di Samuele di Kalamon,* ed. Tito Orlandi and Antonella Campagnano. In *Vite de Monaci Copti.* Rome: Città Nuova Editrice, 1984.

Jerome, *Preface to the Pachomian Rules.* ed. Jacques-Paul Migne, *PL* 23, 65–68. Paris: Imprimerie Catholique, 1883.

John of Ephesus. *Ecclesiastical History,* ed. Robert Payne Smith. In *The Third Part of the Ecclesiastical History of John Bishop of Ephesus.* Oxford: Oxford University Press, 1860.

John of Nikiu. *The Chronicle of John, Bishop of Nikiu,* ed. H. Zotenberg. Paris: Imprimerie Nationale, 1888. English trans.: R.H. Charles. Merchantville, NJ: Evolution Publishing, 2007.

John Rufus. *Life of Peter the Iberian,* eds. Cornelia B. Horn and Robert R. Phenix Jr. In *John Rufus: The Lives of Peter the Iberian, Theodosius of Jerusalem, and the Monk Romanus.* Atlanta, GA: Society of Biblical Literature, 2008.

———. *Plerophoria,* ed. F. Nau. PO 8.1 (1911).

Julian of Halicarnassus, *Fragments,* ed. René Draguet. In *Julien d'Halicarnasse et sa controverse avec Sévère d'Antioche sur l'incorruptibilité du corps du Christ.* Louvain: Imprimérie P. Smeesters, 1924.

Justinian. *Against Origen,* ed. Jacques-Paul Migne, *PG* 86 916–993. Paris: Imprimerie Catholique, 1865.

Liberatus. *Brevarium,* ed. Edward Schwartz. ACO 2.5 (1932).

The Life of Apa Aphou, ed. Lincoln H. Blumell and Thomas A. Wayment, in *Christian Oxyrhynchus: Texts, Documents, and Sources,* 638–657. Waco, TX: Baylor University Press, 2015.

Life of Longinus, ed. Tim Vivian. In *Words to Live By: Journeys in Ancient and Modern Egyptian Monasticism,* 237–82. Kalamazoo, MI: Cistercian Publications, 2005.

Life of Pachomius. Sahidic: L. Lefort in *S. Pachomii Vitae,* CSCO Scriptores Coptici, Sahidice Scriptae 3.8. Paris: E Typographeo Reipublicae, 1933. Bohairic: ed. L. Lefort in *S. Pachomii Vita, Bohairice Scripta,* CSCO Scriptores Coptici 89.7. Louvain: Secrétariat du SCO, 1953. Greek: Apostolos N. Athanassakis, *Vita Prima Graeca.* Missoula, MT: Scholars Press, 1975. English: Armand Veilleux, *Pachomian Koinonia,* vol. I. Kalamazoo, MI: Cistercian Publications, 1980.

Life of Timothy Aelurus, ed. Hugh G. Evelyn White. In *New Texts from the Monastery of Saint Macarius: The Monasteries of Wadi 'n Natrûn,* 1:164–67. New York: Arno Press, 1996.

Martyrdom of John of Phanijoit, ed. Jason Zaborowski. Leiden: Brill, 2005.

Mena of Nikiou. *Vie d'Isaac patriarche d'Alexandrie,* ed. Émile Amélineau. *Histoire du patriarche copte Isaac: Étude critique, texte et traduction.* Paris, Leroux, 1890.

————. *Vie d'Isaac patriarche d'Alexandrie de 686 à 689,* ed. E. Porcher, PO 11 (1915).

————. *Mena of Nikiou: The Life of Isaac of Alexandria and The Martyrdom of Saint Macrobius.* Translated by David N. Bell. Kalamazoo, MI: Cistercian Publications, 1988.

Panegyric on Abraham of Farshut, Life of Manasses and Panegyric on Moses, ed. Émile Amélineau. In *Monuments pour servir a l'histoire de l'Égypte chrétienne aux 4., 5., 6., et 7. siècles.* Mèmoires publiés par les membres de la mission archéologique français au Caire 4/2. Paris, Leroux, 1895.

————, ed. Antonella Campagnano. In *Preliminary Editions of Coptic Codices: Monb. GC: Life of Abraham- Encomium of Abraham,* Corpus dei manoscritti copti letterari. Rome: Centro italiano microfiches, 1985.

Panegyric on Abraham of Farshut, ed. James E. Goehring. In *Politics, Monasticism, and Miracles in Sixth Century Upper Egypt: A Critical Edition and Translation of the Coptic Texts on Abraham of Farshut,* Studien und Texte zu Antike und Christentum. Tübingen: Mohr Siebeck, 2012.

Paralipomena on Saints Pachomius and Theodore, ed. André-Jean Festugière, in *Le Corpus Athénien de Saint Pachome,* 73- 93. Geneva: Patrick Cramer, 1982.

Der Pentateuch Koptisch, ed. Paul de Lagarde. Leipzig: B. G. Teubner, 1867.

Peter of Callinicum. *Anti-Tritheist Dossier,* ed. R. Y. Ebied, A. Van Roey and L. R. Wickham. Leuven: Departement Oriëntalistiek, 1981.

————. *Petri Callinicensis Patriarchae Antiocheni Tractatus contra Damianum,* ed. R. Y. Ebied, A. Van Roey, and L. R. Wickham. 4 vols. CSCO Series Graeca 29. Louvain: Peeters, 1994.

Pseudo-Dioscorus, *Panégyrique de Macaire de Tkoou,* ed. Émile Amélineau. *Monuments pour servir à l'histoire de l'Égypte chrétienne aux 4. et 5. siècles.* Mèmoires publiés par les membres de la mission archéologique français au Caire 4/2. Paris, Leroux, 1895.

————. *Panegyric on Macarius of Tkôw,* ed. David W. Johnson, CSCO 415–416. Louvain: Secrétariat du Corpus SCO, 1980.

————. *Panegyrikos auf Makarios von Tkôōu,* ed. Samuel Moawad. Wiesbaden: Reichert Verlag, 2010.

Pseudo-Leontius, *De sectis.* PG 86: 1193–1268.

Pseudo-Samuel of Kalamun. *L'Apocalypse de Samuel, supérieur de deir-el-Qalamoun,* ed. J. Ziadeh. *ROC* 20 (1915–1917): 374–404.

Pseudo-Theopistus, *Histoire de Dioscore, patriarche d'Alexandrie,* ed. F. Nau. *JA* 10 (1903): 5–108 (text), 241–310 (translation).

Severus ibn al-Muqaffa, *Arabic History of the Patriarchs of Alexandria,* vols. I, III, ed. B. Evetts. PO 1.4, 5.1 (1904, 1947): 381–519, 1–215.

Severus of Antioch. *A Collection of Letters of Severus of Antioch from Numerous Syriac Manuscripts,* ed. E. W. Brooks. PO 12 (1916): 165–342.

————. *The Sixth Book of the Select Letters of Severus, Patriarch of Antioch: In the Syriac Version of Athanasius of Nisibus*. 2 vols. Ed. E. W. Brooks. London: Williams & Norgate, 1904.

Shenoute of Atripe. *I Have Been Reading the Holy Gospels*, in *Sinuthii Archimandritae Vita et Opera Omnia*, vol. III, ed. Johannes Leipoldt, 218–224 (Paris: E Typographeo Reipublicae, 1931); Mark Moussa, "I Have Been Reading the Holy Gospels by Shenoute of Atripe (Discourses 8, Work 1): Coptic Text, Translation, and Commentary." PhD diss. The Catholic University of America, 2010.

————, *Let Our Eyes*, ed. Stephen Emmel, in "Shenoute of Atripe and the Christian Destruction of Temples in Egypt: Rhetoric and Reality." In *From Temple to Church: Destruction and Renewal of Local Cultic Topography in Late Antiquity*, ed. Johannes Hahn Stephen Emmel and Ulrich Gotter, 161–201. Leiden: Brill, 2008.

————, *Not Because a Fox Barks*, ed. Emile Chassinat, in *Le Quatrième Livre des Entretiens et Épîtres de Shenouti: Mémoires publiés par les membres de l'Institut français d'archéologie orientale 23*, 204–216. Cairo: Institut Français d'Archéologie Orientale du Caire, 1911. English trans.: David Brakke and Andrew Crislip, *Selected Discourses of Shenoute the Great: Community, Theology, and Social Conflict in Late Antique Egypt*, 201–205. Cambridge, UK: Cambridge University Press, 2015.

Stephen of Hnēs, *Panegyric on Apollo*, ed. Karl H. Kuhn, CSCO 394–395. Louvain: Secrétariat du Corpus SCO, 1978.

Storio della chiesa di Alessandria, ed. Tito Orlandi. Milano: Istituto Editoriale Cisalpino, 1967.

Synaxarium, ed. Réne Basset. PO 11 (1915): 505–859.

————, ed. Jacques Forget. Louvain: Secrétariat du corpus SCO Scriptores Arabici 18 (text & Latin translation). Rome: Excudebat Karolus de Luigi, 1921.

Theophilus of Alexandria. *Chronicon Paschale*, ed. Bruno Krusch, in *Studien zur Christlich-Mittelalterlichen*, 221–226. Leipzig: Verlag von Veit, 1880.

————. *Letter to Emperor Theodosius*, ed. Bruno Krusch, in *Studien zur Christlich-Mittelalterlichen*, 220–221. Leipzig: Verlag von Veit, 1880. English trans.: Norman Russell, *Theophilus of Alexandria* (New York: Routledge, 2007), 81–82.

————. *On Isaiah 6:1–7*, ed. D. Germani Morin. In *Sancti Hieronymi Presbyteri: Tractatus Siue Homiliae, Anaecdota Maredsolana*, 3.3, 103–128. Maredsoli, 1903.

————. *Second Synodal Letter to the Bishops of Palestine and Cyprus*. Ed. Isidor Hilberg, CSEL 55, 147–155. Leipzig: Temksy, 1912.

Timothy Aelurus. *Against Chalcedon*. Edited by R. Y. Ebied and L. R. Wickham. In *After Chalcedon: Studies in Theology and Church History Offered to Professor Albert van Roey*, edited and translated by C. Laga, J. A. Munitiz, and L. Van Rompay, 115–66. Leuven: Peeters, 1985.

————. "A Collection of Unpublished Syriac Letters of Timothy Aelurus." Edited by R. Y. Ebied and L. R. Wickham. *JTS* 21 (1970): 321–69.

————. "Extraits de Timothée Aelure." Edited by François Nau. PO 13 (1919): 202–18.

Vie et récits de l'Abbé Daniel le Scété (VI Siècle), ed. Ignazio Guidi. *ROC* 5 (1900): 535–64; 6 (1901): 51–53.

———, ed. L. Clugnet, F. Nau, and Ignazio Guidi. Paris: Bibliothèque Hagiographique Orientale 1, 1901.

———, ed. F. M. Esteves Pereira. In *Vida do Abba Daniel do Mosteiro de Sceté*, Lisbon: Imprensa Nacional, 1897.

———, ed. Christa Müller-Kessler and Michael Sokoloff. In *The Forty Martyrs of the Sinai Desert, Eulogios the Stone-Cutter, and Anastasia*. A Corpus of Christian Palestinian Aramaic III. Groningen: Styx, 1996.

———, ed. Britt Dahlman. In *Saint Daniel of Sketis: A Group of Hagiographic Texts with Introduction, Translation, and Commentary*. Studia Byzantina Upsaliensis 10. Uppsala: Acta Universitatis Upsaliensis, 2007.

———, ed. Tim Vivian. In *Witness to Holiness: Abba Daniel of Scetis*. Kalamazoo, MI: Cistercian Publications, 2008.

Vite dei monaci Phif e Longino, ed. Tito Orlandi. Milano: Cisalpino-Goliardica, 1975.

———, ed. Tim Vivian. In *Words to Live By: Journeys in Ancient and Modern Egyptian Monasticism*, 237–282. Kalamazoo, MI: Cistercian Publications, 2005.

Zacharias of Mytilene. *Chronicle of Zachariah Scholasticus*, ed. F. J. Hamilton and E. W. Brooks. London: Methuen & Co, 1899.

———. *The Chronicle of Pseudo-Zachariah Rhetor*, ed. Geoffrey Greatrex. Liverpool: Liverpool University Press, 2011.

———. *Vie de Sévère*, ed. M. A. Kugener. PO 2 (1907): 199–400.

———. *The Life of Severus*, ed. Lena Ambjörn. Piscataway, NJ: Gorgias Press, 2008.

———. *Two Early Lives of Severos, Patriarch of Antioch*, ed. Sebastian Brock and Brian Fitzgerald. Liverpool: Liverpool University Press, 2013.

Zacharias of Sakha, *Vie de Jean Kolobos*, ed. Émile Amélineau. Paris: Annales du Musée Guimet 25, 1894. Trans. Tim Vivian and Maged Mikhail, *CCR* 18 (1997): 3–64.

SECONDARY SOURCES

Abramowski, L. "Ein Text des Johannes Chrysostomus über die Auferstehung in den Belegsammlungen des Timotheus Älurus." In *After Chalcedon: Studies in Theology and Church History Offered to Profesor Albert van Roey*, edited and translated by C. Laga, J. A. Munitiz, and L. Van Rompay, 1–10. Leuven: Peeters, 1985.

Adams, William Y. *Nubia: Corridor to Africa*. Princeton, NJ: Princeton University Press, 1977.

Allen, Pauline, and C. T. R. Hayward. *Severus of Antioch*. New York: Routledge, 2004.

Amélineau, Émile. *Geographie de l'Égypte à l'époque copte*. Paris: Imprimerie nationale, 1893.

———. *Résumé de l'histoire de l'Égypte depuis les temps les plus reculés jusqu'à nos jours*. Paris: Ernest Leroux, 1894.

Anderson, Benedict. *Imagined Communities: Reflections on the Origin and Spread of Nationalism*. New York: Verso, 1983.

Andrade, Nathanael. *Syrian Identity in the Greco-Roman World*. Cambridge, UK: Cambridge University Press, 2013.

Bagnall, Roger. *Egypt in the Byzantine World*. New York: Cambridge University Press, 2007.

Baldwin, James. "Faulkner and Desegregation." *The Partisan Review* (1956): 568–73.

Barclay, John M. G. "Ἰουδαῖος:: Ethnicity and Translation." In *Ethnicity, Race, Religion: Identities and Ideologies in Early Jewish and Christian Texts, and in Modern Biblical Interpretation*, ed. David G. Horrell and Katherine M. Hockey, 46–58. London: Bloomsbury Publishing, 2018.

Barreto, Eric D. *Ethnic Negotiations: The Function of Race and Ethnicity in Acts 16*. Tübingen: Mohr Siebeck, 2010.

Barth, Fredrik. "Boundaries and Connections." In *Signifying Identities: Anthropological Perspectives on Boundaries and Contested Values*, edited by Anthony P. Cohen, 17–36. New York: Routledge, 2000.

———. *Ethnic Groups and Boundaries: The Social Organization of Culture Difference*. Oslo: Universitetsforlaget, 1969.

Beaucamp, Joëlle. "Byzantine Egypt and Imperial Law." In *Egypt in the Byzantine World, 300–700*, edited by Roger S. Bagnall, 271–87. Cambridge, UK: Cambridge Univesity Press, 2007.

Becker, Adam H., and Annette Yoshiko Reed. *The Ways That Never Parted: Jews and Christians in Late Antiquity and the Early Middle Ages*. Minneapolis: Fortress, 2007.

Bert, Michel, and James Costa. "What Counts as a Linguistic Border, for Whom and What Implications? Exploring Occitan and Francoprovençal in Rhône-Aples, France." In *Language, Borders and Identity*, edited by Dominic Watt and Carmen Llamas, 186–205. Edinburgh: Edinburgh University Press, 2014.

Bedjan, Paul. *'Liber superiorum seu Historia Monastica auctore Thoma, Episcopa Margensi' Dicta de Sévres*. Leipzig: Harrassowitz, 1901.

Bell, Harold Idris. *Egypt from Alexander the Great to the Arab Conquest: A Study in the Diffusion and Decay of Hellenism*. Oxford: Clarendon Press, 1948.

Blaudeau, Philippe. "Timothée Aelure et la direction ecclésiale de l'Empire post-chalcédonien." *REB* 54 (1996): 107–33.

Boer, Inge E. *Uncertain Territories: Boundaries in Cultural Analysis*. Amsterdam: Rodopi, 2006.

Bolman, Elizabeth. *Monastic Visions: Wall Paintings in the Monastery of St. Anthony at the Red Sea*. New Haven, CT: Yale University and the American Research Center in Egypt, 2002.

Bond, Sarah E. "Why We Need to Start Seeing the Classical World in Color." *Hyperallergic*, June 7, 2017. https://hyperallergic.com/383776/why-we-need-to-start-seeing-the-classical- world-in-color.

Bowersock, Glen W. *The Throne of Adulis: Red Sea Wars on the Eve of Islam.* Oxford: Oxford University Press, 2013.

Boyarin, Daniel. "Semantic Differences; or 'Judaism/Christianity.'" In *The Ways that Never Parted: Jews and Christians in Late Antiquity and the Early Middle Ages,* edited by Adam H. Becker and Annette Yoshiko Reed, 65–85. Tübingen: Mohr Siebeck, 2003.

Brakke, David. *Athanasius and Asceticism.* Baltimore, MD: The Johns Hopkins University Press, 1995.

Brakmann, Heinzgerd. "Zum Pariser Fragment angeblich des koptischen Patriarchen Agathon: Ein neues Blatt der Vita Benjamin I." *Muséon* 93 (1980): 299–309.

Bright, Pamela. "The Church as 'The House of Truth' in the Letters of Antony of Egypt." In *Origeniana Octava: Origen and the Alexandrian Tradition,* vol. II, edited by L. Perrone, 977–86. Leuven: Leuven University Press, 2003.

Bright, W. "Timotheus." *Dictionary of Christian Biography,* 4:1031–33. London: John Murray, 1887.

Brock, Sebastian. "An Early Syriac Life of Maximus the Confessor." *Analecta Bollandiana* 91 (1975): 299–346.

Brown, Peter. *Poverty and Leadership in the Later Roman Empire.* Hanover, NH: University Press of New England, 2001.

Brubaker, Rogers. "Ethnicity Without Groups." In *Ethnicity, Nationalism, and Minority Rights,* edited by Stephen May, Tariq Modood, and Judith Squires, 50–77. Cambridge, UK: Cambridge University Press, 2004.

Budge, Wallis E. A. *The Earliest Known Coptic Psalter: The Text, in the Dialect of Upper Egypt, Edited from the Unique Papyrus Codex Oriental 5000 in the British Museum.* London: Kegan Paul, Trench, Trübner & Co. Ltd., 1898.

Buell, Denise K. *Why This New Race: Ethnic Reasoning in Early Christianity.* New York: Columbia University Press, 2008.

Burguière, André, and Raymond Grew. *The Construction of Minorities: Cases for Comparison Across Time and Around the World.* Ann Arbor: University of Michigan Press, 2001.

Burstein, Stanley M. *Graeco-Africana: Studies in the History of Greek Relations with Egypt and Nubia.* New Rochelle, NY: Aristide D. Caratzas, 1995.

Butler, Alfred J. *Arab Conquest of Egypt and the Last Thirty Years of the Roman Dominion,* edited by P. M. Fraser. 2nd ed. Oxford: Clarendon Press, 1978.

Byron, Gay L. *Symbolic Blackness and Ethnic Difference in Early Christian Literature.* New York: Routledge, 2002.

Cain, Andrew. *The Greek Historia Monachorum in Aegytpo: Monastic Hagiography in the Late Fourth Century.* Oxford: Oxford University Press, 2016.

Cameron, Averil M. *Byzantine Matters.* Princeton, NJ: Princeton University Press, 2014.

———. *Christianity and the Rhetoric of Empire: The Development of Christian Discourse.* Berkeley: University of California Press, 1991.

Campagnano, Antonella. "Monaci egiziani fra V e VI secolo." *VetChr* 15 (1978): 223–46.

Camplani, Alberto. "A Syriac Fragment from the Liber Historiarum by Timothy Aelurus (CPG 5486), the Coptic Church History, and the Archives of the Bishopric of Alexandria." In *Christianity in Egypt: Literary Production and Intellectual Trends Studies in Honor of Tito Orlandi,* edited by Paola Buzi and Alberto Camplani, 206–26. Roma: Instituta Patristicum Augustinianum, 2011.

Cavallo, Guglielmo. *The Byzantines.* Chicago: University of Chicago Press, 1997.

Chaîne, M. "La durée du patriarcat d'Isaac, XLIe Patriarche d'Alexandrie." *ROC* 23 (1922–23): 214–16.

Cohen, Ronald. "Ethnicity: Problem and Focus in Anthropology." *Annual Review of Anthropology* 7 (1978): 379–403.

Collar, Anna. *Religious Networks in the Roman Empire: The Spread of New Ideas.* Cambridge, UK: Cambridge University Press, 2013.

Cornell, Stephen and Douglas Hartmann. *Ethnicity and Race: Making Identities in a Changing World.* Thousand Oaks, CA: Pine Forge Press, 2007.

Coyle, John Kevin. *Manichaeism and Its Legacy.* Leiden: Koninklijke Brill, 2009.

Crum, Walter E. *A Coptic Dictionary.* Oxford: Oxford University Press, 1939.

———. "Eusebius and Coptic Church Histories." *Society of Biblical Archeology* 24 (1902): 68–84.

Davis, Stephen. *Coptic Christology in Practice.* Oxford: Oxford University Press, 2008.

———. *The Early Coptic Papacy.* Cairo: American University in Cairo Press, 2004.

De Fina, Anna. "Code-Switching and the Construction of Ethnic Identity in a Community of Practice." *Language in Society* 36 (2007): 371–92.

De Vos, George, and Lola Romanucci-Ross, eds. *Ethnic Identity: Creation, Conflict, and Accommodation.* 3rd ed. London: Altamira Press, 1995.

Dench, Emma. *From Barbarians to New Men: Greek, Roman, and Modern Perceptions of Peoples from the Central Apennines.* Oxford: Clarendon Press, 1995.

Derks, Ton, and Nico Roymans. *Ethnic Constructs in Antiquity: The Role of Power and Tradition.* Amsterdam: Amsterdam University Press, 2009.

Despres, Leo A. *Ethnicity and Resource Competition in Plural Societies.* The Hague: Mouton, 1975.

Du Bois, W. E. B. "The Conservation of Races." In *The Oxford W. E. B. DuBois Reader,* edited by Eric Sundquist, 38–47. New York: Oxford University Press, 1996.

Emmel, Stephen. "Immer erst das Kleingedruckte lesen: 'Die Pointe verstehen' in dem koptischen Panegyrikos auf Makarios von Tkōou." In *Ägypten- Münster. Kulturwissenschaftliche Studien zu Ägypten, dem Vorderen Orient und verwandten Gebieten,* edited by Erhart Graefe, Anke I. Blöbaum, Jochem Kahl and Simon D. Schweitzer, 91–104. Wiesbaden: Harrassowitz Verlag, 2003.

Eriksen, Thomas Hylland. *Ethnicity and Nationalism: Anthropological Perspectives.* 2nd ed. London: Pluto Press, 2002.

Evans, Trevor. "Complaints of the Natives in a Greek Dress: The Zenon Archive and the Problem of Egyptian Interference." In *Multilingualism in the Graeco-Roman*

Worlds, edited by Alex Mullen and Patrick James, 106–23. Cambridge, UK: Cambridge University Press, 2012.

Evelyn White, Hugh G. *The Monasteries of the Wadi 'N Natrun.* Vol. 2 of *The History of the Monasteries of Nitria and Scetis.* New York: Arno Press, 1973.

Farag, Mary K. *What Makes a Church Sacred? Legal and Ritual Perspectives from Late Antiquity.* Oakland: University of California Press, 2021.

Flusin, B. "L'Hagiographie palestinienne et la reception du concile de chalcédoine." In *LEIMWN: Studies Presented to Lennart Rydén on His Sixty-Fifth Birthday,* edited by J. O. Rosenqvist, 25–47. Uppsala, 1996.

Foat, Michael. "I Myself Have Seen: The Representation of Humanity in the Writings of Apa Shenoute of Atripe." PhD diss., Brown University, 1996.

Fought, Carmen. *Language and Ethnicity.* Cambridge, UK: Cambridge University Press, 2006.

Frankfurter, David. *Christianizing Egypt: Syncretism and Local Worlds in Late Antiquity.* Princeton, NJ: Princeton University Press, 2018.

———. *Pilgrimage and Holy Space in Late Antique Egypt.* Leiden: Brill, 1998.

Frend, W. H. C. "Heresy and Schism as Social and National Movements." In *Studies in Church History, Vol. 9: Schism, Heresy and Religious Protest,* edited by Derek Baker, 37–56. Cambridge, UK: Cambridge University Press, 1972.

———. "Nationalism as a Factor in Anti-Chalcedonian Feeling in Egypt." In *Studies in Church History vol. 18: Religion and National Identity,* edited by Stuart Mews, 21–38. Oxford: Blackwell, 1982.

———. *The Rise of the Monophysite Movement: Chapters in the History of the Church in the Fifth and Sixth Centuries.* Cambridge, UK: Cambridge University Press, 1972.

Gaddis, Michael. *There is No Crime for Those who Have Christ: Religious Violence in the Christian Roman Empire.* Berkeley: University of California Press, 2005.

Galvao-Sobrinho, Carlos R. *Doctrine and Power: Theological Controversy and Christian Leadership in the Later Roman Empire.* Oakland: University of California Press, 2021.

Garman, Sebastian. "Ethnosymbolism in the Ancient Mediterranean World." In *Nationalism and Ethnosymbolism: History, Culture and Ethnicity in the Formation of Nations,* edited by Athena S. Leoussi and Steven Grosby, 113–125. Edinburgh: Edinburgh University Press, 2007.

Gat, Azar, and Alexander Yakobson. *Nations: The Long History and Deep Roots of Political Ethnicity and Nationalism.* Cambridge, UK: Cambridge University Press, 2013.

———. *Nations and Nationalism.* Ithaca, NY: Cornell University Press, 1983.

Goehring, James E. *Ascetics, Society, and the Desert: Studies in Early Egyptian Monasticism.* Harrisburg, PA: Trinity Press International, 1999.

———. "Chalcedonian Power Politics and the Demise of Pachomian Monasticism." Occasional Paper 15. Claremont, CA: Institute for Antiquity and Christianity, 1989.

———. "Keeping the Monastery Clean: A Cleansing Episode from an Excerpt on Abraham of Farshut and Shenoute's Discourse on Purity." In *The World of Early Egyptian Christianity: Language, Literature, and Social Context*, edited by James E. Goehring and Janet Timbie, 158–75. Washington, DC: The Catholic University of America Press, 2007.

———. "Pachomius' Vision of Heresy: The Development of a Pachomian Tradition." *Le Muséon* 95 (1982): 241–62.

———. "Remembering Abraham of Farshut: History, Hagiography, and the Fate of the Pachomian Tradition." *JECS 14* (2006): 1–26.

Goldschmidt, Lazarus, and F. M. Esteves Pereira. *Vida do Abba Daniel do Mosteiro de Sceté: Versão Ethiopica*. Lisbon: Imprensa Nacional, 1897.

Griffith, Sidney. "The Handwriting on the Wall: Graffiti in the Church of St. Antony." In *Monastic Visions: Wall Paintings in the Monastery of St. Antony at the Red Sea*, edited by Elizabeth Bolman, 185–93. New Haven, CT: American Research Center in Egypt/Yale University Press, 2002.

Grillmeier, Aloys. *Christ in Christian Tradition. Volume Two, Part One: From the Council of Chalcedon (451) to Gregory the Great (590–604): Reception and Contradiction the Development of the Discussion about Chalcedon from 451 to the Beginning of the Reign of Justinian*. Atlanta, GA: John Knox Press, 1996.

Gruen, Erich S. *Rethinking the Other in Antiquity*. Princeton, NJ: Princeton University Press, 2011.

Guibernau, Montserrat, and John Rex, eds. *The Ethnicity Reader: Nationalism, Multiculturalism and Migration*. Cambridge, UK: Polity Press, 1997.

Haar Romeny, Bas ter. "Ethnicity, Ethnogenesis and the Identity of the Syriac Orthodox Christians." In *Visions of Community in the Post-Roman World: The West, Byzantium and the Islamic World, 300–1100*, edited by Walter Pohl, Clemens Gantner, and Richard Payne, 183–204. New York: Routledge, 2012.

———. *Religious Origins of Nations? The Christian Communities of the Middle East*. Leiden: Brill, 2010.

Haldon, John F. *Byzantium: A History*. Stroud: Tempus Publishing, 2000.

Hall, Jonathan M. *Ethnic Identity in Greek Antiquity*. Cambridge, UK: Cambridge University Press, 1997.

———. *Hellenicity: Between Ethnicity and Culture*. Chicago: University of Chicago Press, 2002.

Hall, Stuart. *The Fateful Triangle: Race, Ethnicity, Nation*. Cambridge, MA: Harvard University Press, 2017.

Harmless, William. *Desert Christians: An Introduction to the Literature of Early Monasticism*. Oxford: Oxford University Press, 2004.

Hatke, George. *Aksum and Nubia: Warfare, Commerce, and Political Fictions in Ancient Northeast Africa*. New York: New York University Press, 2013.

Horrell, David G., and Katherine M. Hockey. *Ethnicity, Race, Religion: Identities and Ideologies in Early Jewish and Christian Texts, and in Modern Biblical Interpretation*. London: Bloomsbury Publishing, 2018.

Hovorun, Cyril. *Will, Action, and Freedom: Christological Controversies in the Seventh Century*. Leiden: Brill, 2008.

Hoyland, Robert G. *In God's Path: The Arab Conquests and the Creation of an Islamic Empire*. Oxford: Oxford University Press, 2015.

———. *Seeing Islam as Others Saw It: A Survey and Evaluation of Christian, Jewish and Zoroastrian Writings on Early Islam*. Princeton, NJ: Darwin Press, 1997.

Isaac, Benjamin. *The Invention of Racism in Classical Antiquity*. Princeton, NJ: Princeton University Press, 2004.

Iskander, John. "Islamization in Medieval Egypt: The Copto-Arabic 'Apocalypse of Samuel' as a Source for the Social and Religious History of Medieval Copts." *Medieval Encounters* 4 (1998): 219–27.

Jacobs, Andrew S. *Remains of the Jews: The Holy Land and Christian Empire in Late Antiquity*. Palo Alto, CA: Stanford University Press, 2004.

Jan Mohamed, Abdul, and David Lloyd. "Introduction: Toward a Theory of Minority Discourse." *Cultural Critique* 6 (1987): 5–12.

Jenkins, Richard. *Rethinking Ethnicity*. 2nd ed. London: Sage Publications, 2008.

Johnson, Aaron P. "The Blackness of Ethiopians: Classical Ethnography and Eusebius's Commentary on the Psalms." *The Harvard Theological Review* 99, no. 2 (2006): 165–86.

———. *Ethnicity and Argument in Eusebius' Praeparatio Evangelica*. Oxford: Oxford University Press, 2006.

———. *Religion and Identity in Porphyry of Tyre: The Limits of Hellenism in Late Antiquity*. Cambridge, UK: Cambridge University Press, 2013.

Johnson, David W. "Anti-Chalcedonian Polemics in Coptic Texts." In *Roots of Egyptian Christianity*, edited by. B. A. Pearson and James Goehring, 216–34. Philadelphia, PA: Fortress, 1986.

———. "A Coptic Source for the *History of Patriarchs of Alexandria*." Ph.D. diss., The Catholic University of America, 1973.

———. "The Dossier of Aba Zenobius." *Orientalia* 58 (1989): 193–212.

———. "Further Fragments of a Coptic History of the Church: Cambridge OR. 1699 R." *Enchoria: Zeitschrift für Demotistik und Koptologie* 6 (1976): 7–17.

———. "Pope Timothy II Aelurus: His Life and His Importance for the Development of Christianity in Egypt." *Coptica* 1 (2002): 77–89.

Johnson, Scott F. *Languages and Cultures of Eastern Christianity: Greek*. Burlington, VT: Ashgate Publishing, 2015.

Jones, A. H. M. "Were Ancient Heresies National or Social Movements in Disguise?" *JTS* 10 (1959): 280–98.

Jülicher, A. "Die Liste der alexandrinischen Patriachen im 6. und 7. Jahrhundert." In *Festgabe von Fachgenossen und Freunden Karl Müller*, 7–23. Tübingen, 1922.

Kennedy, Rebecca F. "Why I Teach About Race and Ethnicity in the Classical World." *Eidolon*, 2017. Accessed June 9, 2021. https://eidolon.pub/why-i-teach-about-race-and-ethnicity-in-the-classical-world-abe379722170.

Kennedy, Rebecca F., C. Sydnor Roy, and Max L. Goldman. *Race and Ethnicity in the Classical World: An Anthology of Primary Sources in Translation.* Indianapolis, IN: Hackett Publishing Company, 2013.

Kiss, Zsolt. "Alexandria in the Fourth to Seventh Centuries." In *Egypt in the Byzantine World, 300–700,* edited by Roger S. Bagnall, 187–206. Cambridge, UK: Cambridge University Press, 2007.

Kuhn, Karl H. "Two Further Fragments of a Panegyric on Apollo." *Le Muséon* 95 (1982): 263–68.

Layton, Bentley. *The Canons of Our Fathers: Monastic Rules of Shenoute.* Oxford: Oxford University Press, 2014.

Lebon, Joseph. "La christologie de Timothée Ailure, archevêque monophysite d'Alexandrie, d'après les sources syriaques." *RHE* 9 (1908): 677–702.

———. "Version arménienne et version syriaque de Timothée Elure." *Handes Amsorya: Zeitschrift für armenische Philologie* 41 (1927): 713–22.

Lee, G. M. "Coptic Christianity in a Changing World." In *Studies in Church History Vol. 18: Religion and National Identity,* 39–45. Oxford: Oxford University Press, 1982.

Leipoldt, Johannes. *Schenute von Atripe und die Entstehung des national ägyptischen Christentums.* Leipzig: J. C. Hinrichs'sche Buchhandlung, 1903.

Lieu, Judith M. "Identity Games in Early Christian Texts: The Letter to Diognetus." In *Ethnicity, Race, Religion: Identities and Ideologies in Early Jewish and Christian Texts, and in Modern Biblical Interpretation,* edited by David G. Horrell and Katherine M. Hockey, 59–72. London: Bloomsbury Publishing, 2018.

MacCoull, Leslie S. B. *Documenting Christianity in Egypt, Sixth to Fourteenth Centuries.* Burlington, VT: Ashgate, 2011.

Malešević, Siniša. *The Sociology of Ethnicity.* London: Sage Publications, 2004.

Maspero, Jean. "Horapollon et la fin du paganisme égyptien." *BIFAO* 11 (1914): 163–95.

Mata, Karim. "Of Barbarians and Boundaries: The Making and Remaking of Transcultural Discourse." In *Romans and Barbarians Beyond the Frontiers: Archaeology, Ideology and Identities in the North,* edited by Sergio González Sánchez and Alexandra Guglielmi, 8–33. Philadelphia, PA: Oxbow, 2017.

Mathisen, Ralph, and Danuta Shanzer. *Romans, Barbarians, and the Transformation of the Roman World: Cultural Interaction and the Creation of Identity in Late Antiquity.* Burlington, VT: Ashgate, 2011.

———, and Hagith S. Sivan. *Shifting Frontiers in Late Antiquity.* Aldershot, UK: Variorum, 1996.

May, Stephen, Tariq Modood, and Judith Squires. *Ethnicity, Nationalism, and Minority Rights.* Cambridge, UK: Cambridge University Press, 2004.

McCoskey, Denise Eileen. *Race: Antiquity and Its Legacy.* Oxford: Oxford University Press, 2012.

———. "Race Before 'Whiteness': Studying Identity in Ptolemaic Egypt." In *Critical Sociology* 2, no. 1–2 (2002): 13–39.

Menze, Volker L. *Justinian and the Making of the Syrian Orthodox Church*. Oxford: Oxford University Press, 2008.

Mikhail, Maged S. A. *From Byzantine to Islamic Egypt: Religion, Identity and Politics after the Arab Conquest*. London: I. B. Tauris, 2014.

Millar, Fergus. "The Evolution of the Syrian Orthodox Church in the Pre-Islamic Period: From Greek to Syriac?" *JECS* 21 (2013): 43–92.

Mitchell, Stephen, and Geoffrey Greatrex. *Ethnicity and Culture in Late Antiquity*. London: Duckworth, 2000.

Moawad, Samuel. "John of Shmoun and Coptic Identity." In *Christianity and Monasticism in Middle Egypt: Al-Minya and Asyut,* edited by Gawdat Gabra and Hany N. Takla, 89–98. Cairo: The American University in Cairo Press, 2015.

———. "The Role of the Church in Establishing Coptic Identity." *Coptica* 13 (2014): 11–40.

———. "Some Features of Coptic Identity." *ANES* 53 (2016): 243–74.

Moussa, Mark. "I Have Been Reading the Holy Gospels by Shenoute of Atripe (Discourses 8, Work 1): Coptic Text, Translation, and Commentary." PhD diss., The Catholic University of America, 2010.

Müller, C. D. G. "Benjamin I: 38. Patriarch von Alexandrien." *Le Muséon* 69 (1956): 313–40.

———. "Damian, Papst und Patriarch von Alexandrien." *OC* 70 (1986): 118–42.

———. *Die Kirche in ihrer Geschichte: Geschichte der orientalischen Nationalkirchen*. Göttingen: Vandenhoeck & Ruprecht, 1981.

———. "Neues Über Benjamin I, 38. und Agathon, 39. Patriarchen von Alexandrien." *Le Muséon* 72 (1959): 323–47.

Nau, François. "Sur la christologie de Timothée Aelure." *ROC* 2nd ser. 4.14 (1909): 99–103.

Nicks, Fiona K. "Literary Culture in the Reign of Anastaius I." In *Ethnicity and Culture in Late Antiqiuty,* edited by Stephen Mithcell and Geoffrey Greatrex, 183–204. London: Duckworth, 2000.

Obłuski, Artur. *The Rise of Nobadia: Social Changes in Northern Nubia in Late Antiquity*. Warsaw: University of Warsaw Institute of Archaeology/Department of Papyrology, 2014.

Ok, Janette H. *Constructing Ethnic Identity in 1 Peter*. London: T&T Clark, 2021.

Olick, Jeffrey K., Vered Vinitzky-Seroussi, and Daniel Levy. *The Collective Memory Reader*. Oxford: Oxford University Press, 2011.

Olster, David. "From Periphery to Center: The Transformation of Late Roman Self-Definition in the Seventh Century." In *Shifting Frontiers in Late Antiquity,* edited by Ralph W. Mathisen and Hagith S. Sivan, 93–102. Aldershot: Variorum, 1996.

Orlandi, Tito. "Literature, Coptic." *CE* 5: 1450–60.

———. "The Coptic Ecclesiastical History: A Survey." In *The World of Early Egyptian Christianity: Language, Literature, and Social Context,* edited by James E. Goehring and Janet A. Timbie, 3–24. Washington, DC: The Catholic University of America Press, 2007.

———. "Un Projet Milanais Concernant les Manuscrits Coptes du Monastère Blanc." *Le Muséon* 85 (1972): 403–13.

———. *Vite di Monaci Copti*. Roma: Città Nuova Editrice. 1984.

Papaconstantinou, Arietta. "Historiography, Hagiography, and the Making of the Coptic 'Church of the Martyrs' in Early Islamic Egypt." *DOP* 60 (2006): 65–86.

———. "'They Shall Speak the Arabic Language and Take Pride In It': Reconsidering the Fate of Coptic After the Arab Conquest." *Le Muséon* 120 (2007): 273–99.

Patterson, Paul A. *Visions of Christ: The Anthropomorphite Controversy of 399 CE*. Tübingen: Mohr Siebeck, 2012.

Pohl, Walter, and Gerda Heydemann, eds. *Strategies of Identification: Ethnicity and Religion in Early Medieval Europe*. Turnhout: Brepols, 2013.

Pohl, Walter, Clemens Gantner, and Richard Payne, eds. *Visions of Community in the Post-Roman World: The West, Byzantium and the Islamic World, 300–1100*. Burlington, VT: Ashgate Publishing Company, 2012.

Poo, Mu-Chou. *Enemies of Civilization: Attitudes Toward Foreigners in Ancient Mesopotamia, Egypt, and China*. Albany: State University of New York Press, 2005.

Porcher, E. "Les dates du patriarcat d'Isaac." *ROC* 24 (1924): 219–22.

Prattis, Iain. "Barthing up the Wrong Tree." *American Anthropologist* 85 (1983): 103–9.

Price, Richard. "The Development of a Chalcedonian Identity in Byzantium (451–553)." In *Religious Origins of Nations? The Christian Communities of the Middle East*, edited by Bas ter Haar Romeny, 307–25. Leiden: Brill, 2010.

Quentin, H. J. *Jean-Dominique Mansi et les grandes collections conciliaires*. Whitefish, MT: Kessinger Publishing, 1900.

Rapp, Claudia. "Monastic Jargon and Citizenship Language in Late Antiquity." *Al-Masāq: Journal of the Medieval Mediterranean* 32, no. 1 (2020): 54–63.

Reimitz, Helmut. "Ethnogenesis." In *The Encyclopedia of Ancient History*, edited by Roger Bagnall, et al., 2528–31. Hoboken, NJ: Wiley-Blackwell, 2012.

Rex, John. "The Fundamentals of the Theory of Ethnicty." In *Making Sense of Collectivity: Ethnicity, Nationalism and Globalization*, edited by Siniša Malešević and Mark Haugaard, 88–121. London: Pluto Press, 2002.

Reyes, G. Mitchell. *Public Memory, Race, and Ethnicity*. Newcastle upon Tyne: Cambridge Scholars Publishing, 2010.

Reymond, E. A. E. and J. W. B. Barnes. *Four Martyrdoms from the Pierpont Morgan Coptic Codices*. Oxford: Clarendon Press, 1973.

Riley, Philip. *Language, Culture and Identity: An Ethnolinguistic Perspective*. London: Continuum, 2007.

Romanucci-Ross, Lola, George A. De Vos, and Takeyuki Tsuda, eds. *Ethnic Identity: Problems and Prospects for the Twenty-First Century*. 4th ed. London: Altamira Press, 2006.

Rousseau, Philip. *Pachomius: The Making of a Community in Fourth-Century Egypt*. Berkeley: University of California Press, 1985.

———. "The Successors of Pachomius and the Nag Hammadi Codices: Exegetical Themes and Literary Structures." In *The World of Early Egyptian Christianity: Language, Literature, and Social Context: Essays in Honor of David W. Johnson,* edited by David W. Johnson, James E. Goehring, and Janet A. Timbie, 140–57. Washington, DC: The Catholic University of America Press, 2007.

Roymans, Nico. *Ethnic Identity and Imperial Power: The Batavians in the Early Roman Empire.* Amsterdam: Amsterdam University Press, 2004.

Rowe, Paul S. "The Sheep and the Goats? Christian Groups in Lebanon and Egypt in Comparative Perspective." In *Nationalism and Minority Identities in Islamic Societies,* edited by Maya Shatzmiller, 85–107. Montreal: McGill-Queen's University Press, 2005.

Sarris, Peter. *Economy and Society in the Age of Justinian.* Cambridge, UK: Cambridge University Press, 2006.

Sellers, R. V. *The Council of Chalcedon: A Historical and Doctrinal Survey.* London: SPCK, 1953.

Shatzmiller, Maya, ed. *Nationalism and Minority Identities in Islamic Societies.* Montreal: McGill-Queen's University Press, 2005.

Shepardson, Christina. *Anti-Judaism and Christian Orthodoxy: Ephrem's Hymns in Fourth-Century Syria.* Washington, DC: Catholic University of America Press, 2008.

Simon, Thomas W. *Ethnic Identity and Minority Protection: Designation, Discrimination, and Brutalization.* Lanham, MD: Lexington Books, 2012.

Smelser, Neil J., William Julius Wilson, and Faith Mitchell. *America Becoming: Racial Trends and Their Consequences.* Vol 1. Washington, DC: National Academy Press, 2001.

Smith, Anthony D. *Theories of Nationalism.* New York: Harper & Row, 1971.

Smith, Stuart Tyson. *Wretched Kush: Ethnic Identities and Boundaries in Egypt's Nubian Empire.* New York: Routledge, 2003.

Snowden, Frank M., Jr. *Blacks in Antiquity.* Cambridge, MA: Belknap Press, 1970.

Sonnis-Bell, Marissa, David Elijah Bell, and Michelle Ryan. *Strangers, Aliens, Foreigners: The Politics of Othering from Migrants to Corporations.* Leiden: Brill, 2019.

Street, Jon. "College Professor Says White Marble Statues Promote Racism," Blaze Media, June 8, 2017. Accessed June 9, 2021. https://www.theblaze.com/news/2017/06/08/college-professor-says-white-marble-statues-promote-racism.

Suny, Ron. "Making Minorities: The Politics of National Boundaries in the Soviet Experience." In *The Construction of Minorities: Cases for Comparison Across Time and Around the World,* edited by André Burguière and Raymond Grew, 245–68. Ann Arbor: The University of Michigan Press, 2001.

Tanaseanu-Döbler, Ilinca. *Theurgy in Late Antiquity: The Invention of a Ritual Tradition.* Beiträge zur Europäischen Religionsgeschichte (BERG). Vol. I. Göttingen: Vandenhoeck and Ruprecht, 2013.

Tannous, Jack B. V. "Syria Between Byzantium and Islam: Making Incommensurables Speak." Ph.D. diss., Princeton University, 2010.

Till, Walter. "Koptishe Heiligen- Und Martyrerlegenden: Texte, Übersetzungen und Indices Herausgegeben und Bearbeitet." In *OCA* 102, 126–33. Roma: Pont. Institutum Orientalium Studiorum, 1935.

Tisserant E., and G. Wiet. "La liste des patriarches d'Alexandrie dans Qalqachandi." *ROC* 23 (1922–23): 123–43.

Van Cauwenbergh, Paul. *Étude sur les moines d'Égypte depuis le concile le Concile de Chalcédoine (451) jusqu'à l'invasion arabe (640).* Paris: Imprimerie Nationale, 1914.

Van Doorn-Harder, Pieternella. "Copts: Fully Egyptian, but for a Tattoo?" In *Nationalism and Minority Identities in Islamic Societies,* edited by Maya Shatzmiller, 22–57. Montreal: McGill-Queen's University Press, 2005.

Van Lantschoot, Arnold. "Allocution de Timothée d'Alexandrie prononcée a l'occasion de la dédicace de l'église de Pachome a Pboou." *Le Muséon* 47 (1934): 13–56.

Van Lent, Jos. "The Nineteen Muslim Kings in Coptic Apocalypses." *Parole de l'Orient* 25 (2000): 643–93.

Van Minnen, Peter. "The Other Cities in Later Roman Egypt." In *Egypt in the Byzantine World 300–700,* edited by Roger S. Bagnall, 207–25. Cambridge: Cambridge University Press, 2007.

Van Nuffelen, Peter. "What Happened after Eusebius? Chronicles and Narrative Identities in the Fourth Century." In *Rhetoric and Religious Identity in Late Antiquity,* edited by Richard Lower and Morwenna Ludlow. Oxford: Oxford University Press, 2020.

Van Rompay, Lucas. "Society and Community in the Christian East." In *The Cambridge Companion to the Age of Justinian,* edited by Michael Maas, 239–66. Cambridge, UK: Cambridge University Press, 2005.

Veilleux, Armand. *Pachomian Koinonia I: The Life of Saint Pachomius and His Disciples.* Collegeville, MN: Cistercian Publications, 1980.

Vermeulen, Hans, and Cora Govers. *The Anthropology of Ethnicity: Beyond 'Ethnic Groups and Boundaries.'* Amsterdam: Het Spinhuis, 1994.

Vivian, Tim. "Humility and Resistance in Late Antique Egypt: The Life of Longinus." *CCR* 20 (1999): 4–9.

———. "Witness to Holiness: Abba Daniel of Scetis." *Coptic Church Review* 24 (2003): 2–52.

———. *Witness to Holiness: Abba Daniel of Scetis.* Kalamazoo, MI: Cistercian Publications, 2008.

van der Vliet, Jacques. "Coptic as a Nubian Literary Language: Four Theses for Discussion." In *The Christian Epigraphy of Egypt and Nubia,* edited by Jacques van der Vliet, 269–78. New York: Routledge, 2018.

———. "The Copts: Modern Sons of the Pharaohs?" In *Religious Origins of Nations? The Christian Communities of the Middle East,* edited by Bas ter Haar Romeny, 279–90. Leiden: Brill, 2010.

Watts, Edward J. "John Rufus, Timothy Aelurus, and the Fall of the Western Roman Empire." In *Romans, Barbarians, and the Transformation of the Roman*

World: Cultural Interaction and the Creation of Identity in Late Antiquity, edited by Ralph W. Mathisen and Danuta Shanzer, 97–106. Burlington, VT: Ashgate, 2011.

———. *Riot in Alexandria: Tradition and Group Dynamics in Late Antique Pagan and Christian Communities.* Berkeley: University of California Press, 2010.

Weber, Max. *Economy and Society: An Outline of Interpretive Sociology.* 4th ed. New York: Bedminster Press, 1968.

Wessel, Susan. *Cyril of Alexandria and the Nestorian Controversy: The Making of a Saint and of a Heretic.* Oxford: Oxford University Press, 2004.

Westerfield, Jennifer Taylor. *Egyptian Hieroglyphs in the Late Antique Imagination.* Philadelphia: University of Pennsylvania Press, 2019.

Winkler, Dietmar. "Miaphysitism: A New Term for Use in the History of Dogma and in Ecumenical Theology." *The Harp* 10 (1997): 33–40.

Wipszycka, Ewa. "La christianisation de l'Égypte aux IVe-Vie siècles. Aspects sociaux et ethniques." *Aegyptus* 68 (1988): 117–65.

———. "Le nationalisme a-t-il existé en Égypte byzantine?" In *Études sur le Christianisme dans l'Égypte de l'Antiquité tardive,* 9–61. Roma: Institutum Patristicum Augustinianum, 1996.

Wood, Philip. *History and Identity in the Late Antique Near East.* Oxford: Oxford University Press, 2013.

Woodward, E. L. *Christianity and Nationalism in the Later Roman Empire.* London: Longmans, Green, 1916.

Woolf, Greg. "Becoming Roman, Staying Greek: Culture, Identity and the Civilizing Process in the Roman East." *Proceedings of the Cambridge Philological Society* 40 (1994): 116–43.

Wortley, John. *The Spiritual Meadow by John Moschos.* Collegeville, MN: Cistercian Publishing, 1992.

Young, Iris Marion. "Two Concepts of Self-Determination." In *Ethnicity, Nationalism and Minority Rights,* edited by Stephen May, Tariq Modood and Judith Squires, 176–96. Cambridge, UK: Cambridge University Press, 2004.

Zaborowski, Jason R. "Egyptian Christians Implicating Chalcedonians in the Arab Takeover of Egypt: The Arabic Apocalypse of Samuel of Qalamūn." *OC* 87 (2003): 100–15.

———. "From Coptic to Arabic in Medieval Egypt." *Medieval Encounters* 14 (2008): 15–40.

———. *The Coptic Martyrdom of John of Phanijōit: Assimilation and Conversion to Islam in Thirteenth-Century Egypt.* Leiden: Brill, 2005.

INDEX

'Abd al-'Aziz ibn Marwan, 137–41
Abraham of Farshut, 70–71, 78–92, 115, 121,
    161; abduction of, 87
Acacius, 45, 55, 58–59
Acts of the Council of Chalcedon, 67–68
Agathon of Alexandria, 101–3, 105, 107,
    207n26, 210n69; *Book of the Consecra-*
    tion of the Sanctuary of Benjamin,
    102–6, 108, 110, 207n18, 207n20
akepholai, 220n250, 220n254
Alexander of Alexandria, 27, 109–10
Alexandria, 2, 57–60, 95, 114, 136, 143,
    147–51, 155, 204n161; anchorites in, 18;
    authority of the teaching of, 85; church
    of, 26, 33, 38–39, 41–42, 49, 209n44;
    Church of the Theotokos in, 104; as
    context for sin and temptation, 172n15;
    cultural distinctiveness of, 19–20; episco-
    pal see of, 41–42, 44, 49, 66, 77; Greek-
    speaking Christians of, 18; Greek-speak-
    ing monks of, 18–19; mob violence by the
    Miaphysites of, 45, 55, 59; patriarchate of,
    194n179; synod in, 67. *See also* Egypt
al-Makīn Ibn al-'Amīd, 148
Ambjörn, Lena, 223n6
Amélineau, Émile, 6, 135, 167n19, 190n142,
    214n140, 219n226, 220n250, 221n270,
    221n285
Ammon, bishop of Alexandria, 36
'Amr ibn-al-As, 2, 102, 115–16
Anastasia, 92
Anastasius, bishop of Rome, 26
Anastasius, Emperor, 93

Anatolios, ruler of Pšate, 107
anchorites, 18, 40. *See also* asceticism
Anthony, 40, 145, 195n206. *See also* Egyp-
    tian ascetics
anthropology, 9–10, 157
anthropomorphite controversy, 39, 179n126
anti-Chalcedonian movement, 2–9, 16, 28,
    52–69, 142, 209n55; anti-Palestinian
    sentiment in the Egyptian, 155; confes-
    sion of faith of the, 59, 69; in Coptic
    Christianity, 187n72; cosmopolitanism
    of the, 56; Egyptian resistance of the,
    40, 49–50, 65–69, 84, 97, 105, 108, 114,
    122, 161, 198n52; ethnic rhetoric of the,
    50, 63–66, 69, 157, 160; exiles of the,
    151–53; literature of the, 9, 11, 43–141,
    143, 157, 160; moderates of the, 157;
    multiethnic community of the, 59, 144;
    transregional contact in the, 142–58. *See*
    also Christology; Miaphysite movement
Antioch, 70, 148, 153–54; Severus as the
    true patriarch of, 143, 147. *See also* Syria
Apocalypse of Samuel of Kalamun, 100, 117,
    125–31, 216n168, 217n178, 221n279
Apollinarianism, 148
Apollo of Hnēs, 70, 92, 161
Apophthegmata Patrum, 15, 21, 28–29,
    33–39, 55, 91–94, 159, 172n15, 181n153,
    188n89, 194n180, 205n170, 215n150;
    "Egypt" as an allegory for returning to
    worldly lifestyles in the, 177n101; stories
    about Moses the Black in the, 64. *See*
    also asceticism; Egyptian ascetics

Egypt: Arab Muslim rule in, 66, 102, 108,
112, 115–17, 127–28, 131–41; barbaric
region of, 65; Byzantine, 57, 63, 74; as
the "catholic church," 85; as center of
global orthodoxy, 26, 40–41, 49, 55,
60–63, 78, 89, 97–98, 107–10, 115, 133,
141–44, 156–57; Christian destruction
of the Serapeum in, 32; early medieval,
125–26, 129–30, 162; ethnicity prior to
Chalcedon in, 15–42, 83; geography of,
191n148; Greek-Coptic unity of, 160;
indigenous religious practices of, 6, 8,
29–32, 178n117, 215n145; Lower, 18, 37,
60, 92, 116, 137; marginalization of, 69;
multilingual environment of fifth-
century, 62, 72; Nile Valley of, 83, 139,
141, 201n102; patriarchal authority in,
133; Persian occupation of, 101; post-
Chalcedonian, 21, 37, 40; pre-Chalcedonian, 17, 37, 39–41, 99, 159, 176n79;
relationship between Christians and
Muslims in the seventh-century, 136;
Roman citizenship in fifth-century, 65;
Roman citizenship in sixth-century, 88;
Umayyad rule in, 139; Upper, 6, 18–19,
37, 39, 78, 92–93, 111–13, 118, 122, 137,
147, 204n161, 206n188. See also Alexandria; Coptic literature; Egyptian Christianity; Hnês; Nile River; orthodoxy;
Panopolis; Pbow; Pentapolis; Scetis;
Tabennesi; Thebaid; Tkôw
Egyptian ascetics, 16, 18, 38–39, 162;
Anthony as ethnically Egyptian among,
33; celebration in *Apophthegmata
Patrum* of, 37; Macarius as humble
among, 60–64; Samuel as hero among,
122, 125; social discrimination accepted
by, 64; suffering and martyrdom of, 75.
See also Anthony; *Apophthegmata
Patrum;* asceticism; Egyptian Christianity; Macarius of Tkôw; Pachomius;
Shenoute of Atripe; Timothy Aelurus,
patriarch of Alexandria
Egyptian Chalcedonians, 52, 60, 71, 74–75,
88–91, 99, 101, 121–22, 183n4, 212n123;
as heretical, 106; as result of political
sycophancy or persecution, 186n65. *See
also* Chalcedonianism

Egyptian Christianity: Byzantine persecution of, 70–100; critique by Severus of
Egyptian leaders of, 155; critique of
Roman and Egyptian governmental
leaders of, 29, 106; depiction of Constantinople in, 47; inclusivity and
universality of, 20–22, 54–55; literature
of, 83, 105, 130; medieval Islamic persecution of, 137–38, 140; post-Chalcedonian, 21, 37, 40–69; practice of mummification among, 30; pride in Egyptian
ethnicity of, 34, 42, 83, 157, 159–60;
Roman persecution of, 3, 16, 22, 27, 32.
See also Christianity; Coptic literature;
Egypt; Egyptian ascetics; Egyptian
Miaphysites; Enaton monastic community; martyrdom; miracles
Egyptian Miaphysites, 7, 51, 73–76,
194n185; Chalcedonian persecution of,
101, 105, 115; Egyptian identity of, 3, 10,
15, 17, 43, 47, 75, 90, 97; expressions of
violent rebellion of, 76; as faithful
minority, 198n47. *See also* Egyptian
Christianity; Miaphysite movement
Enaton monastic community, 45, 55, 57–58,
66, 93, 112, 143, 188n92, 224n31. *See also*
Egyptian Christianity
Eriksen, Thomas Hylland, 206n185, 206n2
Ethiopia, 84, 133, 201n102, 218n221. *See also*
Axum
ethnic boundary maintenance, 9–10, 15,
50–76, 80, 85, 88–90, 99, 116, 119, 126,
130, 133, 141–42, 161; and collective
memory, 86; Egyptian Christian, 100,
102, 159, 162; as function of Roman
provincialism, 160; and minority identity, 207n14; rhetoric of, 88–89, 161;
stereotypes as fundamental component
of, 173n32. *See also* ethnicity; identity
ethnicity, 1–14, 211n98; anthropological
conceptions of, 52, 169n44; Coptic, 129;
definition of, 7–8, 199n55; Egyptian, 51,
60–64, 96, 113, 126, 131–34, 142, 151, 156,
161–63, 181n146; exalted, 135; language
and, 62–63, 126; modern concept of, 8,
63, 169n48; and nation, 178n119; para-
digms of, 7–10; race and, 171n60,
179n121, 188n104, 208n42; and resist-

Marcian, Emperor, 2, 51, 58, 62, 65–68,
75–76, 105, 149, 185n37
Marcion, 89
Mark III, Patriarch, 148
Maronites, 157
martyrdom: as central theme in the Coptic
church, 3, 75; Egyptian Christian, 23,
105, 108, 119; of Macarius for the cause of
orthodoxy, 69; of Samuel at the hands of
Roman Chalcedonians, 117, 120, 122;
value of humility and, 137. See also asceti-
cism; Egyptian Christianity; violence
Martyrdom of John of Phanijōit, 138
Martyrios, 82
Maspero, Jean, 6, 167n24
Mauritania, 139–40
Maximian, Emperor, 23
Maximus, 104
Maximus the Confessor, 185n41
Mazices. See barbarians
McCoskey, Denise, 181n146
Meletianism, 40, 71, 78–79, 199n64
Mena, bishop of Pishati: Life of Isaac of
Alexandria, 132–41, 145, 157, 221n268,
221n272
Miaphysite movement, 3, 6, 8, 10, 52, 60, 65;
assumption of uniform adherence
among Egyptians to the, 119, 143; and
Egyptian identity, 43, 46–49, 54, 69, 71,
78, 91, 97, 106, 139, 161, 203n146; ethnic
tension between Egyptian and Syrian
Christians of the, 157; ethnocentrism of
the, 146, 155–58, 160; as international
movement, 54, 64–65, 79–80, 142–58,
162; literature of the, 4–5, 46, 63, 69, 78,
104, 128, 135, 149, 153, 212n123, 217n178;
in minority language groups within the,
223n3; monastic communities of the,
81–83, 86, 97–98, 120; multiethnic
community of the, 144, 146, 151, 154,
157; as orthodox, 42, 66–69, 78, 84–86,
103, 106, 137, 163; Palestinian, 64–65,
149; Syrian, 202n118. See also anti-Chalcedonian movement; Christology;
Egyptian Miaphysites
Miaphysite Trisagion, 65, 193n171
Mikhail, Maged, 115, 209n60, 210nn79,80,
211n87, 216n170, 220n250

Millar, Fergus, 166n4
miracles, 57, 60, 63–64, 68, 79, 83–84, 107,
125; of healing, 124, 138, 209n43; liturgi-
cal celebration of, 108. See also Egyptian
Christianity
Moawad, Samuel, 183n3, 191nn142,143
Monastery of Canopus, 101
Monastery of Isaac, 76, 78–79, 104
Monastery of Meṭrā, 113
Monastery of Saint Antony, 150–51
Monastery of Saint Macarius, 91, 134,
207n18, 220n242
Monastery of Saint Sergius, 136
Monastery of Saint Severus, 147
Monastery of Saint Shenoute, 114,
210n79
Monothelitism, 110–11. See also
Christology

nationalism, 5–8, 51, 63, 67, 126, 129, 156,
160, 207n14; anti-Byzantine, 157; mod-
ern Coptic, 8, 168n40. See also identity;
Pharaonism
nature (physis), 2, 76. See also Christology
Nephalius, 156
Nestorianism, 185n41, 190n132
Nestorius, 26, 28, 41, 66–67, 81, 89, 110, 159;
condemnation of, 145
Nika Revolt, 202n108
Nile River, 93. See also Egypt
Nubia, 34, 84, 133, 201n102

Ok, Janette, 222n1
Origen, 26
Orlandi, Tito, 168n32, 189n120, 196n8,
196n12, 197n29, 198n44
orthodoxy, 21; Coptic, 87, 136; Egypt as
bastion of, 26, 40–41, 49, 55, 60–63, 78,
89; Miaphysite, 42, 66–69, 79, 84–86,
103, 106, 137, 163; Nicene, 27, 159;
Roman imperial authority through the
lens of theological, 28, 51; universal
Christian, 44. See also Egypt; heresy
Osrhoene, 23

Pachomius, 17–18, 20–25, 36, 82, 84–86,
145; ascetic community of, 24, 175n64;
federation of, 89–90; followers of,

Pachomius *(continued)*
174n53; *politeia* of, 73–74, 81. *See also*
Egyptian ascetics
Palestine, 8, 64–65, 142, 144, 149,
152–53, 156; traditions of resistance
of, 149
Panegyric on Abraham of Farshut, 80–91,
200n76, 200n87
Panegyric on Elijah, 71
Panegyric on Manasseh, 87–89, 203n132
Panopolis, 31–32. *See also* Egypt
Papaconstantinou, Arietta, 128, 145,
216n168, 216n170, 217n201
Paphnutius, 38
Paul, Apostle, 52, 56
Paul, patriarch of Alexandria, 145
Pbow, 73–78, 81, 87, 90; anti-Chalcedonian
population around, 82; construction of
a basilica at, 82; Coptic-speaking monks
of, 17–19, 26–27, 41; ethnic diversity of,
20; Greek-speaking monks of, 21,
26–27; monastic community at, 92,
200n94. *See also* Egypt
Pentapolis, 53. *See also* Egypt
Persia, 23–24, 28
person *(hypostasis),* 2. *See also* Christology
person *(prosopōn),* 76. *See also* Christology
Peter, Apostle, 109, 114
Peter Mongus, 156, 220n250
Peter of Alexandria, 23, 105
Peter of Callinicum, 148, 150, 156; *Against
Damian,* 225n54
Peter the Iberian, 45
Petronius, 82
Pharaonism, 161–62. *See also* nationalism
politeia, 73–75, 81; ascetic, 98
political economy, 8
Porcher, E., 135, 221n270, 222n285
Porphyry, 149, 191n149
Proterius, 45, 67, 188n93; murder of,
48, 55
Pseudo-Dioscorus: *Panegyric on Macarius
of Tkôw,* 55, 60–69, 94, 129, 190n136,
192n157, 192n164, 192n167, 193n171,
193n174, 195n206
Pshintbahse, 81
Psote, bishop of Ebsay, 62
Pulcheria, Empress, 47, 51, 62, 68

race, 10–14, 47, 94, 96; definition of, 133;
and ethnicity, 171n60, 179n121, 188n104,
208n42; foreign, 56–57; modern concepts of, 170n48; skin color and, 33–34,
64, 179n123. *See also* ethnicity; identity
Rapp, Claudia, 171n4, 182n157
religion: religious violence against practitioners of Greco-Egyptian, 31–33; traditional Greek, 34; traditional Roman, 32.
See also Christianity; Islam; Judaism
rhetoric: anti-Byzantine, 162; anti-Islamic,
126, 128, 162; anti-Roman, 114; anti-
Sabellian, 225n54; anti-Semitic, 76–78,
122, 198n48, 198n53; Egyptian ethnic,
107, 126, 150, 159–62, 166n10, 168n32,
182n163; of Egyptian martyrdom, 108;
Egyptian resistance, 186n54; religious
polemical, 73, 118
Roman Chalcedonians, 10, 38, 56, 106, 111,
117, 124, 132. *See also* Chalcedonianism
Roman Empire, 1, 15, 19, 23–33, 77; authorities of the, 115–16; Chalcedonian dominance in the, 4, 40, 69; Christian
dominance in the, 29, 31–32; Egypt as
province of the, 7, 59; Egyptian visions
of Christian universalism tied to the
political and theological status of the,
22, 173n27; fall of the, 53; as "godly"
empire, 21, 24–28, 31, 160; identity of
ethnic groups within the, 175n62; as
multiethnic state, 97; persecution of
Christians in the, 3, 23–24; prediction
by Timothy Aelurus of the fall of the
Western, 44–45, 161; religious unity
across the, 175n66. *See also* Byzantine
Empire; Rome
romanitas, 77
Rome: bishop of, 2, 45; dominant church of
the Roman Empire centered in, 26, 33,
42; as a "Greek City," 88. *See also*
Roman Empire
Roymans, Nico, 180n138

Sabinus, bishop of Gangra, 67
Samuel of Kalamun, 99, 117–31, 144, 161;
place in Egyptian Christian memory of,
125
Saracens, 138–39, 157. *See also* Islam

Sarris, Peter, 202n108
Scetis, 36, 204n161; Church of Makarios at, 102–7; monastic community of, 107, 118–20, 123–24, 134–35, 181n143, 208n40. *See also* Egypt
Sebastian, 87
Second Council of Constantinople, 70
Second Council of Ephesus, 2
Septuagint, 107
Severus ibn al-Muqaffa, 101
Severus of Antioch, 8, 48, 72, 77–79, 102, 142–58, 161, 202n118, 223n3, 224n31, 224n41; as ecumenical ambassador, 145; as foundational pillar of Egyptian Christianity, 148; as Greek-speaking representative of Syria, 150, 224n23; as orthodox savior rescuing Egypt from heresy, 154, 226n89
Shenoute of Atripe, 5, 21, 25, 31–32, 64–65, 82, 87, 90, 111–12, 115, 145, 160, 162, 173n39, 173n41, 176n83, 178nn115,116. *See also* Egyptian ascetics
Simon of Cyrene, 185n37
Smith, Stuart Tyson, 227n117
Snowden, Frank, 11
Sokortes, 123–24, 215n152; ethnic group of, 215n150
Sonnis-Bell, Marissa, 208n38
Southern Arabia, 34
Stephen, bishop of Hnēs, 71–80, 196n5, 198n49; *Panegyric on Apollo*, 71–80, 122, 145, 150, 196n8, 196n12, 198n44, 198n46, 198n49, 199n64, 202n118
Synaxarium, 55, 59, 68, 90, 125, 188n92, 195n197, 205n171, 213n125, 216n169
Syria, 8, 79, 142–43, 145–49, 151–56, 191n148, 202n118. *See also* Antioch

Tabennesi, 20, 181n144. *See also* Egypt
Thebaid, 23, 26, 36–37, 53, 73. *See also* Egypt
Theodora, Empress, 84, 86, 90, 94–95
Theodore, 18–21, 40; *politeia* of, 81
Theodore Anagnostes, 44
Theodore of Mopsuestia, 110
Theodoret, 110
Theodosius, patriarch of Alexandria, 77, 84, 102

Theodosius, Emperor, 31–33, 37–38
Theodotus of Ancyra, 50
Theophilus of Alexandria, 22, 26, 30–34, 38–39, 174n49, 177n109, 182n155, 182n166, 183n170
Timothy Aelurus, patriarch of Alexandria, 4, 28, 43–56, 63, 82, 93, 105, 143, 160–61, 184n23, 185n30; *Against Chalcedon*, 46, 50, 184n28; exile of, 45–46, 184n18, 195n201; *On the Unity of Christ*, 46. *See also* Egyptian ascetics
Timothy Salofaciolus, 55, 60, 67–68, 187n82, 195n201
Tkôw, 63, 191n152. *See also* Egypt
Trinity, 76. *See also* Christianity

van Cauwenbergh, Paul, 200n94
van Lantschoot, Arnold, 200n94
Victor, bishop of the Fayyum, 121–22
violence: Christian legitimization of, 178n112; mob, 45, 55, 59; physical, 122; religious, 111; of torture, 124. *See also* martyrdom
Vivian, Tim, 179n121, 188n90, 188n101, 189n120, 204n161, 205n164, 206n188

Weber, Max, 8–9
White, Evelyn, 184n11
White Monastery, 64, 83, 90–91, 111–12, 115, 160, 203n146, 210n79; *Great Euchologion* of the, 187n72
Wickham, L. R., 52, 167n27, 185n43, 225n54
Winkler, Dietmar, 166n4
Wipszycka, Ewa, 6
Woodward, E. L., 6
Woolf, Greg, 180n141

Zaborowski, Jason, 7, 126, 129, 148, 215n150, 217n178
Zacharias of Mytilene: *Chronicle*, 45, 76, 184n13, 188n93; *Life of Severus*, 143, 147, 150, 156, 225n46
Zeno, Emperor, 2, 46, 75–76, 156–57; *Henoticon*, 76

Founded in 1893,
UNIVERSITY OF CALIFORNIA PRESS
publishes bold, progressive books and journals
on topics in the arts, humanities, social sciences,
and natural sciences—with a focus on social
justice issues—that inspire thought and action
among readers worldwide.

The UC PRESS FOUNDATION
raises funds to uphold the press's vital role
as an independent, nonprofit publisher, and
receives philanthropic support from a wide
range of individuals and institutions—and from
committed readers like you. To learn more, visit
ucpress.edu/supportus.